The Ruby Workshop

Develop powerful applications by writing clean, expressive code with Ruby and Ruby on Rails

Akshat Paul

Peter Philips

Dániel Szabó

Cheyne Wallace

The Ruby Workshop

Authors: Akshat Paul, Peter Philips, Dániel Szabó, and Cheyne Wallace

Technical Reviewers: Jonathan Evans, Jagdish Narayandasani, and Dixitkumar N. Patel

Managing Editor: Snehal Tambe

Acquisitions Editor: Alicia Wooding

Production Editor: Samita Warang

Editorial Board: Shubhopriya Banerjee, Bharat Botle, Ewan Buckingham, Megan Carlisle, Mahesh Dhyani, Manasa Kumar, Alex Mazonowicz, Bridget Neale, Dominic Pereira, Shiny Poojary, Abhishek Rane, Erol Staveley, Ankita Thakur, Nitesh Thakur, and Jonathan Wray

First Published: October 2019

Production Reference: 5220221

ISBN: 978-1-83864-236-5

Published by Packt Publishing Ltd.

Livery Place, 35 Livery Street

Birmingham B3 2PB, UK

Why Learn with a Packt Workshop?

Learn by Doing

Packt Workshops are built around the idea that the best way to learn something new is by getting hands-on experience. We know that learning a language or technology isn't just an academic pursuit. It's a journey towards the effective use of a new tool—whether that's to kickstart your career, automate repetitive tasks, or just build some cool stuff.

That's why Workshops are designed to get you writing code from the very beginning. You'll start fairly small—learning how to implement some basic functionality—but once you've completed that, you'll have the confidence and understanding to move onto something slightly more advanced.

As you work through each chapter, you'll build your understanding in a coherent, logical way, adding new skills to your toolkit and working on increasingly complex and challenging problems.

Context is Key

All new concepts are introduced in the context of realistic use-cases, and then demonstrated practically with guided exercises. At the end of each chapter, you'll find an activity that challenges you to draw together what you've learned and apply your new skills to solve a problem or build something new.

We believe this is the most effective way of building your understanding and confidence. Experiencing real applications of the code will help you get used to the syntax and see how the tools and techniques are applied in real projects.

Build Real-World Understanding

Of course, you do need some theory. But unlike many tutorials, which force you to wade through pages and pages of dry technical explanations and assume too much prior knowledge, Workshops only tell you what you actually need to know to be able to get started making things. Explanations are clear, simple, and to-the-point. So you don't need to worry about how everything works under the hood; you can just get on and use it.

Written by industry professionals, you'll see how concepts are relevant to real-world work, helping to get you beyond "Hello, world!" and build relevant, productive skills. Whether you're studying web development, data science, or a core programming language, you'll start to think like a problem solver and build your understanding and confidence through contextual, targeted practice.

Enjoy the Journey

Learning something new is a journey from where you are now to where you want to be, and this Workshop is just a vehicle to get you there. We hope that you find it to be a productive and enjoyable learning experience.

Packt has a wide range of different Workshops available, covering the following topic areas:

- Programming languages
- Web development
- Data science, machine learning, and artificial intelligence
- Containers

Once you've worked your way through this Workshop, why not continue your journey with another? You can find the full range online at http://packt.live/2MNkuyl.

If you could leave us a review while you're there, that would be great. We value all feedback. It helps us to continually improve and make better books for our readers, and also helps prospective customers make an informed decision about their purchase.

Thank you,
The Packt Workshop Team

Table of Contents

Chapter 2: Ruby Data Types and Operations   35

Chapter 5: Object-Oriented programming with Ruby   159

Chapter 6: Modules and Mixins   213

Chapter 9: Ruby Beyond the Basics I   345

Preface

About

This section briefly introduces the coverage of this book, the technical skills you'll need to get started, and the software requirements required to complete all of the included activities and exercises.

About the Book

The beauty of Ruby is its readability and expressiveness. Ruby hides away a lot of the complexity of programming, allowing you to work quickly and 'do more' with fewer lines of code. This makes it a great programming language for beginners, but learning any new skill can still be a daunting task. If you want to learn to code using Ruby, but don't know where to start, *The Ruby Workshop* will help you cut through the noise and make sense of this fun, flexible language.

You'll start by writing and running simple code snippets and Ruby source code files. After learning about strings, numbers, and booleans, you'll see how to store collections of objects with arrays and hashes. You'll then learn how to control the flow of a Ruby program using boolean logic.

The book then delves into OOP and explains inheritance, encapsulation, and polymorphism. Gradually, you'll build your knowledge of advanced concepts by learning how to interact with external APIs, before finally exploring the most popular Ruby framework – Ruby on Rails – and using it for web development.

Throughout this book, you'll work on a series of realistic projects, including simple games, a voting application, and an online blog. By the end of this Ruby book, you'll have the knowledge, skills and confidence to creatively tackle your own ambitious projects with Ruby.

About the Chapters

Chapter 1, Writing and Running Ruby Programs, introduces you to writing and running simple snippets interactively as well as writing and running Ruby source code files.

Chapter 2, Ruby Data types and Operations, will teach you how to work with more complex data types such as arrays and hashes.

Chapter 3, Program Flow, informs you about the different options for controlling how a Ruby program flows: where it branches based on Boolean logic, where it switches tracks based on different cases, and where it circles back on itself to do repetitive work.

Chapter 4, Ruby Methods, builds your understanding of how to construct your own methods and master the concise and elegant syntax that Ruby offers for doing so.

Chapter 5, Object-Oriented Programming with Ruby, familiarizes you with Object-Oriented (OO) programming concepts with Ruby. You will learn how to organize code in a way that sets us up to write larger and more complex applications. We'll also begin looking at a common practice known as Test-Driven Development (TDD), which helps us build better code by getting us to think about our tests first.

Chapter 6, Modules and Mixins, will let you dive deeper into Ruby and OO programming concepts and learn about inheritance, encapsulation, and polymorphism. We will implement these using powerful Ruby language features known as modules and mixins. These will allow us to organize code and teach us deeper concepts of the Ruby object model.

Chapter 7, Introduction to Ruby Gems, focuses on importing data from external sources, processing it using our application and outputting the data in human-readable formats. We'll dive into Ruby's excellent package management system, RubyGems, how to read and write files to the filesystem, and finally how to neatly encapsulate our newly learned service-based code with service classes.

Chapter 8, Debugging with Ruby, instructs you on fundamental logging and debugging concepts and how we debug with Ruby. We'll cover different methods for different purposes and learn real-world techniques that can save you time and effort when it comes to solving problems in both development and production.

Chapter 9, Ruby Beyond the Basics I, teaches you about techniques and concepts such as blocks, procs, and lambdas. We will also learn about a very powerful concept of Ruby called metaprogramming, which is essentially code that writes code.

Chapter 10, Ruby Beyond the Basics II, teaches you how to interact with external APIs. Our code will consume a public API and parse the response. We will then create a reusable module out of this Ruby code and publish it as a Ruby gem.

Chapter 11, Introduction to Ruby on Rails I, introduces you to the most popular Ruby framework, Ruby on Rails. We will learn about the Model-View-Controller (MVC) architecture and how to organize code in Ruby on Rails. When learning about the MVC architecture, we'll see how to keep a fat model and a thin controller. Lastly, we will create a simple Create, Read, Update, and Delete (CRUD) web application with Ruby on Rails.

Chapter 12, Introduction to Ruby on Rails II, continues to build our Rails application and you will learn about REST principles and other fundamental concepts of Ruby on Rails such as routing, the asset pipeline, and ORM (Object Relational Mapping) with ActiveRecord. Finally, we will deploy our Rails application on the server with Heroku.

Conventions

Code words in text, database table names, folder names, filenames, file extensions, pathnames, dummy URLs, user input, and Twitter handles are shown as follows: "We use **puts** to print a string".

Words that you see on the screen, for example, in menus or dialog boxes, also appear in the text like this: "Both of them are inherited by the **Integer** class".

A block of code is set as follows:

```
[1,2,3].each do |i|
  puts "My item: #{i}"
end
```

New terms and important words are shown like this: "With metaprogramming, you can write methods and classes at runtime, which helps us to maintain a **Don't Repeat Yourself** (**DRY**) and maintainable code base".

Long code snippets are truncated and the corresponding names of the code files on GitHub are placed at the top of the truncated code. The permalinks to the entire code are placed below the code snippet. It should look as follows:

inheritancewithmodulemethods.rb

```
1  module Address
2    attr_accessor :address_line1, :address_line2, :city, :state,:postal_code, :country
```

https://packt.live/2o83FC5

Before You Begin

Each great journey begins with a humble step. Our upcoming adventure with Ruby programming is no exception. Before we can do awesome things using Ruby, we need to be prepared with a productive environment. In this small note, we shall see how to do that.

Installing Ruby 2.6

- (Linux/Unix) and macOS:

  To install Ruby on Linux/Unix and macOS, you can use the third-party tools **rbenv** (https://packt.live/32rkVAV) or **RVM** (https://packt.live/2VTQfpu).

- Windows:

  To install Ruby on Windows, you can simply use **RubyInstaller** (https://packt.live/2VTXEp1). Download the file, run it, and you should be done.

All code in this book is Ruby 2.x-compatible. However, we have specifically used Ruby 2.6 in our lab environment for all of the book content. We recommend using Ruby 2.6 to avoid any issues completing the chapter.

Please note that the **bundler** gem, which is used in various chapters of the book, is included within Ruby 2.6, but earlier versions of Ruby will require a manual install by simply running the following code:

```
gem install bundler
gem install rails
```

You can use any editor of your choosing to work with Ruby. However, our editor of choice is Visual Studio Code (https://packt.live/35KD2Ek) combined with the Ruby language extension (https://packt.live/33K0Jui).

For Ruby on Rails, you can simply install the extension for Rails on the Visual Studio Code Editor interface. Make sure you have installed all gems using the bundler so that the enabled extension works. If you have any issues or questions about installation, please email us at **workshops@packt.com**.

Installing the Code Bundle

Download the code and relevant files from GitHub at https://packt.live/2BowSvw and place them in a new folder called **C:\Code**. Refer to these code files for the complete code bundle.

Writing and Running Ruby Programs

Overview

By the end of this chapter, you will be able to use the Interactive Ruby Shell (IRB) to write Ruby programs; execute Ruby code with a Ruby interpreter using Ruby (.rb) files; implement variables, literals, and constants in Ruby programs; use standard data types, such as numbers, Booleans, and strings, in Ruby programs; execute basic arithmetic operations on integer and floating-point numbers, implement string concatenation and interpolation in Ruby programs.

This chapter introduces the basics of Ruby and serves as a firm foundation to build the complex code that you will encounter later in the book.

Introduction

Ruby is a dynamic, interpreted, object-oriented programming language developed by Yukihiro ("Matz") Matsumoto at some point in the mid-1990s, with its first stable release in 1995. According to the creator of Ruby, it is highly influenced by Perl, Smalltalk, Ada, and Lisp. The influence of these languages on Ruby allows it to embrace various programming paradigms, such as functional, object-oriented, and imperative, with dynamic typing (referred to as **duck typing** in popular culture) and automatic memory management.

Being an interpreted scripting language, Ruby has the ability to make system calls directly, and has a long list of useful string operations where variable declaration and variable type are not required. Ruby wholly embraces object-oriented programming because everything in Ruby is an object. Ruby has a long list of keywords that make many operations a piece of cake. This means you can do more with less code.

Whether you are a newbie to the world of programming, or an experienced developer in other languages who is tired of the compilation processes, extra declarations, and the keywords of other languages, Ruby will be a revelation from the point of view of your productivity.

With all these characteristics, Ruby gives developers an enriching experience, making programming productive and fun. In addition to Ruby being a fantastic programming language, the Ruby community is also very friendly and supportive.

Key Features of Ruby

A number of key features of the Ruby language make it really unique in terms of working with it. It has very neatly assimilated the best features of many programming languages. Here are a few features of Ruby that make it a delight to program with:

- Object-oriented
- Interpreted language
- Duck typing and dynamic typing
- Multi-paradigm language
- Reflection
- Metaprogramming

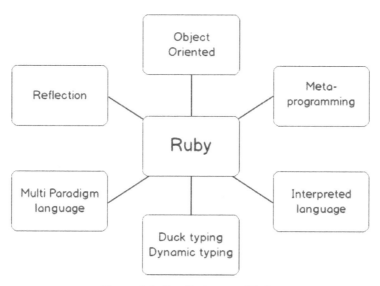

Figure 1.1: Key features of Ruby

Object-Oriented

Ruby is thoroughly object-oriented, and objects are the basic building block of a Ruby program. Every value in Ruby is an object, even data types such as strings, numbers, and Booleans: everything is an object. This means that every object is part of a class that gives access to a wide range of methods to do incredible things. Each class is also an object in Ruby. Here's an example:

```ruby
class Fruit
  #code
end
```

The preceding code defines the **Fruit** class. The following code shows that two new objects, **fruit1** and **fruit2**, are derived from the **Fruit** class:

```ruby
fruit1 = Fruit.new
fruit2 = Fruit.new
```

Interpreted Language

Ruby is an interpreted language, meaning that it's ready to run the program as soon as you finish typing. Unlike programming languages such as **C++**, **Java**, and **Objective-C**, which require code to be compiled before running, this is not the case with Ruby. Look at this example:

```ruby
print "Hello World"
```

This code will immediately print **Hello World**, as follows:

```
Hello World
```

Duck Typing and Dynamic Typing

Dynamic typing means a variable can refer to objects of various types when the program is executed. There is no type checking in Ruby. Duck typing is a principle that denotes that an object is based on the value assigned to it rather than the type of variable. The underlying rule here is: "If it walks like a duck and quacks like a duck, then it must be a duck." Here's an example:

```
x= [:a, :b, :c]
x.map(&:to_s) # => ['a', 'b', 'c']
```

The preceding example illustrates how the **x** variable responds to **map** and returns the expected object. This means that the **x** variable here is considered an **array**.

Multi-paradigm Language

While languages are focused on one type of programming paradigm, besides being object-oriented, Ruby also allows procedural and functional styles of programming. The procedural paradigm refers to an instance where procedure calls are interpreted as function calls. However, functions do not exist in Ruby, and, therefore, methods can be created outside classes. Look at this example:

```
self # => main
def method1
   "John is developing a program."
end
def method2
   "Jane is developing another program."
end

method1 # => "John is developing a program."
method2 # => "Jane is developing another program."
```

Here, **method1** and **method2** are defined outside the classes; however, they are still a part of the **main** object.

Additionally, Ruby also features the functional style of programming, meaning it largely revolves around functions. Consider the following example:

```ruby
def ruby_method(obj)
  obj - 1
end
print ruby_method(5)
=> 4
```

Here, the **ruby_method** always stores the result of the object passed as an argument, subtracting 1.

Reflection

Reflection in Ruby makes it very easy to understand what's happening at runtime because you can get a lot of information, such as class methods, inheritance hierarchies, and all the living objects in your running program. Here's an example:

```ruby
class Box
  def hello
    "hello"
  end
end
# without reflection
obj = Box.new
obj.hello
# with reflection
class_name = "Box"
method_name = :hello
obj = Object.const_get(class_name).new
obj.send method_name
```

This shows that we can inspect every element of the code.

Metaprogramming

Ruby supports metaprogramming, which is a technique that helps you to write code that creates code on its own. This means it is able to create methods and classes dynamically. With metaprogramming, you can write methods and classes at runtime, which helps us to maintain a **Don't Repeat Yourself** (**DRY**) and maintainable code base. Here's an example:

```ruby
['one', 'two', 'three'].each do |num|
  define_method(num) do
    num.upcase
```

```
    end
end
one # => "ONE"
two # => "TWO"
three # => "THREE"
```

The preceding code shows that we can make changes to the core **Array** class at runtime and modify it as required.

Interactive Ruby Shell (IRB)

The easiest way to start playing around with Ruby is by using **IRB**, where **I** stands for **Interactive** and **RB** stand for the **.rb** extension of the Ruby programming files. IRB is a command-line interpreter and is also known as a **REPL** tool in Ruby, which means **Read**, **Eval**, **Print**, and **Loop**, and was inspired by Smalltalk. IRB is very useful for quick experiments, exploring Ruby, and testing fragments of code quickly.

IRB comes out of the box with Ruby, and you can access it using the **irb** command from the Terminal:

1. Go to the Terminal (or Command Prompt) and type the following command:

   ```
   $ irb
   >_
   ```

2. Once the shell is open, you can type commands and get instant results. Try a simple **puts** command in Ruby using IRB:

   ```
   puts "Hello World"
   ```

   The output should be as follows:

   ```
   irb(main):005:0> puts "Hello World"
   Hello World
   => nil
   ```

   Figure 1.2: Output for "Hello World"

> **Note**
>
> **puts** or **p** is used to print any string or value of a variable that follows **puts** or **p**.

Let's do some addition with the Interactive Ruby Shell:

1. Go to the IRB shell.

2. Type the following command:

    ```
    17 + 13
    ```

    The output should be as follows:

    ```
    irb(main):007:0> 17 + 13
    => 30
    ```

    Figure 1.3: Addition output on irb

> **Note**
>
> You can use IRB or any IDE to complete the exercises/activities in this book.

Exercise 1.01: Creating and Assigning Variables

In this exercise, we will create a variable, assign an operation to it, and print it. Let's assign the calculation in the previous example to a variable, such as the number of students, and print it in IRB:

1. Go to the IRB shell or the IDE of your choice.

2. Type the following code:

    ```
    number_of_students = 17 + 13
    ```

    You should get the sum of 17 and 13 in the output.

3. Next, we print the value carried by the **number_of_students** variable:

    ```
    puts number_of_students
    ```

The output should be as follows:

```
irb(main):008:0> number_of_students = 17 + 13
=> 30
irb(main):009:0> puts number_of_students
30
=> nil
```

Figure 1.4: Output for assigning variables

> **Note**
>
> The Ruby variable stores the value assigned to a variable in one IRB session, as seen here with **number_of_students**.

Before we start the next exercise, please note that data types in Ruby symbolize various types of data, such as strings, numbers, decimal numbers, and text. All of these data types are based on classes; for example, **string** is an object of the **String** class, since Ruby is an object-oriented language. We will discuss a variety of data types in Ruby later in this chapter.

Exercise 1.02: Assigning a Variable of One Data Type to a Different Type

In this exercise, we will assign a string value to a variable of the integer data type. It is not necessary that a variable, once assigned, stays the same type forever. Let's assign a variable that holds an integer and another variable that has a string value:

1. Continue from the previous example (if you are starting here, please complete *Exercise 1.01, Creating and Assigning Variables*).

2. Type the following code:

```
number_of_students
```

This should give you an output of **30** as this was the value assigned in the previous exercise.

Next, we assign a different value to the **number_of_students** variable:

```
number_of_students = "not enough for a session"
=> "not enough for a session"
```

The output should be as follows:

```
irb(main):010:0> number_of_students
=> 30
irb(main):011:0> number_of_students = "not enough for a session"
=> "not enough for a session"
```

Figure 1.5: The output for variables assigned to a different data type

We can simply change the data type of a variable with the inbuilt Ruby methods. For example, to convert an integer to a string, we can use **.to_s**, and we can convert a string to an integer with **.to_i**.

We will study Ruby methods in detail in the later sections of this chapter.

Exercise 1.03: Getting the Type of a Variable

In this exercise, we will get information about the data type of a variable. Continuing on from the previous exercise, we can get a lot of information about the variable. First, let's see from which class the variable is derived. This can be achieved using the dot (.) operator on the variable itself.

1. Continue from the previous example (if you are starting here, please complete *Exercises 1.01, Creating and Assigning Variables* and *1.02, Assigning a Variable of One Data Type to a Different Type*).

2. Now, we will try to identify the data type of our **number_of_students** variable using **.class**:

    ```
    number_of_students.class
    ```

    The output should be as follows:

    ```
    irb(main):014:0> number_of_students.class
    => String
    ```

Figure 1.6: Output of the data type of a variable

.class tells us about the class that the variable belongs to.

3. The same can be achieved using the :: operator:

    ```
    number_of_students::class
    ```

In Ruby, the . and :: operators almost work in the same way. There is no major difference between :: and . when calling static methods. However, you may use the :: operator to access constants and other name-spaced things, where using the dot (.) operator is not possible. Aesthetically, . operator is preferable to :: operator.

Getting the Details of the Public Methods of an Object

We will now see various public methods that are available for an object by default from Ruby. Everything in Ruby is an object; the **class** itself is an object of **Class**. We can then check what interfaces are available for an object. Let's now see what public methods are associated with this object:

```
number_of_students.public_methods
```

The output should be as follows:

```
irb(main):017:0> number_of_students.public_methods
=> [:encode, :include?, :%, :*, :+, :to_c, :count, :partition, :sum, :next, :casecmp, :casecmp?, :insert, :bytesize, :matc
h, :match?, :succ!, :<=>, :next!, :index, :rindex, :upto, :==, :===, :chr, :=~, :byteslice, :[], :[]=, :scrub!, :getbyte,
:replace, :clear, :scrub, :empty?, :eql?, :-@, :downcase, :upcase, :dump, :setbyte, :swapcase, :+@, :capitalize, :capitali
ze!, :undump, :downcase!, :oct, :swapcase!, :lines, :bytes, :split, :codepoints, :freeze, :inspect, :reverse!, :grapheme_c
lusters, :reverse, :hex, :scan, :upcase!, :crypt, :ord, :chars, :prepend, :length, :size, :start_with?, :succ, :sub, :inte
rn, :chop, :center, :<<, :concat, :strip, :lstrip, :end_with?, :delete_prefix, :to_str, :to_sym, :gsub!, :rstrip, :gsub, :
delete_suffix, :to_s, :to_i, :rjust, :chomp!, :strip!, :lstrip!, :sub!, :chomp, :chop!, :ljust, :tr_s, :delete, :rstrip!,
:delete_prefix!, :delete_suffix!, :tr, :squeeze!, :each_line, :to_f, :tr!, :tr_s!, :delete!, :slice, :slice!, :each_byte,
:squeeze, :each_codepoint, :each_grapheme_cluster, :valid_encoding?, :ascii_only?, :rpartition, :encoding, :hash, :b, :uni
code_normalize!, :unicode_normalized?, :to_r, :force_encoding, :each_char, :unicode_normalize, :encode!, :unpack, :unpack1
, :<=, :>=, :between?, :<, :>, :clamp, :instance_variable_set, :instance_variable_defined?, :remove_instance_variable, :in
stance_of?, :kind_of?, :is_a?, :tap, :instance_variable_get, :singleton_method, :method, :public_method, :define_singleton
_method, :public_send, :extend, :pp, :to_enum, :enum_for, :!~, :respond_to?, :object_id, :send, :display, :nil?, :class, :
singleton_class, :clone, :dup, :itself, :yield_self, :taint, :tainted?, :untaint, :untrust, :untrusted?, :trust, :frozen?,
:methods, :singleton_methods, :protected_methods, :private_methods, :public_methods, :instance_variables, :!, :equal?, :i
nstance_eval, :instance_exec, :!=, :__id__, :__send__]
```

Figure 1.7: Output for public methods

You can use all of the preceding public methods on this object to execute various operations and manipulate the value set in the object. If you look closely, some of the methods are self-explanatory, such as **upcase**, and **downcase** (we will discuss individual data types and their **class** later in this chapter).

Running Ruby Code from Ruby Files

In the previous section, we used **IRB** to execute some code snippets from the Terminal. But that's not usually the case when you write Ruby code. Whether you use a framework or run a standalone Ruby code, you would keep your code inside a Ruby file, which, in layman's terms, is a file with the **.rb** extension.

Let's try creating a **hello_world.rb** file and place some Ruby code in it. You can use your choice of IDE or simply use the Terminal.

1. Create a new file and add the following code to it:

```
puts "***"
puts  "*****"
puts  "*******"
puts  "Hello World"
```

```
puts  "*******"
puts  "*****"
puts  "***"
```

2. Save this file in the desired location with the **.rb** extension. For example, save it as **hello_world.rb**.

3. To execute this code, fire up your Terminal.

4. Run the following command from root where your Ruby file is saved:

```
$ ruby hello_world.rb
```

The output should be as follows:

```
***
*****
*******
Hello World
*******
*****
***
```

Figure 1.8: Output of the hello world program

So far, we have learned how to print any value from a variable. Now that we know how to write and execute a code from a Ruby file, let's up the ante a bit by getting user input.

Exercise 1.04: Getting User Input in a Ruby Program

In this exercise, we will get the user to input some numerical data and perform a simple addition. To do so, follow these steps:

1. Open your choice of IDE or the Terminal application.

2. Create a new file.

3. Add the following code to it. We use **puts** to print a string. The **gets** function is used to allow the input data to be stored in the **num** variable:

```
puts  "Please enter a number to added to 5"
num = gets
sum = 5 + num.to_i
puts  "The result is"
puts sum
```

We have converted the **num** variable explicitly to an integer using the built-in **to_i** method.

4. Save the file as **sum.rb**.

5. Open the Terminal and execute the following code:

```
$ ruby sum.rb
```

The output should be as follows:

```
Please enter a number to added to 5
10
The result is
15
```

Figure 1.9: Output for user input in Ruby

By using the **gets** method, we were able to capture input from the user. When you executed the Ruby file, the cursor stopped for the input. The same input, as captured by the **gets** method, was used and added to **5**.

Alternatively, there is a method called **gets.chomp** that removes the trailing line character from a string. Typically, the **gets** method will input the entire string, including the line break character. **gets.chomp** will remove line break characters from strings.

Standard Data Types

The three major data types used in Ruby are as follows:

- Number
- String
- Boolean

We shall look at each of these data types in detail in this section.

Number

Numbers in Ruby are objects that derive from the **Numeric** class. Let's look at the class hierarchy for various number types:

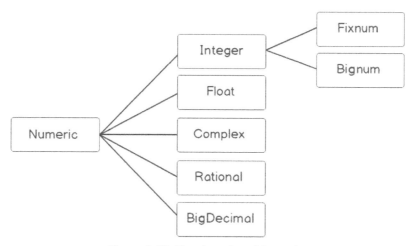

Figure 1.10: Number class hierarchy

Of all of these, two of the most commonly used number types are **integer** and **float**, and there are a number of methods associated with both integer and floating-point numbers. Let's take a look at them one by one.

In Ruby, integers are represented by two classes: **Fixnum** and **Bignum**:

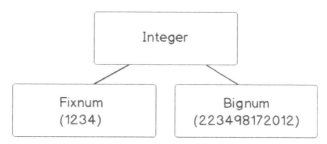

Figure 1.11: Integer types

Both of them are inherited by the **Integer** class. As the name suggests, the **Bignum** class represents big numbers, and **Fixnum** is used to represent small numbers. Ruby manages the conversion between the two automatically. For example, if the result of an operation of two **Fixnum** numbers is outside the **Fixnum** range, it's converted to **Bignum**. From Ruby 2.4 onward, Ruby has unified these classes and automatically uses the **Fixnum** class for small numbers and **Bignum** for large numbers.

Exercise 1.05: Performing Common Integer Operations

In this exercise, we will perform common mathematical operations such as addition (+), subtraction (-), multiplication (*), and division (/) in Ruby:

1. Go to the Terminal.

2. Type **irb** to enter the IRB.

3. Type the following code:

```
1 + 2
```

The output should be as follows:

```
irb(main):014:0> 1+2
=> 3
```

Figure 1.12: Output for the addition operator

4. Perform subtraction using the - operator:

```
3 - 1
```

The output should be as follows:

```
irb(main):018:0> 3-1
=> 2
```

Figure 1.13: Output for the subtraction operator

5. Perform multiplication using the * operator:

```
3 * 3
```

The output should be as follows:

```
irb(main):021:0> 3*3
=> 9
```

Figure 1.14: Output for the multiplication operator

6. Perform division using the / operator:

```
10 / 2
```

The output should be as follows:

```
irb(main):024:0> 10/2
=> 5
```

Figure 1.15: Output for the division operator

You may ask yourself how is the principle of BODMAS (Bracket, Open, Division, Multiplication, Addition, and Subtraction) managed by Ruby automatically. Ruby follows an order of precedence for operators, which defines the order in which the operators will take priority in any equation. We will learn about precedence in *Chapter 3, Program Workflow*.

> **Note**
>
> You can also divide up long integers by separating them with an underscore. For example, 121_334 will be read in Ruby as 121334

Exercise 1.06: Using Common Integer Methods to Perform Complex Arithmetic

In this exercise, we will try some common integer methods to make complex operations trivial. We will perform operations to calculate the next and previous numbers and calculate the Least Common Multiple (LCM) and Greatest Common Denominator (GCD) using built-in methods.

LCM is a method that finds the smallest multiple common to any two or more numbers, whereas GCD finds the largest divisor common to two or more numbers.

The following steps should help you with the solution:

1. Go to the Terminal.

2. Type **irb** to enter the IRB.

3. Type the following code. **.next** will provide the next number:

    ```
    2.next
    ```

    The output should be as follows:

    ```
    irb(main):027:0> 2.next
    => 3
    ```

    Figure 1.16: Output for the next number

4. Next, we will calculate the previous number using **.pred**:

    ```
    2.pred
    ```

The output should be as follows:

```
irb(main):029:0> 2.pred
=> 1
```

Figure 1.17: Output for the previous number

5. Then we calculate the LCM of 2 and 3 using .lcm:

```
2.lcm(3)
```

The output should be as follows:

```
irb(main):032:0> 2.lcm(3)
=> 6
```

Figure 1.18: Output for the LCM of 2 and 3

6. We also calculate the GCD of 2 and 3 using .gcd:

```
2.gcd(3)
```

The output should be as follows:

```
irb(main):036:0> 2.gcd(3)
=> 1
```

Figure 1.19: Output for the GCD of 2 and 3

Most of these methods are self-explanatory, but let's go through each of them:

*   .next provides the next integer value.

*   .pred provides the preceding integer value.

*   .lcm gives us the least common multiple of the integer to which the method is applied and the value passed.

*   .gcd provides the greatest common divisor of the integer to which the method is applied and the value passed.

There are a number of methods available for the integer class, which you can play around with. Simply check them by using .methods on the integer.

Go to the Terminal. Type irb to enter the IRB and type the following code:

```
2.methods
```

The output should be as follows:

```
irb(main):039:0> 2.methods
=> [:-@, :**, :<=>, :upto, :<<, :<=, :>=, :==, :chr, :===, :>>, :[], :%, :&, :inspect, :+, :ord, :-, :numerator, :/, :*, :
rationalize, :gcd, :lcm, :gcdlcm, :denominator, :size, :succ, :<, :>, :to_int, :coerce, :divmod, :to_s, :to_i, :fdiv, :mod
ulo, :remainder, :abs, :magnitude, :integer?, :to_r, :floor, :ceil, :round, :truncate, :to_f, :^, :odd?, :even?, :allbits?
, :anybits?, :nobits?, :downto, :times, :pred, :pow, :bit_length, :digits, :next, :div, :|, :~, :+@, :eql?, :singleton_met
hod_added, :arg, :rectangular, :rect, :polar, :real, :imaginary, :imag, :abs2, :angle, :phase, :conjugate, :to_c, :conj, :
i, :real?, :zero?, :nonzero?, :finite?, :infinite?, :step, :positive?, :negative?, :clone, :dup, :quo, :between?, :clamp,
:instance_variable_set, :instance_variable_defined?, :remove_instance_variable, :instance_of?, :kind_of?, :is_a?, :tap, :i
nstance_variable_get, :singleton_method, :method, :public_method, :define_singleton_method, :public_send, :extend, :pp, :t
o_enum, :enum_for, :=~, :!~, :respond_to?, :freeze, :object_id, :send, :display, :nil?, :hash, :class, :singleton_class, :
itself, :yield_self, :taint, :tainted?, :untaint, :untrust, :untrusted?, :trust, :frozen?, :methods, :singleton_methods, :
protected_methods, :private_methods, :public_methods, :instance_variables, :!, :equal?, :instance_eval, :instance_exec, :!
=, :__id__, :__send__]
```

Figure 1.20: Available methods in Ruby

> **Note**
>
> To know more about all the methods and operations they can perform, refer to the official documentation at https://packt.live/2nc962i.

Floating-Point Numbers

Next, let's look into floating-point numbers. Floats are essentially imprecise decimal numbers in Ruby; we use the **Float** class with 15 digits of precision.

There are two ways to write floating-point numbers:

- 1.121 – with a decimal point

- 1.0e3 – adding an exponent provided there is one number before and after the decimal point

Exercise 1.07: Performing Common Operations for Floating-Point Numbers

In this exercise, we will try some common floating-point methods to make complex operations easy. We will also learn how to calculate the previous and next decimal number, as well as how to round off a decimal number completely or up to a certain decimal point:

1. Go to the Terminal.

2. Type **irb** to enter the IRB.

3. Type the following code. Firstly, we have assigned our floating-point value to a **num** variable and applied various methods to it:

```
num = 2.339
num.ceil
num.floor
```

.ceil returns the closest next integer, and **.floor** returns the closest previous integer.

4. Then we have **.next_float**. This returns the next floating-point value, which is an increment in the last digit of the number to 15 decimal places. Similarly, **.prev_float** returns the previous floating point value to 15 decimal places:

```
num.next_float
num.prev_float
```

5. Next, we have **.round**, which removes the values after the decimal. If the value after the decimal point is less than 5, you get the previous integer, and if it is over 5, you get the next integer. When we pass a number to **.round(2)**, we get a floating-point value to two decimal places:

```
num.round
num.round(2)
```

The output should be as follows:

```
irb(main):043:0> num = 2.339
=> 2.339
irb(main):044:0> num.ceil
=> 3
irb(main):045:0> num.floor
=> 2
irb(main):046:0> num.round
=> 2
irb(main):047:0> num.round(2)
=> 2.34
```

Figure 1.21: Output for floating-point number operations

There are a number of methods available for the **Float** class, which you can play around with. Simply check them against **.methods** on any integer:

1. Go to the Terminal.

2. Type **irb** to enter the IRB.

3. Type the following Ruby code:

```
2.15.methods
```

The output should be as follows:

```
irb(main):052:0> 2.15.methods
=> [:-@, :**, :<=>, :<=, :>=, :==, :===, :eql?, :%, :*, :inspect, :+, :-, :numerator, :/, :denominator, :rationalize, :arg
, :<, :>, :angle, :phase, :to_int, :coerce, :divmod, :to_s, :to_i, :fdiv, :modulo, :abs, :magnitude, :to_r, :zero?, :finit
e?, :infinite?, :floor, :ceil, :round, :truncate, :to_f, :positive?, :negative?, :hash, :quo, :nan?, :next_float, :prev_fl
oat, :+@, :singleton_method_added, :rectangular, :rect, :polar, :real, :imaginary, :imag, :abs2, :conjugate, :to_c, :conj,
 :i, :remainder, :real?, :integer?, :nonzero?, :step, :clone, :dup, :div, :between?, :clamp, :instance_variable_set, :inst
ance_variable_defined?, :remove_instance_variable, :instance_of?, :kind_of?, :is_a?, :tap, :instance_variable_get, :single
ton_method, :method, :public_method, :define_singleton_method, :public_send, :extend, :pp, :to_enum, :enum_for, :=~, :!~,
:respond_to?, :freeze, :object_id, :send, :display, :nil?, :class, :singleton_class, :itself, :yield_self, :taint, :tainte
d?, :untaint, :untrust, :untrusted?, :trust, :frozen?, :methods, :singleton_methods, :protected_methods, :private_methods,
 :public_methods, :instance_variables, :!, :equal?, :instance_eval, :instance_exec, :!=, :__id__, :__send__]
```

Figure 1.22: Methods for the Float class

> **Note**
>
> To find out more about all the methods and the operations they can perform, refer to the official documentation at https://packt.live/2o7rYzS.

String

Strings in Ruby are derived from the **String** class, and there are over 100 methods to manipulate and operate on strings. This is perhaps because, in programming, a lot revolves around strings, and Ruby reduces the headache by managing a lot out of the box.

By default, Ruby comes with UTF-8 encoding, but this can be changed by placing a special comment at the top of a file:

```
# encoding: us-ascii
puts "Hello".encoding
output:
ruby strings.rb
#<Encoding:US-ASCII>
```

> **Note**
>
> If you remove the comment, by default, it will be UTF-8.

There are various ways to write strings in Ruby. These are some of the most common ones:

- We can simply place anything between single quotes ('') and it becomes a string:

  ```
  'Ruby Fundamentals'
    => "Ruby Fundamentals"
  ```

- In order to keep the single quote with the letters, we can escape it using the backslash character (\):

  ```
  '\'Ruby Fundamentals\''
    => "'Ruby Fundamentals'"
  ```

- We can also use **%q**, as shown in the following examples, and place the required string in a delimiter, which can be a bracket, curly brackets, or something else:

  ```
  %q('Ruby' Fundamentals)
    => "'Ruby' Fundamentals"

  %q['Ruby' Fundamentals]
    => "'Ruby' Fundamentals"

  %q{'Ruby' Fundamentals}
    => "'Ruby' Fundamentals"

  %q<'Ruby' Fundamentals>
    => "'Ruby' Fundamentals"
  ```

- We can also use double quotes (""), which is the cleanest way to define a string.

```
"'Ruby' Fundamentals"
 => "'Ruby' Fundamentals"
```

The output of all the preceding code should be as follows:

```
irb(main):001:0> 'Ruby Fundamentals'
=> "Ruby Fundamentals"
irb(main):002:0> '\'Ruby Fundamentals\''
=> "'Ruby Fundamentals'"
irb(main):003:0> %q('Ruby' Fundamentals)
=> "'Ruby' Fundamentals"
irb(main):004:0> %q['Ruby' Fundamentals]
=> "'Ruby' Fundamentals"
irb(main):005:0> %q{'Ruby' Fundamentals}
=> "'Ruby' Fundamentals"
irb(main):006:0> %q<'Ruby' Fundamentals>
=> "'Ruby' Fundamentals"
irb(main):007:0> "'Ruby' Fundamentals"
=> "'Ruby' Fundamentals"
```

Figure 1.23: Ways to write strings in Ruby

Exercise 1.08: Using Common String Methods

In this exercise, we will perform a number of common operations on a string. We will first assign a string to a variable, then find its size and length, and then change the case of the String value. We will then capitalize the string. All this will be done using the **String** class' built-in methods. Lastly, we will discuss the bang (**!**) operator and see how adding it impacts the results:

1. Go to the Terminal.

2. Type **irb** to enter the IRB.

3. Enter the following code to define the string:

```
title = "ruby fundamentals"
```

The output should be as follows:

```
irb(main):011:0> title = "ruby fundamentals"
=> "ruby fundamentals"
```

Figure 1.24: Output for string definition

Here, we are using the **ruby fundamentals** value for the title variable on which all the following operations will be executed.

4. Next, we check the number of characters in this string, including white spaces, using .**size**:

```
title.size
```

The output should be as follows:

```
irb(main):014:0> title.size
=> 17
```

Figure 1.25: Character count of a string

5. Then, we also check the number of characters in this string, including white spaces, using .**length**:

```
title.length
```

The output should be as follows:

```
irb(main):017:0> title.length
=> 17
```

Figure 1.26: String length calculation

.**length** is the same as size, but it is more meaningful in certain situations. Mostly, it is a matter of preference. Some developers prefer using .**size** for large collections of data, such as arrays, and hashes, and .**length** for smaller collections of data, such as strings.

6. Next, we change the case of the string characters to uppercase using .**upcase**:

```
title.upcase
```

The output should be as follows:

```
irb(main):019:0> title.upcase
=> "RUBY FUNDAMENTALS"
```

Figure 1.27: Uppercase string characters

7. Similarly, we can change the casing to lowercase using .**downcase**:

```
title.downcase
```

The output should be as follows:

```
irb(main):022:0> title.downcase
=> "ruby fundamentals"
```

Figure 1.28: Lowercase string characters

8. We can also capitalize the first character of the string using `.capitalize`:

```
title.capitalize
```

The output should be as follows:

```
irb(main):024:0> title.capitalize
=> "Ruby fundamentals"
```

Figure 1.29: Capitalized string characters

Note that even after the operations are applied on the string, the original string object remains the same:

```
title
```

The output should be as follows:

```
irb(main):012:0> title
=> "ruby fundamentals"
```

Figure 1.30: Original string object

9. Let's now try the **bang** method. **Bang** methods end with an exclamation mark (**!**), and we can use them to modify the original object with the result of the operation. Since the **bang** method can permanently modify the receiver (the original value), it should be used carefully:

```
title.capitalize!
title
```

The output should be as follows:

```
irb(main):015:0> title.capitalize!
=> "Ruby fundamentals"
```

Figure 1.31: Bang operation on a string

There are other operations as well that we can perform on strings, a common one being concatenation.

Exercise 1.09: Performing String Concatenation

In this exercise, we will be concatenating two string values that are assigned to different variables. We will solve the same problem in three ways:

- Using the + operator
- Using the .concat method
- Using the << operator

The following steps will help you to perform the exercise:

1. Go to the Terminal.

2. Type **irb** to enter the IRB.

3. Enter the following code. We first define the strings as **var1** and **var2**:

```
var1 = "Ruby"
var2 = "Fundamentals"
```

4. Next, we concatenate the two strings using whitespace:

```
title = var1 + ' ' + var2
```

The output should be as follows:

```
irb(main):017:0> var1 = "Ruby"
=> "Ruby"
irb(main):018:0> var2 = "Fundamentals"
=> "Fundamentals"
irb(main):019:0> title = var1 + ' ' + var2
=> "Ruby Fundamentals"
```

Figure 1.32: Output using whitespace

To add a space between **var1** and **var2** in the final result, you can do this by chain two + operators with a whitespace in-between.

5. We can also do the same with the .**concat** method and modify the Ruby code:

```
title = var1.concat(var2)
```

The output should be as follows:

```
irb(main):021:0> title = var1.concat(var2)
=> "RubyFundamentals"
```

Figure 1.33: Output using the .concat method

6. We can also concatenate the strings using the **<<** operator:

```
title = ""
var1 = "Ruby"
title << var1
title << " "
var2 = "Fundamentals"
title << var2
```

The output should be as follows:

```
irb(main):025:0> title = ""
=> ""
irb(main):026:0> var1 = "Ruby"
=> "Ruby"
irb(main):027:0> title << var1
=> "Ruby"
irb(main):028:0> title << " "
=> "Ruby "
irb(main):029:0> var2 = "Fundamentals"
=> "Fundamentals"
irb(main):030:0> title << var2
=> "Ruby Fundamentals"
```

Figure 1.34: Concatenation using the << operator

Another way of accomplishing string manipulation is by using a technique called string interpolation. This works much more elegantly than the previous methods and allows you to combine the elements of different types together in a string. With string interpolation, we can combine strings and embed Ruby expressions in a string.

Exercise 1.10: Performing String Interpolation

In this exercise, we will use the title variable that contains a value for Ruby Fundamentals and interpolate it in a sentence:

1. Go to the Terminal.

2. Type **irb** to enter the IRB.

3. Define the string:

```
title = "Ruby Fundamentals"
puts "My Favorite Ruby book is #{title}"
```

The output should be as follows:

```
irb(main):033:0> title = "Ruby Fundamentals"
=> "Ruby Fundamentals"
irb(main):034:0> puts "My Favorite Ruby book is #{title}"
My Favorite Ruby book is Ruby Fundamentals
```

Figure 1.35: String interpolation

4. We can also perform operations with string interpolation, for example, addition within a string:

```
puts "My Favorite Ruby book is #{title} and I am using it for last #{10+30} days"
```

The output should be as follows:

```
irb(main):038:0> puts "My Favorite Ruby book is #{title} and I am using it for last #{10+30} days"
My Favorite Ruby book is Ruby Fundamentals and I am using it for last 40 days
```

Figure 1.36: Addition operation in string interpolation

This is how we carry out addition operations with string interpolation.

Exercise 1.11: Extracting and Searching a Substring from a String

To extract certain characters from a string, follow these steps:

1. Go to the Terminal.

2. Type **irb** to enter the IRB.

3. Define the string and then extract the characters, starting from the eighth position in an index to the second position from it:

```
quote = "Just Do IT"
quote[8,2]
```

The output should be as follows:

```
irb(main):048:0> quote = "Just Do IT"
=> "Just Do IT"
irb(main):049:0> quote[8,2]
=> "IT"
```

Figure 1.37: Extracting characters from a string

Thus, we have extracted characters, starting from the eighth position in an index to the second position from it, and hence get the characters **IT**.

4. Now, we will use string methods that can check whether a certain character, or group of characters, exists in a string object:

```
quote = "Just Do IT"
quote.include?("Just")
quote.include?("just")
```

The output should be as follows:

```
irb(main):052:0> quote = "Just Do IT"
=> "Just Do IT"
irb(main):053:0> quote.include?("Just")
=> true
irb(main):054:0> quote.include?("just")
=> false
```

Figure 1.38: Searching a substring from a string

Here, the characters must be together and in exactly the same order.

Exercise 1.12: Replacing Part of a String with Another String

In this exercise, we will replace the word **Java** in the sentence "My favorite book is Java Fundamentals" with the word **Ruby**. To do so, follow these steps:

1. Go to the Terminal.

2. Type **irb** to enter the IRB.

3. Store the sentence **My favorite book is Java Fundamentals** in **title**:

```
title = "My favorite book is Java Fundamentals"
```

4. Type the following code, which replaces the word **Java** with **Ruby** in **title**:

```
title["Java"] = "Ruby"
```

5. Print **title** to confirm the change:

```
title
```

The output should be as follows:

```
irb(main):057:0> title = "My favorite book is Java Fundamentals"
=> "My favorite book is Java Fundamentals"
irb(main):058:0> title["Java"] = "Ruby"
=> "Ruby"
irb(main):059:0> title
=> "My favorite book is Ruby Fundamentals"
```

Figure 1.39: Replacing string characters

We have now easily updated the specific value of the string object in the **title** variable.

If the original title was **My favorite Java book is Java Fundamentals**, we have Java repeated twice. In this case, only the first instance of Java would be replaced. The output would be **My Favorite Ruby book is Java Fundamentals**. This is where the **gsub** method comes into play. It is used to globally substitute a character, or set of characters, with another.

Exercise 1.13: Replacing All the Values inside a String Using gsub

In this exercise, we will use the **gsub** method to replace all the instances of Java with Ruby in a sentence:

1. Go to the Terminal.

2. Type **irb** to enter the IRB.

3. Define the string value and apply the **gsub** method as follows:

```
title = "My Favorite Java book is Java Fundamentals"
title.gsub("Java", "Ruby")
```

The output should be as follows:

```
irb(main):062:0> title = "My Favorite Java book is Java Fundamentals"
=> "My Favorite Java book is Java Fundamentals"
irb(main):063:0> title.gsub("Java", "Ruby")
=> "My Favorite Ruby book is Ruby Fundamentals"
```

Figure 1.40: Using the gsub method to replace characters in a string

This way, we can easily replace the same values across the object using **gsub**. This is very handy when we have to replace one character that is repeated and acts as noise in data with something meaningful.

Exercise 1.14: Splitting a String and Joining a String

In Ruby, we can split a string, which gives the result in an array (we will learn about arrays in the next chapter). In this exercise, we are going to split a string of words into an array of words.

1. Go to the Terminal.

2. Type **irb** to enter the IRB.

3. Define the string and use the **.split** method to divide the string into an array of words:

```
title = "My Favorite book is Ruby Fundamentals"
title.split
```

The output should be as follows:

```
irb(main):067:0> title = "My Favorite book is Ruby Fundamentals"
=> "My Favorite book is Ruby Fundamentals"
irb(main):068:0> title.split
=> ["My", "Favorite", "book", "is", "Ruby", "Fundamentals"]
```

Figure 1.41: Splitting a string

4. Use the **split** method to separate values in a string:

```
months = "Jan; Feb; Mar"
months.split(';')
```

The output should be as follows:

```
irb(main):073:0> months = "Jan; Feb; Mar"
=> "Jan; Feb; Mar"
irb(main):074:0> months.split(';')
=> ["Jan", " Feb", " Mar"]
```

Figure 1.42: Splitting a string using a unique character

5. Join the array values in a string:

```
data = ["My", "Favorite", "book", "is", "Ruby", "Fundamentals"]
data.join
```

The output should be as follows:

```
irb(main):078:0> data = ["My", "Favorite", "book", "is", "Ruby", "Fundamentals"]
=> ["My", "Favorite", "book", "is", "Ruby", "Fundamentals"]
irb(main):079:0> data.join
=> "MyFavoritebookisRubyFundamentals"
```

Figure 1.43: Joining arrays to form a string

Thus, we have successfully used **data.join** to bring together values in a string.

The **string** class has several methods. You can use the following code to check the methods available in the string class:

```
"abc".methods
```

It lists all the methods that are present in the string class:

```
irb(main):084:0> "abc".methods
=> [:encode, :include?, :%, :*, :+, :to_c, :count, :partition, :sum, :next, :casecmp, :casecmp?, :insert, :bytesize, :matc
h, :match?, :succ!, :<=>, :next!, :index, :rindex, :upto, :==, :===, :chr, :=~, :byteslice, :[], :[]=, :scrub!, :getbyte,
:replace, :clear, :scrub, :empty?, :eql?, :-@, :downcase, :upcase, :dump, :setbyte, :swapcase, :+@, :capitalize, :capitali
ze!, :undump, :downcase!, :oct, :swapcase!, :lines, :bytes, :split, :codepoints, :freeze, :inspect, :reverse!, :grapheme_c
lusters, :reverse, :hex, :scan, :upcase!, :crypt, :ord, :chars, :prepend, :length, :size, :start_with?, :succ, :sub, :inte
rn, :chop, :center, :<<, :concat, :strip, :lstrip, :end_with?, :delete_prefix, :to_str, :to_sym, :gsub!, :rstrip, :gsub, :
delete_suffix, :to_s, :to_i, :rjust, :chomp!, :strip!, :lstrip!, :sub!, :chomp, :chop!, :ljust, :tr_s, :delete, :rstrip!,
:delete_prefix!, :delete_suffix!, :tr, :squeeze!, :each_line, :to_f, :tr!, :tr_s!, :delete!, :slice, :slice!, :each_byte,
:squeeze, :each_codepoint, :each_grapheme_cluster, :valid_encoding?, :ascii_only?, :rpartition, :encoding, :hash, :b, :uni
code_normalize!, :unicode_normalized?, :to_r, :force_encoding, :each_char, :unicode_normalize, :encode!, :unpack, :unpack1
, :<=, :>=, :between?, :<, :>, :clamp, :instance_variable_set, :instance_variable_defined?, :remove_instance_variable, :in
stance_of?, :kind_of?, :is_a?, :tap, :instance_variable_get, :singleton_method, :method, :public_method, :define_singleton
_method, :public_send, :extend, :pp, :to_enum, :enum_for, :!~, :respond_to?, :object_id, :send, :display, :nil?, :class, :
singleton_class, :clone, :dup, :itself, :yield_self, :taint, :tainted?, :untaint, :untrust, :untrusted?, :trust, :frozen?,
:methods, :singleton_methods, :protected_methods, :private_methods, :public_methods, :instance_variables, :!, :equal?, :i
nstance_eval, :instance_exec, :!=, :__id__, :__send__]
```

Figure 1.44: String methods

> **Note**
>
> To find out more about all the methods and the operations they can perform, refer to the official documentation at https://packt.live/2pDVtK5.

Activity 1.01: Generating Email Addresses Using Ruby

Imagine you have to write a Ruby program for a company (with the **rubyprograms.com** domain), which will generate a roster of email IDs of the company's employees. For this, we just need to accept user input in the form of the first name and last name of each employee and place them in an email format, which means adding an **@** symbol between the two.

Observe the following steps to complete the activity:

1. Create variables to accept the first names and last names of the individuals.

2. Use **gets.chomp** to accept string input from users.

3. Combine the first name and last name with the domain name and print the result.

   The expected output is as follows:

```
Enter your first name:
akshat
Enter your last name:
paul
akshatpaul@rubyprogram.com
```

Figure 1.45: Output for email address generation

> **Note**
>
> The solution to the activity can be found on page 458.

Boolean

Unlike other languages, Ruby does not have a Boolean type, but it has true and false Boolean values, which are essentially instances of the **TrueClass** and the **FalseClass**, respectively. These are singleton instances, which means that you can't create other instances of these classes.

Let's test this with an example:

```
a = nil
 => nil
a.nil?
 => true
```

The output should be as follows:

```
irb(main):003:0> a = nil
=> nil
irb(main):004:0> a.nil?
=> true
```

Figure 1.46: True and false classes

You get Boolean values when you check whether the **a** variable is **nil**.

We will learn more about the Boolean data type in *Chapter 3, Controlling Program Flow*.

Activity 1.02: Calculating the Area and Perimeter of a Candy Manufacturing Plant

In this activity, we will be using radius as the input to calculate the area and perimeter of a candy manufacturing plant.

Follow these steps to complete the activity:

1. Go to the Terminal and use **irb** to enter the IRB.

2. Define the variables for **radius**, **perimeter**, and **area**.

3. Calculate the value received from user input stored in the radius variable and print the results for **area** and **perimeter**.

   The expected output is as follows:

   ```
   Enter the radius for the circular candy: 1.3
   The perimeter of the candy is 8.1681408978.
   The area of the candy is 5.30929158357.
   ```

   Figure 1.47: Output for area and perimeter

> **Note**
>
> The solution to the activity can be found on page 459.

Summary

In this chapter, we learned about the fundamentals of Ruby and its key features. We started with the history of Ruby and the key programming paradigms the language supports that make it unique and powerful at the same time. We then learned about using Ruby code with the IRB and also learned how to write code in Ruby files and execute it. Next, we delved into the standard data types in Ruby, which are number, Boolean, and string. Here, we implemented various operations on variables along with commonly used string operations, such as string concatenation and interpolation.

In the next chapter, we will learn how to work with data structures such as arrays and hashes. We will explore the details of the various powerful methods associated with them, and we will also learn how to create our own Ruby methods and call them, which is the bedrock of day-to-day programming with Ruby.

Ruby Data Types and Operations

Overview

By the end of this chapter, you will be able to perform operations on arrays and hashes; use Ruby methods on arrays and hashes; create your own Ruby method and write a Ruby program for rolling dice.

Introduction

In the previous chapter, we studied variables, constants, strings, and various data types. We performed various operations on strings and numbers. We were also introduced to the **Interactive Ruby Shell (IRB)**, which makes coding in Ruby easier.

This chapter is dedicated to bringing you up to speed with arrays, hashes, and methods in Ruby. You could say that these are among the most fundamental topics. We will take a closer look at the different ways of creating arrays and hashes, as there are a wide variety of options. We'll also look at methods, which is another essential concept in Ruby and study certain rules about arguments that you should be aware of while creating methods. After that, you have the fundamentals to become a fine Ruby developer.

Arrays

An array is a data structure that contains a list of values called **elements**. Arrays can be an ordered, integer-indexed collection of any object. Ruby arrays can have objects such as **Integer**, **String**, **Symbol**, **Fixnum**, and **Hash**, or even other arrays, as elements. In many languages, arrays are rigid in terms of their size. In Ruby, however, an array increases its size as elements are added.

When we say ordered, we mean that the array will keep track of how the elements are inserted or removed from it. While fetching the data from an array, we can retrieve the values directly based on the position of the element. This will become clearer as we dive into the depths of data extraction and manipulation using arrays.

Integer-indexed means that each element in the array is linked to an index. In Ruby, we can fetch the data from an array based on the index irrespective of the value at that location. Like most other languages, array indexes in Ruby start from zero.

Ruby is very flexible and provides us with many ways in which to create arrays. Let's now look at a few examples in relation to arrays.

> **Note**
>
> We will be using Interactive Ruby Shell (IRB) extensively in this chapter for all examples, exercises, and activities.

Beginning with arrays, here is the code for creating an empty array:

```
my_array = []
```

The output will appear as follows:

```
irb(main):001:0> my_array = []
=> []
```

Figure 2.1: Output for an empty array

To create an array with predefined values, we need to include the values in the parentheses **[]**, as shown in the following code snippet:

```
my_array = [1,2,3]
```

The output will appear as follows:

```
irb(main):002:0> my_array = [1,2,3]
=> [1, 2, 3]
```

Figure 2.2: Output for an array with predefined values

To create an array with default values using a different method that involves the **.new** function in the **Array** class with arguments, consider the following command:

```
my_array = Array.new([1,2,3])
my_array = Array.new(3, "ruby")
```

The output on IRB would appear as follows:

```
irb(main):006:0> my_array = Array.new([1,2,3])
=> [1, 2, 3]
irb(main):007:0> Array.new(3, "ruby")
=> ["ruby", "ruby", "ruby"]
```

Figure 2.3: Output with Array.new

The **.new** function is a constructor for the **Array** class, which can take different arguments based on your current requirements.

If we want to create an array with the first few values as empty and start from a particular index in certain scenarios, we could do so as follows:

```
my_array = []
my_array[4] = "ruby"
my_array
```

The output will be as shown in the following code block:

```
irb(main):008:0> my_array = []
=> []
irb(main):009:0> my_array[4] = "ruby"
=> "ruby"
irb(main):010:0> my_array
=> [nil, nil, nil, nil, "ruby"]
```

Figure 2.4: Output for an array with the first four values empty

Unlike languages such as Java/C, an array in Ruby can contain more than one type of element, as depicted in the following code:

```
my_array = ["ruby", 1, "is", 2, "awesome", 3]
```

The output will appear as follows :

```
irb(main):012:0> my_array = ["ruby", 1, "is", 2, "awesome", 3]
=> ["ruby", 1, "is", 2, "awesome", 3]
```

Figure 2.5: Output for arrays with different types of elements

Iterating Through an Array

Iterating through an array can either be done with or without the index. The code for both scenarios is presented as follows:

- Code for iterating without an index:

```
my_array = [1,2,3,4,5]
my_array.each do |element|
puts element
end
```

The output will be as follows:

```
1
2
3
4
5
```

Figure 2.6: Iterating without an index

- Code for iterating with an index:

```
my_array = ["a","b","c","d","e"]
my_array.each_with_index do |element, index|
    puts "#{element} => #{index}"
end
```

The output will be as follows:

```
a => 0
b => 1
c => 2
d => 3
e => 4
=> ["a", "b", "c", "d", "e"]
```

Figure 2.7: Iterating with an index

As mentioned previously, the index starts from 0. However, note that the index is just a variable and we can play around with it just like any other variable and it will not affect how we iterate over an array. By way of a demonstration, we can create a loop over the **each_with_index** function of an array and show the **index+10** value for the array item. The **each_with_index** function will iterate over each element and create a temporary variable that shows the actual index of the element in the array, before returning a pair of elements (**element**, **index**) for each iteration.

In the first iteration, this will be (**'a',10**). It prints out "index + 10 => element", meaning it will print "10 => a" in the first iteration. As depicted in the following code:

```
my_array = ["a","b","c","d","e"]
my_array.each_with_index do |element, index|
puts "#{element} => #{index + 10}"
end
```

The output will appear as follows:

```
a => 10
b => 11
c => 12
d => 13
e => 14
=> ["a", "b", "c", "d", "e"]
```

Figure 2.8: Output for the each_with_index function

> **Note**
>
> Changing the value of the index variable is only valid during its current iteration and does not affect subsequent iterations of the loop.

Ruby is purely an object-oriented language. This means that arrays are objects themselves. The full **Object Oriented Programming (OOP)** paradigm is valid for Ruby constructs throughout the application. We can use inheritance, polymorphism, and encapsulation in our application.

Now, let's check the base class for our **Array**. The base class is a class from which the specific properties of a data type and methods are inherited in a new instance as a way of reusing code and maintaining functionality.

Use the following code to check the class of the array:

```
my_array.class
```

The output on IRB would appear as follows:

```
irb(main):033:0> my_array.class
=> Array
```

Figure 2.9: Output for the array class

Ruby provides us with inbuilt methods related to a specific data type that allow us to discover the inherited methods, as well as the methods of our instance. This can be achieved using the .**methods** function as follows:

```
my_array.methods
```

The output will be as follows:

```
irb(main):036:0> my_array.methods
=> [:to_h, :include?, :at, :fetch, :last, :push, :append, :pop, :shift, :unshift, :each_index, :
ort!, :sort_by!, :collect!, :map!, :select!, :keep_if, :values_at, :delete_at, :delete_if, :reje
anspose, :-, :uniq!, :compact!, :flatten, :flatten!, :rassoc, :shuffle!, :sample, :permutation,
fle, :repeated_permutation, :repeated_combination, :product, :compact, :bsearch_index, :bsearch,
, :select, :reject, :collect, :map, :first, :any?, :reverse_each, :zip, :take, :take_while, :dro
m, :uniq, :|, :insert, :pack, :<=>, :<<, :index, :rindex, :replace, :==, :clear, :[], :[]=, :emp
rse!, :concat, :inspect, :prepend, :max, :min, :length, :size, :each, :to_ary, :delete, :to_a, :
, :hash, :frozen?, :find, :entries, :sort_by, :grep, :grep_v, :detect, :find_all, :flat_map, :co
uce, :partition, :group_by, :all?, :one?, :none?, :minmax, :min_by, :max_by, :minmax_by, :member
entry, :each_slice, :each_cons, :each_with_object, :chunk, :slice_before, :slice_after, :slice_w
instance_variable_set, :instance_variable_defined?, :remove_instance_variable, :instance_of?, :k
tance_variable_get, :singleton_method, :method, :public_method, :define_singleton_method, :publi
num, :enum_for, :===, :=~, :!~, :respond_to?, :freeze, :object_id, :send, :display, :nil?, :clas
, :dup, :itself, :yield_self, :taint, :tainted?, :untaint, :untrust, :untrusted?, :trust, :metho
otected_methods, :private_methods, :public_methods, :instance_variables, :!, :equal?, :instance_
:__id__, :__send__]
```

Figure 2.10: Methods for an array

As can be seen from the preceding output, **.methods** will return all the method names the object can be called upon. The preceding screenshot shows **169** methods, but we'll dig deep into just a few of the most common and important methods.

Ruby allows us to check whether a method is implemented in the instance we created, and thus inherited from its base class. This can be checked on an array using the **.respond_to** function. Consider the following example:

```
my_array = ["I", "love", "ruby"]
my_array.respond_to?("length")
my_array.respond_to?("garbage")
```

The output will appear as follows:

```
irb(main):040:0> my_array.respond_to?("length")
=> true
irb(main):041:0> my_array.respond_to?("garbage")
=> false
```

Figure 2.11: Output using the .respond_to? function on an array

In the preceding example, we define a set of variables in an array and check how the array responds to the methods called on the array. If you see the output, Ruby returns **true** when the **length** method is called on the array and **false** when a non-existent **garbage** method is called on the array. This clearly means that the array will only *respond to* the defined methods and return **false** for anything other than that.

Let's now move on to implementing some operations on arrays.

Operations on Arrays

Arrays are the Swiss army knife of every programming language. They are usually used to store values or different types, to calculate intermediate or final results, and even to send data to other functions or classes. This section shows you how we can harness the power of arrays for this purpose.

In this section, we are going to study how to perform various operations on arrays.

Merging Two Arrays

Different values held in arrays can be merged, as shown in the following code:

```
my_array_first_half = [1,2,3]
my_array_second_half = [4, 5, 6]
my_array_first_half + my_array_second_half
```

The output will appear as follows:

```
irb(main):044:0> my_array_first_half + my_array_second_half
=> [1, 2, 3, 4, 5, 6]
```

Figure 2.12: Merging two arrays

From the preceding code, you can clearly discern that the two arrays have been merged together using the + operator.

Note that even different values, belonging to different data types, that are held in arrays can be merged.

Removing Occurrences of Similar Elements from an Array

Values that have multiple instances in the array can be removed, as shown in the following code:

```
my_array_with_duplicates = [1, 1, 4, 5, 6]
my_array_to_be_removed = [1,2,3]
my_array_with_duplicates - my_array_to_be_removed
```

The output will be as shown in the following code block:

```
irb(main):054:0> my_array_with_duplicates - my_array_to_be_removed
=> [4, 5, 6]
```

Figure 2.13: Removing similar elements from the array

In the preceding code, we defined two arrays with a few variables. Using the - operator, all the occurrences of the second array were removed from the resulting array.

If you notice, all the occurrences of **1** are removed from the result.

Inserting Elements into an Array at the End

There are many ways in which you can insert elements in an array. The following code shows how to insert elements using the **push** method. This will extend the current array with the new elements specified as arguments to the **push** function. They can be of any type; it is not necessary to have the same type of elements as the values already in the array:

```
my_array  = [1,2,3]
my_array.push(4)
```

The output will be as shown in the following code block:

```
irb(main):059:0> my_array.push(4)
=> [1, 2, 3, 4]
```

Figure 2.14: Inserting elements into an array using the push method

Here, we have defined an array and pushed the variable **4** into the array using the .**push** method.

Another way to add elements to an array is by means of the **<<** operator. There are operators in Ruby that are aliases to functions or methods, and they are used to achieve the same result, but with shortcuts:

```
my_array  = [1,2,3]
my_array  << 4
```

The output will be as shown in the following code block:

```
irb(main):064:0> my_array  << 4
=> [1, 2, 3, 4]
```

Figure 2.15: Inserting elements into an array using the << operator

As you can see, the variable **4** is added to the array using the **<<** operator.

Finding the Last Element of an Array without Modifying It

You can find the last element of the array as shown in the following code:

```
my_array  = [1,2,3]
my_array.last
my_array
```

The output will be as shown in the following code block:

```
irb(main):069:0> my_array.last
=> 3
```

Figure 2.16: Finding the last element of the array

As shown in the preceding diagram, the .last method displays the last element of the array.

Finding the Last Element of an Array and Removing it

You can find the last element of the array and eliminate it, as shown in the following code:

```
my_array  = [1,2,3]
my_array.pop
my_array
```

The output will be as shown in the following code block:

```
irb(main):006:0> my_array.pop
=> 3
irb(main):007:0> my_array
=> [1, 2]
```

Figure 2.17: Eliminating the last element from an array

The .pop method has picked up the last element and removed it from the array.

Let's now solve an exercise to deepen our understanding of operations performed on arrays.

Exercise 2.01: Performing Simple Operations on Arrays

In this exercise, we are going to execute the following operations on an array:

- Merge arrays.
- Remove the repeated occurrences of elements in two arrays.
- Insert new elements into an array.
- Find the last element of the array without modifying it.
- Find the last element of the array and remove it.

We will define two arrays, **colors_1** and **colors_2**, in which we will store colors of the visible light spectrum as elements, and then perform the aforementioned operations on these arrays.

The following steps will help you to complete the exercise:

1. Go to the Terminal and enter **irb** for Interactive Ruby Shell.

2. Define the two arrays that you wish to merge and merge them into one array, to be termed as **colors_3**:

```
colors_1 = ['violet', 'indigo', 'blue', 'green']
colors_2 = ['yellow', 'violet', 'orange', 'red', 'violet']
colors_3 = colors_1 + colors_2
```

The output of the colors_3 array would be as follows:

```
irb(main):084:0> colors_3 = colors_1 + colors_2
=> ["violet", "indigo", "blue", "green", "yellow", "violet", "orange", "red", "violet"]
```

Figure 2.18: Output of the colors_3 array

As can be seen in the output, the new array includes elements from both the **colors_1** and **colors_2** arrays. However, as you might notice, some colors are repeated. We will eliminate the duplicates in the next step.

3. Next, use the - operator to remove the repeated occurrences of the elements in the two arrays:

```
colors_repeated = ['violet']
colors_new = colors_3 - colors_repeated
```

The output of the **colors_new** array would be as follows:

```
irb(main):088:0> colors_new = colors_3 - colors_repeated
=> ["indigo", "blue", "green", "yellow", "orange", "red"]
```

Figure 2.19: Output of the colors_new array

You can see that the array only has unique elements. Now, let's try inserting new elements into our arrays.

4. Then, insert new elements into the array:

```
colors_1.push('yellow')
colors_1.push('red')
colors_2.push('green')
colors_2.push('blue')
```

The new **colors_1** and **colors_2** arrays will be as follows:

```
irb(main):092:0> colors_1.push('yellow')
=> ["violet", "indigo", "blue", "green", "yellow"]
irb(main):093:0> colors_1.push('red')
=> ["violet", "indigo", "blue", "green", "yellow", "red"]
irb(main):094:0> colors_2.push('green')
=> ["yellow", "violet", "orange", "red", "violet", "green"]
irb(main):095:0> colors_2.push('blue')
=> ["yellow", "violet", "orange", "red", "violet", "green", "blue"]
```

Figure 2.20: Output of the colors_1 and colors_2 arrays

You can now see how the **yellow**, **red** elements have been added to the **colors_1** array, and how the **green**, **blue** elements have been added to the **colors_2** array.

5. Now, we will trace the last element of the array without modifying the array:

```
colors_1 = ['violet', 'indigo', 'blue', 'green']
colors_1.last
```

The output will be as follows:

```
irb(main):099:0> colors_1.last
=> "green"
```

Figure 2.21: Last element of the array

As you can see from the output, the **.last** method has picked up the last element of the array.

6. Next, we will find the last element in the array and remove it:

```
colors_1 = ['violet', 'indigo', 'blue', 'green']
colors_1.pop
colors_1
```

The output should be as follows:

```
irb(main):104:0> colors_1.pop
=> "green"
irb(main):105:0> colors_1
=> ["violet", "indigo", "blue"]
```

Figure 2.22: Output of the colors_2 array without the last element

As you can see from the output, the **.pop** method has removed the last element from the array.

Thus, we have successfully performed basic operations on arrays.

Until now, we have only performed basic operations on arrays. However, there are many more operations, such as "freezing" an array, finding unique elements, and sorting elements.

Let's now look at each of these in more detail.

Creating an Array That Cannot Be Modified

This can come in handy when we want to limit the size of an array or prevent further modification. The **freeze** function can be used on objects other than arrays with the same result:

```
my_array  = [1,2,3]
my_array.freeze
my_array << 4
```

The output will be as shown in the following code block:

```
Traceback (most recent call last):
        2: from C:/Ruby25-x64/bin/irb.cmd:19:in `<main>'
        1: from (irb):111
FrozenError (can't modify frozen Array)
```

Figure 2.23: FrozenError

As we can see, the error in the output clearly implies that a frozen array cannot be modified.

Finding All the Unique Elements in an Array

uniq means we want to have every occurrence of an element only once in our array. We can retrieve a different object with the results or just modify our original list in place.

Consider the following example:

```
my_array  = [1,2,3, 4,3,2]
unique_array = my_array.uniq
my_array
```

The output will be as shown in the following code block:

```
irb(main):117:0> unique_array = my_array.uniq
=> [1, 2, 3, 4]
```

Figure 2.24: Output of the uniq function

Note that in the preceding case, we do not modify the existing array, rather a new array is returned by the **uniq** method. If we want to modify the existing array, we can use **!** as follows:

```
my_array  = [1,2,3, 4,3,2]
my_array.uniq!
my_array
```

The output will be as shown in the following code block:

```
irb(main):123:0> my_array.uniq!
=> [1, 2, 3, 4]
```

Figure 2.25: Output for the uniq! function

As you can see, **uniq!** has modified the array, keeping only one instance of each element.

Sorting the Elements of an Array

Remember that if we have to modify the existing array, we need to use **!**, as in **sort!**. We can also reverse sort an array. Sorting comes in handy when we do not have any control over the order in which the array elements arrive, but we want to process them in some kind of order. **.reverse** will give us the reverse order of the elements after sorting them, so it's two steps behind the scenes:

```
my_array = [3,6,23, 1]
my_array.sort
my_array.sort.reverse
```

The output will be as shown in the following code block:

```
irb(main):126:0> my_array.sort
=> [1, 3, 6, 23]
irb(main):127:0> my_array.sort.reverse
=> [23, 6, 3, 1]
```

Figure 2.26: Sorting elements

As you see in the preceding output, the array has been arranged in ascending order and also reversed using **.reverse**.

Finding the Number of Elements in an Array

The .**length** and .**size** methods do exactly the same thing and we can use either of them. Consider the following example:

```
my_array  = [1,2,3]
my_array.length
my_array.size
```

The output will be as shown in the following code block:

```
irb(main):131:0> my_array.length
=> 3
irb(main):132:0> my_array.size
=> 3
```

Figure 2.27: Output for the length and size methods

As you can see, the .**length** and .**size** methods have returned the size and length of the array.

> **Note**
>
> In Ruby convention, any method that ends with ? implies that it will return a Boolean value. While writing our own methods, we should observe the same practice.

Establishing Whether an Element Exists in an Array (Case-Sensitive)

include? is used to find the occurrences of an element in an array. It is case-sensitive and is an extremely useful method when it comes to large arrays.

Consider the following example where we will call the **include?** method on two variables with different cases:

```
my_array = ["I", "love", "ruby"]
my_array.include?("ruby")
my_array.include?("Ruby")
```

The output will be as shown in the following code block:

```
irb(main):136:0> my_array.include?("ruby")
=> true
irb(main):137:0> my_array.include?("Ruby")
=> false
```

Figure 2.28: Output of the include? method

As you can see, **include?** has identified the element mentioned in the array and stated the output accordingly as per the element that is being searched for. The array contains **ruby** and, hence, the method has returned **true** for **ruby**, and **false** for **Ruby**.

Converting Elements of an Array into a String

The purpose of **join** here is to combine each element of the array with the string that is passed as a parameter to the **join** method.

Consider the following example:

```
my_array = ["I", "love", "ruby"]
my_array.join(",")
my_array.join(" ")
```

The output will be as shown in the following code block:

```
irb(main):144:0> my_array.join(",")
=> "I,love,ruby"
irb(main):145:0> my_array.join(" ")
=> "I love ruby"
```

Figure 2.29: Output of the join method

As we can see, the element , has been added to the variables in the array in the first case, and a whitespace has been added, in the second case. **join** has successfully combined the elements with a string passed as a parameter.

Exercise 2.02: Performing Complex Operations on Arrays

In this exercise, we will implement all the array operations discussed in the preceding section. We will define an array having numbers as elements for this purpose and then proceed to perform the various array operations.

The following steps will help you to complete the exercise:

1. Go to the Terminal and enter **irb** for Interactive Ruby Shell.

2. Define the array and use **.freeze** to make it unchangeable. Make sure you use a different notation for the new array so that you can use the original array in subsequent steps:

```
my_array = [1,2,3,4,5,6,6,4,3,2,1]
my_array.freeze
```

The output will appear as shown in the following code block:

```
irb(main):150:0> my_array.freeze
=> [1, 2, 3, 4, 5, 6, 6, 4, 3, 2, 1]
```

Figure 2.30: Output of the frozen array

Now that we have frozen the array, it is not possible to make any changes to this array or perform any operations on it.

3. You may have observed that there are a few values that are repeated in our array. Now, let's write the code to list the unique elements in the array using **.uniq**:

```
my_uniq_arry = my_array.uniq
```

The array should now be as shown in the following code block:

```
irb(main):153:0> my_uniq_arry = my_array.uniq
=> [1, 2, 3, 4, 5, 6]
```

Figure 2.31: Output for .uniq

You can see that the new array has eliminated the repeat occurrences of the variables and returned only the unique elements of the array.

4. Next, we use .**sort** to arrange the elements in alphabetical order:

```
my_sorted_array = my_array.sort
```

The output for the .**sort** method will be as follows:

```
irb(main):158:0> my_sorted_array = my_array.sort
=> [1, 1, 2, 2, 3, 3, 4, 4, 5, 6, 6]
```

Figure 2.32: Output for the .sort method

As can be seen in the preceding figure, the array has now sorted the elements in ascending order.

5. Now, we find the total number of elements in the array using .**length** and .**size**:

```
my_array.size
my_array.length
```

The array size and length are as shown in the following code block:

```
irb(main):161:0> my_array.size
=> 11
irb(main):162:0> my_array.length
=> 11
```

Figure 2.33: Output for the size and length of the array

With .**length** and .**size**, we have derived the actual length and size of the array.

6. Next, we shall use .**include** to establish whether a particular element exists in the array:

```
my_array.include?(1)
my_array.include?(11)
```

The output will be as shown in the following code block:

```
irb(main):165:0> my_array.include?(1)
=> true
irb(main):166:0> my_array.include?(11)
=> false
```

Figure 2.34: Output for the .include method

As you can see, the .**include?** method returns **true** when checked for the element 1, and false for the element 11.

7. Lastly, we shall be converting the elements of the array into a string:

```
my_array.inspect
```

The output will be as shown in the following code block:

```
irb(main):170:0> my_array.inspect
=> "[1, 2, 3, 4, 5, 6, 6, 4, 3, 2, 1]"
```

Figure 2.35: Output for .inspect

With the completion this exercise, we have successfully implemented all the aforementioned methods on an array and established a basic understanding of arrays in Ruby.

Hashes

Hashes are collections that save data as key-value pairs. This means that a key will identify every value that we want to save. This also means that keys within a hash have to be unique, otherwise we will overwrite the old values.

In terms of performance, hashes have a lookup time of **O(1)**, which means that finding a value in a hash by its key will not be dependent on the size of the hash, nor on the order in which the hash was created. **O(1)** means a constant lookup time for the operation performed on a hash, irrespective of the data size. This differs from arrays, where finding a value in an **O(n)** operation means that the time taken to find an element in an array will be dependent on the length of an array. This means that we are looking for an element and we are going to find it on the *nth* location; the **n** does not denote the size of the array, but the location of the element.

An empty hash can be created as follows:

```
my_hash = {}
my_hash = Hash.new
```

The output will be as follows:

```
irb(main):004:0> my_hash = {}
=> {}
irb(main):005:0> my_hash = Hash.new
=> {}
```

Figure 2.36: Output for the Hash.new method

We can also create hashes that have a default value, as shown in the following code snippet:

```ruby
my_hash = Hash.new("No Value")
my_hash["Non existent key"]
my_hash = Hash.new("test")
my_hash["No such key"]
```

The output with default values would be as follows:

```
irb(main):008:0> my_hash = Hash.new("No Value")
=> {}
irb(main):009:0> my_hash["Non existent key"]
=> "No Value"
irb(main):010:0> my_hash = Hash.new("test")
=> {}
irb(main):011:0> my_hash["No such key"]
=> "test"
```

Figure 2.37: Output for default values in hashes

We can also initialize hashes when creating them as well, as you will see in the following code:

```ruby
my_hash = {"jan" => 1, "feb" => 2, "mar" => 3}
```

The initialized hash would now appear as follows:

```
irb(main):014:0> my_hash = {"jan" => 1, "feb" => 2, "mar" => 3}
=> {"jan"=>1, "feb"=>2, "mar"=>3}
```

Figure 2.38: Output for initialized hashes

We can also add values to the hash. When adding values to the hash, we can use two syntaxes. When the keys are symbols, values can be assigned to the hash as follows:

```ruby
my_hash = {}
my_hash[:jan] = 1
my_hash[:feb] = 2
my_hash[:mar] = 3
my_hash
```

:jan is called a symbol, and it's very similar to a string; however, strings are used to store data, while symbols are used as identifiers in Ruby.

The updated hash will now appear as follows:

```
irb(main):022:0> my_hash
=> {:jan=>1, :feb=>2, :mar=>3}
```

Figure 2.39: Output for the hash with assigned values

> **Note**
>
> Keys are preceded with a : and not with double quotes.

When the keys are strings, values are assigned to the hash as follows:

```
my_hash = {}
my_hash["jan"] = 1
my_hash["feb"] = 2
my_hash["mar"] = 3
my_hash
```

The output, when keys are strings, would be as follows:

```
irb(main):030:0> my_hash
=> {"jan"=>1, "feb"=>2, "mar"=>3}
```

Figure 2.40: Output for the hash when keys are strings

As you can see, we have used both symbols and strings as keys in the hash. While we can use symbols and strings in a single hash, it is not advisable as the person reading our code would not be able to guess what we are using, and this would always be a source of confusion when retrieving values.

The value in the key-value pair inside a hash can be any data type, such as an array of our custom object, or even an array of our custom class objects.

We can use whichever method we want, but while using the hash, we must stick to just one. If the key is a symbol and we try to retrieve it as a string, the hash will return **nil**. The following code will show you the same:

```
my_hash = {}
my_hash[:jan] = 1
my_hash[:feb] = 2
my_hash[:mar] = 3
my_hash[:mar]
my_hash[:mar.to_s]
my_hash[:jan.to_s]
```

The output will now appear as follows:

```
irb(main):038:0> my_hash[:mar] = 3
=> 3
irb(main):039:0> my_hash[:mar]
=> 3
irb(main):040:0> my_hash[:mar.to_s]
=> nil
```

Figure 2.41: Output for the hash when the symbol is retrieved as a string

Note how referring to :mar gives us the correct value. However, when we convert the keys to the :mar.to_s string, it fails to find the appropriate value.

The most common way to iterate through a hash is to use the .each iterator, which gives access to both keys and values of a hash while iterating.

Consider the following example:

```
my_hash = {}
my_hash[:jan] = 1
my_hash[:feb] = 2
my_hash[:mar] = 3
my_hash.each do |key, value|
puts "#{key} => #{value}"
end
```

The output will be as follows:

```
jan => 1
feb => 2
mar => 3
=> {:jan=>1, :feb=>2, :mar=>3}
```

Figure 2.42: Output using the .each iterator

In the preceding code, we have created a hash and defined the keys – :jan, :feb, and :mar, with values. We have used the .each iterator to iterate through the key-value pairs.

As you can see, the .each iterator has pulled up both the keys and values of the hash through the iteration.

Ruby is purely an object-oriented language, which means that basic data types such as hashes are also objects in Ruby. This can be realized by the following code snippet:

```
my_hash = {}
my_hash.class
```

The object type of **hash** is displayed as follows:

```
irb(main):059:0> my_hash = {}
=> {}
irb(main):060:0> my_hash.class
=> Hash
```

Figure 2.43: Object type of hash

As you can see, the hash belongs to the **Hash** class. This also means that we can figure out which methods the **Hash** class responds to as well, as shown in the following code:

```
my_hash = {}
my_hash.methods
```

The output will be as follows:

```
irb(main):064:0> my_hash.methods
=> [:index, :<=, :replace, :==, :clear, :>=, :[], :to_h, :[]=, :include?, :empty?, :eql?, :fetch, :shift, :selec
t!, :keep_if, :values_at, :inspect, :delete_if, :reject!, :assoc, :rassoc, :compact, :compact!, :flatten, :lengt
h, :size, :each, :<, :>, :default, :rehash, :store, :default=, :default_proc, :default_proc=, :to_hash, :to_proc
, :each_key, :to_a, :to_s, :each_pair, :transform_values, :transform_keys!, :values, :transform_values!, :fetch_
values, :slice, :update, :transform_keys, :select, :each_value, :invert, :keys, :merge!, :merge, :reject, :delet
e, :key?, :value?, :has_key?, :has_value?, :any?, :compare_by_identity, :compare_by_identity?, :member?, :dig, :
hash, :key, :max, :min, :find, :entries, :sort, :sort_by, :grep, :grep_v, :count, :detect, :find_index, :find_al
l, :collect, :map, :flat_map, :collect_concat, :inject, :reduce, :partition, :group_by, :first, :all?, :one?, :n
one?, :minmax, :min_by, :max_by, :minmax_by, :each_with_index, :reverse_each, :each_entry, :each_slice, :each_co
ns, :each_with_object, :zip, :take, :take_while, :drop, :drop_while, :cycle, :chunk, :slice_before, :slice_after
, :slice_when, :chunk_while, :sum, :uniq, :lazy, :instance_variable_set, :instance_variable_defined?, :remove_in
stance_variable, :instance_of?, :kind_of?, :is_a?, :tap, :instance_variable_get, :singleton_method, :method, :pu
blic_method, :define_singleton_method, :public_send, :extend, :pp, :to_enum, :enum_for, :<=>, :===, :=~, :!~, :r
espond_to?, :freeze, :object_id, :send, :display, :nil?, :class, :singleton_class, :clone, :dup, :itself, :yield
_self, :taint, :tainted?, :untaint, :untrust, :untrusted?, :trust, :frozen?, :methods, :singleton_methods, :prot
ected_methods, :private_methods, :public_methods, :instance_variables, :!, :equal?, :instance_eval, :instance_ex
ec, :!=, :__id__, :__send__]
```

Figure 2.44: Output for methods on hashes

In Ruby, **.methods** will return all the method names on which the object can be called. The preceding figure has **147** methods, so we'll just dig deep into a few of the most common and important methods.

Soon, when we familiarize ourselves with functions and methods in Ruby that can be called on objects, we need to learn **respond_to?**, which will tell us what functionality is implemented or inherited in our instance of a specific class. In this case, we inspect the **my_hash** variable, whose functionality is supported as shown in the following code:

```
my_hash = {}
my_hash.respond_to?("length")
my_hash.respond_to?("garbage")
```

respond_to? will provide the following output:

```
irb(main):069:0> my_hash = {}
=> {}
irb(main):070:0> my_hash.respond_to?("length")
=> true
irb(main):071:0> my_hash.respond_to?("garbage")
=> false
```

Figure 2.45: Output for respond_to?

Just as for arrays, the **respond_to?** method will return the values for methods that are defined for hashes. As you can see in the preceding diagram, **respond_to?** returns **true** for the **length** method and **false** for the **garbage** method.

Operations on Hashes

In this section, we will perform various operations on hashes, just like we did for arrays, as mentioned in the following list:

- Getting values based on keys
- Setting values for keys
- Sorting
- Merging
- Deleting values of a key
- Removing or rejecting keys
- Searching for values or keys

Let's have a look at each of these in detail.

Getting Values from the Hash

It's the key that fetches the value from the hash. If the key does not exist, a nil value will be returned:

```
my_hash = {:jan => 1, :feb => 2}
my_hash[:feb]
my_hash[:march]
```

The output will be as follows:

```
irb(main):074:0> my_hash = {:jan => 1, :feb => 2}
=> {:jan=>1, :feb=>2}
irb(main):075:0> my_hash[:feb]
=> 2
irb(main):076:0> my_hash[:march]
=> nil
```

Figure 2.46: Retrieving values from the hash

As you can see, the hash returns the value 2 for the :feb key, but **false** for the :march key as the latter is not a part of the hash.

Sorting a Hash

Sorting a hash is not as simple as it is in an array. You can sort a hash by value by using .**sort_by**. The result of .**sort_by** is an array, with each key-value pair as an array element in a sorted manner. The .**sort_by** function operates differently based on which object is called.

The following code will show you how you can iterate over the |**key,value**| pairs of a hash, and then sort based on the second argument, which will be **age**, which is the value for the given hash key:

```
my_hash = {:bill => 34, :steve => 66, :eric => 6}
my_hash.sort_by { |name, age| age }
my_hash.sort_by { |name, age| age }.reverse
```

The output will be as follows:

```
irb(main):080:0> my_hash = {:bill => 34, :steve => 66, :eric => 6}
=> {:bill=>34, :steve=>66, :eric=>6}
irb(main):081:0> my_hash.sort_by { |name, age| age }
=> [[:eric, 6], [:bill, 34], [:steve, 66]]
irb(main):082:0> my_hash.sort_by { |name, age| age }.reverse
=> [[:steve, 66], [:bill, 34], [:eric, 6]]
```

Figure 2.47: Output for sorting and reversing arrays

As can be seen from the output, you can infer that the keys have been sorted and arranged as defined by the key-value pair by using the .**sort_by** method. The same hash is now reversed using the .**reverse** method.

Sorting can even be done on a more complex hash. It can be sorted by what we provide as a parameter in the .**sort_by** method.

Our next hash is a nested hash, where each key holds a small hash. We will sort the hash based on the :**age** of the hashes located inside the keys:

```
my_hash = {:bill => {:name => "Bill", :age => 55}, :steve => {:name => "Steve", :age => 60}, :eric => {:name =>"Eric", :age => 50}}
my_hash.sort_by {|key, value| value[:age]}
```

The output will be as follows:

```
irb(main):101:0> my_hash.sort_by {|key, value| value[:age]}
=> [[:eric, {:name=>"Eric", :age=>50}], [:bill, {:name=>"Bill", :age=>55}], [:steve, {:name=>"Steve", :age=>60}]]
```

Figure 2.48: Sorting keys in a hash

Merging Hashes

Hashes can be merged together just like arrays, but there is something you need to be mindful of the order in which the keys are passed within the hash. To understand this, let's look at the following example:

```
my_hash_1 = {:a => 10, :b => 20}
my_hash_2 = {:c => 30, :d => 40}
my_hash_1.merge(my_hash_2)
```

The output will be as follows:

```
irb(main):004:0> my_hash_1.merge(my_hash_2)
=> {:a=>10, :b=>20, :c=>30, :d=>40}
```

Figure 2.49: Output for merging hashes

In the preceding example, we merged two hashes with unique keys. However, when merging hashes with common keys, the latter will override the former.

As shown in the following example, the value in the resulting hash would be **my_hash_2** instead of **my_hash_1**. We are going to overwrite the value in the first hash with the value in the second hash as follows:

```
my_hash_1 = {:a => 10, :b => 20}
my_hash_2 = {:c => 30, :d => 40, :a => 33}
my_hash_1.merge(my_hash_2)
```

The output will be as follows:

```
irb(main):009:0> my_hash_1.merge(my_hash_2)
=> {:a=>33, :b=>20, :c=>30, :d=>40}
```

Figure 2.50: Output depicting the overriding of hashes

Retrieving Keys or Values from a Hash

We can also get all the keys or values from a hash using **.keys** and **.values**, as shown in the following code:

```
my_hash= {:a => 10, :b => 20}
my_hash.keys
my_hash.values
```

The keys and values of the hash will be as follows:

```
irb(main):014:0> my_hash.keys
=> [:a, :b]
irb(main):015:0> my_hash.values
=> [10, 20]
```

Figure 2.51: Keys and values of a hash

Deleting a Value from a Hash by Key

If the key is found, it will return the value. If the key is not found, **nil** would be returned. Look at the following example:

```
my_hash= {:a => 10, :b => 20}
my_hash.delete(:b)
my_hash
my_hash.delete(:c)
```

The output will be as follows:

```
irb(main):020:0> my_hash
=> {:a=>10}
irb(main):021:0> my_hash.delete(:c)
=> nil
```

Figure 2.52: Deleting a value from a hash

You can see how the value for **:b** is deleted and also **nil** is returned when **:c** is called.

Removing or Rejecting Elements from a Hash

Based on a logical condition, if the value of a specific key is below a threshold, .reject returns a new copy with the elements omitted, while reject! actually removes them from the hash. Consider the following example:

```
my_hash= {:a => 10, :b => 20, :c => 23, :d => 2}
my_hash.reject   { |key, value| value < 20 }
```

The output will be as follows:

```
irb(main):027:0> my_hash.reject   { |key, value| value < 20 }
=> {:b=>20, :c=>23}
```

Figure 2.53: Using reject on a hash

As you can see in the preceding code, the values below **20** were removed from the hash.

Establishing whether a Hash Contains a Particular Value

This operation will compare the value to the predefined value and display the result accordingly:

Consider the following example:

```
my_hash= {:a => 10, :b => 20}
my_hash.has_value?(10)
my_hash.has_value?(100)
```

The output will be as follows:

```
irb(main):032:0> my_hash.has_value?(10)
=> true
irb(main):033:0> my_hash.has_value?(100)
=> false
```

Figure 2.54: Finding values within the hash

The preceding output shows that the .has_value? method has returned **true** for the key **10**, as it is a part of the hash. It has subsequently returned **false** for the key **100**.

Let's now solve an exercise that will strengthen our understanding of hashes.

Exercise 2.03: Converting a Time String to a Hash

In this exercise, we will write a program to standardize the input time to **hh:mm:ss.s** format. The following steps will help with the solution:

1. Go to the Terminal and use **irb** to enter the Interactive Ruby Shell.

2. Define a string, which may be the following format – **hh:mm:ss.s**.

```
my_string_time = "00:05:23.323"
my_hash_time = {}
```

3. Split the string into appropriate keys and update the hash:

```
my_hash_time["hh"] = my_string_time.split(":")[0]
my_hash_time["mm"] = my_string_time.split(":")[1]
my_hash_time["ss"] = my_string_time.split(":")[2].split(".")[0]
my_hash_time["s"] = my_string_time.split(":")[2].split(".")[1]
```

The output will be as follows:

```
irb(main):015:0> my_hash_time["hh"] = my_string_time.split(":")[0]
=> "00"
irb(main):016:0> my_hash_time["mm"] = my_string_time.split(":")[1]
=> "05"
irb(main):017:0> my_hash_time["ss"] = my_string_time.split(":")[2].split(".")[0]
=> "23"
irb(main):018:0> my_hash_time["s"] = my_string_time.split(":")[2].split(".")[1]
=> "323"
```

Figure 2.55: Splitting the string

4. Inspect the hash to see the standardized input:

```
my_hash_time.inspect
```

The output will now appear as follows:

```
irb(main):019:0> my_hash_time.inspect
=> "{\"hh\"=>\"00\", \"mm\"=>\"05\", \"ss\"=>\"23\", \"s\"=>\"323\"}"
```

Figure 2.56: Output for the inspect method

Make sure you follow the original time format, as the program would fail if you changed it. But this exercise shows you how to convert the time string to a hash, and then refer to each part of the string as you would like to, as shown in the following code:

```
my_hash_time["hh"]
my_hash_time["mm"]
my_hash_time["ss"]
my_hash_time["s"]
```

The output will now look like the following code block:

```
irb(main):011:0> my_hash_time["hh"]
=> "00"
irb(main):012:0> my_hash_time["mm"]
=> "05"
irb(main):013:0> my_hash_time["ss"]
=> "23"
irb(main):014:0> my_hash_time["s"]
=> "323"
```

Figure 2.57: Separating strings from a hash

Ruby Methods

A method in Ruby is a set of expressions that return a value. These are similar to functions in other programming languages. Methods are defined using the **def** keyword, followed by the method name and then by optional parameters. The method body is enclosed between the preceding definition and the **end** keyword at the bottom:

```
def my_method
##method body
end
```

By convention, method names should begin with a lowercase letter, otherwise Ruby might consider it to be a constant while parsing. Also, names that have multiple words should be separated by an underscore. As in the preceding examples, the method name – **my_method**, has an underscore between two words.

Passing Arguments to a Method

We can pass arguments to the method on which a method has to operate. There is no limit in terms of the number of parameters that we can pass to a method. The following is a simple example of how we can create our own methods in Ruby:

```ruby
def add_two_numbers a, b
  puts "Sum of the number is #{a+b}"
end
add_two_numbers(10, 20)
```

The output will appear as follows:

```
Sum of the number is 30
```

Figure 2.58: Output for adding two numbers

As we can see from the preceding example, a method, **add_two_numbers**, is defined with the variables **a** and **b**. The method body comprises the display message, suggesting what method is used. The use of the parentheses (and) is optional. As a good practice, we should choose one approach in a project and follow it throughout.

Ruby Methods with Default Values

We can also define default values as parameters in the methods. In case the caller wants to use the default values, they may choose not to pass any parameter to the optional one. In case the caller wants to override it, they can always do that by passing that extra parameter.

Let's take this up with an example where we almost always want to calculate 50% of a particular value. In only 5% of the cases, this value goes to 70%:

```ruby
def percent_of_value a, b=50
  puts "Percent value is #{(a*b)/100}"
end
percent_of_value 10
percent_of_value 10, 70
```

The output will be as follows:

```
Percent value is 5
Percent value is 7
```

Figure 2.59: Output for percentage values

As we can see in the preceding example, in the first call, we do not provide the value of **b**. Since **b** is an optional value, the default value is taken, and the answer turns out to be **5**. However, in the second call, we are explicitly passing the value of **b**. This value overrides the default value and, hence, the output is evaluated to **7**.

However, these default values should always be the last parameter. Currently, there is no way where a value on the left can be a default and, when we pass just one parameter, as in the preceding case, it takes that value as a mandatory field. So, we have a default value that is stated by **a=50** and a mandatory argument, which is the **b**.

Now, let's make our problem a little more difficult. Reverse the optional and required values and see the output:

```ruby
def print_values a = 50, b
  puts "value of a is #{a}"
  puts "value of b is #{b}"
end
print_values 1
```

The output will be as follows:

```
value of a is 50
value of b is 1
```

Figure 2.60: Output after reversing the optional and required values

As we can see from the preceding example, the Ruby program was smart enough to decide which value should be given to which parameter. But actually, it shows the internal logic of Ruby; if we have an argument with a default value, it is skipped from being assigned an argument value until there are arguments without default values that can be mapped to actual arguments passed. Let's now make our problem more complex, and throw in another optional parameter:

```ruby
def print_values a = 50, b = 100, c
  puts "value of a is #{a}"
  puts "value of b is #{b}"
  puts "value of c is #{c}"
end
print_values 1, 2
```

The output will be printed as follows:

```
value of a is 1
value of b is 100
value of c is 2
```

Figure 2.61: Output with three parameters

The preceding example is very interesting since our Ruby program skipped the assigning of the middle parameter. We can first deduce from the preceding example the value of the non-optional element that is committed (from right to left), and then the optional parameters from left to right.

However, we cannot mix and match the way in which we use optional and required parameters.

Let's now add one more parameter to the code and see what output is generated:

```ruby
def print_values a = 50, b = 100, c, d=100
  puts "value of a is #{a}"
  puts "value of b is #{b}"
  puts "value of c is #{c}"
end
print_values 1, 2
```

The output will be as follows:

```
syntax error, unexpected '=', expecting ';' or '\n'
```

Figure 2.62: Syntax error

Along similar lines, if we try to pass an incorrect number of arguments, we'll get the **ArgumentError** exception. Consider the following example:

```ruby
def no_parameters
  puts "I do not take any parameters"
end
no_parameters "Hello"
```

The output will be as follows:

```
ArgumentError (wrong number of arguments (given 1, expected 0))
```

Figure 2.63: The ArgumentError exception with no parameters

Look at another example with two parameters:

```ruby
def add_two_numbers a, b
  puts "The sum is #{a + b}"
end
add_two_numbers 10
```

The output will be as follows:

```
ArgumentError (wrong number of arguments (given 1, expected 2))
```

Figure 2.64: The ArgumentError exception with two parameters

Ruby also allows us to send an unknown number of parameters to the method. This is done with the help of a splat argument represented by an asterisk, *. Splatting means that whatever we pass as an argument is going to be treated as an array. Each value or argument passed will be stored in an array called **my_params**. Let's look at how this works in the following example:

```ruby
def any_parameters(*my_params)
  puts my_params.inspect
end
any_parameters "any", "number", "of", "parameters"
```

The output will be as follows:

```
["any", "number", "of", "parameters"]
```

Figure 2.65: Using a splat operator

The .**inspect** function is a little helper that converts the input object to a string temporarily, enabling us to print all the arguments that were passed.

If we look at the output, we can see that it is an array. So, what Ruby does internally is convert all the parameters that we are passing to a method and converting the parameters into an array. Once this is done, the method can access this array and take decisions based on accordingly.

This splat operator is very handy in many situations. Let's take a look at the following examples:

```ruby
first_element, *rest_of_them = ["a", "b", "c", "d"]
puts first_element
puts rest_of_them
```

The output will be as follows:

```
irb(main):009:0> puts first_element
a
=> nil
irb(main):010:0> puts rest_of_them
b
c
d
```

Figure 2.66: Output using a splat operator

There are two things to note here. The first is that the **first_element** variable gets the first element and it is not an array. The second is that the **rest_of_them** variable is an array because of the splat operator. We can also use this splat operator to force variables into an array. Consider the following example:

```
a = "Hi".to_a
```

The output will show up an error as follows:

```
NoMethodError (undefined method `to_a' for "Hi":String)
```

Figure 2.67: Undefined method error

Now, we use a splat operator as shown in the following code:

```
a = *"Hello"
```

The output will be as follows:

```
["Hello"]
```

Figure 2.68: Using a splat operator

This is how the splat operator will force elements into an array.

Return Value(s) from Methods

Methods return the output of the last statement that is executed. Look at the following example:

```
def welcome_to_city
    city = "New York"
    "Welcome to " + city
end
  puts welcome_to_city
```

The output will be as follows:

Welcome to New York

Figure 2.69: Output for the return statement

If we want to compare this with other languages where the **return** statement is required, the program would look like this:

```
def welcome_to_city
    city = "New York"
    result = "Welcome to " + city
    return result
end
  puts welcome_to_city
```

The output will be as follows:

Welcome to New York

Figure 2.70: Output for the return statement

The preceding code is valid Ruby code as well. As with everything in Ruby, it is developer-friendly and   minimizes the typing effort required.

An explicit **return** statement before the end of the function definition can also be used to return from the function. This is useful to terminate from a loop or return from a function if a condition is satisfied. Consider the   following example:

```
def welcome_to_city city
    return city if city == "Garbage"
    "Welcome to " + city
end
puts welcome_to_city "Garbage"
puts welcome_to_city "New York"
```

The output will now be as follows:

Garbage
Welcome to New York

Figure 2.71: Using the explicit return statement

The next obvious question that comes to mind is how we can return more than one value from a method. The answer to that question is that we can trick the system by returning an object, which can contain multiple   values.

The most common and obvious way to do this is to return an array containing all the values that we need. The following example shows how to return an array with all the requisite values:

```ruby
def return_multiple_values a, b
  result_array = []
  result_array << a + b
  result_array << b - a
end
puts return_multiple_values 10, 20
```

The output will be as follows:

```
30
10
```

Figure 2.72: Returning multiple required values in an array

Let's take a look at this example and try to understand what is happening. When the last statement of the method is executed, it is returning **result_array**, which happens to contain two values. We can have multiple values in that array and then return that object. Instead of an array, we can use **hash** or even a custom object that we want to return and have values associated with it.

Naming Conventions for Methods

Methods that act as queries and return a Boolean value should be named with a trailing ?. This convention is followed within Ruby as well. For example, look at the **include?** method. When we are using this method, we do not have to worry about the return type as we know it's going to be of the Boolean type.

The following is an example of how we use this. Note that this is not a strict rule and the program will not fail if we do not use **?** at the end of the method that returns a Boolean value. It is a convention that makes our code more readable and helps our fellow developers:

```ruby
def check_presence?
    ["New York", "Abu Dhabi"].include? "New Delhi"
end
puts check_presence?
#false
```

Another convention is the bang(!) method. What this means is that if a method ends with (!), it will modify the object on which it is working. The following is an example to reflect this:

```ruby
def find_unique! test_array
   test_array.uniq!
end
test_array = [1, 2, 3, 1, 2, 3]
puts find_unique! test_array
#[1,2,3]
```

Since our method is changing the value of the **test_array** array, it should end with (!).

Activity 2.01: Dice Roller Program

In this activity, we will simulate a dice roller program that has three objectives:

- Roll a die

- Roll a die with any number of sides

- Roll any number of dice

This activity will test you in terms of performing operations on arrays and using the .each iterator. Here are some steps that will help you to complete this activity:

1. First, create a **roller.rb** file.

2. Use the **rand** method to return a random number. Ruby has a built-in **rand** method, which returns a random number. It takes an argument as an integer and returns a random number.

3. Type **rand 2** and you'll notice that the numbers you get in response are either **0** or **1**, never **2**. This is what 0-indexing means.

4. Create a method roll to simulate the rolling of a die.

5. Next, add an argument to the roll to enable the die to roll.

6. Then, add another argument along with the dice to roll any number of dice.

Upon successful completion of the activity, you should obtain a random number printed on the screen for two scenarios: rolling a five-sided die and rolling two six-sided dice.

The output should be similar to the following:

```
Rolling a 5 sided die!
2
Rolling two 6 sided dice!
9
```

Figure 2.73: Output for dice roller

> **Note**
>
> The solution to this activity can be found on page 460.

Summary

In this chapter, we took a journey into data types and some very common operations that can be performed on them. We started out with array operations and took a closer look at adding, removing, and iterating over this data type. Then, we moved on to the hash data type and discovered the hidden magic that powers most of the web and desktop applications written in Ruby. Hashes are a very common way to store and manipulate data inside web applications. We added, removed, and iterated over hashes, and then performed some symbol-based sorting with nested hashes. Our final destination in this chapter was the methods and functions that allow us to create either functional or procedural applications in Ruby. Functions and methods in themselves are not of much use, so we imbued them with arguments. We also took a closer look at how optional and default arguments are handled in case multiple arguments are passed. This constituted a very important chapter, namely, how the extra arguments are mapped to the predefined arguments. In the next chapter, we will be studying methods in detail and how they define the program workflows.

3

Program Flow

Overview

By the end of the chapter, you will be able to utilize Boolean operators in Ruby programs; create and implement conditional expressions in Ruby; utilize ternary operators and ranges for programs; implement iterators on arrays and hashes and create programmatic loops with while, for, and until. The chapter aims to introduce us to different methods and entities involved in the Ruby program workflow.

Introduction

In the previous chapter, we studied the concept of arrays and hashes in Ruby. We also looked at different methods applied to arrays and hashes. In this chapter, we will be looking at how programs in Ruby are designed and used in applications.

Useful software programs are not simply a linear set of instructions; they make decisions about what code to run at any given time based on a set of conditions or criteria. Different programming languages have different types of program flow options. Two of the most common types of program flow options are **conditionals** and **loops**, which we will cover in this chapter.

Conditionals, also known as branches, are like a fork in the road. Do you turn left, or do you turn right? In the case of programming, for instance, you can decide what to do if a variable equals a value or is less than or greater than a certain value. Software simplifies the problem and makes the decision simply about truthiness: whether a condition is satisfied or not. A common example is evaluating a user's password and logging them in if the user-supplied value matches the value in the database or showing an error message if it does not.

Loops are another way to control program flow. A section of code will be repeated in a loop until a condition is met. In programming, you often want to loop over a collection of data such as an array and process the values in that collection. In some cases, the condition may never be met as the program may be configured to run forever. A web server, for instance, loops forever, waiting for new requests to come in to serve content.

In all types of program flow decisions, the fundamental unit is the Boolean. The Boolean represents truthiness or true or false values. We use the word "truthiness" to express that some values may not be an exact true or false Boolean but will be considered by the language as behaving as "true" or "false".

Since program flow is decided by truthiness, which is represented by Booleans, we need to learn how Booleans operate. We can do this by first learning about Boolean operators; there are three: AND, OR, and NOT. This is how we will begin our chapter.

Boolean Operators

As we know, Booleans tell us whether a value or condition is **true** and **false**. We can work with Booleans using the following three operators:

- AND
- OR
- NOT

The AND Operator

In Ruby, the AND operator is represented by a double ampersand, **&&**. It represents what the truthiness is across two values if both are **true**. Consider the following sample code snippet:

```
var1 = true
var2 = true
var1 && var2

var1 = false
var2 = true
var1 && var2

var1 = false
var2 = false
var1 && var2
```

The output should look like this:

```
irb(main):001:0> var1 = true
=> true
irb(main):002:0> var2 = true
=> true
irb(main):003:0> var1 && var2
=> true
irb(main):004:0>
irb(main):005:0> var1 = false
=> false
irb(main):006:0> var2 = true
=> true
irb(main):007:0> var1 && var2
=> false
irb(main):008:0>
irb(main):009:0> var1 = false
=> false
irb(main):010:0> var2 = false
=> false
irb(main):011:0> var1 && var2
=> false
```

Figure 3.1: Output for the Boolean AND operator

In the preceding example, the **var1** and **var2** variables depict **true** and **false** Boolean states in different combinations and the **&&** operator gives results as per the combination.

The OR Operator

In Ruby, the OR operator is represented by a double pipe, ||. It represents what the truthiness is across two values if one is **true**. Consider the following sample code snippet:

```
var1 = true
var2 = true
var1 || var2

var1 = false
var2 = true
var1 || var2

var1 = false
var2 = false
var1 || var2
```

The output should look like this:

```
irb(main):019:0> var1 = false
=> false
irb(main):020:0> var2 = true
=> true
irb(main):021:0> var1 || var2
=> true
irb(main):022:0>
irb(main):023:0> var1 = false
=> false
irb(main):024:0> var2 = false
=> false
irb(main):025:0> var1 || var2
=> false
```

Figure 3.2: Output for the Boolean OR operator

As depicted in the previous example, the **var1** and **var2** variables depict **true** and **false** Boolean states in different combinations and the || operator gives results as per the combination.

The NOT Operator

In Ruby, the NOT or negation operator is represented by a bang or exclamation point (**!**). It represents the opposite of a value. If a value is **true**, the negation of it is **false**, and if a value is **false**, the negation of it is **true**:

```
var1 = true
!var1
var1 = false
!var1
```

The output should look like this:

```
irb(main):001:0> var1 = true
=> true
irb(main):002:0> !var1
=> false
irb(main):003:0> var1 = false
=> false
irb(main):004:0> !var1
=> true
```

Figure 3.3: Output for the Boolean NOT operator

Truth Tables

The possibilities of these operators are best described with a truth table. Here is a sample truth table for the **AND** and **OR** operators:

x	y	x && y	x || y
F	F	F	F
T	F	F	T
F	T	F	T
T	T	T	T

Figure 3.4: Truth table for the AND and OR operators

As you can see from this table, there are some rules that can be inferred:

- With **AND**, the result is **true** only if both are **true**.

- Conversely, with **AND**, the result is **false** if either of the variables is **false**.

- With **OR**, the result is **true** if either of the variables is **true**.

- Conversely, with **OR**, the result is only **false** if both variables are **false**.

The following table is a truth table for the **NOT** operator:

x	!x
F	T
T	F

Figure 3.5: Truth table for the NOT operator

As seen in the preceding table, the following statements can be inferred:

- The result is **true** if the variable is **false**.

- The result is **false** if the variable is **true**.

Truth tables are the base of Boolean algebra, which is beyond the scope of this book. However, let's cover two additional interesting properties that occur when we combine the negation operator with the AND and OR operators.

Consider the following statements:

- `!(x && y)` is the same as saying `!x || !y`

- `!(x || y)` is the same as saying `!x && !y`

Another way of looking at this is to say if you want to negate an operator used with two variables, then you distribute the negation to each variable and "flip" the operator. Flipping the operator means to switch between `&&` and `||`.

We can confirm this with a truth table, which is just a representation of two variables and all the possible combinations of **true** and **false** and the result of each operator:

x	y	x && y	!(x && y)	!x || !y	!y	!x
F	F	F	T	T	T	T
T	F	F	T	T	T	F
F	T	F	T	T	F	T
T	T	T	F	F	F	F

Figure 3.6: Truth table of flipped operators

Here is another truth table:

x	y	x || y	!(x || y)	!x || !y	!y	!x
F	F	F	T	T	T	T
T	F	T	F	T	T	F
F	T	T	F	T	F	T
T	T	T	F	F	F	F

Figure 3.7: Truth table of flipped operators

This is an example of one of the many laws of Boolean algebra.

Understanding Booleans and truthiness is a foundational concept that will lead us through to the use of all other aspects of program flow in Ruby.

Truthiness

As we mentioned, in Ruby, you can have Booleans that are direct representations of **true** and **false**. However, other values, such as strings and numbers, can be evaluated as to whether they should be **true** or **false**.

Take the number 0, for instance. Is the number 0 a **true** or **false** value? In other words, if we had an **if** condition statement that evaluated 0, Ruby should choose the **true** branch or the **false** branch. This is what we mean by "truthy." If a variable is "truthy," it means it doesn't contain a direct true value but will be treated as true for the purposes of program flow or Boolean evaluation. Different languages handle truthiness in different ways. Here is the truthiness table for Ruby:

Value	Truthy?
0	yes
""	yes
"hello"	yes
nil	no
6.7	yes
true	yes
false	no
[1,2]	yes
{:hi=>"there"}	yes

Figure 3.8: Truthiness table for Ruby

As you can see, **0** evaluates to **truthy** In fact, in Ruby, almost everything evaluates to true except for **nil** and **false**. We can see this in an IRB console using a special trick: the bang, (**!**), and the double bang, (**!!**).

! is the negation operator in Ruby and therefore gives us the Boolean opposite of whatever value we are evaluating. When we apply the double bang operator, **!!**, we will get the Boolean opposite of the variable, which if you are following, gives us the Boolean value of the variable.

Let's look at the following example:

```
def is_truthy(var)
  if var
    puts "The var #{var} is truthy!"
  else
    puts "The var #{var} is falsey"
  end
end
is_truthy(0) # "The var 0 is truthy
is_truthy(nil) # "The var is falsey"
is_truthy(false) # "The var false is falsey"
is_truthy("") # "The var  is truthy!"
```

```
is_truthy(5) # "The var 5 is truthy!"
is_truthy("hello") # "The var hello is truthy!"
is_truthy(!0) # "The var false is falsey"
is_truthy(!!0) # "The var true is truthy!"
is_truthy(!nil) # "The var true is truthy!"
is_truthy(!!nil) # "The var false is falsey"
```

The output should look like this:

```
irb(main):079:0> is_truthy(0) # "The var 0 is truthy
The var 0 is truthy!
=> nil
irb(main):080:0> is_truthy(nil) # "The var is falsey"
The var
=> nil
irb(main):081:0> is_truthy(false) # "The var false is falsey"
The var
=> nil
irb(main):082:0> is_truthy("") # "The var  is truthy!"
The var  is truthy!
=> nil
irb(main):083:0> is_truthy(5) # "The var 5 is truthy!"
The var 5 is truthy!
=> nil
irb(main):084:0> is_truthy("hello") # "The var hello is truthy!"
The var hello is truthy!
=> nil
irb(main):085:0> is_truthy(!0) # "The var false is falsey"
The var
=> nil
irb(main):086:0> is_truthy(!!0) # "The var true is truthy!"
The var true is truthy!
=> nil
irb(main):087:0> is_truthy(!nil) # "The var true is truthy!"
The var true is truthy!
=> nil
irb(main):088:0> is_truthy(!!nil) # "The var false is falsey"
The var
=> nil
```

Figure 3.9: Output for truthiness

Precedence

In Ruby, there are both **&&** and **and** as well as the **||** and **or** syntaxes. They serve the same purpose in that they both do a logical comparison, however, there is a small and notable difference in how they are interpreted by Ruby. The difference lies in the precedence of operators. In other words, Ruby will process some operators sooner than other operators.

The following is a table on operator precedence in Ruby

Operator	Description
[] [] =	Element reference, element set
**	Exponentiation
! ~ + -	Not, complement, unary plus and minus (method names for the last two are +@ and -@)
* / %	Multiply, divide, and modulo
+ -	Plus and minus
>> <<	Right and left shift
&	Bitwise 'and'
^ |	Bitwise exclusive 'or' and regular 'or'
<=< >>=	Comparison operators
<=> == === != =~ !~	Equality and pattern match operators (!= and !~ may not be defined as methods)
&&	Logical 'and'
||	Logical 'or'
.. ...	Range (inclusive and exclusive)
? :	Ternary if-then-else
= %= { /= _= += |= &= >>= <<= *= &&= ||= **=D22	Assignment
defined?	Check if symbol defined
not	Logical negation
or and	Logical composition
if unless while until	Expression modifiers
begin/end	Block expression

Figure 3.10: Operator precedence

We can see that the logical **&&** and **||** operators have higher precedence than the **AND** and **OR** operators. In most cases, the difference in precedence is negligible. However, there are a couple of situations where it is important, particularly when doing variable assignment:

```
var1 = true AND 1 # var1 == true
var2 = true && 2 # var2 == 2
```

In the preceding example, **var1** is **true** because the variable assignment has higher precedence than the"**and** operator. However, **var2** is equal to **2** because the **&&** operator is evaluated first and is then assigned to the variable. The astute reader will note that even though **true && 2** is a logical comparison, the assigned value is **2**. Ruby will return the actual value of logical comparison if it is **true**. The value it returns depends on the operator.

Consider the following example:

```
var1 = 5 || true # var1 == 5
var2 = true or 5 # var2 == true
var3 = false || nil # nil
```

In the case of **var1**, we see that even though we are using the **||** operator, which has high precedence, **var1** is getting assigned **5**. This is because when Ruby processes the **||** operator, it will stop processing once it has satisfied the **||** operator (that is, it has reached a **true** condition). In the case of **var2**, the assignment operation happens first (**var2** is assigned to true) and then is *or'd* with **5** (which is also true). In the case of **var3**, the Ruby interpreter can't satisfy the **or** condition with **false**, so it proceeds and then hits **nil**, which is then returned to the assignment operation and gets assigned to **var3**.

The general rule of thumb is that it is safe to use **and** and **or** in a program flow (for example, **if**/**else** conditions), whereas you always use **&&** and **||** when doing variable assignment. While the **and** and **or** syntax is more readable than **&&** and **||**, it avoids sinister bugs that come up due to oversights in the order of precedence. Therefore, it is recommended to always use **&&** and **||**.

Exercise 3.01: Implementing Boolean Operators

In this exercise, we will demonstrate how Boolean operators work by creating a method that evaluates each of the operators. We can then pass different values in to see how the Boolean operators work. The following steps will help you with the solution:

1. Open a new session on IRB.

2. We first create a method that runs through all the scenarios of Boolean operators using two arguments. As you already know, **puts** is used to print the result of the operation:

```
def truthiness(x, y)
  puts "AND: ", x && y
  puts "OR: ", x || y
  puts "!AND: ", !(x && y)
  puts "!OR: ", !(x || Y)
end
```

3. Apply the operators to different values for **x** and **y**:

```
truthiness(true, true)
truthiness(true, false)
truthiness(false, true
truthiness(false, false)
truthiness(0, true)
truthiness(nil, false)
```

Here's the expected output:

```
irb(main):014:0> puts truthiness(true, true)
AND:
true
OR:
true
!AND:
false
!OR:
false

=> nil
irb(main):015:0> puts truthiness(true, false)
AND:
false
OR:
true
!AND:
true
!OR:
false
```

Figure 3.11: Output for Boolean operators

Conditional Expressions

Now that we are well-versed in Booleans and truthiness, we can begin to dive into program flow. We'll begin by discussing branches, which are also known as conditionals.

There are several keywords that denote conditionals:

- `if`
- `else`
- `elsif`
- `unless`

In Ruby, conditionals are structured into blocks of code that begin with a conditional keyword and end with an **end** keyword.

Let's look at each of them, one by one.

The if Statement

The **if** conditional is used to evaluate the existing condition of a variable and display the result accordingly. Consider the following example:

```
good_weather = true
if good_weather
  puts "Go outside"
end
```

The output should look like this:

```
irb(main):092:0> good_weather = true
=> true
irb(main):093:0> if good_weather
irb(main):094:1>   puts "Go outside"
irb(main):095:1> end
Go outside
```

Figure 3.12: Output for the if statement

Here, we initialize a **good_weather** variable, which will represent whether the weather is good. If it's good weather, we will output a statement telling us to go outside.

Next, we will see how to branch our code to handle good and bad, which are the weather conditions.

The else Statement

An **else** condition will help provide an alternate result if the desired condition is not satisfied. Consider the   following example:

```
good_weather = true
if good_weather
   puts "Go outside"
else
   puts "Stay inside"
end
```

The output should look like this:

<code>Go outside</code>

Figure 3.13: Output for the else statement

In this example, if the weather is good, we will get an output statement: **Go outside**. If not, the statement will be **Stay inside**.

The elsif Statement

We can use the **else** keyword to represent an either/or conditional. If we have more than two choices, we can use the **elsif** keyword to match multiple conditions. Look at the following example:

```
bananas_are_fresh = true
oranges_are_fresh = true
if bananas_are_fresh
   puts "Make a smoothie"
elsif oranges_are_fresh
   puts "Make orange juice"
else
   puts "Go to the farmers market to get more fresh fruit"
end
```

In the preceding example, there are two variables, **bananas_are_fresh** and **oranges_are_fresh**, which are set to **true**. If the first condition is met, the output statement will be **Make a smoothie**. If the second condition is also met, the output will be **Make orange juice**. If both conditions are not met, the output will be **Go to the farmers market to get more fresh fruit**.

The output should look like this:

Make a smoothie

Figure 3.14: Output for the elsif statement

The unless Statement

If statements, like most other programming languages, are saying if the following evaluation is **true**, then execute the next block of code. Ruby has an additional keyword to express a conditional when something is **false**. That keyword is **unless**. Look at the following example:

```
its_raining = false
unless its_raining
   puts "Go outside"
end
```

The output should look like this:

Go outside

Figure 3.15: Output for the unless statement

As you might guess, the **unless** keyword is the same as saying **if** not. While Ruby has **elsif** for additional conditions within an **if**/**else** block, there is no corresponding keyword for **unless**. Therefore, **unless** can only be paired with **else**, as in the following example:

```
its_raining = false
unless its_raining
   puts "Go outside"
else
   puts "Stay inside"
end
```

When deciding which keyword to use, one of the considerations should be readability. Which form makes it more readable to you and/or for others later on?

Let's look at an example that combines conditional keywords with Boolean operators:

```
its_raining = false
its_cold = true
if its_raining && its_cold
   puts "Bring rain jacket"
elsif its_raining
   puts "Bring umbrella"
```

```
else
   puts "It's nice outside, just don't forget your wallet"
end
```

The preceding code clearly depicts the use of the **&&** Boolean operator to combine two conditions and give out the result accordingly. Additionally, if one of the conditions is met, the output will be **Bring umbrella**. If both conditions are not met, the output would be **It's nice outside, just don't forget your wallet**.

The output should look like this:

```
It's nice outside, just don't forget your wallet
```

Figure 3.16: Output for the if statement

> **Note**
>
> It's good practice to steer clear of excessively lengthy and nested **if/else** statements. This is called a "code smell" because it makes you wince when you try to understand it. It's a good time to consider whether there is a better way to organize the code.

Comparison

We've learned how to evaluate the truthiness of a statement and how to branch code based on that truthiness. The last foundational concept in conditional program flow is how to compare two variables. We need to be able to determine whether two variables are the same, are not the same, or are less than or greater than each other.

Let's look at the operators used for comparison in Ruby.

Comparison Operators

The following are the operators most commonly used for comparison in Ruby:

Greater than:	>
Greater than or equal to:	>=
Less than:	<
Less than or equal to:	<=
Equal to:	==
Not equal to:	!=

Figure 3.17: Comparison operators

Let's now write a method that combines all of the concepts in this chapter. We will be comparing two variables, **x** and **y**, and putting them through different comparison conditions:

```
def compare(x, y)
  if x < y
    puts "#{x} < #{y}"
  elsif x <= y
    puts "#{x} <= #{y}"
  elsif x == y
    puts "#{x} == #{y}"
  elsif x >= y
    puts "#{x} >= #{y}"
  elsif x > y
    puts "#{x} > #{y}"
  end
end
```

While this code appears to represent all the cases of each operator, it's actually problematic. We won't possibly encounter the == case, because if we evaluate to **true** for <=, this will evaluate first and we won't encounter the == case. In fact, we won't even run into the >= case.

Hence, a better way to write a comparison method would be as follows:

```
def compare(x,y)
  if x==y
    puts "x and y are equal"
  elsif x < y
    puts "x is less than y"
  else
    puts "x is greater than y"
  end
end
```

The choice of whether to use > and >= or < and <= depends on the situation and the problem you are trying to solve. This is called a boundary condition.

Comparing Strings

It is convenient to use comparison operators with integers, but it can be difficult with other types of variables, such as strings. Each object type (or class) in Ruby will define how to compare itself to other objects of the same type. For instance, when it comes to comparing two strings, we can think of it as follows:

```
"this string" == "something else" # false
```

That is straightforward, but the following condition is unrealistic:

```
"apples" > "oranges"
```

Let's use our **compare** method from the previous example to see how lots of different inputs behave:

```
compare("apples", "oranges") # x is less than y
compare("a", "a") # x and y are equal
compare("a", "A") # x is greater than y
compare("a", "b") # x is less than y
```

We are seeing some surprising things here. Why is **a** greater than **A** but less than **b**? The reason is because of how Ruby implements that comparison operator on strings. Most people will not memorize the internal algorithms of Ruby, so this is a good opportunity to *read the docs*.

When you go to the online Ruby documentation at https://packt.live/35mif9C, search for the type of object (or class) that you are looking for. In this case, **string**. There will be several results, usually for different versions of Ruby. Find your version of Ruby and dive into the **string** class. You will notice that there isn't an entry for <, >, or ==. Instead, Ruby implements all comparison operators with a single method: <=>, which returns -1, 0, and 1 to indicate less than, equal to, or greater than. All the other comparison operators (which really are just methods) are based on this central comparison operator. When you click on <=>, you will get an explanation of how Ruby decides to compare strings.

Exercise 3.02: Creating a Method to Check Your Balance

In this exercise, we will write a method to determine whether you have enough money to purchase something. We will determine the logic necessary for our balancer checker method and then implement it using conditionals and comparison operators:

1. Open a new session on IRB.

2. First, we determine the method. If you have more than enough money, you can make a purchase. If you have exactly enough money, you can make a purchase. If you do not have enough money, you cannot make a purchase:

```
def can_purchase?(amount_in_bank, cost_of_item)
  if amount_in_bank >= cost_of_item
    return true
  else
    return false
  end
end
```

Here, we use the >= operator because as long as we have an amount equal to or greater than the cost of the item, we are okay to purchase it.

3. We can also create an alternative implementation using a different operator:

```
def can_purchase?(amount_in_bank, cost_of_item)
  if amount_in_bank < cost_of_item
    return false
  else
    return true
  end
end
```

> **Note**
>
> It's up to you as the programmer to decide which is easier to read. You will also notice that we named our method with a question mark. This is good practice with methods that return Boolean values.

4. Let's see how we can call this method in a conditional:

```
bank_balance = 100
cost_of_item = 200
if can_purchase?(bank_balance, cost_of_item)
  puts "You can purchase this item"
else
  puts "Sorry, you don't have enough money to buy this item"
end
```

You can see how when you write code with clearly named variables and method names, the resulting code is quite readable, even to people who are new to Ruby.

Here's the expected output:

```
Sorry, you don't have enough money to buy this item
```

Figure 3.18: Output for balance checking

Thus, we have successfully created a method to initiate/decline a purchase after checking the balance amount of the bank account by using conditionals and comparison operators.

The case/when Statement

Often, when programming, you will need to branch code based on many conditions. Using lots of **if**/**else** statements can result in *spaghetti code*, which is not easy to read or understand.

Spaghetti code refers to a pejorative term where the code is unstructured and normally has many **goto** statements, making it difficult to interpret.

An alternative to lots of **if/else** statements is to use the **case/when** keywords. Here is an example:

```
def get_animal_sound(animal_type)
  case animal_type
  when :dog
    "woof"
  when :cat
    "meow"
  when :cow
    "moo"
  when :bird
    "tweet"
  else
```

```
      nil
    end
  end
```

Here, we have a method that depends on the type of animal we pass into it and returns a string with the sound it makes. This works by doing a comparison of the **animal_type** variable against each value in the **case/when** statement, going from top to bottom.

Try calling the methods with the following values:

```
puts get_animal_sound(:dog) # woof
puts get_animal_sound(:bird) # tweet
puts get_animal_sound("dog") # nil
```

The last call did not return the correct sound because strings and symbols are unequal and so the execution will continue until it hits the final **else** condition in the block.

An alternative format in the **case/when** statement is to leave out the variable to the right of the **case** keyword. In this format, Ruby will execute the statement following an evaluation to **true**.

Consider the following example:

```
def get_animal_sound(animal_type)
  case
  when animal_type == :dog
    "woof"
  when animal_type == :cat
    "meow"
  when animal_type == :cow
    "moo"
  when animal_type == :bird
    "tweet"
      else
    nil
  end
end
```

In this case, the expanded format is less ideal than the first since we are repeating the **animal_type** variable for each condition. However, this format can come in handy when you don't know all the cases ahead of time or need to do more complex logic such as doing a greater than or less than comparison.

The === Operator

You might naturally wonder about the difference between == and ===. First, let's remember that the == operator is actually a method that each Ruby object type (class) defines for itself so it knows how to compare two objects of the same type. The === operator is an additional method that Ruby gives us to do a similar but slightly different equality comparison. The === operator is often called the "case equality" operator or the "identity" operator. It allows comparison based on the type of object passed into it. Another way to put it is that the === operator determines whether the input passed to it is part of the set of what it's being compared to.

Consider the following example:

```ruby
def guess_type(input)
  case input
  when String
    puts "It's a string!"
  when Integer
    puts "It's a number!"
  when Array
    puts "It's an array"
  when Hash
    puts "It's a hash"
  else
    puts "Not sure what you passed: #{input}"
  end
end
guess_type(5)
guess_type("5")
guess_type([1,2,3])
guess_type({foo: :bar})
```

The output should look like this:

```
irb(main):060:0> guess_type(5)
It's a number!
=> nil
irb(main):061:0> guess_type("5")
It's a string!
=> nil
irb(main):062:0> guess_type([1,2,3])
It's an array
=> nil
irb(main):063:0> guess_type({foo: :bar})
It's a hash
=> nil
```

Figure 3.19: Output for input type determination

What's happening here is the **case** statement is calling the **===** operator on the input and determining whether the input is part of the set. In this case, it is determining whether the type of object passed in is a type that belongs to the class it's being compared to.

Here are some further examples of the **===** operator:

```
String === "mystring" # true
Integer === 5  # true
5 === Integer # false?
```

Here, you can see in the last statement that something strange is going on. **Integer === 5** holds true but **5 === Integer** is shown as **false**. The reason is, while **5** is a type of **Integer**, **Integer** is a class and is not a type of **5**. This concept will become clearer as we cover classes and ranges in upcoming chapters.

The Ternary Operator

Ternary means composed of three parts. In Ruby (and also in other programming languages), there is a common programming idiom called the ternary operator, which allows a quick **if/else** conditional to be put on one line by breaking it into three parts:

```
user_input = 'password'
secret = 'password'
user_has_access = user_input == secret ? true : false
```

The three parts are the condition (**user_input == secret**), the statement if true (**true**), and the statement if false (**false**). The three parts are separated first by a **?** and secondly by a **:** notation.

While Ruby doesn't always require syntax such as parentheses, the preceding statement may be a bit hard to read unless you are very familiar with how Ruby handles the order of operations. Here is a clearer way of writing the preceding code:

```
user_has_access = (user_input == secret) ? true : false
```

The ternary operator is great for quick one-liners. However, if lots of complex logic is starting to creep into any of the three parts, this may be considered a code smell and the code will need refactoring into simpler logic. You can either refactor it into a proper **if/else** statement or you can refactor the complex logic into separate variables that are then evaluated in the ternary condition.

Consider the following example:

```
user_input = 'secret'
password = 'secret'
def login_user
  puts "logging in user"
end
def show_access_denied
  puts "Password was incorrect, try again"
end
user_has_access = user_input == secret
user_has_access ? login_user : show_access_denied
```

By using clearly labeled method names and simplifying the ternary statement, we can clearly see that if the user has access, we will log them in; otherwise, we will ask them to re-input their password.

Exercise 3.03: Speed Determiner

Write a method that determines the speed that a self-driving car should adjust to, based on environmental conditions, as well as the traffic status and distance to a traffic light. The method should return the new speed. Perform the following steps:

1. Open a new session on IRB.

2. First, we write the logic in pseudocode:

```
Green light:
        Sunny, all conditions: speed_limit
        Rainy, distance >= 50ft: speed_limit
        Rainy, distance < 50ft: 90% speed_limit
   Yellow light:
        Sunny, distance >= 50ft: 80% speed_limit
        Sunny, distance < 50ft: 50% speed_limit
```

```
        Rainy, distance >= 50f: 80% speed_limit
        Rainy, distance < 50f: 25% speed limit
   Red light:
        Sunny, distance >= 50ft: 50% speed limit
        Sunny, distance <= 50ft: 0% speed limit
        Rainy, distance >= 50ft: 25% speed limit
        Rainy, distance <= 50ft: 0% speed limit
```

3. Implement the logic in a method. Define the method as **drive_decision** and also the parameters we consider in the method.

> **Note**
>
> We are introducing **raise** here, which will fatally exit the program if the code is encountered. This is a basic way to make sure that if a parameter is not passed in correctly, we get notified about it.

```ruby
def drive_decision(traffic_signal, weather, distance_to_signal, speed_limit)
  if traffic_signal == :green
    if weather == :sunny
      speed_limit
    elsif distance_to_signal >= 50
      speed_limit
    else
      speed_limit * 0.9
    end
  elsif traffic_signal == :yellow
    if weather == :sunny && distance_to_signal >= 50
      speed_limit * 0.8
    elsif weather == :sunny && distance_to_signal < 50
      speed_limit * 0.5
    elsif weather == :rainy && distance_to_signal >= 50
      speed_limit * 0.8
    elsif weather == :rainy && distance_to_signal < 50
      speed_limit * 0.25
    else
      raise "Condition not handled"
    end
  else # red light
    if weather == :sunny && distance_to_signal >= 50
      speed_limit * 0.5
    elsif weather == :rainy && distance_to_signal >= 50
```

```
            speed_limit * 0.25
        else
            0 # all other conditions should stop the car
        end
    end
end
```

> **Note**
>
> **raise** is a keyword that raises exceptions. Exceptions can be caught and handled –
> this topic is covered later in the book.

4. Evaluate the method with different variables:

    ```
    drive_decision(:green, :sunny, 100, 50)
    drive_decision(:yellow, :rainy, 50, 25)
    ```

5. Refactor the method using **case/when** and additional methods. First, we determine
    the method for **drive_decision_when_green**:

    ```
    def drive_decision_when_green(weather, distance_to_signal, speed_limit)
        case weather
        when :sunny
            speed_limit
        when :rainy
            if distance_to_signal >= 50
                speed_limit
            else
                speed_limit * 0.9
            end
        else
            raise "Not handled"
        end
    end
    ```

6. Similarly, we define the method for **drive_decision_when_yellow**:

    ```
    def drive_decision_when_yellow(weather, distance_to_signal, speed_limit)
        case weather
        when :sunny
            if distance_to_signal >= 50
                speed_limit * 0.8
            else
    ```

```
                speed_limit * 0.5
            end
    when :rainy
            if distance_to_signal >= 50
                speed_limit * 0.8
            else
                speed_limit * 0.25
            end
    else
            raise "Not handled"
    end
end
```

7. We also define the method for **drive_decision_when_red**:

```
def drive_decision_when_red(weather, distance_to_signal, speed_limit)
    if distance_to_signal >= 50
        case weather
        when :sunny
                speed_limit * 0.5
        when :rainy
                speed_limit * 0.25
        else
                raise "Not handled"
        end
    else
        0
    end
end
```

8. Lastly, we define the **drive_decision** method depending on the three conditions defined before:

```
def drive_decision(traffic_signal, weather, distance_to_signal, speed_limit)
    case traffic_signal
    when :green
            drive_decision_when_green(weather, distance_to_signal, speed_limit)
    when :yellow
```

```
      drive_decision_when_yellow(weather, distance_to_signal, speed_limit)
         else
                drive_decision_when_red(weather, distance_to_signal, speed_limit)
         end
      end
```

Here's the expected output:

```
      irb(main):295:0> drive_decision(:yellow, :sunny, 25, 35)
      => 17.5
      irb(main):296:0> drive_decision(:red, :rainy, 25, 35)
      => 0
      irb(main):297:0> drive_decision(:green, :rainy, 25, 35)
      => 31.5
      irb(main):298:0> drive_decision(:green, :sunny, 25, 35)
      => 35
```

Figure 3.20: Output for driving decisions

We can see, in the preceding code, that we are repeating code in the **case** statement. We can refactor this code by creating a new method that checks for valid traffic, weather states and writing this as a one-liner at the top of a method definition like this:

```
def drive_decision(traffic_signal, weather, distance_to_signal, speed_limit)
  raise "Unhandled weather condition" unless valid_weather_condition?(weather)
  #...rest of the method implementation...
end
def valid_weather_condition?(weather)
  [:sunny, :rainy].include?(weather.to_sym)
end
```

This line of code, which starts off a method implementation, is called a guard clause because it makes a quick decision about whether we should proceed with the method implementation. In other words, it guards the method implementation by making sure only valid parameters are passed in. Guard clauses are a great way to refactor complicated **if**/**else** conditionals by checking for these conditions at the top of a method implementation with a guard clause. Then, you can keep the rest of your method implementation clean of additional checks on the data.

Loops

Loops are a type of program flow that repeat blocks of code. The ability to repeat a block of code allows us to do things such as processing collections of data. Typically, loops will run until a condition is satisfied. For instance, a loop may be run until it has run a certain number of times, or a loop may be run until it has processed all the items in a collection of data. Let's look at the following types of loops in Ruby:

- **while/do** loops
- **until/do** loops
- **do/while** loops

The while/do Loop

Another foundational concept for program flow is being able to repeat sections of code until a condition is met. These are called loops and in Ruby there are many ways to create loops. The most basic structure of a loop contains two things:

- The condition that will be evaluated to determine whether to repeat the code
- The block of code to be repeated

Here is a simple block using the **while** keyword:

```
while true do
  puts Time.now
end
```

It should be fairly clear what this loop does. We can write this loop in English by saying, *while true, output the current time*:

- **while** is the keyword that says evaluate while a condition is **true**.
- **do** is the keyword that establishes the start of the potentially repeated block of code.
- **end** is the keyword the declares the end of the repeated block of code.

In this case, **true** is obviously always evaluated to true and therefore this will loop forever. In other words, this is an infinite loop. Infinite loops are important concepts because they should either be intentional in the design of the program or otherwise avoided. An intentional infinite loop might be a program that runs forever, such as a web server.

Let's try another **while** loop that gets user input each time, which will determine whether we keep looping again or not.

Exercise 3.04: Developing a Mind Reader

In this exercise, we will write a method that picks a random number and asks us, the user, to try to guess it. The random number will be picked from a range of numbers supplied as a parameter to the method.

The following steps will help you to complete the exercise:

1. Open a new session on IRB.

2. Begin by creating the basic **mind_reader** method:

```
def mind_reader
end
```

3. Define a method to pick a random number from a range and print it using **puts**:

```
def mind_reader(range)
  magic_number = rand(range)
  puts "The magic number is #{magic_number}"
end
```

4. Now we get user input and check it against a random number. For that, we define **guess** to accept user input using **gets.chomp** and use conditionals to display the corresponding output statements:

```
def mind_reader(range)
  magic_number = rand(range)
  puts "What's your guess?"
  guess = gets.chomp.to_i
  if guess == magic_number
    puts "That's right!"
  else
    puts "Sorry, that's not correct. The correct number is: #{magic_number}"
  end
end
```

The output should look as follows:

```
irb(main):317:0> mind_reader(30)
What's your guess?
24
Sorry, that's not correct. The correct number is: 6
=> nil
irb(main):318:0> mind_reader(10)
What's your guess?
3
Sorry, that's not correct. The correct number is: 1
=> nil
irb(main):319:0> mind_reader(5)
What's your guess?
4
Sorry, that's not correct. The correct number is: 0
=> nil
```

Figure 3.21: Output for the incorrect number

5. Write a loop to allow continued guessing until it's correct using the **unless** conditional. Once the guess matches the number, the output will show the corresponding output statement:

```
def mind_reader
  magic_number = 7
  guess = nil
  while guess != magic_number do
    print "Nope! Try again! " unless guess.nil?
    puts "What's your guess?"
    guess = gets.chomp.to_i
  end
  puts "That's right!"
end
```

The output should look as follows:

```
irb(main):336:0> mind_reader
What's your guess?
3
Nope! Try again! What's your guess?
1
Nope! Try again! What's your guess?
7
That's right!
=> nil
```

Figure 3.22: Output for the correct number

6. Expand this loop to only give the user a certain number of guesses by using the comparison operator. That is how we limit the number of guesses:

```
def mind_reader
  magic_number = 7
  max_guesses = 3
  attempts = 0
  guess = nil
  while guess != magic_number do
    print "Nope! Try again! " unless guess.nil?
    puts "What's your guess?"
    guess = gets.chomp.to_i
    break if attempts >= max_guesses
  end
  puts guess == magic_number ? "That's right!" : "You ran out of guesses, try again later!"
end
```

In this iteration, we establish the maximum number of guesses and keep track of how many attempts the user has made. However, this code could result in an infinite loop if the user never guesses the right number. We need to increment the number of guesses we are on. Let's add that in.

7. Next, we increment the number of attempts:

```
def mind_reader
  magic_number = 7
  max_guesses = 3
  attempts = 0
```

```ruby
  guess = nil
  while guess != magic_number do
    print "Nope! Try again! " unless guess.nil?
    puts "What's your guess?"
    guess = gets.chomp.to_i
    break if attempts >= max_guesses
    attempts += 1
  end
  winner = "You've guessed it!"
  loser = "You ran out of guesses, try again later!"
  puts guess == magic_number ? winner : loser
end
```

Here's the output:

```
irb(main):360:0> mind_reader
What's your guess?
1
Nope! Try again! What's your guess?
4
Nope! Try again! What's your guess?
5
Nope! Try again! What's your guess?
2
You ran out of guesses, try again later!
=> nil
irb(main):361:0> mind_reader
What's your guess?
2
Nope! Try again! What's your guess?
7
You'guessed it!
=> nil
```

Figure 3.23: Output for incrementing the number of attempts at guessing

Thus, we have created a method where we cover all the different conditions of guessing a number.

The until/do Loop

while loops run while a condition is true. Conversely, Ruby has included the **until/do** construct, which runs code while a condition is not true or rather until the code becomes true. It is understandable that this converse logic can get confusing. It is similar to **if** and **unless** statements though. **if** statement blocks are run when a condition is **true**, whereas **unless** statement blocks are only run when a condition is **false**.

Consider the following example:

```
bank_balance = 0
cost_of_vacation = 1000
until bank_balance >= cost_of_vacation do
  bank_balance += 50
end
```

The loop clearly indicates that until **bank_balance** is greater than the defined **cost_of_vacation** variable, it will keep incrementing **bank_balance**.

The output should look like this:

```
irb(main):030:0> bank_balance = 0
=> 0
irb(main):031:0> cost_of_vacation = 1000
=> 1000
irb(main):032:0> until bank_balance >= cost_of_vacation do
irb(main):033:1* bank_balance += 50
irb(main):034:1> end
=> nil
```

Figure 3.24: Output for the until/do loop

The do/while Loop

The previous loops first evaluate the condition before running the block of code. Sometimes, you want to run the block of code at least once before evaluating whether you would like to repeat it. Let's refactor our **mind_reader** method to do this:

```
def mind_reader magic_number
  max_attempts = 3
  attempt = 0
  guess = nil
  loop do
    print "What's your guess?"
    guess = gets.chomp.to_i
```

```
    break if attempt >= max_attempts
    break if guess == magic_number
    attempt += 1
    puts "Nope! Try again"
  end
  puts guess == magic_number ? "That's right!" : "You ran out of guesses, try again
later!"
end
```

Here, we are using the **break** keyword to exit the loop based on a condition. The **break** keyword is useful because it allows us to jump out of the loop at any time, not just after the full block has been executed. This allows us to output the **Try again** statement at the end but only if we really are trying again.

The output should look like this:

```
irb(main):392:0> mind_reader 37
What's your guess?22
Nope! Try again
What's your guess?35
Nope! Try again
What's your guess?37
That's right!
=> nil
irb(main):393:0> mind_reader 37
What's your guess?4
Nope! Try again
What's your guess?3
Nope! Try again
What's your guess?6
Nope! Try again
What's your guess?4
You ran out of guesses, try again later!
=> nil
```

Figure 3.25: Output for the do/while loop using the break keyword

Here is another form of the **do/while** syntax:

```
keep_looping = :yes
begin
  print "Should we keep looping? "
  keep_looping = gets.chomp.downcase.to_sym
end while keep_looping == :yes
```

The output should look like this:

```
Should we keep looping?
```

Figure 3.26: Output for the do/while loop

Here, we are establishing a block of code using the **begin** and **end** keywords. **Begin** and **end** blocks are useful not just for **do/while** loops but also for defining blocks of code for catching exceptions or errors in code. We will learn more about this later in the book.

Iterators and Enumerators

The loops we've seen so far are based on a condition that determines whether we should repeat the block of code or not. We can also decide to loop code blocks based on a set of data such as an array. This is known as iterating over a set. The following are common methods used to iterate over collections of data:

- **each**
- **each_with_index**
- **map/collect**
- **select/reject**

The each Method

each is one of the most common methods for iterating over sets of data in Ruby. For instance, if we have an array of three items, we can decide to loop over each item in the array:

```
[1,2,3].each do |i|
  puts "My item: #{i}"
end
```

The output should look like this:

```
My item: 1
My item: 2
My item: 3
=> [1, 2, 3]
```

Figure 3.27: Iteration output for the each method

Here, we have a three-item array and we call the **each** method on the array. This method returns an **Enumerator**, as follows:

```
[1,2,3].each.class #Enumerator
```

An enumerator is a Ruby class that allows iterations across a set of data. In order to iterate across a set of data, we also need a block of code and that block of code needs access to the singular item that is being worked on (or iterated over). This is where the **do |i|** syntax comes in. **Do** defines the block of code and **|i|** is the item in the array that the iterator is passing to the block of code. This is known as yielding a variable to the block.

The **each** method, as the name implies, simply iterates over each item in the array, passing it to the block. **each** is a core method that operates not just on arrays, but also any collection of data that includes hashes. Consider the following example:

```
parameters = {id: 1, email: "dany@example.com", first_name: "Dany", last_name:
"Targaryen"}
parameters.each do |key, value|
  puts "#{key} has value: #{value}"
end
```

In the preceding code, we start by initializing a hash called **parameters** with some basic data of key-value pairs. We then call the **each** method on the **parameters** hash. Each key-value pair is yielded as separate arguments to the block within **||** characters. In the preceding example, the arguments are called **key** and **value**, but they can be have different names.

The output should look like this:

```
id has value: 1
email has value: dany@example.com
first_name has value: Dany
last_name has value: Targaryen
```

Figure 3.28: Output for the each method

We can see that when we iterate over a hash, the block takes two arguments, the key and the value for each key/value pair in the hash. It's up to each collection type to decide how it implements the **each** method and what arguments it will provide to the block. There is no limit to the number of arguments; it just depends on what is appropriate for the collection type. In most cases, there will either be one or two arguments in the block.

The each_with_index Method

The **each_with_index** method is very similar to the **each** method. However, as the name implies, this method not only provides the enumerated item in the loop but also the index of the item in the array. An example of when this is useful is when you may need to know the next or previous item in the array:

```ruby
order_queue = ["bob", "mary", "suzie", "charles"]
order_queue.each_with_index do |person, index|
  puts "Processing order for #{person} at index: #{index}"
  if index < order_queue.length - 1
    puts "Next up is: #{order_queue[index+1]}"
  else
    puts "#{person} is last in the queue"
  end
end
```

The output should look like this:

```
Processing order for bob at index: 0
Next up is: mary
Processing order for mary at index: 1
Next up is: suzie
Processing order for suzie at index: 2
Next up is: charles
Processing order for charles at index: 3
charles is last in the queue
```

Figure 3.29: Output for the each_with_index method

Now, let's call **each_with_index** on a hash:

```ruby
parameters = {id: 1, email: "bob@example.com", first_name: "Bob"}
parameters.each_with_index do |key, value|
  puts "Key: #{key}, Value: #{value}"
end
```

The output should look like this:

```
Key: [:id, 1], Value: 0
Key: [:email, "bob@example.com"], Value: 1
Key: [:first_name, "Bob"], Value: 2
=> {:id=>1, :email=>"bob@example.com", :first_name=>"Bob"}
```

Figure 3.30: Output with index of items in hash

Here, we see that the key is actually an array of the key/value pair, and the value is the index. This is interesting. What's happening here is that the hash implements the **each** method so that it returns a key and value to the iterator block. Now that we are calling **each_with_index**, the implementation is also going to send through the index to the block. You might be tempted to do the following to get each key, value, and index in separate variables:

```ruby
parameters = {id: 1, email: "bob@example.com", first_name: "Bob"}
parameters.each_with_index do |key, value, index|
  puts "Key: #{key}, Value: #{value}, index: #{index}"
end
```

The output should look like this:

```
Key: [:id, 1], Value: 0, index:
Key: [:email, "bob@example.com"], Value: 1, index:
Key: [:first_name, "Bob"], Value: 2, index:
=> {:id=>1, :email=>"bob@example.com", :first_name=>"Bob"}
```

Figure 3.31: Output with separate variables

We can see this doesn't get us what we want. Let's try it differently:

```ruby
parameters = {id: 1, email: "bob@example.com", first_name: "Bob"}
parameters.each_with_index do |(key, value), index|
  puts "Key: #{key}, Value: #{value}, index: #{index}"
end
```

The output should look like this:

```
Key: id, Value: 1, index: 0
Key: email, Value: bob@example.com, index: 1
Key: first_name, Value: Bob, index: 2
=> {:id=>1, :email=>"bob@example.com", :first_name=>"Bob"}
```

Figure 3.32: Output with separate variables using parentheses

There we go. We've got each key, value, and index into separate variables by wrapping the key and value in parentheses in the block parameters. This is a special syntax in block parameters that allows arrays to be split into separate variables.

The map/collect Loop

Often, we want to iterate on a collection, process those items, and return a new collection of items. This is where the **map** and **collect** methods come in. The following is the implementation of the **map** method:

```
[1,2,3].map do |i|
  i + 5
end # [6,7,8]
```

The output should look like this:

=> [6, 7, 8]

Figure 3.33: Output for the map method

The **map** method, similar to the **each** method, iterates over each item in the array, but it collects the result of each iteration of the block in a new array. As you can see in the preceding example, the new array is the result of each item plus five.

Something to keep in mind here that is not obvious about Ruby is that the last line of the block is what's returned to the iterator. You might think that you should use the **return** keyword but that is not how Ruby is implemented. We will learn more about methods and the **return** keyword in the next chapter.

Also, an alternative syntax you can use to define the iteration loop is with curly braces, as follows:

```
[1,2,3].each {|i| puts i}
```

The output should look like this:

1
2
3
=> [1, 2, 3]

Figure 3.34: Output for the each method

In most cases in Ruby, you can replace **do/end** blocks with **{}** but there are some nuances, especially when working within IRB, to look out for.

Iterators are extremely handy for looping over any set or collection of data. For instance, here is how you can iterate over a hash that is really a collection of key/value pairs:

```
address = {country: "Spain",city: "Barcelona", post_code: "08001"}
address.each do |key, value|
  puts "#{key}: #{value}"
end
```

The output should look like this:

```
country: Spain
city: Barcelona
post_code: 08001
=> {:country=>"Spain", :city=>"Barcelona", :post_code=>"08001"}
```

Figure 3.35: Output after using iterators

Here, we call the **each** method on the hash, and what is yielded to the block are two variables. Of course, the names of the variables passed to the block do not matter, but the position of them does. The Ruby hash is implemented such that it iterates over each key/value pair, and, for each pair, the key is yielded as the first variable and the value is yielded as the second variable.

There is no limit to what can be yielded to the block; it just depends on the collection being iterated over and how it is implemented. Let's take a look at how to implement our own iterator to learn more about how yielding works.

Imagine you have an array of product prices and you want to write a method that applies an arbitrary tax rate to them:

```
def with_sales_tax array
  array.map do |item|
    yield item.to_f
  end
end


prices = [5,25,"20",3.75,"5.25"]
sales_tax = 0.25
new_prices = with_sales_tax prices do |price|
  price * sales_tax
end
```

The output should look like this:

```
=> [1.25, 6.25, 5.0, 0.9375, 1.3125]
```

Figure 3.36: Output for the yield method

Here, we have implemented a method that loops over the array passed in as a variable to the method and performs a common operation, **.to_f**, in order to sanitize the input and make sure all the items are floating-point numbers. Then, the method yields to the block associated with the call to the method. The transformation (adding a sales tax percentage) is the last line of the block, which is then passed as the last line of the call to **map** inside the method, which collects the sanitized and transformed prices and passes them back as the result of the method.

Blocks and yielding are one of the trickiest parts of learning Ruby when you first get started. Let's explore another way of writing the same code:

```ruby
def with_sales_tax(array, &block)
  array.map do |item|
    block.call(item.to_f)
  end
end
prices = [5,25,"20",3.75,"5.25"]
sales_tax = 0.25
new_prices = with_sales_tax prices do |price|
  price * sales_tax
end
```

The output should look like this:

```
=> [1.25, 6.25, 5.0, 0.9375, 1.3125]
```

Figure 3.37: Output for block as an argument

In this form, the **block** is explicitly passed as an argument to the method. An ampersand is used as a prefix to tell the Ruby interpreter that the argument is a **proc** object. A **proc** object is a block of transportable, runnable code and will be covered in *Chapter 11, Introduction to Ruby on Rails I*.

Exercise 3.05: Developing an Arbitrary Math Method

In this exercise, we will develop a method that accepts an array of numbers. It will yield two elements in the array to a block that performs a mathematical operation on them (addition, subtraction, division, and so on) and returns the result to be processed in the next iteration:

1. Define the **math** method:

```
def math(array)
end
```

2. Implement the method. In order to yield two items from an array, process the result and then take the result and apply it again to the next item in the array. The easiest way is to continue to shift items out of the array. We begin by shifting the first item out of the array:

```
def math(array)
  first_item = array.shift
```

3. Then, we continue to loop over the array while there are items in the array with the **while** loop:

```
while(array.length > 0) do
```

4. Then, we need to get the value of the **second_item** variable from the array:

```
second_item = array.shift
```

5. Pass the two items to the block by yielding them individually as arguments to **yield**:

```
    first_item = yield first_item, second_item
  end
  return first_item
end
```

The output should look like this:

```
irb(main):040:0> math([4,5,6]) { |a,b| a + b}
=> 15
irb(main):041:0> math([4,5,6]) { |a,b| a * b}
=> 120
irb(main):042:0> math([4,5,6]) { |a,b| a - b}
=> -7
irb(main):043:0> math([4,5,6]) { |a,b| a / b}
=> 0
irb(main):044:0> math([4,5,6]) { |a,b| a / b.to_f}
=> 0.13333333333333333
```

Figure 3.38: Output for the math method

You'll notice that we capture the result of the block in the **first_item** variable. This is an important point. The **return** value of the block (even though you don't specify the **return** keyword) is what comes back from **yield** and you can capture it in a variable.

In our exercise, we then return to the top of the **while** block and evaluate whether there are items in the array to continue processing. If so, we shift the next one along as our second argument. In this case, now, our first argument is actually the result of the previous **yield** call.

While we've called this an arbitrary **math** function, really this implementation can be used for any processing of subsequent items in a set of data. This is actually how you could implement **map/reduce**, which is a programming paradigm for processing large datasets very quickly and is a common paradigm in functional programming languages.

6. Process three variables at a time:

```
def math(array)
  first_item = array.shift
  while(array.length > 1) do
    second_item = array.shift || 0
    third_item = array.shift || 0
    first_item = yield first_item, second_item, third_item
  end
  return first_item
end
```

The output should look like this:

```
irb(main):066:0> math([3,4,5]) { |a,b,c| a + b + c}
=> 12
irb(main):067:0> math([3,4,5,6]) { |a,b,c| a + b + c}
=> 18
irb(main):068:0> math([3,4,5,6,7]) { |a,b,c| a + b + c}
=> 25
irb(main):069:0> math([3,4,5,6,7,8]) { |a,b,c| a + b + c}
=> 33
```

Figure 3.39: Output for the math array

You'll notice that we modified a couple of lines to handle nil references:

```
second_item = array.shift || 0
third_item = array.shift || 0
```

Because we are processing three items at a time, this allows arrays with lengths that do not divide evenly into three to still be processed. This works great for addition, but will it work for all the other mathematical operations?

Also, a good follow-up exercise would be to implement this method and parameterize the number of items to process at a given time. As such, the usage would look like this:

```
math([3,4,5,6], 2) { |a,b| a + b }
math([3,4,5,6], 4) { |a,b,c,d| a + b + c + d }
```

Activity 3.01: Number-Guessing Game

In this activity, write a high/low guessing game. The computer will pick a random number and the player needs to guess what it is. If the player guesses incorrectly, the computer will respond with a higher or lower statement, indicating that the player should guess a higher or lower number, respectively. The program exits when the player guesses correctly.

The following steps will help you with the solution of the activity:

1. Open a new session on IRB.

2. Create a **play_choice** method that allows a user to choose to play or exit. It should define the variable used for the **Yes** condition and continue to play:

```
Welcome to HiLow - Shall we play? [Y/n]y
I'm going to pick a random number that you will have to guess. Please enter the maximum number for the guessing range.
```

Figure 3.40: Output for the yes input

Similarly, if the input is **No**, display a **thank you** message, as shown in the following figure:

```
Welcome to HiLow - Shall we play? [Y/n]n
Thanks for playing!
```

Figure 3.41: Output for a no input

3. Implement a single **guess** method. This method will employ various conditions for guessing a number. It will suggest that the player guesses lower/higher if their guess is incorrect. Also, it will print a message saying **You guessed correctly!** when the guess is correct, as shown in the following figure:

```
What's your guess? 2
Guess higher
What's your guess? 5
Guess lower
What's your guess? 3
Guess higher
What's your guess? 4
You guessed correctly!
```

Figure 3.42: Outputs displayed for the guessing attempts

4. Put the whole program together with a **play_game** method, where the game is initiated using a **while** loop and the conditions are followed.

Here's the expected output:

```
Welcome to HiLow - Shall we play? [Y/n]y
I'm going to pick a random number that you will have to guess. Please enter the maximum number for the guessing range.6
What's your guess? 2
Guess higher
What's your guess? 5
Guess lower
What's your guess? 3
Guess higher
What's your guess? 4
You guessed correctly!
```

Figure 3.43: Output for the HiLow game

> **Note**
>
> The solution for the activity can be found on page 462.

Summary

In this chapter, we learned about program flow. Program flow is a foundational concept in programming that allows programmers to change execution paths dynamically depending on any number of conditions. A core concept within program flow is understanding the Boolean data type along with its truthy operators, AND (**&&**) and OR (**||**).

We learned that Ruby supports different program flow options, such as `if` and `unless`, which are logical inverses of each other. The decision to use one or the other depends on the programmer, who should opt for readability and maintainability.

We also learned how to loop and were introduced to Ruby blocks, which are bundles of code that get executed along with each iteration of a loop. Bundling code into reusable chunks is also a foundational concept. Another way to bundle code is by using methods, which we've looked at only briefly so far. In the next chapter, we will go into greater depth about methods by learning how to define them, how to set different types of parameters, and how to return values from them.

4

Ruby Methods

Overview

By the end of this chapter, you will be able to define and call your own methods for Ruby programs; set parameters for methods in Ruby; provide default values for a parameter in Ruby; implement methods in Ruby that return multiple values and write code using the built-in modules of Time and Math.

Introduction

In the previous chapter, we learned about Boolean variables, conditional expressions, and loops, including the core Ruby concepts of using blocks. We will now zoom out a little in the Ruby world and learn about methods. In fact, we've been using methods in the previous chapters, and we will look at them in more depth now.

Methods are foundational units in Ruby. They allow you to wrap code in chunks that can be called with different parameters to get different outputs. Methods commonly have descriptive names and, as such, make clear what the underlying bundle of code does. For instance, we previously learned about the **each** method on arrays. This method enumerates over each item in the array, and so is very descriptive. In fact, method naming is an art where you balance simplicity with descriptiveness. It is considered that the difficult things in computer science are caching, naming things, and off-by-one errors. Commonly known as OBOB errors, off-by-one bugs are logical errors that occur when there are too many iterations in a program or when there are mistakes in the comparisons in code.

Methods are like atoms. They have can have internal parts; however, for the most part, they are fundamental units of code with a defined interface. In addition to this, methods are the building blocks for classes, which are the higher-order building blocks for Ruby programs.

Methods should be designed so that they are simple and can accomplish a basic purpose. If a method gets too long or complicated, then that is a good sign that you need to break up the method into smaller, more clearly labeled methods. By having clearly labeled single-purpose methods, readability, maintainability, and testability are increased. These three attributes are the cornerstones of great code.

Additionally, by defining a clear interface to the method, we can change the implementation at any time without fear of breaking any code that calls the method. In Ruby, this can be a bit trickier because Ruby is a dynamically typed language. This means that the arguments passed to a method or the values returned from a method can be of any type. For instance, a method can accept a string or an integer or any other type of object in its arguments. It's up to the method's implementation to handle each of these cases. A common approach to handling all these cases is actually not to worry about the specific types of arguments, but to worry about whether the arguments behave as we need them to instead. This is called **duck typing** and will be covered in this chapter.

The Basic Structure of the Ruby Method

As we have seen, the basic structure of a method is as follows:

```
def echo(var)
  puts var
end
```

We are defining a method named **echo** that accepts the **var** variable as a parameter or argument. The **end** keyword marks the end of the block of code. The code between the **def** and **end** statements is known as the **method body** or the **method implementation**.

Methods are always called on an object. In Ruby, a method is called a message, and the object is called the receiver. The online Ruby documentation uses this language specifically, so it is good to get used to this vocabulary.

In the previous example, however, it doesn't seem like there is an object. Let's investigate this through IRB:

```
def echo(var)
  puts var
end
=> :echo
echo "helloooo!"
helloooo!
=> nil
self
=> main
self.class
=> Object
```

Here, we've defined and called our **echo** method in IRB. We use the **self** keyword, which is a reference to the current object. In IRB, when we call **self**, we can see that the current object is **main**. We can call **class** on any object to find out what type of object it is. Here, the **main** object is simply a type of the Ruby **Object** class.

In Ruby, everything is an object; even classes are objects. This can be a bit confusing and we will discuss more about classes in the next chapter, *Chapter 5, Object-Oriented Programming with Ruby*. For now, just know that we can call methods on objects. Or, in Ruby parlance, we can send messages to receivers, or an object can receive a message.

In Ruby, the . (dot) notation is the syntax for how we send a message to a receiver.

When you call a method without a dot notation, there is an implicit lookup to find the method. This implicit lookup is the same as calling **self.method**.

Consider the following line of code:

```
irb(main):013:0> self.echo("test 1-2, is there anyone in here?")
```

The output should be as follows:

```
irb(main):077:0> self.echo("test 1-2, is there anyone in here?")
test 1-2, is there anyone in here?
=> nil
```

Figure 4.1: The self method output

Here, we can see that calling **echo** on **self** gives us the same behavior.

Method Components: Signature and Implementation

A method is composed of two parts: its signature and its implementation. A method signature is basically the first line of a method, which defines the following:

- How the method is called (as a class, instance, module, or anonymously)

- Name of the method

- Arguments (also known as parameters)

A method implementation is simply the body of the method after the signature (that is, everything after the first line of the method).

The Method Signature

A method signature is a combination of how the method is defined, its name, and its arguments. A method signature defines everything that is unique about the method and tells us everything we need to know in order to call the method. In **Object-Oriented Programming** (OOP), in order to utilize methods from other libraries or sections of code, we learn their signatures. As long as the signature of a method remains the same, a developer can feel free to reimplement a method however they wish, and we can count on our code not breaking from this change. This is called encapsulation and is a core concept in OOP. We will talk more about method signatures throughout this chapter, while we will talk more about encapsulation in the next chapter, *Chapter 5, Object-Oriented Programming with Ruby*.

There is a nuance about method signatures, implementations, and encapsulations to be aware of. Ruby is not statically typed, which means a method could be reimplemented such that the return value could change. The same method could be reimplemented where it previously returned a number and now returns a string. Ruby does not enforce return types; so, as a method developer, it is your responsibility to manage what types of values are being returned and to keep things consistent.

Here are some quick examples from the Ruby library:

```
Dir.entries("./")
```

The output should be as follows:

```
irb(main):082:0> Dir. entries(" ./")
=> ["app" , ". rspec", " . generators", ". DS_Store", " .jshintrc", "Testing.md", "script" ,
"nclouds", "Rakefile", " . dockerignore", "public", " .gitignore" ,
"README. md", txt" ,"Jenkinsfile", "ruby-version", "test", "bin", "config", "config. ru", " . bundle", " .byebug_history", "spec",
"package. json", " .env", " .erdconfig", "rdoc", "Gemfile", " . rubocop .yml " ,
"Gemfile. lock" , "Capfile", " .git", "erd.pdf" , "log" , "doc", "knapsack_rspec_report. json" , "tmp", " . travis.yml " . sourcelevel .yml " ,
"vendor" , " reports , " README" ]
```

Figure 4.2: Directory entries

The preceding example calls the **entries** method on the **Dir** class; it accepts a single **String** argument and it returns an array of the entries in the current directory. Contrast this with an instance method on **Array**:

```
[1,2,3].length
```

The output should be as follows:

```
irb(main):085:0> [1,2,3].length
=> 3
```

Figure 4.3: The length method of an array

Here, we call the **length** method on an actual instance of an array; it does not take any arguments and returns an integer.

> **Note**
>
> To learn more about method signatures, refer to https://packt.live/2p3kw9a.

Method Arguments

As we discovered in the previous section, a method signature is one of the most important parts of a method, defining how it's called, what its name is, and what arguments it can take. Let's dive deeper into method arguments now.

Ruby methods can take any number of arguments. There are also different approaches to specifying arguments, with pros and cons to each. These approaches to specifying arguments are known as the method signatures.

There are different types of arguments available for Ruby methods:

- Positional arguments
- Optional parentheses
- Mandatory and optional arguments
- Keyword arguments

Let's take a look at each of these argument types one by one.

Positional Arguments

Positional arguments are arguments that are listed in the method signature and rely on their ordering in the signature. In other words, if a method signature has multiple arguments listed in a particular order, when the method is called with those arguments, Ruby will assign the arguments passed into the variables in the signature in the exact same order as they are specified.

Consider the following example:

```ruby
def adjust_thermostat(temperature, fan_speed)
  puts "Temperature is now: #{temperature}"
  puts "Fan speed is now: #{fan_speed}"
end
adjust_thermostat(50, :low)
adjust_thermostat(:low, 50)
```

Here, we have a method with two positional arguments. In the first example, we call the method correctly by passing the temperature first and the fan speed second. However, in the second call, the parameters are called in the incorrect order and could have unintended consequences. The output should be as follows:

```
irb(main):158:0> adjust_thermostat(50, :low)
Temperature is now: 50
Fan speed is now: low
=> nil
irb(main):159:0> adjust_thermostat(:low, 50)
Temperature is now: low
Fan speed is now: 50
```

Figure 4.4: Output for positional arguments

In this case, we are just outputting the values, so there is no issue. However, if we were doing any kind of calculation on the temperature, we could encounter an error when doing a mathematical operation on a symbol.

Variable Scope

Before we move on to discussing the other types of arguments, let's first talk about variable scope. Variable scope can be defined as the parts of code that are able to have access to certain variables. Variable scope is a much larger topic that is discussed throughout this book as we talk about the different fundamentals of Ruby code. For the purposes of methods and arguments, we need to know that method arguments are local to the method implementation.

In other words, these variables are not available outside the scope of the method block. Here is an example:

```
def adjust_temperature(temperature, adjustment)
  current_temperature += adjustment
  return current_temperature
end
puts adjust_temperature(50,5)
puts current_temperature
puts adjust_temperature(50,-5)
puts current_temperature
```

The output should be as follows:

```
irb(main):194:0> puts adjust_temperature(50, 5)
55
=> nil
irb(main):195:0> puts current_temperature
50
=> nil
irb(main):196:0> puts adjust_temperature(50, -5)
45
=> nil
irb(main):197:0> puts current_temperature
50
=> nil
```

Figure 4.5: Variable scope arguments

Here, we define a variable called **current_temperature** outside the method block. We have a variable with the same name inside the method block. However, they are really two different variables, as we can see in the preceding example: the **current_temperature** variable outside the block never gets modified despite being modified inside the method block.

That said, there is a nuance here as regards objects that are passed as arguments. For instance, if you pass a hash as an argument and modify it in the method, it will be modified outside the method. Consider the following example:

```
def adjust_temperature(climate_options, desired_temperature)
  climate_options[:temperature] = desired_temperature
  return nil
end
climate_options = {temperature: 50, fan_speed: :low}
adjust_temperature(climate_options, 55)
climate_options
```

The output would be as follows:

```
irb(main):216:0> climate_options = {temperature: 50, fan_speed: :low}
=> {:temperature=>50, :fan_speed=>:low}
irb(main):217:0> adjust_temperature(climate_options, 55)
=> nil
irb(main):218:0> climate_options
=> {:temperature=>55, :fan_speed=>:low}
```

Figure 4.6: Modifying the hash inside a method

In this case, we modified the hash that was passed as an argument inside the method block. This is because the hash is passed to the method in a particular way, called **pass by reference**. This is in contrast to the previous example, which is **pass by value**.

> **Note**
>
> For further reading, search for "pass by value" and "pass by reference" in Google to learn more about variable scope and passing arguments to methods.

Understanding variable scope is important to consider as each new concept of Ruby is learned. Variable scope will depend on the context. We will learn more about variable scope in the next chapter, *Chapter 5, Object-Oriented Programming with Ruby*.

Optional Parentheses and Code Style

In Ruby, as we have already seen, we have defined method signatures as having a name, followed by parentheses, and then the arguments within the parentheses. However, it is optional to include parentheses in the method signature:

```ruby
def hello! # no parameters, no parentheses, no worries
  puts "hello!"
end
def hello() # valid syntax, bad style
  puts "hello!"
end
def echo age1, age2 # valid syntax, bad style.
  puts age1, age2
end
```

In any programming language, there are many ways to write code, and this gives rise to "coding style." In Ruby, there is a generally accepted style guide, which can be found here: https://packt.live/2Vr542N. The Ruby style guide advises us to not use parentheses when there are no parameters and to always use parentheses when there are parameters.

Mandatory and Optional Arguments

So far, we have learned how to call methods with arguments. Let's see what happens when we try to call a method without passing in an argument:

```
ArgumentError (wrong number of arguments (given 0, expected 2))
```

The output should be as follows:

```
irb(main):220:0> adjust_temperature
Traceback (most recent call last):
        3: from /Users/peter/.rbenv/versions/2.5.1/bin/irb:11:in `<main>'
        2: from (irb):220
        1: from (irb):211:in `adjust_temperature'
ArgumentError (wrong number of arguments (given 0, expected 2))
```

Figure 4.7: Calling a method without an argument

By declaring the variables as we have done so far in the preceding method signatures, we are making them mandatory arguments.

We can also declare variables in a method signature to be optional. By making variables optional, we have to supply a default value for them:

```
def log(message, time = Time.now)
  return "[#{time}] #{message}"
end
```

Here, we've defined a method to return a string to be entered into a **log** file. It accepts the **log** message and an optional argument of **time**. In order for a variable to be optional, it has to have a default value. In this case, the current time is the default value.

> **Note**
>
> The default value in the method signature is always executed at runtime. Also, the default value can be any value, including nil. Just make sure that you handle those possible values in your method implementation.

The optional arguments must always be listed last and cannot be in the middle of mandatory arguments.

Keyword Arguments

Ruby 2.0 introduced keyword arguments. Keyword arguments, in contrast to positional arguments, allow arguments to be specified in the method signature by keyword instead of by their position in the signature.

Consider a method to process a payment by subtracting the price of an item from a balance. Prior to Ruby 2.0, the code to implement such a method would have been the following:

```
def process_payment(options = {})
  price = options[:price]
  balance = options[:balance]
  return balance - price
end
process_payment(price: 5, balance: 20)
```

The balance and price of the item are passed in a single hash argument. The default **options** argument is replaced by the argument that is passed in during the method call.

However, with Ruby 2.0, named arguments allow us to refactor the method as follows:

```
def process_payment(price:, balance: )
  return balance - price
end
process_payment(price: 5, balance: 20)
```

The invocation is the same, but the implementation of the method is much cleaner because the arguments are named ahead of time. We don't need to extract them from a hash. The other advantage here is that keyword arguments can be listed in any order in the method signature or the method invocation. Contrast this with the positional arguments that we learned about in the first section of this chapter.

This advantage allows us to add or remove arguments from the method signature without having to worry about other code that may reference this method. This is a huge advantage.

You can, of course, use default options with named arguments just as with positional arguments:

```
def log_message(message: ,time: Time.now)
  return "[#{time}] #{message}"
end
log_message(message: "This is the message to log")
```

Sometimes, named arguments can be more verbose than using positional arguments. So, the choice to use one or the other is up to the developer and the use case.

> **Note**
>
> Positional arguments are easier, more lightweight, and less verbose. Keyword arguments are more explicit and verbose, but allow the reordering of parameters.

Return Values

Methods are great for wrapping up blocks of code that accomplish some purpose. In many cases, we want to capture the results of that code execution in one or more variables. As such, the method can return these variables to the caller of the method. Conveniently enough, the keyword for returning variables is **return**.

Here is a basic case of adding two numbers:

```ruby
def sum(var1, var2)
    return var1 + var2
end
```

In Ruby, the value of the last line of code in a method is implicitly returned, so we also write this as follows:

```ruby
def sum(var1, var2)
    var1 + var2
end
total = sum(1, 3)
```

The choice to do one or the other depends on the developer's style and the requirements of the program.

The Ruby style guide says to avoid the use of the **return** keyword when not required for flow control.

Multiple Return Values

Ruby methods can also return multiple values. Let's take a look at some simple examples.

The following method returns a pair of random numbers:

```ruby
def get_random_pair
    return rand(10), rand(10)
end
```

There are a few ways to capture these return values:

```
pair = get_random_pair
  item1, item2 = get_random_pair
```

As we can see, Ruby is smart enough to figure out what type of assignment we are trying to do. Ruby knows we have an array of two and we are trying to assign values to two variables. Let's see what happens when there is not a 1:1 ratio of **return** values to variable assignments:

```
def get_three_items
  return rand(10), rand(10), rand(10)
end
item1, item2 = get_three_items
```

We can see here that Ruby put a single value for the **item1** and **item2** variables. The third item was discarded. If you run this code, you will see something similar to the following:

```
irb(main):262:0> item1, item2 = get_three_items
=> [4, 0, 2]
```

Figure 4.8: Multiple return values

IRB is outputting an array of three items. The method returns the three items no matter what, but Ruby can only assign them to two variables. However, the entire line of code still has a separate return value. We can demonstrate this with the following:

```
overall_return = (item1, item2 = get_three_items)
```

The output should be as follows:

```
irb(main):266:0> overall_return
=> [5, 1, 9]
```

Figure 4.9: The overall return value

This demonstrates that we can do variable assignment from the return value(s) of a method and still have an **overall_return** value from the whole statement. In most cases, the **overall_return** value is the same as the individual variable assignment; however, this demonstrates that it doesn't have to be, especially when you have multiple return values.

Also, as we can see, the **overall_return** value is an array, even though we listed the return values as a list of variables. This is because Ruby implements any set of multiple values as an array. Convenient, right? This means that we can also return an array and do the same thing with variable assignment and **overall_return** values.

We can list the return values in an array very easily using the **Array#last** method. Consider a basic array with five items:

```
array = [1,2,3,4,5]
```

We can use the following code to obtain the last two items from the array and assign them to a single variable:

```
top2 = array.last(2)
```

The output should be as follows:

```
irb(main):270:0> top2 = array.last(2)
=> [4, 5]
```

Figure 4.10: Output for the array.last method

Use the following code to assign variables individually:

```
var1, var2 = array.last(2)
```

The output should be as follows:

```
irb(main):276:0> var1, var2 = array.last(2)
=> [4, 5]
```

Figure 4.11: Individual variable assignment

We can use the following code to assign variables individually, discarding the last item:

```
var1, var2 = array.last(3)
```

The output should be as follows:

```
irb(main):281:0> var1, var2 = array.last(3)
=> [3, 4, 5]
```

Figure 4.12: Output after discarding the last item from an array

Until now, we have discussed the components of a method and how to implement them in Ruby. We have looked at various types of arguments and learned how to pass these arguments to methods. We also discussed how the **return** keyword can be used to capture the results from a method's execution in a variable. Now we will implement these concepts in an exercise.

Exercise 4.01: Performing Operations on an Array

In this exercise, we will be creating a method that returns the sum, mean, and median values of an array.

The following steps will help you to complete the exercise:

1. Create a new Ruby file. Define the method and the **return** variables:

```
def array_stats(input_array)
  return sum, median, mean
end
```

2. Then, we define a method that will calculate the **sum** value using the **inject** method. The **inject** method is used to sequentially add values, one by one, from the array:

```
def array_stats(input_array)
  sum = input_array.inject(0){|total, i| total + i }
  return sum
end
```

3. We modify the method that will calculate the **mean** value:

```
def array_stats(input_array)
  sum = input_array.inject(0){|total, i| total + i }
  mean = sum/input_array.length
  return sum, mean
end
```

4. Calculate **median** by creating another method that is dedicated to that purpose.

> **Note**
>
> The median is essentially the middle number in a sorted set of numbers. It is the value that separates the top half from the bottom half. As such, we need to write a method that calculates this. The median or middle number will depend on whether the set of numbers has an odd number or even number of elements.

Hence, we have used an **if/else** block in the method to address these two scenarios:

```ruby
def calculate_median(array)
  array = array.sort
  if array.length.odd?
    array[(array.length - 1) / 2]
  else array.length.even?
    (array[array.length/2] + array[array.length/2 - 1])/2.to_f
  end
end
```

5. Bring all the code together for **sum**, **mean**, and **median**:

```ruby
def array_stats(input_array)
  sum = input_array.inject(0){|total, i| total + i }
  mean = sum/input_array.length
  median = calculate_median(input_array)
    return sum, mean, median
end
```

6. Call **sum**, **mean** and **median** with different input arrays and capture the values into variables:

```ruby
array_stats([1,2,3])
stats = array_stats([500, 12, 1, 99, 55, 12, 12])
sum, mean, median = array_stats([500, 12, 1, 99, 55, 12, 12])
```

The output should be as follows:

```
=> :calculate_median
irb(main):016:0> sum, mean, median = array_stats([500, 12, 1, 99, 55, 12, 12])
=> [691, 98, 12]
irb(main):017:0> array_stats([500, 12, 1, 99, 55, 12, 12])
=> [691, 98, 12]
```

Figure 4.13: Output for sum, mean, and median

Note

The order of return values is important because they are similar to positional arguments. The order of how you list them will determine how they get assigned.

The Splat Operator

Suppose you want a method to have arguments and you want to accept a varying number of them. Ruby has a special syntax to account for this case. It is called the **splat** operator and is denoted as *. Actually, this is called the single splat operator. Since Ruby 2.0, there is also a double splat operator, **. Let's take a look at both of these.

The Single Splat (*) Operator

The single splat operator, *, is actually a way to work with arrays. Remember from earlier that Ruby really implements arguments as arrays behind the scenes? The splat operator allows us to build arrays together into a single variable or to splat them out into multiple variables. One of the main uses of the splat operator is to use it as a catch-all method argument. In other words, you can pass multiple arguments to a method call, and if the method signature defines an argument with the splat operator, it will combine all those arguments into the one variable.

Consider the following example:

```
def method_with_any_number_of_args(*args)
  puts args.class
  puts args
end
```

In this method signature, we have a single argument called **args**, which is denoted by the splat operator. This tells Ruby that the method can be called with any number of arguments and to splat them into a variable as an array.

It's not very common to use this form of method signature. Using this form requires more code to parse the array for specific arguments and can lend the code to be more error-prone and hard to debug. It's also not clear by reading the method signature what types of arguments the method can handle.

That said, knowing the splat operator exists and how it works can come in handy. We'll learn in the final chapter about a special Ruby method called **method_missing**, which uses the splat operator. In brief, this method is called by Ruby on an object when the object receives a message (method) that is not defined.

Let's take a look at some uses of the splat operator:

```
method_with_any_number_of_args(5, "asdf", [1,2,3])
```

Here, we pass three arguments of varying types and all arguments are put into the **args** variable as an array that can be further processed.

A useful usage of the splat operator is to assemble arguments as an array, and then to splat them out as arguments:

```ruby
args = []
args << 5
args << "asdf"
args << [1,2,3]
method_with_any_number_of_args(*args)
```

We can also use the splat operator to send our assembled arguments, even if the method signature has traditional positional arguments:

```ruby
def foo(arg1, arg2)
  puts arg1, arg2
end
args = [1,2]
foo(*args)
```

The Double Splat (**) Operator

The double splat operator arrived with Ruby 2.0 and pairs with its keyword arguments. Whereas the single splat operator can be used for splatting positional arguments into a single argument, the double splat operator is used for splatting keyword arguments into a single argument.

Let's take look at a method with keyword arguments:

```ruby
def log_message(message:, time: Time.now)
  return "[#{time}] #{message}"
end
log_message(message: "This is the message to log")
```

The output should be as follows:

```
irb(main):313:0> log_message(message: "This is the message to log")
=> "[2019-08-10 16:19:28 -0700] This is the message to log"
```

Figure 4.14: Output with keyword arguments

Now let's implement the same method with the double splat operator:

```
def log_message(**params)
  puts params.inspect
end
log_message(message: "This is the message to log", time: Time.now)
```

The output should be as follows:

```
irb(main):319:0> log_message(message: "This is the message to log", time: Time.now)
{:message=>"This is the message to log", :time=>2019-08-10 16:20:48 -0700}
```

Figure 4.15: Using the double splat operator

Let's perform an exercise in which we will implement the splat operator.

Exercise 4.02: Creating a Method to Take Any Number of Parameters

In this exercise, we will write a method that emulates an API client that can take any number of parameters. Additionally, we will call the method using the single splat operator.

A common idiom is to assemble arguments in this way if there are conditions determining which arguments to pass to the method. Let's take a look at an example using an API client that makes a web request. The web request method can take any number of arguments:

1. Open the IDE and create a new file. First, we need to create a method that implements a method called **get_data** and takes the **url**, **headers**, and **params** variables, which use the splat operator:

```
def get_data(url, headers = {}, *params)
  puts "Calling #{url}"
  if headers.length > 0
  puts "Headers: #{headers}"
  else
  puts "No headers"
end
  params.each do |param|
    puts "Found param: #{param}"
  end
end
```

2. Write a method that assembles parameters into an array:

```ruby
def assemble_params(include_headers = false, include_date_in_search = false, only_
show_my_records = true)
  headers = {accept: "application/json"}
  url = "https://exampleapi.com"
  args = [url]
  args << headers if include_headers
  params = []
  params << "date=#{Time.now}" if include_date_in_search
  params << "myrecords=true" if only_show_my_records
  args << params if params.length > 0
end
```

3. Call methods with different values using the splat operator:

```ruby
get_data(*assemble_params)
get_data(*assemble_params(true))
get_data(*assemble_params(false, true, false))
```

The output should be as follows:

```
irb(main):426:0> get_data(*assemble_params)
Calling https://exampleapi.com
Headers: ["myrecords=true"]
=> []
irb(main):427:0> get_data(*assemble_params(true))
Calling https://exampleapi.com
Headers: {:accept=>"application/json"}
Found param: ["myrecords=true"]
=> [["myrecords=true"]]
irb(main):428:0> get_data(*assemble_params(false, true, false))
Calling https://exampleapi.com
Headers: ["date=2019-08-10 16:27:02 -0700"]
```

Figure 4.16: Output of the method taking multiple parameters

We have written a method that emulates an API client that can take any number of parameters.

Duck Typing

Ruby is a dynamically typed language. Other languages are statically typed. The difference comes down to whether, and how, the language enforces the consistency of the type of variables. The consistency can be enforced (or not, as in Ruby) on the method arguments.

For example, a method can have a single argument, and there is nothing that restricts the code from calling that method and passing a variable of any data type. You can pass strings, arrays, and integers into any argument you want and Ruby will not complain. However, the method implementation may complain if you pass it a type that it cannot handle.

While this behavior leads to very flexible code, it can also lead to vulnerable code or code that needs to accommodate many different types. There is a split among developers, with some who prefer dynamically typed languages over statically typed languages.

As Ruby enthusiasts, we love dynamic typing because of its flexibility and expressiveness. In statically typed languages, you often have to declare the type ahead of time. However, you may not know or care about the type. If the variable passed into a method can be anything, then that would mean that we need to handle lots of different cases in code.

As long as the variable passed in behaves as you need it to, it doesn't matter what type is passed in. That is what is termed as duck typing.

For instance, say you implement a logging method that outputs the length of an object passed into it, as in the following example:

```ruby
def log_items(myvar)
  if myvar.kind_of?(Array) || myvar.kind_of?(Hash) || myvar.kind_of?(String)
    puts "Logging item with length: #{myvar.length}"
  end
end
```

In the preceding method, we are only logging items that respond to the **length** method. But what if there is a new type of object that also responds to **length**? Well, we would then have to add to the already quite long **if** conditional.

Instead, we can duck type the method so that it checks whether the variable responds to the method we need, in this case, **length**, as shown in the following code:

```ruby
def log_items(myvar)
  raise "Unhandled type" unless myvar.respond_to?(:length)
  puts "Logging item with length: #{myvar.length}"
end
```

That is a lot cleaner and allows any object to be passed into the method and it will succeed as long as the object responds to the **length** method. **respond_to?** is a special Ruby method on all objects that allows code to check whether the method is defined or, rather, can **respond_to** the method in question, which is passed in as a symbol.

Duck typing gets its name from the old adage, "*If it looks like a duck and it walks like a duck, then it is a duck.*" In other words, if an object has the characteristics that the method needs, we don't care about its type.

Sending a Message

So far, we've seen the standard way to send a message to Ruby objects using the dot (.) notation. Another way to send a message to a Ruby object is through the **send** method, as shown in the following code:

```
array = [1,2,3]
array.length # standard way of sending a message to an object
array.send(:length) # using the send method
array.send("length") # You can send a symbol or a string
```

send also supports passing arguments to methods:

```
array.send(:last, 2)
```

send will pass the positional arguments to the method in the same order that the method defines them. In other words, the second argument to **send** is really the first argument to the method that is actually being called. The third argument to **send** is the second argument to the method being called, and so on.

Let's take a look at some additional cases.

In the following example, we **send** the **each** method and can still pass a block:

```
[1,2,3].send(:each) do |i|
puts i
end
```

Let's take a look at a method that has keyword arguments:

```
irb(main):068:0> def foo(arg1: , arg2: )
irb(main):069:1> puts arg1, arg2
irb(main):070:1> end
=> :foo
irb(main):071:0> send(:foo, 1, 2)
```

```
Traceback (most recent call last):
  3: from /Users/peter/.rbenv/versions/2.5.1/bin/irb:11:in '<main>'
  2: from (irb):71
  1: from (irb):68:in 'foo'
ArgumentError (wrong number of arguments (given 2, expected 0; required keywords: arg1,
arg2))
```

We tried to call **send** with positional arguments, but Ruby is telling us we need to call with keyword arguments, and even tells us the names. So, let's try again:

```
send(:foo, arg1: 1, arg2: 2)
1
2
=> nil
```

send isn't used too often and is used in advanced Ruby programming. However, it's good to be introduced to it as it does have some interesting properties. One reason you might want to use **send** is if you don't know the method ahead of time. For instance, the actual method called might depend on some conditions, be assembled dynamically, or you might receive the method from user input.

The following is an interesting example of using **send** to create a method that can call any method passed in from user input:

```
def call_anything(object, method)
  object.send(method)
end
call_anything([1,2,3], gets.chomp.to_sym) # try it with sum
call_anything({a: 1, b: 2},gets.chomp.to_sym)
```

Additionally, we will learn, in Chapter 5, Object-Oriented Programming with Ruby, how **send** can bypass method visibility when using OOP in Ruby.

> **Note**
>
> Passing user input to **send** is inadvisable because, if you pass a variable that comes from user input to **send**, it could lead to a security vulnerability for remote code execution. It also leads to unclear and unpredictable code.

Using Built-In Modules: Time and Math

The Ruby language is composed of both a core set of libraries and a standard set. The Ruby Core library contains libraries that are always available in any Ruby interpreter. These libraries cover the basic programming constructs such as working with files, objects, arrays, hashes, and other primitives. The Ruby Standard Library contains additional libraries that you will find useful as a developer but are not considered core to the language. Examples of these include temp files, web servers (`WEBrick`), matrices, networking libraries (`net/http` or `net/ftp`), and more.

As you learn Ruby, you should take the time to see which libraries are included in Core and which are included in the Ruby Standard Library. You will use these libraries frequently. For instance, you could implement your own library to parse URLs, but the Ruby development team knows this is a very common task and has provided the URI module in the standard library. In your humble author's opinion, the best developer is not the one who knows how to write low-level routines, but the one who has the best fluency in the libraries at their disposal. In this section, we will cover how to use two libraries from the Core library: `Math` and `Time`.

While `Math` and `Time` are both libraries in the Ruby Core library, they are different types of libraries. `Math` is a module and `Time` is a class. We will elaborate more deeply on classes and modules in the next two chapters. For now, all you need to know is that they exist and that methods are called in a slightly differently way.

Math

The `Math` library is a library in the Ruby core set of libraries that provides methods for many mathematical functions. In this section, we will learn how to see what's available in this library.

Let's solve an exercise to acquaint ourselves better with the library.

Exercise 4.03: Using the Math Library to Perform Mathematical Operations

In this exercise, we will be using the `Math` library from Ruby to perform basic mathematical operations:

1. Open up an IRB console.

2. Begin by typing the following command to identify the class:

    ```
    Math.class
    ```

The output should be as follows:

```
irb(main):001:0> Math.class
=> Module
```

Figure 4.17: The Math module in Ruby

This confirms to us that **Math** is indeed a module. This fact, combined with the fact that our preceding list of methods is of "module methods" (prefixed with the scoping operator, ::), tells us that we can call these methods directly on **Math**.

3. Perform the sine operation on an integer:

```
Math.sin(45)
```

The output should be as follows:

```
irb(main):003:0> Math.sin(45)
=> 0.8509035245341184
```

Figure 4.18: The sine operation

4. Next, calculate the square root of an integer value:

```
Math.sqrt(144)
```

The output should be as follows:

```
irb(main):004:0> Math.sqrt(144)
=> 12.0
```

Figure 4.19: The square root function

5. Next, build the numbers for a sine wave. Begin by creating a start value and an increment:

```
x = -10
increment = 0.25
```

6. Now let's write a **while** loop to create a set of **x-y** pairs for the sine wave:

```
while(x<10) do
y = Math.sin(x)
puts "#{x} #{y}"
x += increment
end
```

In this example, our sine wave will go from **-10** to **10**. The **while** loop will simply output the **x-y** pair with a space in between. The output would look as follows:

```
-10 0.5440211108893699
-9.75 0.3195191936222736
-9.5 0.07515112046180931
-9.25 -0.17388948538043356
-9.0 -0.4121184852417566
-8.75 -0.6247239537541924
-8.5 -0.7984871126234903
-8.25 -0.9226042102393402
-8.0 -0.9893582466233818
-7.75 -0.9945987791111761
-7.5 -0.9379999767747389
-7.25 -0.8230808790115054
-7.0 -0.6569865987187891
-6.75 -0.4500440737806176
-6.5 -0.21511998808781552
-6.25 0.03317921654755682
-6.0 0.27941549819892586
-5.75 0.5082790774992583
```

Figure 4.20: Output for x,y pairs

Here, we can see that the **y** value starts at **0.554** when the **x** value is **-10**, and that by an **x** value of **-5.75**, the **y** value has gone through being negative back to being around **0.5**, which is characteristic of half of the wavelength of a sine wave.

7. Next, let's visualize this is in a spreadsheet such as Google Docs or Microsoft Excel. The following instructions may vary depending on your spreadsheet software. First, select and copy all the **x-y** pairs into your clipboard. Next, paste this into your spreadsheet software. It should show up as follows:

fx -10 0.5440211108893699

	A	B
1	-10 0.5440211108893699	
2	-9.75 0.3195191936222736	
3	-9.5 0.07515112046180931	
4	-9.25 -0.17388948538043356	
5	-9.0 -0.4121184852417566	
6	-8.75 -0.6247239537541924	
7	-8.5 -0.7984871126234903	
8	-8.25 -0.9226042102393402	
9	-8.0 -0.9893582466233818	
10	-7.75 -0.9945987791111761	
11	-7.5 -0.9379999767747389	
12	-7.25 -0.8230808790115054	
13	-7.0 -0.6569865987187891	
14	-6.75 -0.4500440737806176	

Figure 4.21: x-y pairs

8. Next, we need to split our **x-y** pair into separate columns. The command will vary depending on your spreadsheet software.

   For Google Docs, enter **=SPLIT(A1, " ")** into cell **B1**.

   For Microsoft Excel, you can use the **Text to Columns** feature on the **Data** tab.

   Follow the wizard and make sure to pick **Space** as your delimiter:

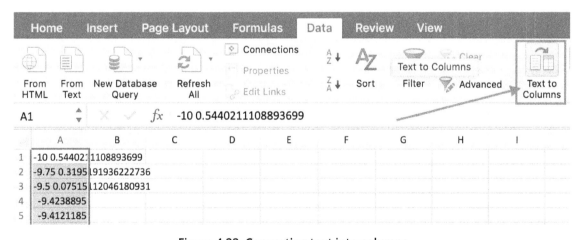

Figure 4.22: Converting text into columns

You should end up with two columns of **x-y** value pairs. Next, highlight your two **x-y** pair columns, click on **Insert > Chart**, and then choose the **line** chart. Depending on your spreadsheet software, you may end up with two series (make sure to remove the straight-line series). You should end up with a nice-looking sine wave:

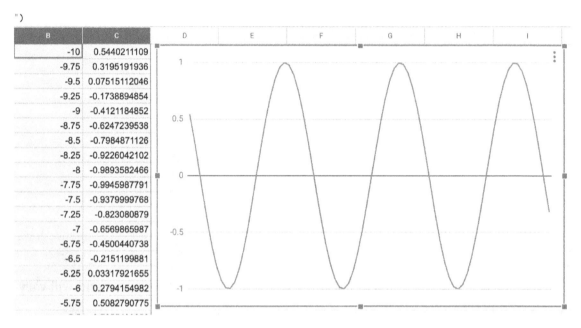

Figure 4.23: Sine-wave output

Thus, we have successfully used the **Math** module to perform mathematical operations and we have also generated a sine wave.

Time

The **Time** library is probably one of the most commonly used Ruby libraries. Almost every project you will work on will likely need to incorporate some concept of **Time**. As mentioned previously, **Time** is implemented as a class, not as a module.

This is actually something into which we will go deeper over the next two chapters. However, for now, we will cover the differences briefly. Consider that **Math** and mathematical functions never change. **sine(45)** will always have the same answer. However, time is fluid. Yesterday is different than today. 5 minutes ago is different than last year. **Time**, as a class, is used to represent a particular state of time. To do that, we have to create different instances of time. These are also known as **objects**. Let's investigate this by way of an exercise.

Exercise 4.04: Performing Method Operations with the Time Module

In this exercise, we will explore the built-in **Time** module of Ruby and perform various operations with it:

1. Jump into an IRB session and play around with **Time**. First, we will check the type of the module:

    ```
    Time.class
    ```

    The output should be as follows:

    ```
    irb(main):019:0> Time.class
    => Class
    ```

    Figure 4.24: Time.class

    By calling **Time.class**, we see that **Class** is returned, which confirms that **Time** is indeed a class.

2. Call one of those methods that were prefixed by the scoping operator, ::, straight on the **Time** class:

    ```
    Time.now
    ```

    The output should be as follows:

    ```
    irb(main):021:0> Time.now
    => 2019-08-18 16:19:59 -0700
    ```

    Figure 4.25: Time.now

    We called **Time.now** and it returned some output, which seems like a string that represents the current time.

3. Call the **.class** method on the value returned by **Time.now**:

    ```
    Time.now.class
    ```

    The output should be as follows:

    ```
    irb(main):022:0> Time.now.class
    => Time
    ```

    Figure 4.26: The .class method on time.now

Here, we can see that `Time.now` is not a string after all but an object that is a `Time` class. This can be a little difficult to rationalize at this point before we have learned about classes, objects, and instances, but bear with us here. `Time` is a class (really, it's a class constant) and `Time.now` returns an instance of the `Time` class.

Because we know that `Time.now` returns an instance of `Time`, we know that we can now call any of the instances on this object.

4. Save `Time.now` to a variable. Additionally, try calling `Time.now` successively after that:

```
t = Time.now
```

The output should be as follows:

```
irb(main):023:0> t = Time.now
=> 2019-08-18 16:24:55 -0700
irb(main):024:0> Time.now
=> 2019-08-18 16:25:10 -0700
irb(main):025:0> Time.now
=> 2019-08-18 16:25:11 -0700
irb(main):026:0> Time.now
=> 2019-08-18 16:25:13 -0700
irb(main):027:0> t
=> 2019-08-18 16:24:55 -0700
```

Figure 4.27: Methods on time.now

By saving `Time.now` to a variable, we've saved that exact instance of time; that variable will always represent that instance. As long as we don't mutate that variable, that instance of time is stopped.

Calling `Time.now` successively, though, shows that each call returns a new instance of time that represents the time at the exact instant it was called. We can see time advance with each successive call. That is what we would expect with the semantic call to `Time.now`.

When we call the **t** variable, it's holding the original time that was saved when we called `Time.now` several seconds prior.

Let's play with a few more methods.

5. Call the **hour**, **min**, and **day** methods on time instance **t**:

```
t.hour
t.min
t.min
```

The output should be as follows:

```
irb(main):032:0> t
=> 2019-08-18 16:24:55 -0700
irb(main):033:0> t.hour
=> 16
irb(main):034:0> t.min
=> 24
irb(main):035:0> t.day
=> 18
```

Figure 4.28: Methods on time instance t

Here we are calling several methods on time instance **t**, which are returning different values depending on what we are asking: the hour, the minute, or the day of the month.

We can go further with **Time**. The astute reader will have noticed that the first few instance methods on **Time** are the symbols **+**, **-**, and **<=>**.

The **+** and **-** symbols are the standard math operators for addition and subtraction. Let's explore this further by creating two **Time** instances and storing them in variables and then performing the addition and subtraction operations on them.

6. Call **Time.now** at different intervals and calculate the difference:

```
t1 = Time.now
t2 = Time.now
```

The output should be as follows:

```
irb(main):036:0> t1 = Time.now
=> 2019-08-18 16:33:17 -0700
irb(main):037:0> t2 = Time.now
=> 2019-08-18 16:33:24 -0700
```

Figure 4.29: Difference in Time instances

Here, there are two **Time** instances that are roughly 7 seconds apart. Add the instances and check the result:

```
t1 + t2
```

The output should be as follows:

```
irb(main):038:0> t1 + t2
Traceback (most recent call last):
        3: from /Users/peter/.rbenv/versions/2.5.1/bin/irb:11:in `<main>'
        2: from (irb):38
        1: from (irb):38:in `+'
TypeError (time + time?)
```

Figure 4.30: Sum of the two Time instances

We get an error. We're not actually adding two **Time** instances together, but we're adding a number of seconds to a time. This makes more sense. Let's try it:

```
t1 + 7
```

The output should be as follows:

```
irb(main):040:0> t1 + 7
=> 2019-08-18 16:33:24 -0700
```

Figure 4.31: Adding two Time instances

7. When we subtract two **Time** instances, we get a floating-point number, and when we subtract a number from a **Time** instance, we get another time.

```
t2 - t1
```

The output should be as follows:

```
irb(main):042:0> t2 - t1
=> 7.023575
irb(main):043:0> t2 - 7
=> 2019-08-18 16:33:17 -0700
```

Figure 4.32: Subtracting two Time instances

With this, we have successfully explored the **Time** module of Ruby.

Activity 4.01: Blackjack Card Game

Write a program that allows us to play the card game Blackjack. This version of Blackjack will be played with a single player and a computer dealer. The objective is for the player to get their cards as close to 21 as possible, without going over, and to beat the dealer's hand. Each player will be dealt a hand and the player will only be able to see one card from the dealer. The player can decide to hit or to stay, making a judgment based on what the dealer is showing and their own hand.

You can represent a single card as a number between 1 and 13. The four suits are diamonds, clubs, hearts, and spades:

1. Write a method to generate a deck of cards.

2. Write a method to shuffle the deck of cards.

3. Write a method to identify the cards drawn in a hand.

4. Write a method to label the cards based on their numbers and suits.

5. Write a method that defines the card value and displays a hand of cards with its total.

6. Write a method that determines the winner based on two hands (that is, two sets of cards). You will need a way to ask the user whether they want to hit or stay. `Hitting` means adding another card to the player's hand. `Staying` means keeping the current hand.

   Additionally, you will need a way for the dealer to determine whether it should hit or stay. The dealer could follow a fixed set of rules. If the total of the current hand is less than 17, it must hit. If the dealer's hand totals 17 or higher, it must stay.

7. Write a loop that allows a player to continue playing as long as there are enough cards in the deck. The minimum number of cards for a hand is 4 (2 for the player and 2 for the dealer).

> **Note**
>
> In the middle of a hand, the deck may run out of cards. This case should be handled.

You can extend the activity and make it more interesting by altering the solution to include the following scenarios:

- **Bonus 1**: Allow playing with more than one deck of cards or more than one player.

- **Bonus 2**: After every hand, place the used cards in a discard array that can be used and shuffled when the main deck has run out.

Here is the expected output:

```
Do you want to play a hand?[Yn]Y
Player has: 9♠,Jack♦ (19)
Dealer has: 10♣ (10), <other card hidden>
Do you want to hit or stay?stay
Your cards are now: 9♠,Jack♦ (19)
It's a tie!
Dealer hand: 19 (10♣,9♣ (19))
Player hand: 19 (9♠,Jack♦ (19))
Deck has: 48 cards left
Do you want to play a hand?[Yn]Y
Player has: Jack♥,3♣ (13)
Dealer has: 9♦ (9), <other card hidden>
Do you want to hit or stay?hit
Your cards are now: Jack♥,3♣,7♥ (20)
Do you want to hit or stay?stay
Your cards are now: Jack♥,3♣,7♥ (20)
Player wins!
Dealer hand: 19 (9♦,Jack♣ (19))
Player hand: 20 (Jack♥,3♣,7♥ (20))
Deck has: 43 cards left
```

Figure 4.33: Output for Blackjack

> **Note**
>
> The solution for this activity can be found on page 464.

Summary

In this chapter, we covered the significance of methods, how to define them, and the different ways to send arguments to them. Indeed, methods are one of the foundational concepts of Ruby, so it's important to feel comfortable using them. The main purpose of a method is to wrap up a chunk of code to accomplish a small task. You do not want to create methods with lots of code. If you do end up with a method that has lots of code, you can refactor it into multiple, smaller methods.

Methods take arguments and can return values. As long as the method signature and return values stay the same, it makes it very easy to change the implementation later on, which is a core virtue of methods.

Methods, like atoms, are building blocks of software programming. Once we start having a lot of methods, we will want to bundle them up into a higher-order concept. In Ruby, there are two higher-order concepts in which to group methods: classes and modules. We will look at both of these in the next chapter, beginning with classes.

5

Object-Oriented programming with Ruby

Overview

By the end of this chapter you will be able to describe the basics of object-oriented programming using Ruby; model data with classes; implement instance and class variables in Ruby programs; write instance and class methods in application programs; and evaluate getters and setters in Ruby.

Introduction

In the previous chapter, we studied different methods and parameters of Ruby. We also learned about the built-in libraries of `Math` and `Time` in Ruby. It was here that we began to introduce the concepts of classes and modules. In this chapter, we will dive deeper into Ruby classes using object-oriented programming (OOP) concepts as our guide.

OOP is where the rubber meets the road in programming. In other words, this is where the action happens. If you want to write a quick script or a full-fledged application, the chances are you will use OOP. OOP has the following benefits:

- It is easy to design programs, as OOP concepts help greatly in the organization of concepts in everyday life.

- It breaks hard problems down into manageable pieces for coding.

- It is easy to test.

- It is easy for others to read and learn how the program works.

- It provides foundational units that can be easily extended or built upon, so as to construct robust applications.

OOP facilitates writing code in a way that allows you to think about, and model, the concepts that you are working with in your program. For instance, imagine that you are tasked to write an application that allows all your coworkers to vote on who they think should be the employee of the month. You are most likely going to need code that deals with the abstract concepts in a voting system such as a user, a vote, and some code for grouping votes in a certain time period.

This kind of thinking and modeling is also known as domain modeling. The problem domain is everything involved in trying to solve the problem. In the preceding case, the problem domain is an employee-of-the-month voting system. OOP is the tactical way of solving that problem by splitting our problem domain specifically into domain models using objects and classes.

In our example, our concepts, users, and votes are classes. Our code will generate specific instances of users and votes and these are called objects. In English, we might say "*Mary (object) is a type of User (class)*" or "*Bob (User) voted (Vote) for Suzie (User)*". In this chapter, we'll learn how to model this voting application while learning the basics of OOP using classes and objects in Ruby.

> **Note**
>
> OOP is a large discipline and we will cover this topic in enough detail to understand Ruby and learn how to build applications.

Classes and Objects

Classes are abstract templates for objects. You can also say that objects are instances of classes. Classes contain the template for a set of behaviors (such as methods) and data (such as variables). As mentioned in the preceding example, at our company, we want to let everyone vote, so we need a way to keep track of those users and we need to model each user's behavior, such as the ability to vote. Here is an example of how we can create a **User** class to do this:

```
class User
  def initialize(name)
    @name = name
  end
end
```

We've created the base template for a user by using the **class** keyword and have given it the name **User**. Based on what we've learned so far, we can tell right off the bat that we have a **User** class with a method called **initialize**, which takes an argument of **name**. The body of the **User** class is concluded as usual with an **end** keyword. Additionally, we should note that the name of the **User** class is stored as an uppercase word, which means it's a constant.

The **initialize** method is a special method in Ruby that is placed inside the class definition. In other languages, the **initialize** method is known as the "constructor." This method is called automatically when we "instantiate" this class, meaning when we create objects from this class. The purpose of a constructor is to "initialize" some state (such as variables) for every object that is instantiated.

The user's name is stored in an "instance variable" denoted by the **@var** syntax. Instance variables are as the name suggests – they are "available to instances." We'll learn more about instance variables in the next section. Let's first create an instance of the **User** class:

```
u = User.new("Suzanne")
```

Here, we've created an object (that is, an instance) of a **User** class by calling the **new** method on **User** and passing in the name as a string. We've stored the result of this method in the **u** variable. Let's inspect this object:

```
irb(main):011:0> puts u.class
User
```

Figure 5.1: Output for the initialize method

Instance Methods

As we learned in the previous chapter with regard to the **Time** class, instance methods are methods that are available on a specific instance or object of a class. Instances have states that are held in instance variables. As you would expect, instance methods have access to these instance variables.

We've begun by modeling a **User** class with its own class and an instance variable, **@name**. This isn't very useful by itself, so let's add some useful methods (or behaviors), such as being able to return the name.

Consider the following example:

```ruby
class User
  def initialize(name)
    @name = name
  end
  def name
    @name
  end
end
```

We have defined the **name** method in the preceding snippet. Now, we will invoke it, as shown in the following code:

```ruby
u= User.new("Suzanne")
u.name
```

The output will be as follows:

```
irb(main):023:0> u.name
=> "Suzanne"
```

Figure 5.2: Output for the instance method

Here, we've added an instance method called **name**, which returns the instance variable, **@name**. Instance variables are useful because they are held separately in each object and are accessible to the object in any method. This is why you can assign the variable in the **initialize** method and access that same variable in another method. Look at the following example:

```ruby
u1 = User.new("Suzanne")
u2 = User.new("Mary")
u1.name
u2.name
```

The output would now show up as follows:

```
irb(main):025:0> u1.name
=> "Suzanne"
irb(main):026:0> u2.name
=> "Mary"
```

Figure 5.3: Output for the multiple instance classes

Let's add another method for updating the name:

```
class User
  def initialize(name)
    @name = name
  end
  def name
    @name
  end
  def set_name(new_name)
    @name = new_name
  end
end
u = User.new("Suzanne")
u.name
u.set_name("Suzie")
u.name
```

The output will be as follows:

```
irb(main):047:0> u.name
=> "Suzanne"
irb(main):048:0> u.set_name("Suzie")
=> "Suzie"
irb(main):049:0> u.name
=> "Suzie"
```

Figure 5.4: Modifying the instance variables

Here, we can see that we can modify the instance variable in a different method and this is reflected when we call the **name** method.

Getters and Setters

Since we are often getting (that is, retrieving) and setting (that is, assigning) variables with objects, it's common to define the methods that get and set those variables. In the previous section, the **name** method was a getter, and the **set_name** method was the setter.

Getting and setting variables are quite a common occurrence, and Ruby has a number of different ways for us to set and get variables. One quick improvement is to rewrite the setter method to use the assignment operator.

Let's consider the following example:

```ruby
class User
  def initialize(name)
    @name = name
  end
  def name
    @name
  end
  def name=(new_name)
    @name = new_name
  end
end
u = User.new("Suzanne")
u.name = "Suzie"
```

The output will be as follows:

```
irb(main):066:0> u.name = "Suzie"
=> "Suzie"
```

Figure 5.5: Output using = in the method signature

Adding = to the method signature tells Ruby that this method is to be used with the assignment operator.

If we try to call this method as a typical method, we'll get an **ArgumentError** error as follows:

```ruby
u.name("Suz")
```

The output will be as follows:

```
irb(main):069:0> u.name("Suz")
Traceback (most recent call last):
        3: from C:/Ruby25-x64/bin/irb.cmd:19:in `<main>'
        2: from (irb):69
        1: from (irb):56:in `name'
ArgumentError (wrong number of arguments (given 1, expected 0))
```

Figure 5.6: Output with a typical method

Here is a very common idiom to define your class with some instance variables:

```ruby
class User
  attr_accessor :name
  def initialize(name)
    @name = name
  end
end
u = User.new("Marlon")
u.name
```

The output will be as follows:

```
irb(main):084:0> u.name
=> "Marlon"
```

Figure 5.7: Defining a class with instance methods

attr_accessor is a keyword that tells Ruby to define "accessor" methods on the instance. Accessor methods are both the "get" and "set" method for the symbol passed in. In other words, they can be depicted as follows:

```ruby
attr_accessor :name
```

Note that **#** is used as shorthand for :. Let's look at an example:

```ruby
def name
  @name
end
def name=(new_name)
  @name = new_name
end
```

You can now quickly define lots of getters and setters just by listing them as symbols to **attr_accessor**, as shown in the following code:

```ruby
class User
   attr_accessor :name, :address, :birthday, :zodiac_sign
end
u = User.new
u.name = "Cleo"
u.zodiac_sign = "Libra"
```

In the preceding format, you will notice that we left out the **initialize** method, which shows that it is optional.

As you can see, **attr_accessor** defines both the getter and the setter. However, there may be instances where we only want to define one or the other, as shown in the following code:

```ruby
class User
   attr_reader :first_name
   attr_writer :last_name
   def initialize(first_name)
      @first_name = first_name
   end
   def full_name
      #{first_name} #{last_name}"
   end
   def last_name
      @last_name
   end
end
u = User.new("Sophia")
u.first_name # Sophia
u.full_name # Sophia
u.last_name = "Khan"
u.full_name # Sophia Khan
```

The output will be as follows:

```
irb(main):150:0> u.first_name # Sophia
=> "Sophia"
irb(main):151:0> u.full_name # Sophia
=> nil
irb(main):152:0> u.last_name = "Khan"
=> "Khan"
irb(main):153:0> u.full_name # Sophia Khan
=> nil
```

Figure 5.8: Using attr_accessor

In this case, we've written a contrived class in which the first name is immutable, meaning it can't be changed once the object has been instantiated. However, we can read the first name, update the last name, and display the full name by calling the corresponding instance method.

attr_accessor is used when you want to have both a setter and getter defined for you. **attr_writer** is rarely used as there aren't many cases when you want a class to write to an instance variable but not have access to it. **attr_reader** is very commonly used to provide access to an instance variable but not allow it to be changed directly.

Let's now solve an exercise to implement the **attr_accessor** method.

Exercise 5.01: Modeling a Company's Organizational Chart Using Classes

In this exercise, we are going to create some classes that model a company's organizational chart. In a company, there can be many departments, and each department can have many users. We will be creating a model for this structure. The following steps will help you to complete the exercise:

1. Create classes to represent the company, department, and users, as shown in the following code:

```
class User
end
class Company
end
class Department
end
```

2. Add an initiating implementation for each class. We're iterating on these classes and adding functionality (that is, methods) as we go:

Exercise5.01.rb

```
10 class User
11
12   attr_accessor :name, :address, :department
13   def initialize(name, address, department)
14
15     @name = name
16
17     @address = address
18
19     @department = department
20
21   end
22
23 end
24
```

https://packt.live/2IWUf3v

As you can see in the preceding code, we have initialized the classes and specified the variables corresponding to each class. The **User** class will be defined by the name, address, and department variables. The **Company** class will be specified by :name, company :url, and :department. Additionally, the **Department** class will be defined by the :name and :users variables.

> **Note**
>
> We are using the Ruby library, **URI**, to parse the company URL into a proper **URI** object. The **URI** library is available in the Ruby Standard Library.

3. Instantiate a company by passing a name and URL to the constructor:

```
c = Company.new("Acme Inc", "https://example.com")
```

4. Instantiate two department instances by passing a name as the argument:

```
sales = Department.new("Sales")
engineering = Department.new("Engineering")
```

5. Instantiate two users by passing in the name and address strings, alongside the department object instances, to the **User** constructor:

```
bob = User.new("Bob Smith", "1 Main Street", sales)
mary = User.new("Mary Jane", "10 Independence Blvd", engineering)
```

6. Assign department instances to the company through the department's accessor method:

```
c.departments = [sales, engineering]
```

To recap, we've created a company that can be instantiated with a name and URL; a user that can be instantiated with a name and address; a department instance variable that holds a department object instance; a department that can be created with a name; and a company that can have departments assigned to it through its accessor method

7. A company should be able to provide a list of all its users. Since this seems like it will be a common use case, let's write a new method for **Company** that makes it easy to obtain a list of users. Since a company has a reference to its departments, we can simply iterate over the **departments** instance variable and collect all the users in each department, as shown in the following code:

```
class Company
  attr_accessor :name, :url, :departments
  def initialize(name, url)
    @name = name
    @url = URI.parse(url)
  end
  def users
    departments.map(&:users)
  end
end
```

However, can you spot the problem with the preceding method we just wrote? The observant reader will realize that if we map or collect users, which is itself an array, we will end up with an array of arrays. Luckily, Ruby provides a convenient method for dealing with this situation, called the **.flatten** method. The **.flatten** method takes arrays that have any level of nesting within them and flattens all the items into a single-dimensional array, which is exactly what we want in this case.

8. Apply the **.flatten** method to the **departments** array, which itself is an array of users, as shown in the following code:

```
class Company
  # Other code omitted for brevity
  def users
    departments.map(&:users).flatten
  end
end
```

Next, let's take a look at the **Department** class. The **Department** class has an accessor for :**users** but, currently, it's possible that :**users** may be nil. As good programmers, we want to protect against nil conditions where we can. If we protect against nil during object creation, it makes it unlikely or even unnecessary to write **if** conditions checking for nil in other parts of code. This results in much cleaner code. To avoid this, we want to make sure that the **Department** instance always returns an array when :**users** is called. There are two approaches to this – seeding the user's instance variable at object creation or seeding the user's instance variable at runtime when called.

The code for seeding the users instance variable at object creation is as follows:

```
class Department
  attr_accessor :name, :users
  def initialize(name)
    @name = name
    @users = []
  end
end
```

The code for seeding the users instance variable at runtime is as follows:

```
class Department
  attr_accessor :name, :users
  def initialize(name)
    @name = name
  end
  def users
    # override the accessor,
    # to make sure we always have an array to work with to avoid nil conditions
    @users ||= []
  end
end
```

Seeding the user's instance variable during object creation in a constructor means that the **@users** instance variable is set once and is slightly cleaner code. However, the approach of overriding the accessor has the benefit of only being called at runtime. If the **Department** instance never has **users** called on it, then the array is never assigned to **@users** and saves on memory and performance. In this case, it's negligible, but if you are seeding with a large object or array, there is a considerable benefit to this approach. For instance, imagine if you were seeding the variable with data from a file. It is a very common paradigm to seed variables at runtime, as in the second approach.

We will be using the second approach, where we seed instance variables at runtime for this exercise.

9. Finally, let's add some behavior to the **User** class. One thing that is missing in our model is that when a **User** class is created and assigned to a department, the department's instance variable that points to users can get out of sync. We could maintain the relationship manually, which would require a lot of code; alternatively, we can add the user to the department's instance variable when the user is created. In the following code, we are following the second approach, where we assign the user to the instance variable of the department, when the user is created:

```ruby
class User
  attr_accessor :name, :address, :department
  def initialize(name, address, department)
    @name = name
    @address = address
    @department = department
    @department.users << self
  end
end
```

In the **initialize** method for the **User** class, we make a reference to **self** and assign to it the **department.users** attribute. We can do this because, in the **initialize** method, **self** is an already instantiated object. As we discussed previously when discussing the difference between **new** and **initialize**, **initialize** is actually called after the object is instantiated and allows for code to customize (or **initialize**) the state of the object.

This is distinct from other programming languages, where the constructor is responsible for instantiating the object.

10. Let's test the new class code we've written, as shown in the following code:

```ruby
# setup data
c = Company.new("Acme Inc", "https://example.com")
sales = Department.new("Sales")
engineering = Department.new("Engineering")
bob = User.new("Bob Smith", "1 Main Street", sales)
mary = User.new("Mary Jane", "10 Independence Blvd", engineering)
c.departments = [sales, engineering]
# play with new methods
c.users
sales.users
engineering.users
```

The output for the new class code will be as follows:

```
irb(main):259:0> c = Company.new("Acme Inc", "https://example.com")
=> #<Company:0x00007fac5118c2c0 @name="Acme Inc", @url=#<URI::HTTPS https://example.com>>
irb(main):260:0> sales = Department.new("Sales")
=> #<Department:0x00007fac511158a0 @name="Sales">
irb(main):261:0> engineering = Department.new("Engineering")
=> #<Department:0x00007fac51326ea0 @name="Engineering">
irb(main):262:0> bob = User.new("Bob Smith", "1 Main Street", sales)
=> #<User:0x00007fac513177e8 @name="Bob Smith", @address="1 Main Street", @department=#<Department:0x00007fac511158a0 @name="Sales", @us
ers=[#<User:0x00007fac513177e8 ...>]>>
irb(main):263:0> mary = User.new("Mary Jane", "10 Independence Blvd", engineering)
=> #<User:0x00007fac51307028 @name="Mary Jane", @address="10 Independence Blvd", @department=#<Department:0x00007fac51326ea0 @name="Engi
neering", @users=[#<User:0x00007fac51307028 ...>]>>
irb(main):264:0> c.departments = [sales, engineering]
=> [#<Department:0x00007fac511158a0 @name="Sales", @users=[#<User:0x00007fac513177e8 @name="Bob Smith", @address="1 Main Street", @depar
tment=#<Department:0x00007fac511158a0 ...>>]>, #<Department:0x00007fac51326ea0 @name="Engineering", @users=[#<User:0x00007fac51307028 @n
ame="Mary Jane", @address="10 Independence Blvd", @department=#<Department:0x00007fac51326ea0 ...>>]>]
irb(main):265:0> # play with new methods
=> nil
irb(main):266:0> c.users
=> [#<User:0x00007fac513177e8 @name="Bob Smith", @address="1 Main Street", @department=#<Department:0x00007fac511158a0 @name="Sales", @u
sers=[#<User:0x00007fac513177e8 ...>]>>, #<User:0x00007fac51307028 @name="Mary Jane", @address="10 Independence Blvd", @department=#<Dep
artment:0x00007fac51326ea0 @name="Engineering", @users=[#<User:0x00007fac51307028 ...>]>>]
irb(main):267:0> sales.users
=> [#<User:0x00007fac513177e8 @name="Bob Smith", @address="1 Main Street", @department=#<Department:0x00007fac511158a0 @name="Sales", @u
sers=[...]>>]
irb(main):268:0> engineering.users
=> [#<User:0x00007fac51307028 @name="Mary Jane", @address="10 Independence Blvd", @department=#<Department:0x00007fac51326ea0 @name="Eng
ineering", @users=[...]>>]
irb(main):269:0> 
```

Figure 5.9: Output for the class codes

Here, we can see that our data model is correct, as users are added to the proper department instance variable when the user is instantiated with that same department object instance.

11. Let's complete the data model by adding a number of relevant accessor methods and refactoring:

```ruby
class User
  attr_accessor :name, :address
  attr_reader :department
  def initialize(name, address, department)
    @name = name
    @address = address
    @department = department
    department.users << self
  end
  # New method to keep the department's users up to date
  # when a user's department instance variable is changed
  def department=(new_department)
    @department.users.delete(self)
```

```
      @department = new_department
      @department.users << self
   end
 end
```

As you can see, some of the data attributes are dependent on one another. For instance, a user's department should be consistent with the users in that department. This means that we need to make sure that when we change a user's department, we also update the user's attribute of that department.

12. We need to verify whether this works as expected. First, let's make sure we are set up again on an IRB console:

```
c = Company.new("Acme Inc", "https://example.com")
engineering = Department.new("Engineering")
sales = Department.new("Sales")
bob = User.new("Bob Smith", "1 Main Street", sales)
mary = User.new("Mary Jane", "10 Independence Blvd", engineering)
```

13. Next, let's take a look at the users in the **Engineering** department instance (we collect the **User#name** attribute to make it more readable in the output):

```
Engineering.users.map(&:name)
```

The output will be as follows:

```
irb(main):275:0> engineering.users.map(&:name)
=> ["Mary Jane"]
```

Figure 5.10: Output for engineering.users.map

14. Next, let's assign Bob (who was previously in Sales) to the **engineering** department:

```
bob.department = engineering
```

The output will be as follows:

```
irb(main):282:0> bob.department  = engineering
=> #<Department:0x00007fac512ae0e0 @name="Engineering", @users=[#<User:0x00007fac512780f8 @name="Mary Jane", @address="10 Independence
lvd", @department=#<Department:0x00007fac512ae0e0 ...>>, #<User:0x00007fac512891a0 @name="Bob Smith", @address="1 Main Street", @departm
ent=#<Department:0x00007fac512ae0e0 ...>>]>
```

Figure 5.11: Output after assigning a user from one department to another department

15. If you look at the preceding output closely, you can see that the **engineering** department references both Bob and Mary. However, let's examine this on the console as well:

```
engineering.users.map(&:name)
sales.users.map(&:name)
```

The output will be as follows:

```
irb(main):283:0> engineering.users.map(&:name)
=> ["Mary Jane", "Bob Smith"]
irb(main):284:0> sales.users.map(&:name)
=> []
```

Figure 5.12: Output after assigning a user from one department to another department

We can see that both **engineering** and **sales** had their **@users** attribute updated appropriately.

Thus, we have successfully built a model for the company's organizational structure using the **initialize** and **attr_accessor** methods.

Class Methods

We've seen how to create a class, instantiate it, and work with instance variables and instance methods. Now, let's learn about class variables and class methods. As their names imply, these are variables and methods that operate at the class level rather than the instance level. Since classes are templates for objects, class methods and variables typically represent unchanging data or methods that belong to that class and could apply to all instances of that class.

Let's start by defining a class method:

```
class User
  def self.roles
    ["Employee", "Manager", "Director", "Executive"]
  end
end
User.roles
```

Here, we've defined a **User** class, which has a class method called **.roles** that returns an array of strings that represent certain roles a user may have in a company. The method is defined by prefixing it with the **self** keyword. We call the method directly on the class and thus we have a class method.

There are other ways to define class methods in Ruby, as mentioned in the following sections.

Method 1: Calling a Method Directly on the Class

A class method can be defined by calling the method directly on the class. In the following example, we call the `.roles` method on the **User** class:

```
class User
  def User.roles
    ["Employee", "Manager", "Director", "Executive"]
  end
end
```

Method 2: Using the self Keyword

In this method, the **self** keyword is used to define a class method. Take a look at the following example:

```
class User
  class << self
    def roles
        ["Employee", "Manager", "Director", "Executive"]
    end
  end
end
```

The first class method is very similar to the method we defined previously. In fact, **self** in **User.roles** is synonymous with the **User** class constant. We're defining the method on the class constant. Note that this syntax isn't used too often, whereas **def self.<method_ name>** is the most common way of defining class methods.

The syntax used with **class << self** is used fairly frequently. However, if you are searching for class methods, you won't be able to distinguish them from instance methods, whereas in the first invocation, you can search for **def self** and find all the class methods. However, proponents of **class << self** argue that to find a specific method, you don't need to worry about prefixing the **self** keyword in your search query.

Class Variables

Class variables are variables that belong to the class. Contrast this with instance variables that belong to an object instance. Because class variables belong to a class, and a class definition does not change, class variables do not change either.

> **Note**
>
> It is not strictly true that class definitions and class variables do not change in Ruby. Ruby is very flexible; however, the ability to change class variables is strongly discouraged and is a highly advanced topic, which is beyond the scope of this chapter. For now, consider them as variables that are set up when loading the class constant.

The syntax for a class variable is the **@@** sign, as depicted in the following code:

```ruby
class User
  @@roles = ["Employee", "Manager", "Director", "Executive"]
  def self.roles
    return @@roles
  end
end
```

Here, we've replicated our **User** class, stored the user roles in a class variable, and used the **class** method to return the roles. The class variable is available to us within the class context or class methods, and it is also available to us within an instance method:

```ruby
class User
  @@roles = ["Employee", "Manager", "Director", "Executive"]
  def self.roles
    @@roles
  end
  def initialize(role)
    @role = role
  end
```

```
  def get_roles
    @@roles
  end
end
u = User.new("employee")
puts u.get_roles
```

The output will be as follows:

```
                    Employee
                    Manager
                    Director
                    Executive
```

Figure 5.13: User roles

It is important to note that **self** changes here based on the context. For instance, consider writing a method as follows:

```
class User
  @@roles = ["Employee", "Manager", "Director", "Executive"]
  def self.roles
    @@roles
  end
  def get_roles
    self.roles
  end
end
u = User.new("manager")
puts s.get_roles
```

The output will be as follows:

```
 NoMethodError: undefined method `roles for #<User:0x00007fbc13845ec8 @type="manager">
```

Figure 5.14: The NoMethod error

This is because **self** in the instance method refers to the object instance. When we defined the **class** method, we are in a class context, and **self** refers to the **class** constant. If you want to call a **class** method from an instance method, you need to be explicit, as shown in the following code:

```
def get_roles
  User.roles
end
# or
def get_roles
  self.class.roles
end
```

> **Note**
>
> You have to be careful about class variables in multithreaded or multiprocess environments.

Class variables can be dangerous if they are changed by the code. The class variable can be changed in one thread or process and not be changed in another thread or process, and so you may get unexpected results.

> **Note**
>
> Thread safety is a complex topic. You can read more about it at https://packt. live/2Mutq7S.

It is very common for applications to provide links to share their own web pages on social platforms such as Facebook, Twitter, or LinkedIn. These are called social sharing links. There are many libraries and utilities on the internet for doing this. Let's solve an exercise to design our class in an object-oriented way.

Exercise 5.02: Generating URLs for Sharing Content on Social Platforms

In this exercise, we will implement our own Ruby class that allows us to pass in a URL and some other data and generate a URL that can be used to share that content on a social platform. The following steps will help you to complete the exercise:

1. Create a new Ruby file.

2. Create a class called **SocialShare**. This will be the class that we use to generate social links for different social platforms:

```
class SocialShare
end
```

3. Create a class variable that will hold a hash of key-value pairs of social platforms with their social sharing URL templates. Each URL template will use a special Ruby syntax for replacing parts of the string with what's called a "named placement." This is accomplished by using the **%{var}** syntax. The **%{url}**, **%{title}**, and **%{summary}** templates can be called by name to get replaced with another variable:

```
class SocialShare
  @@platforms = {
    facebook: "https://www.facebook.com/sharer/sharer.php?u=%{url}",
    twitter: "https://twitter.com/intent/tweet?text=%{url} %{title}",
    linkedin: "http://www.linkedin.com/shareArticle?mini=true&url=%
    {url}&title=%{title}&summary=%{summary}&source=Recognize"
  }
end
```

4. Implement the **initialize** method to receive the arguments necessary to share a URL. The arguments will include the platform we want a link for, the URL to share, the title for the post that will be shared, and an optional summary. Different platforms support a different set of options when it comes to the sharing utility. Our method will support these different styles, as shown in the following code:

```
class SocialShare
  # @@platforms code omitted for brevity
  def initialize(platform, url, title, summary = "")
    @platform = platform.to_sym
    @share_url = url
    @title = title
    @summary = summary
  end
end
```

5. Implement a **generate_url** method that interpolates the template for the appropriate platform with the arguments used to initialize the object. To do this, we will use a special Ruby syntax that uses the **%** sign as an operator. This is used in conjunction with the **%{var}** templates we set up in *step* 3. The left-hand side of the **%** sign is the string to interpolate, and the right-hand side is a map of key-value pairs. The key should map to the named variable in **%{var}** and the value will be the value that is interpolated into the string:

```ruby
class SocialShare
  # previous code omitted for brevity
  def generate_url
    @@platforms[@platform] % {title: @title, url: @share_url, summary: @summary}
  end
end
```

In the preceding code, we reference the **@@platforms** class variable. Then, we do a hash lookup for the string template value for a particular platform set by the **@platform** instance variable. So, for example, this lookup would look like the following:

```
irb(main):070:0>   platforms = {
irb(main):071:1*     facebook: "https://www.facebook.com/sharer/sharer.php?u=%{url}",
irb(main):072:1*     twitter: "https://twitter.com/intent/tweet?text=%{url} %{title}",
irb(main):073:1*     linkedin: "http://www.linkedin.com/shareArticle?mini=true&url=%{url}&title=%{title}&summary=%{summary}&source=Recognize"
irb(main):074:1>   }
=> {:facebook=>"https://www.facebook.com/sharer/sharer.php?u=%{url}", :twitter=>"https://twitter.com/intent/tweet?text=%{url} %{title}", :linke
y}&source=Recognize"}
irb(main):075:0> platforms[:facebook]
=> "https://www.facebook.com/sharer/sharer.php?u=%{url}"
```

Figure 5.15: Output for the platform lookup

Here, we can see that the template string for the Facebook share URL is returned when we pass **:facebook** as the key in the **@@platforms** class variable.

On the right-hand side of the **%** sign is a hash where the keys are **:title**, **:url**, and **:summary**. Essentially, this line is instructing Ruby to replace any reference to each of these variables with their corresponding values.

6. Implement a reader method, **url**, which memorizes the variable to an instance variable to make the usage more semantic and performant. We do this because we should expect the same output for the same set of parameters. Therefore, if we work with the same instance, we save the results to an instance variable for a quick lookup, as the **generate_url** method will only be called on the first invocation:

```ruby
class SocialShare
  def url
    @url ||= generate_url
  end
end
```

This method is straightforward. We are using the **||=** (which is pronounced "or equal") operator to memorize or cache the results of a call to **generate_url**. The **||=** operator is like saying *if not nil, then assign*. By memorizing the URL for a given platform and set of parameters, we are essentially making the instance "immutable." This means it cannot be changed. Because we expect this object to never change once it's been instantiated, this means we can do performance enhancements, such as memorizing potentially long-running method calls. This particular method call to interpolate may seem very quick when run in isolation, but perhaps you are building a large web application with a lot of traffic that generates a lot of shareable URLs. This time can quickly add up.

7. Test out the class's implementation by instantiating the class in an IRB session with different parameters. To do this, we will first set up some variables to represent the title and URL to share. Then, we will write a loop over all the platforms and make the appropriate method calls on each instance. First, let's take a look at our fully assembled class:

```ruby
class SocialShare
  platforms = {
    facebook: "https://www.facebook.com/sharer/sharer.php?u=%{url}",
    twitter: "https://twitter.com/intent/tweet?text=%{url} %{title}",
    linkedin: "http://www.linkedin.com/shareArticle?mini=true&url=%
    {url}&title=%{title}&summary=%{summary}&source=Recognize"
  }
  def initialize(platform, title, url, summary = "")
    @platform, @title, @share_url, @summary = platform.to_sym, title, url, summary
  end
```

```ruby
  def url
    @url ||= generate_url
  end
  def generate_url
    url_string = @@platforms[@platform] % {title: @title, url: @share_url, summary:
@summary}
  end
end
```

Then, in an IRB console, let's set up some variables that we will reuse when testing:

```ruby
title = "Check out this great coding website!"
url = "packt.com"
```

8. Now, let's loop over an array of platforms (represented by symbols) and instantiate our **SocialShare** class and call the **url** method:

```ruby
[:twitter, :facebook, :linkedin].each.do |platform|
  puts SocialShare.new(platform, title, url).url
end
```

The output will be as follows:

```
irb(main):122:0> [:twitter, :facebook, :linkedin].each do |platform|
irb(main):123:1*   puts SocialShare.new(platform, title, url).url
irb(main):124:1> end
https://twitter.com/intent/tweet?text=packt.com Check out this great coding website!
https://www.facebook.com/sharer/sharer.php?u=packt.com
http://www.linkedin.com/shareArticle?mini=true&url=packt.com&title=Check out this great coding website!&summary=&source=Recognize
=> [:twitter, :facebook, :linkedin]
```

Figure 5.16: Output for calling the URL method

9. Next, let's add a class method to make it easy to call and get a share URL.

    We do this because it makes the usage of this class much easier and cleaner. The class method will be responsible for the code that does the actual instantiation of the class:

```ruby
class SocialShare
  def self.url(platform, title, url, summary = "")
    new(platform, title, url, summary).url
  end
end
```

10. Finally, let's add another class method that could be classified as a *convenience method*. This method will do what our test code does, looping over all the platforms and returning an array with the share links for each of them:

```
class SocialShare
  def self.get_links_for_all(title, url, summary = "")
    @@platforms.keys.map do |platform|
      url(platform, title, url, summary)
    end
  end
end
pp SocialShare.get_links_for_all(title,url)
```

The output for the **get_links_for_all** method will appear as follows:

```
irb(main):160:0> pp SocialShare.get_links_for_all(title, url)
["https://www.facebook.com/sharer/sharer.php?u=packt.com",
 "https://twitter.com/intent/tweet?text=packt.com Check out this great coding website!",
 "http://www.linkedin.com/shareArticle?mini=true&url=packt.com&title=Check out this great coding website!&summary=&source=Recognize"]
=> ["https://www.facebook.com/sharer/sharer.php?u=packt.com", "https://twitter.com/intent/tweet?text=packt.com Check out this great
coding website!&summary=&source=Recognize"]
```

Figure 5.17: Output for a class with share links

And there we go. We have written a class to generate share links on different platforms. This class lends itself well to provide extensions for other platforms. All you need to do is add to the class variable, **@@platforms**, and the rest of the code in the class will work perfectly. This is the beauty of OOP. When you have a well-designed code, it makes it really easy to extend functionality without having to change a lot of other dependent code.

Inheritance

So far, we've learned the basics of objects and classes, as well as their class methods and variables, and instance methods and variables. We've learned that classes are templates for objects, and that we can create classes to represent data and behavior that can be grouped together in order to model a higher-level concept such as a user. This allows us to keep our code clean, organized, and extensible.

Just as we've learned that classes are templates for objects, we can go one step further by learning how to use classes as templates for other classes. This is particularly useful for when you want to have several classes that all share common data and behaviors. Conceptually, think of these "subclasses" as types of a class. A common example of this is vehicles. Vehicles share characteristics, for example, they travel at a certain speed, in a certain direction, and perhaps have a number of wheels. A car generally has four wheels, a bicycle has two, and a boat doesn't have any wheels, but all of them are types of vehicles.

When you create a class that serves as a template (or a base class) for another class, this is called inheritance. Cars, bicycles, and boats are all "types" of vehicles; so, we might have a base vehicle class and then a subclass of the vehicle class to create each of the types of vehicles, respectively.

When a class inherits from a parent class, it inherits both variables and methods from the parent class. For example, the vehicle class might define an instance variable for the number of wheels and an instance method for calculating the speed. Since the subclass (that is, the class that inherits from the base/parent class) is still a class, that means it is still used to create object instances. The object instances from the subclass, therefore, inherit those variables and methods, such as the number of wheels and the speed. Inheritance is a fundamental OOP concept and it is worth calling special attention to it.

As mentioned already, you can think about subclasses as being "types" of the base class. In the following chapter, we will model people in an organization. What are the common characteristics of persons in an organization? At a minimum, they likely all have a name, an email address, and a role in the organization. Can you think of other common attributes or behaviors?

So, inheritance governs both data (that is, variables) and behavior (that is, methods). Let's now dive into how inheritance works with each.

The Inheritance of Methods

In the previous example, we had a **User** class, along with separate **Employee**, **Manager**, **Director**, and **Executive** classes. However, employees, managers, directors, and executives are all types of users, so we can use inheritance to share behavior among them.

Consider the following code snippet:

```ruby
class User
  @@roles = ["Employee", "Manager", "Director", "Executive"]
  attr_reader :address
  def self.roles
    @@roles
  end
  def initialize(address)
    @address = address
  end
end
```

The preceding class describes a simple **User** class with a class variable of **roles** and an instance variable of **address**.

Let's create subclasses of **User** to describe each type of user. To do this, we use the **<** operator to subclass the base **User** class:

```
class Employee < User
end
class Manager < User
end
class Director < User
end
class Executive < User
end
```

Here, we've defined **Employee**, **Manager**, **Director**, and **Executive** classes to "derive" off of the **User** class.

Let's now call the **address** method on the variable using the console, as shown in the following code:

```
e = Employee.new("1 main street")
e.address
```

The output will be as follows:

```
irb(main):053:0>    e = Employee.new("1 main street")
=> #<Employee:0x000000000326fc20 @address="1 main street">
irb(main):054:0>    e.address
=> "1 main street"
```

Figure 5.18: Output for the inheritance method

Here, we see that the **Employee** instance has inherited several things. We did not define an **initialize** method on **Employee**, but it inherited it from the base **User** class. It has inherited the **initialize** method as well as the **@address** instance variable. Accordingly, any instance method or variable you define on a parent class will be available on the instance.

Now, take a look at the following code:

```
class User
  attr_accessor :first_name, :last_name, :address
  def initialize(first_name, last_name, address)
    @first_name = first_name
    @last_name = last_name
    @address = address
  end
```

```
  def label
    "#{first_name} #{last_name}"
  end
end
```

In the preceding **User** class, we have added some additional accessors (:**first_name**, :**last_name**) and created an instance method called **label**, which returns a string that interpolates those variables. Next, let's create our **Employee** subclass:

```
class Employee < User
end
```

Now, let's investigate this on an IRB console. We will call the **label** method on the variables, as shown in the following code:

```
e = Employee.new("Bob", "Smith", "1 Main street")
e.label
```

The console would call the method as shown in the following diagram:

```
irb(main):076:0> e = Employee.new("Bob", "Smith", "1 Main street")
=> #<Employee:0x0000000002f47660 @address="1 Main street", @first_name="Bob", @last_name="Smith">
irb(main):077:0> e.label
=> "Bob Smith"
```

Figure 5.19: Output for the inheritance of all variables and methods

Here, we can see that the **Employee** subclass inherited all the instance variables and methods.

Often, you will want to call the parent's method and customize it in the subclass. You can do this by calling the **super** keyword. We'll learn more about **super** in the next section.

Now, take a look at the following example:

```
class Employee < User
  def label
    "Employee: #{super}"
  end
end
```

We can also call the base class's **class** methods from the subclass. Consider a **User** class with the following class method:

```
class User
  def self.types
    ["Employee", "Manager", "Director", "Executive"]
  end
```

```
end
class Employee < User
end
Employee.types # ["Employee", "Manager", "Director", "Executive"]
```

Employee.types will show up on the console as follows:

```
irb(main):050:0> Employee.types
=> ["Employee", "Manager", "Director", "Executive"]
```

Figure 5.20: Output by calling the class method from the subclass

The Inheritance of Variables

Just as methods are inherited, so too are variables. The inheritance of variables is important because data can be initialized in the parent class and accessed by the subclass. As well as this, data can be set or modified in the subclass and accessed by the parent.

Consider the following example:

```
class Employee < User
  def employee_email
    # first.last_name@example.com
    "#{@first_name}.#{@last_name[0]}@example.com"
  end
end
```

Here, we are creating a convention for employee emails based on a **first_name.last_name** pattern. This shows that we have access to the variables that were created in the parent class. We can also modify the variables in the child class, as follows:

```
e = Employee.new("Bob", "Smith", "1 Main Street")
e.first_name = "Bob"
e.employee_email
```

The console would call the method, as shown in the following diagram:

```
irb(main):059:0> e = Employee.new("Bob", "Smith", "1 Main Street")
=> #<Employee:0x00007f9cd70dbda0 @first_name="Bob", @last_name="Smith", @address="1 Main Street">
irb(main):060:0> e.first_name
=> "Bob"
irb(main):061:0> e.employee_email
=> "Bob.S@example.com"
```

Figure 5.21: Output for the inheritance of variables

We can take this two steps further by subclassing our subclass and completely overriding the **employee_email** method to specialize its behavior in the sub-subclass:

```ruby
class ExecutiveLeadership < Employee
  def employee_email
    "#{@first_name}@example.com"
  end
end
e = ExecutiveLeadership.new("Steve", "Jobs", "1 Infinite Loop")
e.employee_email
```

The output will be as follows:

```
irb(main):091:0> e = ExecutiveLeadership.new("Steve", "Jobs", "1 Infinite Loop")
=> #<ExecutiveLeadership:0x00007f9cd702bef0 @first_name="Steve", @last_name="Jobs", @address="1 Infinite Loop">
irb(main):092:0> e.employee_email
=> "Steve@example.com"
```

Figure 5.22: Output for subclassing a subclass

Here, we've created a special type of employee called **ExecutiveLeadership** by subclassing the **Employee** class. Executives in our application get the coveted first-name-only email address. Now, when we call **employee_email** on an **ExecutiveLeadership** instance, it will still use the inherited variables, but only use the implementation in its class.

Calling super

One of the advantages of inheritance is not only the ability to override behavior and variables in parent classes, but also to customize them. In order to customize them, you need the ability to call the parent method's version of the method you are in and capture the result. The **super** keyword is what calls the parent class's implementation of that method. It is called **super**, because a synonym of the parent class is a "superclass". First, we'll explore **super** in the **initialize** method by modeling a role class to encapsulate all the role-based functionality within this class.

Take a look at the following example:

```ruby
class User
  attr_accessor :name, :address
  def initialize(name, address)
    puts "In User#initialize"
    @name = name
    @address = address
  end
end
```

The preceding example is the standard **User** class we have been working with. It has been simplified to just have **name** and **address** accessors and attributes. Now, let's create a subclass that calls the parent class's implementation of **initialize**, as shown in the following code:

```ruby
class Employee < User
  attr_accessor :on_payroll
  def initialize(name, address)
    puts "In Employee#initialize"
    @on_payroll = true
    super
  end
end
```

In our **Employee** subclass, we defined a new accessor called **:on_payroll**. Also, in our **Employee** subclass, we've overridden the **initialize** method from **User** and set the **@on_payroll** instance variable to **true**. Then, we call the **super** keyword. Let's take a look at this on the console:

```
irb(main):021:0> Employee.new("Jeanine", "1 Main St")
In Employee#initialize
In User#initialize
=> #<Employee:0x00007f9a78804200 @on_payroll=true, @name="Jeanine", @address="1 Main St">
```

Figure 5.23: Output for overriding the initialize method

We can see that when we **initialize** an **Employee subclass**, the **Employee** implementation of **initialize** is called first. Then, we see that the **User** implementation of **initialize** is also called, which is a result of us calling the **super** keyword.

Another thing to point out about this code, which can often be confusing, is when parent classes and subclasses each have access to their respective instance variables and methods. Let's take a look at this by way of an example of what not to do. Consider the following code:

```ruby
class User
  def taxes
    tax_rate = 0.15
    salary * tax_rate
  end
end
class Employee < User
  attr_accessor :salary
end
```

In the preceding code, we've created an **Employee** subclass of **User**, which sets employee users as having a salary accessor. We've also written our **User** base class to have an instance method that uses this accessor, **salary**, to calculate a relevant amount of taxes based on a fixed tax rate. Let's take a look at this behavior in a console:

```
irb(main):011:0> e = Employee.new
=> #<Employee:0x00007fd3ba1d5200>
irb(main):012:0> e.salary = 100000
=> 100000
irb(main):013:0> e.taxes
=> 15000.0
```

Figure 5.24: Output of an instance calling its parent class method

This works as we expect. The **employee** instance is able to call its parent class method, and the implementation of the parent class is able to access the subclass's accessor of **salary**. So, why is this bad code, or an anti-pattern?

This is an anti-pattern for a few reasons:

- The parent class needs to have knowledge of the implementation of the subclass. If the subclass changes its implementation, this could break the parent class's code.

- The **User** class could theoretically be instantiated on its own. Then, it would give out an error referencing a salary method that doesn't exist, as shown in the following diagram:

```
irb(main):014:0> u = User.new
=> #<User:0x00007fd3ba1a2d00>
irb(main):015:0> u.taxes
Traceback (most recent call last):
        5: from /Users/peter/.rbenv/versions/2.6.1/bin/irb:23:in `<main>'
        4: from /Users/peter/.rbenv/versions/2.6.1/bin/irb:23:in `load'
        3: from /Users/peter/.rbenv/versions/2.6.1/lib/ruby/gems/2.6.0/gems/irb-1.0.0/exe/irb:11:in `<top (required)>'
        2: from (irb):15
        1: from (irb):4:in `taxes'
NameError (undefined local variable or method `salary' for #<User:0x00007fd3ba1a2d00>)
```

Figure 5.25: NameError

The Different Ways to Call super

There are several ways that **super** can be called to call the superclass's implementation. They are as follows:

- Without arguments
- With arguments
- With the splat operator

Calling super without Arguments

super can be called without arguments as depicted in the *Calling super* section. However, what's really happening is that the arguments to the current method are implicitly passed to the **super** class's version of the method.

Calling super with Arguments

If the arguments of the child class method do not match **super**, then you can explicitly pass the arguments to **super** (and thus the parent's `initialize` method). In the following code, we create another sub-subclass called **Manager**. **Manager** is subclassed from **Employee**, which, in turn, is subclassed from **User**. We then call **super** and pass in an explicit set of arguments. This is usually done when the subclass method signature has a different number of arguments to the super class's method signature:

```
class Manager < Employee
  attr_reader :department
  def initialize(name, address, department)
    @department = department
    super(name, address)
  end
end
```

Calling super with the Naked Splat Operator

Earlier, we said that when calling **super** with implicit arguments, the method signature to the child class method must match that of the parent. This can be somewhat limiting or cumbersome for a child class to always have to be aware of a specific parent method signature. Of course, Ruby provides a way around this with what's known as "the naked splat operator."

Take a look at the following code:

```
class Employee < User
  attr_accessor :on_payroll
  def initialize(*)
    @on_payroll = true
    super
  end
end
```

Here, the method signature just contains an asterisk (*), which is also known as the splat operator. As we learned in the first section, the splat operator can be used to capture a varying number of arguments. Since we don't need the variables in the child class method, we can capture them as unnamed arguments, which will get passed automatically to **super**.

> **Note**
>
> This syntax is used occasionally and can always be written in a more concise manner that is clearer to read, making use of explicit parameters to **super**. It is up to the developer to decide which syntax is better to use for a particular use case.

Another way to understand the naked splat operator is to look at what happens when you don't use it. Consider the following implementation:

```ruby
class User
  def initialize(name)
    @name = name
  end
end
class Employee < User
  def initialize(name)
    @on_payroll = true
    super
  end
end
Employee.new("Mary")
```

The output will be as follows:

```
irb(main):013:0> Employee.new("Mary")
=> #<Employee:0x00007ff32b9c9ca0 @on_payroll=true, @name="Mary">
```

Figure 5.26: Output when the splat operator is used

So far, there is nothing special about this implementation. The preceding usage is calling **super** without any arguments and, therefore, is implicitly passing the name argument to the superclass's **initialize** method.

However, imagine you work on a large application and there are many developers also working on this code base. Another developer wants to extend the **User** class by adding an address accessor, as follows:

```
class User
  def initialize(name, address)
    @name = name
    @address = address
  end
end
```

Now, when we go to instantiate an **Employee** class with the same implementation as before, let's see what happens:

```
class Employee < User
  def initialize(name)
    @on_payroll = true
    super
  end
end
Employee.new("Mary")
```

The output will be as follows:

```
irb(main):014:0> Employee.new("Mary")
Traceback (most recent call last):
        7: from /Users/peter/.rbenv/versions/2.6.1/bin/irb:23:in `<main>'
        6: from /Users/peter/.rbenv/versions/2.6.1/bin/irb:23:in `load'
        5: from /Users/peter/.rbenv/versions/2.6.1/lib/ruby/gems/2.6.0/gems/irb-1.0.0/exe/irb:11:in `<top (required)>'
        4: from (irb):14
        3: from (irb):14:in `new'
        2: from (irb):10:in `initialize'
        1: from (irb):2:in `initialize'
ArgumentError (wrong number of arguments (given 1, expected 2))
```

Figure 5.27: ArgumentError for the Employee class

The **Employee** class's call to **super** is sending the same arguments to the **User** class's **initialize** method as the **Employee** class, and so is only passing one argument. As such, we get the preceding error telling us that we are not sending the arguments correctly. To fix this, we could do either of the following:

- Call super with explicit arguments
- Use the naked splat operator

Consider the following example where we use the splat operator with the **initialize** method:

```ruby
class Employee < User
  def initialize(*)
      @on_payroll = true
    super
  end
end
Employee.new("Bob")
```

Here, the naked splat operator futureproofs us against additional changes to the parent class, which is a good way to object-orient a program:

```
irb(main):068:0> Employee.new("Bob")
Traceback (most recent call last):
        7: from /Users/peter/.rbenv/versions/2.6.1/bin/irb:23:in `<main>'
        6: from /Users/peter/.rbenv/versions/2.6.1/bin/irb:23:in `load'
        5: from /Users/peter/.rbenv/versions/2.6.1/lib/ruby/gems/2.6.0/gems/irb-1.0.0/exe/irb:11:in `<top (required)>'
        4: from (irb):68
        3: from (irb):68:in `new'
        2: from (irb):65:in `initialize'
        1: from (irb):57:in `initialize'
ArgumentError (wrong number of arguments (given 1, expected 2))
```

Figure 5.28: Using the splat operator

So, what happened here? We are getting an argument error because the naked splat operator is simply passing along the arguments as given to the **initialize** method of **Employee** straight to **User**, which is expecting two arguments. The code that calls the subclass still needs to know to send the appropriate arguments that the base class expects in this case:

```ruby
Employee.new("Bob", "125 Main Street")
```

The console would respond to the call as follows:

```
irb(main):069:0> Employee.new("Bob", "125 Main Street")
=> #<Employee:0x00007ff9fc81d988 @on_payroll=true, @name="Bob", @address="125 Main Street">
```

Figure 5.29: Output for the Employee call

In the previous sections, we modeled a **User** class with name and address instance variables. The address was represented as a string variable. In reality, addresses can be modeled as more sophisticated data structures. Let's conduct an exercise to see how that can be done.

Exercise 5.03: Modelling a Class for Location Addresses

In this exercise, we will use our knowledge of OOP to model an **Address** class to give us a class that will split out the different parts of an address into instance variables and also to add some methods that make working with addresses easier and more useful:

1. Open the Terminal and create a new file.

2. Create the **Address** class and expand on this by modeling a user's address.

   An address is made up of several components and can belong to different types of things such as users and buildings. So, we'll model an address with its own class, as shown in the following code:

   ```ruby
   class Address
     attr_accessor :street_address, :city, :post_code
     def initialize(street_address, city, post_code)
       @street_address = street_address
       @city = city
       @post_code = post_code
     end
   end
   ```

   We've created a class for **Address** that stores each component of a basic address. The preceding code uses a common pattern to define some variables as accessors and to initialize the class with those variables. This makes the resulting object very easy to use with a minimal class definition.

3. Next, we instantiate the class in a Terminal:

   ```ruby
   a = Address.new("25 Martin Luther King Jr Blvd", "Oakland", "94008")
   a.street_address
   a.post_code
   a.street_address = "5 Broadway"
   a.street_address
   ```

The output will be as follows:

```
irb(main):021:0>    puts a = Address.new("25 Martin Luther King Jr Blvd", "Oakland", "94008")
#<Address:0x000000000301ae48>
=> nil
irb(main):022:0>    puts a.street_address
25 Martin Luther King Jr Blvd
=> nil
irb(main):023:0>    puts a.post_code
94008
=> nil
irb(main):024:0>    puts a.street_address = "5 Broadway"
5 Broadway
=> nil
irb(main):025:0>    puts a.street_address
5 Broadway
=> nil
```

Figure 5.30: Output for the Address class

4. Create an immutable class. You may want to make objects immutable, which means that they can't be changed once they are created. You can easily change this by changing **attr_accessor** to **attr_reader**, as shown in the following code:

```
class Address
  attr_reader :street_address, :city, :post_code
  def initialize(street_address, city, post_code)
    @street_address = street_address
    @city = city
    @post_code = post_code
  end
end
```

5. Next, we will be creating subclasses of the **Address** class. We want to create subclasses of **Address** because we want to model different types of addresses, such as international addresses, which have slightly different data and behavior.

Most addresses have three basic components: a street address, a city, and a postcode. For addresses in the United States, you may also want to include a state. For Canadian addresses, you may want to include a province:

Exercise 5.03.rb

```
26 class Address
27   attr_reader :street_address, :city, :post_code, :country
28   def initialize(street_address, city, post_code, country)
29     @street_address = street_address
30     @city = city
31     @post_code = post_code
32   end
33 end
34
35 class UnitedStatesAddress < Address
36   attr_reader :state
37
38   def initialize(street_address, city, state, post_code)
39     @state = state
40     @country = "UnitedStates"
41     super
```

https://packt.live/2IVYA79

6. Now, let's instantiate each type of address, **UnitedStatesAddress** and **CanadianAddress**, and inspect the Terminal to see how the instance variables look:

```
irb(main):090:0> UnitedStatesAddress.new("1 Broadway", "New York", "New York",
10010)
=> #<UnitedStatesAddress:0x00007ffca2a87b08 @state="New York", @
country="UnitedStates", @street_address="1 Broadway", @city="New York", @post_
code="New York">

irb(main):091:0> CanadianAddress.new

=> #<CanadianAddress:0x00007ffca2a84160 @country="Canada", @street_address=nil, @
city=nil, @post_code=nil>
```

The output will be as follows:

```
irb(main):033:0> UnitedStatesAddress.new("1 Broadway", "New York",
=> #<UnitedStatesAddress:0x00000000032ec450 @state="NewYork", @coun
et_address="1 Broadway", @city="New York", @post_code="NewYork">
irb(main):034:0> CanadianAddress.new
=> #<CanadianAddress:0x00000000032a57d0 @country="Canada", @street_
post_code=nil>
```

Figure 5.31: Output for the different types of addresses

There are a few things to point out about the preceding code.

The **UnitedStatesAddress** and **CanadianAddress** addresses implemented their own versions of the **initialize** method. Canadian addresses are constructed using a hash map, whereas the **UnitedStatesAddress** address has named parameters.

The **UnitedStatesAddress** address calls **super** without any arguments, whereas the **CanadianAddress** address is explicit about the **super** arguments. In the first case, the arguments to **super** are implicit based on the arguments in the method signature of the subclass's **initialize** method. In the case of **UnitedStatesAddress**, the method signature is defined (**street_address**, **city**, **state**, **post_code**), but the base class had this as its **initialize** method signature: **street_address**, **city**, **post_code**, **country**). In the preceding Terminal output, there is an error – did you catch it? The **post_code** variable is **New York**. The reason for this is that the implicit arguments are based upon the positional parameters.

In this exercise, we have created an **Address** class to create a data model that gives us more sophisticated functionality regarding addresses that could not be achieved with a simple string. We also created subclasses of this base class to give rise to special types of addresses, such as different international addresses that require special handling.

Encapsulation

Encapsulation is a fundamental concept in OOP that deals with keeping some data (variables) and behavior (methods) private and protected from the other code that interacts with our class. We want to design our classes in such a way that we create a well-defined interface for them that rarely, or never, changes. This is so other code that relies on these classes is not dependent on the low-level implementation details of those classes. Therefore, we need a way to designate whether a method is public or private inside a class. In Ruby, there are three levels of privacy (also known as visibility) of methods:

- Public
- Private
- Protected

Public Methods

This is the default level of the visibility of methods in Ruby classes. When we define a method on a class, or use any of the **attr_** methods, such as **attr_accessor**, **attr_reader**, and **attr_writer**, we are declaring public methods.

Consider the following code for the **User** class:

```ruby
class User
  def initialize(email)
    @email = email
  end
end
```

Here, we've defined a **User** class that can be initialized with an email instance variable. As you can see (notice that we did not define **attr_accessor**), the **@email** instance variable is not accessible to anyone and is, therefore, considered to be *encapsulated* or a private variable to the class:

```
u = User.new("test@example.com")
```

The output will be as follows:

```
irb(main):135:0> u = User.new("test@example.com")
=> #<User:0x00007ff9fca18b70 @email="test@example.com">
irb(main):136:0> u.email
Traceback (most recent call last):
        4: from /Users/peter/.rbenv/versions/2.6.1/bin/irb:23:in `<main>'
        3: from /Users/peter/.rbenv/versions/2.6.1/bin/irb:23:in `load'
        2: from /Users/peter/.rbenv/versions/2.6.1/lib/ruby/gems/2.6.0/gems/irb-1.0.0/exe/irb:11:in `<top (required)>'
        1: from (irb):136
NoMethodError (undefined method `email' for #<User:0x00007ff9fca18b70 @email="test@example.com">)
```

Figure 5.32: Output for the public method

If we define a method on the **User** class, the method is considered a public method and can be accessed by any code that has access to the object, as shown in the following code:

```
class User
  def initialize(email)
    @email = email
  end
  def email
    @email
  end
end
```

The output will appear as follows:

```
irb(main):090:0> u = User.new("test@example.com")
=> #<User:0x0000000003256fe0 @email="test@example.com">
irb(main):091:0> u.email
=> "test@example.com"
```

Figure 5.33: Output for the public method when accessed by any code

Private Methods

Often in our classes, we have several methods that are not meant to be accessible to the general population of code. We only want to call those methods from within the class itself. These are private methods. We designate private methods with the **private** keyword. As you can see, the **private** keyword stands alone, and all methods that are defined below it within the class are considered private.

Consider the following example:

```ruby
class BankAccount
  attr_accessor :transactions
  def balance
    calculate_balance
  end
  private
  def calculate_balance
    transactions.inject(0){|sum, txn| sum + txn }
  end
end
```

The output will be as follows:

```
irb(main):108:0> b = BankAccount.new
=> #<BankAccount:0x000000000326d1f0>
irb(main):109:0> b.transactions = [5,10,7, -2, 3,-4]
=> [5, 10, 7, -2, 3, -4]
irb(main):110:0> b.balance
=> 19
irb(main):111:0> b.calculate_balance
Traceback (most recent call last):
        2: from C:/Ruby25-x64/bin/irb.cmd:19:in `<main>'
        1: from (irb):111
NoMethodError (private method `calculate_balance' called for #<BankAccount:0x000000000326d1f0>)
```

Figure 5.34: Output of the public method calling the private method

In the preceding **BankAccount** class, we defined a **public** method balance that calls the **private** method, **calculate_balance**. If we try to call the private method from outside the object, we get a **NoMethodError** exception telling us we called a private method.

Protected Methods

A lot of programming languages just have two levels of encapsulation: **public** and **private**. However, Ruby provides a third level called **protected**. Protected methods are a middle ground between public and private and are meant to give a moderate level of encapsulation rather than going fully public or private.

Protected methods are declared in a similar way to **private** methods with the **protected** keyword, as shown in the following code snippet:

```ruby
class User
  def this_is_a_public_method
    self.protected_method
  end
  protected
```

```
  def protected_method
    puts "This is protected but still accessible"
  end
end
```

The output will be as follows:

```
irb(main):014:0> u = User.new
=> #<User:0x00007fd15b9a2480>
irb(main):015:0> u.this_is_a_public_method
This is protected but still accessible
=> nil
irb(main):016:0> u.protected_method
Traceback (most recent call last):
        4: from /Users/peter/.rbenv/versions/2.6.1/bin/irb:23:in `<main>'
        3: from /Users/peter/.rbenv/versions/2.6.1/bin/irb:23:in `load'
        2: from /Users/peter/.rbenv/versions/2.6.1/lib/ruby/gems/2.6.0/gems/irb-1.0.0/exe/irb:11:in `<top (required)>'
        1: from (irb):16
NoMethodError (protected method `protected_method' called for #<User:0x00007fd15b9a2480>)
Did you mean?  protected_methods
```

Figure 5.35: Using the protected method

What makes a protected method different from a private method can be a bit confusing and requires a better understanding of the **self** method. Let's take a look at this in the following exercise.

Exercise 5.04: Demonstrate the Visibility Rules of Ruby Methods

In this exercise, we will be using encapsulation and protected methods to maintain the privacy of methods.

1. Open the Terminal and create a new file.

2. First, we create a class to work with that has a public, protected, and private method:

```
class User
  def public_method
    puts "This is a public method"
  end
  protected
  def protected_method
    puts "This is a protected method"
  end
  private
  def private_method
    puts "This is a private method"
  end
end
```

3. Let's call each of the preceding methods to see how they behave. We anticipate that the public methods are accessible to the outside interface of the object instances, while the protected and private methods are only available inside the scope of the object instance:

```
irb(main):131:0> u.public_method
This is a public method
=> nil
irb(main):132:0> u.protected_method
Traceback (most recent call last):
        2: from C:/Ruby25-x64/bin/irb.cmd:19:in `<main>'
        1: from (irb):132
NoMethodError (protected method `protected_method' called for #<User:0x0000000003256fe0 @email="test@example.com">)
Did you mean?  protected_methods
irb(main):133:0> u.private_method
Traceback (most recent call last):
        2: from C:/Ruby25-x64/bin/irb.cmd:19:in `<main>'
        1: from (irb):133
NoMethodError (private method `private_method' called for #<User:0x0000000003256fe0 @email="test@example.com">)
Did you mean?  private_methods
```

Figure 5.36: Output for the method behaviors

Here, we see that we can call the public method from outside the object, but we cannot call the protected method or private methods.

4. Create a new method inside the class that calls each of the previous methods we created:

```
class User
  def call_each
    public_method
    protected_method
    private_method
  end
  def public_method
    puts "This is a public method"
  end
  protected
  def protected_method
    puts "This is a protected method"
  end
  private
  def private_method
    puts "This is a private method"
  end
end
```

5. Instantiate the object again and call the **call_each** method:

```
u = User.new
u.call_each.
```

The output will be as follows:

```
irb(main):027:0> u = User.new
=> #<User:0x000000000319dba8>
irb(main):028:0> u.call_each
This is a public method
This is a protected method
This is a private method
=> nil
```

Figure 5.37: Output after calling each method

Here, we see that each of the methods is accessible from inside the class. Let's make a small change here and use the **self** method to call each of the methods instead.

6. Revise the **call_each** method to use the **self** keyword:

```
class User
  def call_each
    self.public_method
    self.protected_method
    self.private_method
  end
  def public_method
    puts "This is a public method"
  end
#protected
  def protected_method
    puts "This is a protected method"
  end
#private
  def private_method
    puts "This is a private method"
  end
end
u.call_each
```

The output will be as follows:

```
irb(main):052:0> u.call_each
This is a public method
This is a protected method
Traceback (most recent call last):
        3: from C:/Ruby25-x64/bin/irb.cmd:19:in `<main>'
        2: from (irb):52
        1: from (irb):34:in `call_each'
NoMethodError (private method `private_method' called for #<User:0x000000000319dba8>)
Did you mean?  private_methods
```

Figure 5.38: Output for calling the call_each method using self

Here, we see that the public and protected methods are called, but the private method cannot be called even though we are inside the class. Why is this?

This is because, when we call the private method with the **self** keyword, **self** is simply a reference to the object, and so this is essentially like calling it as if we are outside the class; therefore, Ruby will enforce the privacy restrictions on the method. However, there is a special exception to **protected** methods. **Protected** methods can be called on the **self** keyword, but only when inside the object instance scope.

So, what this exercise demonstrates is that **protected** methods can be called with the **self** keyword when inside the method. This is called an explicit self-invocation. When we do not include the **self** keyword and we call a method on the class, **self** is considered **implicit** and, as such, Ruby knows to allow access to the private methods.

There is another magical property of **protected** methods in Ruby. We can call protected methods on another object as long as it's the same type of object. Let's examine this while implementing an equality operator.

7. Let's implement an equality operator. Implementing equality operators is necessary if you want to compare two objects and need special comparison logic, such as comparing against an internal identifier:

```
require 'digest'
class User
  def initialize(email)
    @email = email
  end
  def ==(other)
    self.unique_id == other.unique_id
  end
  protected
```

```
  def unique_id
    Digest::MD5.hexdigest @email.downcase
  end
end
u = User.new("test@example.com")
u2 = User.new("foo@example.com")
u3 = User.new("TesT@EXAMPLE.COM")
u == u2
u == u3
```

The output will be as follows:

```
irb(main):073:0> u = User.new("test@example.com")
=> #<User:0x00000000030de230 @email="test@example.com">
irb(main):074:0> u2 = User.new("foo@example.com")
=> #<User:0x00000000030cc2b0 @email="foo@example.com">
irb(main):075:0> u3 = User.new("TesT@EXAMPLE.COM")
=> #<User:0x0000000002ca9700 @email="TesT@EXAMPLE.COM">
irb(main):076:0> u == u2
=> false
irb(main):077:0> u == u3
=> true
```

Figure 5.39: Output after using the equality operator

Here, first, we implement a unique internal identifier, which is the md5 hash of the lowercase version of the email. This allows us to compare equality based on a case-insensitive comparison of the email.

Then, we implement an equality operator by defining a method called **==**, which has an argument of another object that is assumed to have a unique ID method.

If we call **unique_id** on an object directly, we will get an error. However, because the method is defined as **protected**, and because we are inside a **User** class and the passed-in object is also a **User** object, Ruby allows us to call the protected method. Let's see what happens if we send in a subclass and a completely different class altogether.

8. Create a subclass and a new class. Then, compare them:

```ruby
class Admin < User
end
class Department
  def initialize(name)
    @name = name
  end
  protected
  def unique_id
    Digest::MD5.hexdigest @name.downcase
  end
end
admin = Admin.new("admin@example.com")
admin2 = Admin.new("test@example.com")
u == admin
u == admin2
u == sales
```

The output will be as follows:

```
irb(main):093:0> admin = Admin.new("admin@example.com")
=> #<Admin:0x00000000031263f0 @email="admin@example.com">
irb(main):094:0> admin2 = Admin.new("test@example.com")
=> #<Admin:0x00000000030fce60 @email="test@example.com">
irb(main):095:0> u == admin
=> false
irb(main):096:0> => false
Traceback (most recent call last):
        1: from C:/Ruby25-x64/bin/irb.cmd:19:in `<main>'
SyntaxError ((irb):96: syntax error, unexpected =>)
=> false
^~
irb(main):097:0> u == admin2
=> true
irb(main):098:0> u == sales
Traceback (most recent call last):
        2: from C:/Ruby25-x64/bin/irb.cmd:19:in `<main>'
        1: from (irb):98
NameError (undefined local variable or method `sales' for main:Object)
```

Figure 5.40: Calling the protected method on a different class

Here, we can compare subclasses without any difficulty. However, we cannot call a protected method on a completely different class.

Bypassing Visibility

Even though Ruby does provide the mechanism for encapsulation to follow OOP best practices, Ruby was designed knowing that there may be times when we need to bypass encapsulation. In most cases, if you are bypassing encapsulation of classes that you yourself have written, this may indicate a "code smell" and may need some refactoring. However, you may want to bypass the encapsulation of a library author to debug or introspect their code. Let's use introspection to learn more about visibility and how we can bypass it. For this, we will examine the **URI** module, which is part of the Ruby standard library:

```
irb(main):013:0> uri = URI.parse("http://google.com")
=> #<URI::HTTP http://google.com>
irb(main):014:0> uri.protected_methods(false)
=> [:set_scheme, :set_userinfo, :set_host, :set_port, :set_path, :set_opaque, :set_user,
:set_password, :set_registry, :component_ary]
```

Here, we are using **URI** to parse a string that represents a URL to Google. This returns an instance of the **URI::HTTP** object. We then call **protected_methods** to see the protected methods on the object. We pass **false** in as the argument to find only the protected methods that the class itself has defined (as opposed to other modules and libraries it may have included).

It is really cool that we have the ability to peek into the innards of any class in Ruby. We can see that this class defines a number of protected methods that we can use if need be:

```
uri.set_port 443
uri.send(:set_port, 443)
uri
```

You should be able to see the following output:

```
irb(main):103:0> uri.set_port 443
Traceback (most recent call last):
        2: from C:/Ruby25-x64/bin/irb.cmd:19:in `<main>'
        1: from (irb):103
NoMethodError (protected method `set_port' called for #<URI::HTTP http://google.com>)
Did you mean?  set_host
irb(main):104:0> uri.send(:set_port, 443)
=> 443
irb(main):105:0> uri
=> #<URI::HTTP http://google.com:443>
```

Figure 5.41: Using the URI module

> **Note**
>
> The **send** method is useful for debugging and exploring Ruby. However, it should be used with caution in application code, as it can introduce security vulnerabilities. This is because it can be used to bypass visibility and can be used to call any available method on the object.

Here, we tried to call the **set_port** method directly and get the protected method error. However, we can bypass it by using the **send** method, which we learned about in the last chapter, to directly call any method in Ruby. When we call a method using it, it bypasses encapsulation and visibility rules so it should be used with caution.

Send can also be used to call private methods on a class:

```
class User
  private
  def launch_code
    return "supersecretlaunchcode"
  end
end
u = User.new
u.send(:launch_code)
```

The output will be as follows:

```
irb(main):128:0> u.send(:launch_code)
=> "supersecretlaunchcode"
```

Figure 5.42: Output for send on private methods

A Quick Note about File Organization

At a certain point, your applications will start to grow in size and it's usually a best practice to follow the single responsibility principle with your classes (within reason). Similarly, you will likely want to keep one class per file and, therefore, file and folder organization becomes important. A common design pattern for large applications is the MVC design pattern, which yields folders for models, views, and controllers. You will see this predominantly in the Ruby on Rails web framework. For the purposes of this book, we are just making Terminal applications and we are working with models, so we'll structure our applications with a file that handles the main entry point and control flow and uses classes that are kept inside a models folder. We'll use this approach in the next activity.

Activity 5.01: Voting Application for Employee of the Month

In this activity, we are going to build a program that allows voting on users to be the employee of the month. This is a Terminal program that will be run on a shared machine where people can walk up and vote for their colleagues to be the employee of the month. The program will ask users to identify themselves by name and will then ask for a colleague's name for whom to cast a vote. Each vote for the same user increments that user's total. The program will allow you to display the leaderboard of votes at any time. The leaderboard will be a list of people who received votes, which is sorted by the count of votes.

This activity will use a basic Terminal framework written by the author for the purpose of this activity. This framework uses a model-controller pattern that is based on the popular model-view-controller pattern, which is used by the Ruby on Rails framework. You will check out the framework from the source control (GitHub) and use your knowledge of OOP, such as inheritance, to create additional models and controllers that will be used in the voting machine.

> **Note**
>
> The solution involves using the Lightweight Terminal Framework written by the author. This code can be sourced from GitHub. You can find the Lightweight Terminal Framework here: https://packt.live/2VuZ2yc.

The following steps will help you to complete the activity:

1. Create a new file.

2. Open the Terminal and use the following command to clone the **Lightweight Terminal Framework** from GitHub:

```
git clone https://github.com/PacktWorkshops/The-Ruby-Workshop/tree/master/Chapter05/
Activity5.01/framework
```

3. Create a **VotingMachine** model class to create a model for the application.

4. Create a **VoteController** class to receive votes.

5. Add menu choices to **MenuController** for setting up the menu.

6. Add **LeaderboardController** to manage the leaderboard functionality.

7. Add **LeaderboardController** to **MenuController** so that it is added to the menu.

8. Add tests to **test_controller.rb**.

9. Run tests with the Ruby **test.rb** file.

10. Run the application with the Ruby **application.rb** file.

The output for the activity will be displayed as follows:

```
** Welcome to the Employee Of The Month Votathon **
** Please enter your choice **
   1. Place a vote for a colleague
   2. See current leaderboard
   3. Exit
choice> 1
What's your name? John
Who do you want to vote for? Mary
Vote recorded!
```

Figure 5.43: Output for the voting application

> **Note**
>
> The solution to this activity can be found on page 468.

Summary

In this chapter, we learned about the beginnings of OOP using Ruby. Ruby helps massively when you need to understand OOP in a far easier way due to Ruby's easy-to-understand syntax and the ability to introspect into methods and data.

By the end of the chapter, you should feel comfortable using objects and classes and calling methods on them. By calling a method on any object (or, in Ruby parlance, sending a message to any receiver), you are automatically using OOP since you are working with objects. When you create a subclass, you are using inheritance, which is a core concept of OOP. When you decide to make some methods accessible and some methods private, you are mastering encapsulation, which is another core concept of OOP.

In the next chapter, we will go further into OOP with Ruby by learning about modules and mixins.

Modules and Mixins

Overview

By the end of the chapter, you will be able to implement modules within the Ruby object model; add instance methods by including a module into a class; add class methods by extending a class with a module; create a namespace with a module; distinguish between prepending modules into classes and including and extending them and use modules to address multiple inheritance in Ruby.

Introduction

In the previous chapter, we learned about the basics of object-oriented programming using Ruby. We learned that classes serve as templates for objects. We also learned that classes can also serve as templates for other classes by using the mechanism of inheritance. However, there may be situations where we might have to share code among different classes that don't really fit into an inheritance architecture. For example, we could be designing a reality simulator. In the previous chapter, we talked about how cars have four wheels, bicycles have two wheels, and boats have no wheels, but they still fall under the "Vehicles" class. Imagine that we had previously been tasked with modeling houses or places to live, which we can easily do using classes. Now we are tasked with modeling a mobile home or RV, which serves as both a vehicle and a home.

In other object-oriented languages, this problem is solved with a concept known as "multiple inheritance". For instance, in C++, a class could inherit from more than one base class. Ruby does not support multiple inheritance. Instead, Ruby solves this code reusability problem using the concept of modules.

Modules provide a way to conveniently wrap code in a way that can be shared among many other pieces of code. Modules can be included, extended, and prepended into other code. Modules can also serve as a way to namespace code. The nuances of each of these approaches require a bit more discussion of the Ruby object model. We'll be talking about the Ruby object model. This will give us a foundation for understanding how modules work so we can then learn about **extend** and **prepend** and how and when to use them. We will also study the mixin characteristic of modules. The idea of mixins essentially refers to the property of multiple modules being used by a class to improve code functionality and provide multiple inheritance in Ruby.

Let's begin with the `include` functionality of modules.

Including Modules

Modules, in their simplest definition, are a way to wrap code into a bundle so the code can be reused within other code without needing to be duplicated.

This definition sounds very similar to that of a Ruby class. Specifically, what makes a Ruby module distinct is that it cannot be instantiated into an object like a class. It can, however, be included in a class so the methods and variables defined in the module are accessible by the class. This refers to the mixin property of modules. Also, the methods and variables in a class can also be accessible to the code in the module. Essentially, when a module is included in a class, Ruby treats that code as if it were written right into that class. All the previous concepts we learned about classes and inheritance still apply to the module code when called.

For instance, if you call a module method from inside a class, that module method calls **super** and it will call the **super** class method of the class that the module was included in. This will be made clearer through the following example.

Let's assume we have a **User** class in which every user has a postal address. It can be realized as shown in the following code block:

```
class User
  attr_accessor :address_line1, :address_line2, :city, :state, :postal_code, :country
  def mailing_label
    label = []
    label << address_line1
    label << address_line2
    label << "#{city}, #{state} #{postal_code}"
    label << country
    label.join("\n")
  end
end
```

Now, say we need to add the concept of buildings to our application. Buildings should also have addresses associated with them. We don't want to repeat ourselves and yet we still want to make sure that our **User** class and **Building** class both have this same functionality. We could theoretically do this with inheritance, but it doesn't really make sense to subclass the **User** class and **Building** class from an **Address** class as they aren't "types" of addresses. Instead, we will wrap this functionality in a module and include it in both classes.

Look at the following code:

```
module Address
  attr_accessor :address_line1, :address_line2, :city, :state, :postal_code, :country
  def mailing_label
    label = []
    label << @address_line1
    label << @address_line2
    label << "#{@city}, #{@state} #{@postal_code}"
    label << @country
    label.join("\n")
  end
end
class User
  include Address
```

```
end
class Building
   include Address
end
```

As we can see, modules are declared using the **module** keyword, and they are included in classes using the **include** keyword. Defining methods is done similarly as they are inside a class definition.

The preceding code is using instance variables in the module to demonstrate a point but could also use the accessor methods created by **attr_accessor**.

This is a great way of sharing code. It is a clean way to reuse code. If any new models are necessary in the future and they need an address, we basically get it for free by simply including the module. This is the power of Ruby and object-oriented programming in action.

Let's dive deeper into how this works by working with some objects.

Consider the following code example:

```
u = User.new
b = Building.new
u.address_line1 = "123 Main Street"
b.address_line1 = "987 Broadway"
puts u.address_line1
puts b.address_line1
puts u.instance_variable_get("@address_line1")
puts u.instance_variable_get("@address_line1").object_id
puts b.instance_variable_get("@address_line1")
puts b.instance_variable_get("@address_line1").object_id
```

The output would show up as follows:

```
123 Main Street
987 Broadway
123 Main Street
1641200
987 Broadway
1640220
```

Figure 6.1: Output after including modules

There is an important point in the preceding output. While the module is the same code and, in essence, referencing an instance variable with the same name, it is, indeed, a completely different object instance. This is demonstrated by grabbing the instance variable and outputting the **object_id** attribute of that object. The **object_id** attribute on any object is a unique ID maintained by Ruby. You can think of this as Ruby copying and pasting the module code into the class that we included the module in. So, any variables and code that are included are actually separate across different classes that include them.

Exercise 6.01: Controlling the Operations of Services in an Application

In this exercise, we will extend the **Service** class with a module called **Logger** and take a look at how the inclusion of the module modifies the inner workings of our application.

> **Note**
>
> The **Logger** module is a tool used for debugging in Ruby. We will be looking at the **Logger** module in more detail in *Chapter 8, Debugging with Ruby*.

The following steps will help you complete the exercise:

1. Open up a new file, **Exercise6.01.rb**.

2. Define the **Logger** module:

```
module Logger
  def log_message(level, message)
    File.open("ServiceLogs.txt", "a") do |f|
        f.write "#{level}: #{message}\n"
    end
  end
end
```

3. Now we can define the **Service** class:

```
class Service
  include Logger
  def stop_service(service_name)
    log_message :info, "Stopping service: #{service_name}"
    sleep 3
    log_message :info, "The service: #{service_name} was stopped!"
  end
  def start_service(service_name)
```

```
        log_message :inf, "Starting the service: #{service_name}"
        sleep 2
        log_message :info, "The service: #{service_name} was started!"
    end
end
```

4. Now we instantiate the class and call the functions on the service called **Windows Update**:

```
TestService = Service.new
TestService.stop_service("Windows Update")
TestService.start_service("Windows Update")
```

5. Invoke the code with **ruby Exercise6.01.rb**.

The contents of the **ServiceLogs.txt** file should be as follows:

```
  ServiceLogs.txt
1    info: Stopping service: Windows Update
2    info: The service: Windows Update was stopped!
3    inf: Starting the service: Windows Update
4    info: The service: Windows Update was started!
```

Figure 6.2: Service logs output

Thus, we have successfully used the **Logger** module to generate a service update on an application.

Inheritance with Module Methods

When we include a module in a class, we are basically copying the instance methods into a class. This is a very important point in understanding modules. **include** brings in the methods of a module into a class as instance methods.Because they are brought in as instance methods, all of the concepts that we learned about in the previous chapter about object-oriented programming and inheritance will apply to these methods.

Consider the following code block:

inheritancewithmodulemethods.rb

```
1  module Address
2    attr_accessor :address_line1, :address_line2, :city, :state,:postal_code, :country
3
4    def region
5      return nil if country.nil? || country == ""
6      case country
7      when "United States", "Canada", "Mexico"
8        "North America"
9      else
10          "Global"
11     end
12   end
13 end
14
```

https://packt.live/322sM7Y

Here, we've amended our **Address** module to include a **region** method. We've also created a **Department** class and subclassed **User** to create an **Employee** class that has a **Department** attribute. The **Employee** class has implemented its own **region** method and is delegating **region** to the department. If the department does not have a region, it calls **super**, which will, in effect, call the original **Address** class's method, which was included in the **User** class. Let's see this on the console:

```
e = Employee.new
e.region
e.country = "Mexico"
e.region
e.department = Department.new
e.region
e.department.country = "England"
e.region
```

The output would be as follows:

```
North America
North America
Global
```

Figure 6.3: Output for subclass overriding a method

Our subclass has overridden a method defined in the module and is able to call **super** to that method if necessary.

Inclusion Ordering

The "copying and pasting" that's happening occurs at runtime, so the order of the inclusion of modules is important. Let's examine a case in which two modules have a method called **email**. One module returns a formatted email address, and the other sends an email:

```
module EmailFormatter
  def email
    "#{first_name}.#{last_name}@#{domain}"
  end
end
module EmailSender
  def email(msg, sender, recipient)
    # contrived implementation for now
    puts "Delivering email to #{recipient} from #{sender} with message: #{msg}"
  end
end
class User
  attr_accessor :first_name, :last_name, :domain
  include EmailFormatter
  include EmailSender
end
u = User.new
u.first_name = "John"
u.last_name = "Smith"
u.domain = "example.com"
puts u.email
```

The output will be as follows:

```
Traceback (most recent call last):
        1: from mail.rb:25:in `<main>'
mail.rb:9:in `email': wrong number of arguments (given 0, expected 3) (ArgumentError)
```

Figure 6.4: Output error for inclusion ordering

Here, we can see that the implementation from the **EmailSender** module is being called. Let's reverse it. Please restart IRB for this to work properly:

```ruby
class User
  attr_accessor :first_name, :last_name, :domain
  include EmailSender
  include EmailFormatter
end
u = User.new
u.first_name = "John"
u.last_name = "Smith"
u.domain = "example.com"
puts u.email
```

The output would be as follows:

John.Smith@example.com

Figure 6.5: Output after changing the order

And now the implementation we expected is being called. The second module would have done better to call its **send_email** method instead of just the generic **email** name.

> **Note**
>
> Avoid using methods names that are generic and may be used in other modules or classes. This will help to avoid name conflicts, especially if the module you are writing is intended to be used for a large application or will be publicly released.

Inclusion ordering is also important if the module contains class methods that can be called at the class level. You won't be able to call a class-level method that the module provides if the module has not yet been included. We'll take a look at this in the next section, which discusses adding class methods with modules using **extend**.

extend

In the previous section, we learned about including methods from a module for instances of a class using the **include** keyword. Modules can also be used to add class methods to a class. This can be accomplished by using the **extend** keyword.

Consider the following example:

```
module HelperMethods
  def attributes_for_json
    [:id, :name, :created_at]
  end
end
class User
  extend HelperMethods
end
class Company
  extend HelperMethods
end
irb(main):014:0> User.attributes_for_json
=> [:id, :name, :created_at]
irb(main):015:0> Company.attributes_for_json
=> [:id, :name, :created_at]
```

Here, we've defined a module called **HelperMethods**, which defines a single method called **attributes_for_json**. The intention is that these are a common set of attributes that will be used to convert objects into JSON. Because these attributes are global, in the sense that they apply to all objects, this method should be defined as a class method.

You can see, though, that in the module, the method is just defined as a straightforward method. There is no **self.** that precedes it. When the module is extended inside of a class, all of the methods that are defined as basic methods get extended into the class, meaning that they are added as class methods.

When working with modules, it's important to consider how the methods are defined inside the module. This information, along with how you want the methods to be defined, will inform whether you **include** the module or **extend** it.

There is nothing stopping you from including the preceding module as follows (restart IRB for this chapter):

```
class User
  include HelperMethods
end
class Company
  include HelperMethods
end
```

However, now these methods are defined as instance methods:

```
irb(main):013:0> User.attributes_for_json
Traceback (most recent call last):
    2: from /Users/peter/.rbenv/versions/2.5.1/bin/irb:11:in '<main>'
    1: from (irb):13
NoMethodError (undefined method 'attributes_for_json' for User:Class)
irb(main):014:0> User.new.attributes_for_json
=> [:id, :name, :created_at]
```

Module authors will usually include in their **README** file or documentation as to how their module should be used by other developers.

Often, sophisticated modules add both class methods and instance methods. In the following exercise, we'll take a look at a couple of approaches.

Exercise 6.02: Extending Your Modules with Class and Instance Methods

In this exercise, we will be creating a user module that implements the **User** class and instance methods to display the name and email address of an individual. We will be using the **HelperMethods** module extensively to map the hashes for all the variables. The following steps will help you to complete the exercise:

1. Define a **HelperMethods** module that outputs a hash map of all the instance variables using the **inject** method:

    ```
    module HelperMethods
      def to_hash
        self.instance_variables.inject({}) do |map, iv|
            map[iv] = self.instance_variable_get(iv)
            map
        end
      end
    end
    ```

2. Define a **User** class with **attr_accessors**:

    ```
    class User
      include HelperMethods
      attr_accessor :id, :name, :email
    end
    ```

3. Test the **to_hash** method on variables:

```
u = User.new
u.id = 1
u.name = "Bob"
u.email = "bob@example.com"
u.to_hash
```

The output will be as follows:

```
#<User:0x0000000000463d68>
1
Bob
bob@example.com
{:@id=>1, :@name=>"Bob", :@email=>"bob@example.com"}
```

Figure 6.6: Output for the hash method on variables

4. Next, we create a submodule within the **HelperMethods** module to contain the class methods:

```
module HelperMethods
  def to_hash
    self.instance_variables.inject({}) do |map, iv|
        map[iv] = self.instance_variable_get(iv)
        map
    end
  end
    module ClassMethods
      def attributes_for_json
          [:name, :email]
      end
    end
end
```

The intention here is to only allow some attributes to be output in the **to_hash** method.

5. Amend the **to_hash** method to only use the attributes allowed by the class method:

```
module HelperMethods
  def to_hash
    formatted_class_attributes = self.class.attributes_for_json.map{|attr|
"@#{attr}".to_sym}
    filtered_ivars = self.instance_variables & formatted_class_attributes
    filtered_ivars.inject({}) do |map, iv|
        map[iv] = self.instance_variable_get(iv)
        map
    end
  end
end
module ClassMethods
  def attributes_for_json
    [:name, :email]
  end
end
end
```

We use **&** to get the set intersection of two arrays. In other words, we're filtering for elements that exist in both arrays.

6. Amend the **User** class to include the instance methods, and extend the **ClassMethods** submodule:

```
class User
  include HelperMethods
  extend HelperMethods::ClassMethods
  attr_accessor :id, :name, :email
end
```

7. Let's now test our **User** module:

```
u = User.new
u.id = 1
u.name = "Bob"
u.email = "bob@example.com"
u.to_hash
```

The output should be as follows:

```
#<User:0x00000000004720c0>
1
Bob
bob@example.com
{:@name=>"Bob", :@email=>"bob@example.com"}
```

Figure 6.7: Output for extending classes

And we're in business. We wrote a module that has both instance methods and class methods available. Our **to_hash** instance method brought in by the module calls the class method. However, in the current form, our client code, the **User** class, has to both **include** and **extend** the submodule. This is a bit verbose and since our instance methods require the class method to be there, it would be nice if, as module authors, we didn't leave it up to other developers to write both lines of **include** and **extend**.

Luckily, Ruby provides a way for us to detect when a module has been included, and so we can write code to automatically extend the class methods for us. Let's learn about this in the next section.

Module Callbacks

Callbacks, in general, are an architectural paradigm where a method or function is "called back" to act upon some life cycle event. Web frameworks have callbacks to allow code to be called before and/or after a web request is processed. Database frameworks usually have callbacks to call code before a record is created, updated, or deleted. You can even think of the standard **initialize** method as a callback because Ruby is "calling back" to this method when an object is created. Callbacks allow developers to "hook into" those life cycle events and execute any code they wish.

In Ruby, there are a number of different types of callbacks to hook into Ruby object's life cycle events, but here we're going to focus on module callbacks. Ruby triggers a callback when a module has been either included or extended. This ability gives rise

to a massively useful paradigm, as we will see later. But first, let's see each callback in action.

Exercise 6.03: Using Module Functions to Extend Classes

In this exercise, we will extend the **Facebook** class with two functions from the **ApiWrapper** module, which are called **send_message** and **new_post**:

1. Create a new file, **Exercise6.03.rb**.

2. Define the **ApiWrapper** module with the **send_message** and **new_post** functions:

```ruby
module ApiWrapper
  def send_message(from, to, message)
    puts "Hi #{to}, I wanna say #{message}"
  end
  def new_post(from, title, description)
    puts "This is a post from #{from}, with title: #{title} and #{description}"
  end
end
```

3. Define the **Facebook** class. We will extend **ApiWrapper** within this class:

```ruby
class Facebook
  extend ApiWrapper
end
```

> **Note**
>
> Read more about Ruby life cycle callbacks here: https://packt.live/35ts4D4.

4. Add testing code to the file:

```ruby
Facebook.send_message("Packt","Students","thank you!")
Facebook.new_post("Author","Extending your classes","Extend imports functions from modules as class methods!")
```

5.   Invoke the test code with **ruby Exercise6.03.rb**. The output will be as follows:

```
Hi Students, I wanna say thank you!
This is a post from Author, with title: Extending your classes and Extend imports functions from modules as clas
s methods!
```

Figure 6.8: Output for the Facebook class extension

We have successfully extended the class functionality using module functions.

The **include** keyword extends the namespace of a specific class or module with extra functionality. Consider the following example:

```
module SpyModule
  def self.included(base_class)
    puts "I've been included into: #{base_class}"
  end
end
class User
  include SpyModule
end
```

Here, we've defined our **SpyModule** module, which has a **self.included** method, which takes an argument of the base class. There are a few things to point out here:

- The **included** method callback is defined with **self.** in front of it. This is known as a module method, and we will cover it in the next chapter.

- The **base_class** argument can be called anything. However, it will always represent the class that did the including of the module.

- The **included** method is called as soon as the class definition is loaded. Since class definitions are usually loaded earlier on in program execution, it makes it for an ideal time to further modify class definitions within the module.

Understanding class loading is a complex topic, especially when using a framework such as Ruby on Rails. For the purposes of this book, we can consider that all class loading will be done ahead of all program execution; however, it should be noted that, in reality, class loading is much more dynamic and can occur anywhere in program execution, even near the end.

Importing Modules as Class Methods using Extended

The **extended** callback works identically to the **included** callback. Look at the following example:

```ruby
module SpyModule
  def self.extended(base_class)
    puts "I've been extended into: #{base_class}"
  end
end
class User
  extend SpyModule
end
```

In the preceding code, we have defined the **SpyModule** module, which defines the **self. extended** method. This method, in turn, takes the argument of **base_class**.

Combining include and extend

As we saw in the previous exercise, module authors usually want to add both instance and class methods. Module authors also want to make it convenient and less error-prone for client code to leverage their module. We can refactor the code from the previous exercise, so that client code can simply **include** our module, and then our module takes care of everything else. The magic is actually pretty simple. We will just add the following code to our module:

```ruby
  def self.included(base_class)
    base_class.extend(ClassMethods)
  end
```

Altogether, this code would look like the following:

```ruby
module HelperMethods
  def self.included(base_class)
    puts "#{base_class} has included HelperMethods. We're also going to extend
ClassMethods into it as well"
    base_class.extend(ClassMethods)
  end
  def to_hash
    formatted_class_attributes = self.class.attributes_for_json.map{|attr| "@#{attr}".
to_sym}
    filtered_ivars = self.instance_variables & formatted_class_attributes
    filtered_ivars.inject({}) do |map, iv|
        map[iv] = self.instance_variable_get(iv)
        map
  end
```

```
  end
module ClassMethods
  def attributes_for_json
    [:name, :email]
  end
end
end
```

Now, when our **User** class includes the **HelperMethods** module and completes its class loading, the **included** callback will be called and the calling class (**User**) will be passed as an argument. The **User** class constant will then be sent **extend** with the **ClassMethods** submodule passed to it:

```
class User
  include HelperMethods
end
```

The output will be as follows:

```
User has included HelperMethods. We're also going to extend ClassMethods into it as well
```

Figure 6.9: Output for the User class

As you can see, the **included** callback is called, and we then extend **ClassMethods** into the **User** class. We can infer the following points:

- This is a simple example, but this paradigm provides the basis to leverage some powerful features of Ruby to write useful modules that add diverse functionality to lots of different classes.

- We are calling the **ClassMethods** submodule due to common convention, but this is arbitrary.

- In the preceding example, we are using **include** as the entry point for the class to interact with the module, and thus we use the **included** callback and call **extend** to add class methods. However, module authors can do the converse by telling developers to use **extend** instead, which then calls the **self.extended** callback, which then calls **include** on the class that did the extending. Again, the reason for using one approach over the other is merely convention and possibly for semantics, as it makes slightly more sense linguistically to include a module than to extend it.

Enumerated Types

Enumerated types are not specific to modules, but will come in handy for the next exercise, so let's take a brief moment to talk about them in Ruby. An enumerated type is a data type consisting of a set of named values. In other words, enumerated types, or, as they are commonly called, enums, are custom data types that consist of a set of predefined, or enumerated values.

A common example of an enumerated type is a status. For instance, if you have an e-commerce application, you might have an order status that is comprised of [`:draft`, `:ordered`, `:delivered`, `:canceled`]. It is useful to fix those values to an integer, although a symbol value can work just as well. Integers are commonly used because they are performant for storing in a database, so comparisons and queries are much faster. In Ruby, symbols are more performant than strings, but if you had to save a status in a database, that symbol would get converted to a string. Therefore, it's good practice for enums to have integer values.

To summarize:

- Enumerated types allow you to explicitly list the set of possible values that
- can occur.
- Enumerated types allow you to change the name at any time as long as the value remains the same.
- Enumerated types are commonly referred to as enums.

> **Note**
>
> Enumerated types should not be confused with the Ruby **Enumerable** module.

In practice, enumerated types rarely change, but when they do, it is usually to add an additional type into the set of values.

Here is an example of a **PaymentTypes** enum:

```
class PaymentTypes
  CREDIT_CARD = 1
  CHECK = 2
  WIRE = 3
  TYPES = [CREDIT_CARD, CHECK, WIRE]
end
```

Here, we've defined the possible payment types as named constants and the named constants are assigned an integer value. We've also created a **TYPES** constant so we can easily iterate over the possible types that are defined.

Designing enums in this way is a bit cumbersome and is only mildly useful. Let's design a module that makes working with enums far more useful and makes it quick and easy to define classes as enums.

Exercise 6.04: Writing a Module to Define Payment Methods for a Product Application

In this exercise, we are going to write a module that defines what payment types will be accepted at a product application store. We are going to write a utility module, called **Enum**, that allows for any class to be turned into an enumerated data type. The requirements for our module will be such that the enum classes will be defined with a **DATA** constant, which is an array of all the values of our enum. Each element of the **DATA** array will itself be an array with the integer value, symbol, and label. This gives us the flexibility to store the value in a database, work with it in Ruby as a symbol, or output a human-readable label:

1. Create a class that includes the **Enum** module and defines the enum types in the **DATA** array:

```
class PaymentTypes
  include Enum
  DATA = [
    [ WIRE = 1, :wire, "Wire"],
    [ CHECK = 2, :check, "Check"],
    [ CREDIT = 3, :credit, "Credit card"],
  ]
end
```

Here, we have a basic Ruby class that includes the **Enum** module (to be defined). Then, we declare a **DATA** constant that has our actual **Enum** types of :`wire`, :`check`, and :`credit` with associated values and labels.

2. Build out the module with a basic **included** callback:

```
module Enum
  def self.included(base_class)
    base_class.extend ClassMethods
    base_class.class_eval do
      attr_reader :id, :name, :label
```

```
      end
    end
    module ClassMethods
    end
  end
```

Here, we've added some new magic. As discussed in the previous chapter, using the **included** callback is a powerful paradigm for modules. As we've seen, we first extend **ClassMethods**; we're going to leave the **ClassMethods** submodule empty for now. The next line runs **class_eval** and passes a block to it.

class_eval is a special Ruby method that will run the code contained in the preceding block in the context of the class definition. Running **attr_reader** in the **class_eval** block is the same as if we called it normally in a basic class definition. So, essentially, we are just adding reader methods on whatever class includes **Enum** for **:id**, **:name**, and **:label**.

3. Add a constructor to the module:

```
module Enum
# ... omitted for brevity
  def initialize(id, name, label=nil)
    @id = id
    @name = name
    @label = label
  end
end
```

This is a basic constructor and uses the basic **include** module principles we learned at the beginning of the chapter. The **initialize** method will be added to all instances of the class that include **Enum**.

4. Test out the instantiation:

```
pt = PaymentType.new(1, :wire, "Wire")
pt.id
pt.name
pt.label
```

The output would be as follows:

```
irb(main):074:0> pt = PaymentType.new(1, :wire, "Wire")
=> #<PaymentType:0x00007f921816f538 @id=1, @name=:wire, @label="Wire">
irb(main):075:0> pt.id
=> 1
irb(main):076:0> pt.name
=> :wire
irb(main):077:0> pt.label
=> "Wire"
```

Figure 6.10: Output for payment details

Okay, so we can see our module is basically working. We properly extended the class with the **attr_reader** method and our constructor was added as well. However, we can also do something weird, such as this:

```
pt = PaymentTypes.new(nil, :foo, "Huh?")
```

On the console, it would look as follows:

```
irb(main):081:0> pt = PaymentType.new(nil, :foo, "Huh?")
=> #<PaymentType:0x00007f92181a7ac8 @id=nil, @name=:foo, @label="Huh?">
```

Figure 6.11: Payment type details

We just created a weird payment type that isn't really an enumerable that we expect. We could add a validation to the constructor, but we'll leave that as an exercise for you, dear reader.

5. Add a **ClassMethod** module to get all the types:

```
module ClassMethods
  def all
    @all ||= begin
        self::DATA.map { |args| new(*args) }
    end
  end
end
```

Here, we've defined an **all** class method that loops over the **DATA** constants, instantiates each one and assigns it to a class instance variable. Let's test it out:

```
PaymentTypes.all
```

The output would be as follows:

```
irb(main):414:0> PaymentTypes.all
=> [#<PaymentTypes:0x0000000003444168 @id=1, @name=:
wire, @label="Wire">, #<PaymentTypes:0x0000000003444
140 @id=2, @name=:check, @label="Check">, #<PaymentT
ypes:0x0000000003444118 @id=3, @name=:credit, @label
="Credit card">]
```

Figure 6.12: Output for all payment types

Isn't this amazing? We wrote a module that allows us to easily define enums as an array in any class. Our module adds an **all** method that returns all of the types for us as instances of objects. When we started with enums, they were just integers stored in constants. But now with our module, they are instances of objects and we have all the power of object-oriented programming behind us to work with these types.

6. Add some instance methods to **PaymentTypes**:

```
class PaymentTypes
  include Enum
  DATA = [
    [ WIRE = 1, :wire, "Wire"],
    [ CHECK = 2, :check, "Check"],
    [ CREDIT = 3, :credit, "Credit card"],
  ]
  def wire?
    id == WIRE
  end
  def check?
    id == CHECK
  end
  def credit?
    id == CREDIT
  end
end
```

We've added some methods here. These methods are called **interrogation** methods because they ask the instances what they are. Is it a wire? Is it a credit card? Because our enum is a plain old Ruby class, we have full flexibility for the behavior of this type.

If we were to create more and more enums, the chances are high that we would also create interrogation methods on each of those types. Can we write code in our module that automatically creates those interrogation methods for us? If you've been paying attention, then you'll know the answer is yes. There are a few approaches here, but we'll use our old friend **method_missing** from the previous chapter.

7. Respond to interrogation methods using **method_missing**:

```ruby
module Enum
  def is_type?(type)
    name.to_sym == type.to_sym
  end
  def method_missing(method, *args, &block)
    interrogation_methods = self.class.all.map{|type| "#{type.name}?".to_sym}
    if interrogation_methods.include?(method)
        type = method.to_s.gsub("?", '').to_sym
        is_type?(type)
    else
        super
    end
  end
end
```

Great, so we added a **is_type?** method, which is our comparison method. We overrode **method_missing** to check whether the missing method that was called was an interrogation method to a valid type, and if so, formatted it and passed it to the **is_type?** method:

```ruby
PaymentTypes.all[0].wire?
PaymentTypes.all[0].credit?
PaymentTypes.all[2].wire?
PaymentTypes.all[2].credit?
```

The output would be as follows:

```
irb(main):059:0> PaymentType.all[0].wire?
=> true
irb(main):060:0> PaymentType.all[0].credit?
=> false
irb(main):061:0> PaymentType.all[2].wire?
=> false
irb(main):062:0> PaymentType.all[2].credit?
=> true
```

Figure 6.13: Output for checking the payment type

Now we get these interrogator methods for free with any enum class that includes our module. This module is quite often used in production applications, although it contains quite a few more utility methods.

Module Methods

As we've learned so far, modules have primarily been used to add instance or class methods to other classes. You can add instance or class methods depending on whether you **include** or **extend** that module into your class. In both cases, though, the methods to be added are always defined as basic methods. This is in contrast to class methods in a class definition, which have the **self.** prefix for their declaration.

However, we also saw that the module callbacks were declared differently using the **self.** prefix. Let's see what happens if we define other methods using the **self.** prefix on a module like so:

```
module BabelFish
  def self.the_answer
    return 42
  end
end
```

What we're doing here is defining static module methods. These are very similar to class methods but on a module. They don't contain any state. They are called straight onto the module constant itself:

```
irb(main):058:0> BabelFish.the_answer
=> 42
```

So, module methods are pretty straightforward. Here are a few modules that are defined in the Ruby Core and Standard libraries that have module methods:

- The **URI** module:

```
irb(main):061:0> URI.parse("https://google.com")
=> #<URI::HTTPS https://google.com>
```

- The **FileTest** module:

```
irb(main):003:0> FileTest.directory?("specs")
=> false
```

- The **Math** module:

```
irb(main):005:0> Math.atan(45)
=> 1.5485777614681775
```

> **Note**
>
> You can explore more modules by going to the Ruby documentation here: https://packt.live/2M6n8MM. Modules have an "M" next to them.

Namespaces

In addition to adding methods to classes and providing out-of-the-box functionality as part of the module, another major purpose of modules is to provide a namespace. A namespace is just what it sounds like: it provides a scope or space for naming. In particular, it provides a space for constants. With the exception of raw global methods, the entry point for most code will be through a constant, whether it be a class constant or a module constant.

We've learned how to create classes and modules. Really, what we are doing is creating constants that point to those objects in memory. When we create constants (classes, modules, or otherwise) in IRB, we are creating a constant in the global namespace. This can quickly get crowded, especially if you are creating a class or module constant that may have a common name.

For instance, in the previous topic, we created an **Enum** module. **Enum** is a very common word in the Ruby world, and do we really think our **Enum** module is the best and that we should own that word? It is possible there is a more official **Enum** library, or that Ruby may use it as a global constant in the future. Therefore, it's a good practice to name your global constants with a name that is more unique. By doing this, you are also declaring a unique namespace that you can then put other constants inside of to make them safe from name collision.

As such, let's rename our **Enum** module to be a bit more specific to what the module is doing:

```
module ActsAsEnum
end
class PaymentTypes
  include ActsAsEnum
end
```

The name **ActsAsEnum** is not very inspired, but it is descriptive and as such makes it easy to read and understand what might be happening. While **ActsAsEnum** is more unique than **Enum**, in the Ruby world, lots of people use the **ActsAs** convention, so this may still have issues. We'll go with it for now.

Now that we've defined our **ActsAsEnum** module, assuming it's unique, we are free to add constants inside the **module** namespace and we can be sure to avoid name conflicts. In fact, we can use modules for no other purpose than to define namespaces:

```
module Zippy
  SKIPPY = "skippy"
  class Zappy
end
module Dappy
  def self.say_something
    puts "doo"
  end
end
end
```

We defined our arbitrary namespace, **Zippy**, and created the **Skippy**, **Zappy**, and **Dappy** classes. If we need to access the classes within the namespace, we use the scoping operator, ::, as follows:

```
Zippy::SKIPPY
Zippy::Zappy.new
Zippy::Dappy.say_something
```

The output would be something as follows:

```
irb(main):104:0> Zippy::SKIPPY
=> "skippy"
irb(main):105:0> Zippy::Zappy.new
=> #<Zippy::Zappy:0x00007f9d86040e90>
irb(main):106:0> Zippy::Dappy.say_something
doo
=> nil
```

Figure 6.14: Output after using the scoping operator

We can see that it doesn't matter whether we're accessing a constant with all caps, a class constant, or a module constant – we still use the :: scoping operator to access it.

Ruby is pretty smart about its constant lookup, but sometimes it can get confused, or sometimes you have to override its lookup behavior. The following exercise will show you the problem and provide you with a solution.

Exercise 6.05: How to Reuse Constants with a Namespace

In this exercise, we will be reusing the global **User** constants. We will be using the global scoping operator for this purpose:

1. Write a global class constant that is also a constant inside a module:

```ruby
class User
  def self.output
    return "Global User"
  end
end
module Report
  def self.test_namespace
    User.output
  end
  class User
    def self.output
        return "Report::User"
    end
  end
end
```

Here, we've got two classes with the commonly labeled **User** constant. However, the second **User** class is present within the **Report** module namespace.

2. Call the **Report** module of the **test** method:

```
Report.test_namespace
```

The output will be returned as follows:

```
irb(main):124:0> Report.test_namespace
=> "Report::User"
```

Figure 6.15: Output after applying the namespace method

This is as expected. You would expect to call **User**, which is inside the module, to be called by the module itself. What if we want the global **User** constant, though?

3. Add a method to access the global constant from inside the **module** namespace:

```
class User
  def self.output
    return "Global User"
  end
end
module Report
  def self.test_namespace
    User.output
  end
  def self.test_global
    ::User.output
  end
  class User
    def self.output
      return "Report::User"
    end
  end
end
```

We've added a **test_global** module method that references the global **User** constant by using the scoping operator, : :, but without anything before it. This is the global scoping operator. The output would now be as follows:

```
irb(main):146:0> Report.test_namespace
=> "Report::User"
irb(main):147:0> Report.test_global
=> "Global User"
```

Figure 6.16: Output for the test_global module

We have thus reused the **User** global constant as a common constant for all methods.

prepend

So far, we've discussed the **include**, **extend**, and **module** methods and namespaces. There is one more aspect to modules that came with the Ruby 2.0 release several years ago: **prepend**. **prepend** is not often used, perhaps because it is not well understood. Let's change that.

First, let's consider the following example:

```ruby
module ClassLogger
  def log(msg)
    "[#{self.class}] #{msg}"
  end
end
class User
  include ClassLogger
  def log(msg)
    "[#{Time.now.to_f.to_s}] #{super(msg)}"
  end
end
class Company
  prepend ClassLogger
  def log(msg)
    "[#{Time.now.to_f.to_s}] #{super(msg)}"
  end
end
```

We've created a module called **ClassLogger**, which implements a **log** method. This method wraps a string and outputs the current class. We've also created two classes, **Company** and **User**, which implement an identical **log** method that first calls **super** with the **msg** argument, then adds a prefix of the current time to the log message.

The difference is that **User** calls **include** to this module, whereas **Company** calls **prepend**:

```ruby
User.new.log("hi")
Company.new.log("hi")
```

The output would be as follows:

```
[1567570378.077541] [User] hi
[Company] hi
```

Figure 6.17: Output after prepend

The **User** implementation (**include**) got both the **time** and **class** prefixes, whereas **Company** only has the **time** prefix. What's going on here? The answer lies in how Ruby dispatches methods, as shown in the following code:

```
User.ancestors
```

The **ancestors** method output for the **User** class will be displayed as follows:

```
User
ClassLogger
Object
Kernel
BasicObject
```

Figure 6.18: The ancestor output for the User class

Similarly, the **ancestors** for the **Company** class will be:

```
Company.ancestors
```

```
ClassLogger
Company
Object
Kernel
BasicObject
```

Figure 6.19: The ancestor methods for the Company class

We call the **ancestors** method, which is an introspection method Ruby provides us with on class objects. We can see a significant difference here. The **User** class ancestors have **User** first and then **ClassLogger** second. The **Company** class has **ClassLogger** first and then **Company** second. As such, Ruby calls methods from each of these classes in this hierarchy in that order. The **ClassLogger** implementation doesn't call **super**, so the chain stops there, which is why we only see that particular output. When **User** calls **log**, it first calls the **User** implementation (the **time** prefix) and then calls **super**, which then calls the **ClassLogger** implementation. This is why we see the string output with **time** first and then **class** second.

When we started this chapter, we said that calling **include** was essentially like copying and pasting the code into the class. This isn't entirely true. As we can see, what's actually happening is that it's being added into the class hierarchy in an ordered fashion. That is, it adds the methods to the class hierarchy after the class itself. **prepend**, on the other hand, is adding to the class hierarchy before the class itself.

Prepending methods to the class hierarchy gives rise to some very important behaviors. Primarily, it allows modules to have their methods called first. By being called first, modules then have complete control of the original implementation. They can preprocess or postprocess data and behavior. Module authors should dutifully call **super** to make sure that the original implementation is called or have a good reason to not do it.

prepend with Subclasses

We've said that **prepend** adds module methods to the top of the class hierarchy. However, what happens when we subclass a class that has prepended a module? First, let's look at the subclass hierarchy in the following code:

```
class ParentClass
end
class ChildClass < ParentClass
end
ParentClass.ancestors
```

The ancestors for **ParentClass** will be as follows:

```
ParentClass
Object
Kernel
BasicObject
```

Figure 6.20: The ancestor method output for ParentClass

Similarly, the output for **ChildClass** will be as follows:

```
ChildClass.ancestors
```

```
ChildClass
ParentClass
Object
Kernel
BasicObject
```

Figure 6.21: The ancestor method output for ChildClass

This makes sense. The child class is higher up in the class hierarchy than **ParentClass**, which is what explains basic inheritance behavior in Ruby. Now add a module to prepend, as shown in the following code:

```ruby
module PrependedModule
  def output
    puts "Outputting from the PrependedModule"
    super
  end
end
class ParentClass
  prepend PrependedModule
  def output
    puts "Outputting from the parent class"
  end
end
class ChildClass < ParentClass
  def output
    puts "Outputting from the child class"
  end
end
ChildClass.new.output
```

ChildClass will now look as follows:

```
Outputting from the child class
```

Figure 6.22: ChildClass

```
ChildClass.ancestors
```

The **ancestors** method on **ChildClass** will respond as follows

```
ChildClass
PrependedModule
ParentClass
Object
Kernel
BasicObject
```

Figure 6.23: The ancestor method output for prepended ChildClass

Similarly, for **ParentClass**, the **ancestors** method will respond as follows:

```
ParentClass.ancestors
```

The output would be as follows:

```
PrependedModule
ParentClass
Object
Kernel
BasicObject
```

Figure 6.24: The ancestor method output for prepended ParentClass

As we can see, **ChildClass** appears higher up in the hierarchy than the prepended module. This means the module's function will not be called unless **ChildClass** calls **super**, as shown in the following code:

```
class ChildClass < ParentClass
  def output
    super
    puts "Outputting from the child class"
  end
end
puts ChildClass.new.output
```

The output would now be as follows:

```
Outputting from the PrependedModule
Outputting from the parent class
Outputting from the child class
```

Figure 6.25: Output for the prepended module

If we want our module to work for subclasses too, we have another Ruby callback: **inherited**. Consider the following code:

inheritedcallback.rb

```
1  module PrependedModule
2
3   def output
4     puts "Outputting from the PrependedModule"
5     super
6   end
7  end
8
9  class ParentClass
10   prepend PrependedModule
11
12   def self.inherited(klass)
13     klass.send(:prepend, PrependedModule)
14   end
15
```

https://packt.live/2IH18pl

The output would be as follows:

```
Outputting from the PrependedModule
Outputting from the child class
```

Figure 6.26: Output for the inherited callback

This type of coding is very advanced, and care should be taken to make sure that the method chain is understood well. In other words, take care to understand how **super** is placed in the method chain so that the module method is not called multiple times if that is not desired.

The preceding code still requires **ParentClass** to define the **inherited** callback. We can go even further with our module with the following code:

inheritedcallback_withparentclass.rb

```
1  module PrependedModule
2   def output
3     puts "Outputting from the PrependedModule"
4     super
5   end
6   def self.prepended(base_class)
7     puts "Included: #{base_class}"
8     base_class.instance_eval do
9       def self.inherited(klass)
10        puts "Inherited: #{klass}"
11        klass.send(:prepend, PrependedModule)
12      end
13    end
14   end
15 end
```

https://packt.live/2VDaTKz

The output would be as follows:

```
Outputting from the PrependedModule
Outputting from the child class
```

Figure 6.27: Using the prepended module

Here, we have done some really advanced Ruby coding by using the prepended callback to know when our module was prepended. We also use **instance_eval** to evaluate a block of code in the context of the class constant instance. This allows us to dynamically define the inherited callback method, which then allows us to prepend our module on the subclass.

Exercise 6.06: Prepending Modules to Classes

In this exercise, we will prepend **ApplicationDebugger** to the **Application** class and define the **debug** function, which takes **application_name** and debugs the application:

1. Create a new Ruby file, **Exercise6.06.rb**.

2. Define the **ApplicationDebugger** module with the **debug** function:

```
module ApplicationDebugger
  def debug(args)
    puts "Application debug start: #{args.inspect}"
    result = super
    puts "Application debug finished: #{result}"
  end
end
```

3. Define the **Application** class:

```
class Application
  prepend ApplicationDebugger
  def debug(args)
    {result: "ok"}
  end
end
```

4. Add the invocation code:

```
DBugger = Application.new
DBugger.debug("NotePad")
```

5. Invoke the script with ruby **Exercise6.06.rb**. The output would be as follows:

```
Application debug start: "NotePad"
Application debug finished: {:result=>"ok"}
```

Figure 6.28: Output for prepending ApplicationDebugger

Activity 6.01: Implementing Categories on the Voting Application Program

In this activity, we're going to expand the voting program we wrote in *Chapter 5, Object-Oriented Programming with Ruby*. We will enable the voting program to allow multiple categories and make it so that users can create categories via the menu. Once a category is created, votes can start being recorded for that category. A category could be something such as "Employee of the Month," "Innovation Leader of Q1," or "Best Collaborator." Make sure that there are no duplicate categories. Add a module to the controller base class that handles the logging of each controller run.

The following steps will help you to complete the activity:

1. Open the Terminal and create a new file.

2. Write a new test for **VotingMachine** to add a category.

3. Implement the **add_category** method on the voting machine. Run tests when complete.

4. Write a test for **record_vote** that adds the **category** argument.

5. Amend the **record_vote** implementation to include **category**.

6. Amend the **test_run_vote_controller** test to include **category**.

7. Implement category choosing in the **VoteController**.

8. Implement the **ControllerLogging** module.

Here is the expected output:

```
         ** Please enter your choice **
            1. Place a vote for a colleague
            2. See current leaderboard
            3. Add category
            4. Exit
      choice> 1
      You can vote for:
      Which category would you like to vote for? Best Employee
      What's your name? Jane
      Who do you want to vote for? James
```

Figure 6.29: Voting application with categories

> **Note**
>
> The solution to the activity can be found on page 472.

Summary

This chapter aimed to provide you with the knowledge necessary to create modules with the Ruby object model. We have added instance methods by including modules into classes. We have added class methods to extend class functionality. We have created namespaces for our modules. As a very crucial part, we have made a distinction between prepending modules into classes and how you can extend and include functionality. Modules in Ruby accomplish multiple purposes such as creating namespaces, creating reusable class and instance methods, and modifying a class's code at runtime. Modules are Ruby's answer to multiple inheritance, in that they allow classes to incorporate code from multiple sources. As we saw in the last section, when a module is included or prepended, it affects the class hierarchy, which is what Ruby uses to do method lookup and dispatch. The ordering of this hierarchy is important and something to keep in mind as you start using third-party modules in your application code.

Now that we've covered all the major fundamentals in Ruby, in the next chapter, we'll use what we have learned to focus on importing data from external sources, processing it using the models we'll create, and outputting that data in a common format such as CSV.

Introduction to Ruby Gems

Overview

By the end of this chapter, you will be able to import external data and code to improve the functionality of an application; use Ruby gems in programs; interact with file systems and file modes in Ruby; read and write files to and from disk using Ruby; import and export external CSV data into Ruby applications and use service objects to package code for reuse within applications.

Introduction

In the previous chapter, we learned about code reusability and how to clean up our code base by extracting common functionality and logic from modules that can be included as needed throughout our project, preventing unnecessary code duplication.

This is an important concept to grasp as it forms the base for Ruby's excellent package management system known as **RubyGems**, which we will dive into further in this chapter.

Most applications consist of inputs and outputs. Facebook will have data in the form of photos and status updates (as input), and users, in turn, will see other users' photos and status updates (as output). Additionally, a banking application will load data from a database (as input) and present it to the user in the form of charts and tables (as output). The input data sources will vary per application, but the concept of inputs and outputs is essentially the same.

Data is fed into the application, some sort of processing is performed, and there is an output action, be it saving to a database, exporting data to another format, or simply printing out a processed version of the input.

A common scenario in the workplace is the need to process data in the form of

comma-separated values (CSV) that may have been imported from another system. Following this, some sort of processing is then performed on the values and, finally, a result is outputted to the user in a way that helps them to understand the data.

In this chapter, we will look at handling this exact type of scenario. We will look at importing and exporting CSV data, processing it, and then outputting a result using an external library that's going to format the data into a nice readable table for us.

We will also take a closer look at **RubyGems**, how we can interact with the package manager, and how to utilize external gems in our own code base. We'll then wrap everything up by implementing everything we've learned about as a service object in our code.

RubyGems and the require Method

Similar to the concept of including modules, Ruby has another way of including external code into your project, which is known as a gem. Essentially, a Ruby gem is a package of code that can be included in your project, much like a module, with a few key differences such as the ability to version a particular package and the ability to load other dependent gems at the same time.

Generally speaking, a gem is more of a collection of modules and classes than a single module or class. Gems can be tiny and can solve a single problem, such as formatting screen output, or they can be an entire application framework. The Ruby on Rails framework, for example, is a gem itself.

Most modern languages have an equivalent way of loading external code packages into an application. These are commonly referred to as package managers.

For Node.js, you would use `npm` or `yarn`; for Python, you would use `PIP`; for C#, you would use NuGet; and for Ruby, we use `RubyGems`.

So, why would we want to include other external code and libraries in our own code base? Well, quite simply, to save us time and effort. Consider the following examples.

You're building a new application and you want to allow for user registration so that customers can sign in to your website. Creating a robust user authentication and registration system is no small task. You would probably need to answer the following questions before you begin:

- Do you understand cryptography well enough to implement a secure password hashing algorithm?

- What about allowing users to reset their password?

- How about sending a user a confirmation email on sign up?

- What if you want to allow people to sign in with Facebook or Twitter?

You could write these yourself, but it would take a lot of time and effort and you'll more than likely make mistakes that could compromise the security of your application. Thankfully, with RubyGems, we can simply include the `devise` gem (https://packt.live/318fy8k) into our project and have a fully featured authentication and user registration system that solves our problems in a matter of minutes.

But why stop at user authentication? Let's say our application needs to upload files to a remote location; well, we can just add the `carrierwave` gem (https://packt.live/33nzOV2).

What if you need to paginate the results of your web page? In that case, you just add the `will_paginate` gem (https://packt.live/2VuQuYa).

You can begin to see how we can create a very functional application in no time at all by leveraging this external code in the form of gems. This allows us to focus on what our core application functionality needs to do, rather than the standard functionality that we all expect from any application, such as being able to sign up and log in.

Now let's take a look at how we can interact with Ruby gems. The following are the gem functions we are going to study next:

- `gem search`

- `gem install`

- `gem dependency`

- `gem Versioning`

- `gem list`

Let's take a look at how we can interact with each of these Ruby gems, one by one.

gem search

gem search is used to search for available gems by name. Run the following command on the Terminal:

```
$ gem search terminal-table
```

The output would be as follows:

```
$ gem search terminal-table

*** REMOTE GEMS ***

leifcr-terminal-table (1.5.3)
smtlaissezfaire-terminal-table (1.0.5)
terminal-table (1.8.0)
terminal-table-unicode (0.1.9)
terminal-tableofhashes (0.1.0)
visionmedia-terminal-table (1.2.0)
```

Figure 7.1: Output for gem search

> **Note**
>
> Search for locally installed gems by passing the **--local** flag or search only for remote gems by passing the **--remote** flag, to the **gem search** command.

gem install

As you might expect, **gem install** will install a gem. It does so when you simply pass in the name of a gem to the command. By default, it will install the latest version of the gem:

```
$ gem install terminal-table
```

To install a specific version of a gem with the **--version** flag, use the following command:

```
$ gem install terminal-table --version
```

The output would be as follows:

```
$ gem install terminal-table --version 1.8.0
Fetching: unicode-display_width-1.6.0.gem (100%)
Successfully installed unicode-display_width-1.6.0
Fetching: terminal-table-1.8.0.gem (100%)
Successfully installed terminal-table-1.8.0
Parsing documentation for unicode-display_width-1.6.0
Installing ri documentation for unicode-display_width-1.6.0
Parsing documentation for terminal-table-1.8.0
Installing ri documentation for terminal-table-1.8.0
Done installing documentation for unicode-display_width, terminal-table after 0 seconds
2 gems installed
```

Figure 7.2: Output for gem install

As you can see, there are two gems installed – **terminal table** and **unicode-display-width**. The **unicode-display-width** gem is a dependency, which simply means that the creators of the **terminal-table** gem are using (much like including) the **unicode-display-width** gem in their own code and have listed it as a dependent gem in their own gem's definition.

RubyGems is intelligent enough to figure out all of these dependency chains and install them as required. As you can imagine, gems depending on other gems can go many levels deep, which would be a pain to manage yourself. Thankfully, we don't need to think about that with RubyGems.

gem dependency

As we saw previously, gems can have dependencies on other gems. You can view a gem dependency with the **gem dependency** command as follows:

```
$ gem dependency terminal-table
```

The output would be as follows:

```
$ gem dependency terminal-table
Gem terminal-table-1.8.0
  bundler (~> 1.10, development)
  pry (>= 0, development)
  rake (~> 10.0, development)
  rspec (>= 3.0, development)
  term-ansicolor (>= 0, development)
  unicode-display_width (>= 1.1.1, ~> 1.1)
```

Figure 7.3: Output for gem dependency

You'll notice that there are several gems listed here; however, all but one are assigned to the **development** group. This is essentially saying that those gems are only required in the development environment for the **terminal-table** gem.

By default, these will not be installed when installing the **terminal-table** gem, as only a gem's non-development dependency is installed by default.

gem Versioning

In the following command, notice the numbers with the arrows next to the gem names in some of the gem commands:

```
$ gem dependency terminal-table
Gem terminal-table-1.8.0
  bundler (~> 1.10, development)
  pry (>= 0, development)
  rake (~> 10.0, development)
  rspec (>= 3.0, development)
  term-ansicolor (>= 0, development)
  unicode-display_width (>= 1.1.1, ~> 1.1)
```

Figure 7.4: Output for gem versioning

These are known as semantic versioning constraints. They essentially tell RubyGems what range of versions of that gem is required to be installed. RubyGems is able to read these numbers and select a compatible version of that gem to download and install.

You can translate them to mean "*I need a version equal to or greater than version 1.10,*" or "*I need a version that is no older than version 3.0.*"

> **Note**
>
> More information on how this works can be found at https://packt.live/2IF9wWq.

The ~> symbol in the semantic versioning constraints is called a **twiddle-wakka**.

gem list

gem list lists locally installed gems. It is extremely helpful when we are trying to understand what gems and their versions are installed:

```
$ gem list

*** LOCAL GEMS ***

bigdecimal (default: 1.3.4)
cmath (default: 1.0.0)
csv (default: 1.0.0)
date (default: 1.0.0)
dbm (default: 1.0.0)
did_you_mean (1.2.0)
etc (default: 1.0.0)
fcntl (default: 1.0.0)
fiddle (default: 1.0.0)
fileutils (default: 1.0.2)
gdbm (default: 2.0.0)
io-console (default: 0.4.6)
ipaddr (default: 1.2.0)
json (default: 2.1.0)
minitest (5.10.3)
net-telnet (0.1.1)
openssl (default: 2.1.0)
power_assert (1.1.1)
psych (default: 3.0.2)
rake (12.3.0)
rdoc (default: 6.0.1)
scanf (default: 1.0.0)
sdbm (default: 1.0.0)
stringio (default: 0.0.1)
strscan (default: 1.0.0)
test-unit (3.2.7)
webrick (default: 1.4.2)
xmlrpc (0.3.0)
zlib (default: 1.0.0)
```

Figure 7.5: Output for gem list

You'll notice that there are a lot of gems listed even though you may have only installed one. The gems with **default:** included in the brackets are part of the Ruby core library. They come installed with Ruby and cannot be removed.

You can see from the preceding output that the two gems at the bottom are the ones that we installed previously and do not have the **default:** label attached to them.

> **Note**
>
> Depending on the version of Ruby you are using, this gem listing may appear differently. Newer versions of Ruby may include additional default gems.

Using Gems in Your Code

To use a gem, you simply **require** the gem in your code, which is similar to how you would **include** a module. Consider the following example:

```
user = { name: 'John Smith', age: '35', address: { home: '1 kings cross road' }}
puts JSON.pretty_generate(user)
# NameError (uninitialized constant JSON)
require 'json'
puts JSON.pretty_generate(user)
{
  "name": "John Smith",
  "age": "35",
  "address": {
    "home": "1 kings cross road"
  }
}
```

In the preceding example, we create a simple hash containing some user information and we attempt to convert it to JSON and display it in a formatted way using the **JSON. pretty_generate** function.

We can then see that it throws a **NameError** error because the **JSON** gem has not been required and is, therefore, not available. This is very much like trying to use a method from a module before you've included it.

In the preceding lines of code, we require the **JSON** gem (which is a default Ruby gem). Then, we call the **JSON.pretty_generate** method again; we can see it now works and formats our hash into a pretty **JSON** format.

It really is that simple to load other libraries into our code and extend the functionality of our application.

So, we've learned what Ruby gems are now and how they can be used to extend the functionality of our application by simply "requiring" them in our code. Let's try it out for ourselves now.

In the following exercise, we'll learn how to use a Ruby gem to format and present a basic data structure in our Terminal windows in a readable format. Creating a neatly presented table of information in a Terminal window is a tricky task; it's not something we would want to repeat for every project, so let's make it easier for ourselves and use one that has already been built.

Exercise 7.01: Installing and Using a Ruby Gem

In this exercise, we will be installing a Ruby gem, **terminal-table**, to generate a table of individuals and their locations and then print it.

The following steps will help you to complete this exercise:

1. Install the **terminal-table** gem. From your Terminal, run the following command:

   ```
   gem install terminal-table
   ```

2. Create a **exercise_1.rb** script that will require the **terminal-table** gem. Generate a collection of users and print them to the Terminal as a table:

   ```
   require "terminal-table"
   headings = ["Name", "City"]
   users = [
           ["James", "Sydney"],
           ["Chris", "New York"]
   ]
   table = Terminal::Table.new rows: users,  headings: headings
   puts table
   ```

3. Run the script with the following command:

   ```
   ruby exercise_1.rb
   ```

You should see a table printout of our users with a heading row, as follows:

```
$ ruby exercise_1.rb
+--------+----------+
| Name   | City     |
+--------+----------+
| James  | Sydney   |
| Chris  | New York |
+--------+----------+
```

Figure 7.6: Table using a Ruby gem

Thus, we have successfully represented data in a tabular form, using the

terminal-table gem.

File I/O

The ability to open, read, and write from the filesystem is an important part of any language. Thankfully, Ruby has quite an extensive and user-friendly file **I/O** interface.

The **IO** class is responsible for all input and output operations in Ruby. The **File** class is a subclass of the **IO** class:

```
File.superclass
=> IO
```

When we interact with the filesystem, we are generally always working with the **File** class, although it is helpful to understand where it sits in the class hierarchy.

Let's take a look at some common file operations:

- Creating files
- Reading from files
- Writing to files

Creating Files

We can create new files by instantiating a **File** object and passing the name of the file and the file mode to the initializer:

```
file = File.new("new.txt", "w")
=> #<File:new.txt>
file.close
```

When we create or open files using the `File.new` method, we also need to call **close** afterward to tell Ruby to release the handle it has opened for the file. When using the `File.open` method with a block, **close** is automatically called for us. We shall discuss this in more detail later on in the chapter.

You might be wondering what that **w** parameter that appears after the filename is. This tells Ruby what mode we want to use. In this example, we've set the mode to **w**, which means we want to write to a new file. By default, unless we supply this parameter, the file mode will be **r**, which is short for **READ**. The **READ** file mode is only for, as you may have guessed, reading files.Attempting to create a new file using this mode will give you an error like the following:

```
$ irb
irb(main):001:0> file = File.new("new.txt")
Traceback (most recent call last):
        4: from /Users/cheyne/.rbenv/versions/2.5.0/bin/irb:11:in `<main>'
        3: from (irb):1
        2: from (irb):1:in `new'
        1: from (irb):1:in `initialize'
Errno::ENOENT (No_such file or directory @ rb_sysopen - new.txt)
```

Figure 7.7: An ENOENT error

We will cover file modes more extensively later.

Reading Files

Reading the contents of files is quite a simple process with Ruby. There are a few different methods for reading and processing files:

- Using the `File.read` method

- Using the `File.open` method

- Using the `File.foreach` method

We'll use a test file named `company.txt` for this section that contains the

following content:

```
ACME Company
555 Mystery Lane
2010
```

Let's take a look at each of these file reading methods in turn.

Using the File.read Method

The **File.read** method will read the whole file into memory at once and handle

the file just like a large string:

```
File.read("company.txt")
=> "ACME Company\n555 Mystery Lane\n2010"
```

We see that the entire file is loaded into memory and returned as a single string.

The newline characters are represented as **\n** in the string.

Some potential issues may arise from the **File.read** method. When it comes to the loading of a large file into memory, it can be an inefficient method. In such cases, we can prompt for a more optimized solution for larger files, which leads into the next section of using **File.open** and **File.foreach**.

Using the File.open Method

The **File.open** method on its own simply returns an instance of the **File** class indicating we have an open file handle on the **company.txt** file:

```
File.open("company.txt")
=> #<File:company.txt>
```

Passing a block to the **File.open** method, however, allows us to iterate over the contents of the file one line at a time and process the contents. The block will automatically close the file when it exits:

```
File.open('company.txt').each do |row|
   puts row
end
```

The output would be the following:

```
ACME Company
555 Mystery Lane
2010
```

Using the File.foreach Method

Much like the **File.open().each** method, we can use the slightly more succinct **File.foreach** method, which does essentially the same thing without the need to specifically call **.each**:

```
File.foreach('company.txt') do |row|
   puts row
end
```

The output would be the following:

```
ACME Company
555 Mystery Lane
2010
```

read versus open versus foreach

You could easily be forgiven for being confused about these methods that seemingly do the exact same thing. From an end user's point of view, that's true; however, from a programming perspective, they are quite different.

The `File.read` method will load the entire contents of a file into memory for us to process at once. This may be suitable for smaller files, but for anything larger, this can have a serious impact on your system and application performance.

The `File.open` method with a block and the `File.foreach` method, however, process the contents of a file one line at a time. This allows Ruby to manage memory more efficiently, and they are generally a safer option for when your files are of varying sizes.

We will cover more on this topic of loading and processing data one row at a time in the *Handling CSV Data* section.

> **Note**
>
> Loading external data can have a detrimental effect on application performance if it is not done correctly. Understanding how data is being allocated and cleaned up by Ruby is a key factor in ensuring consistent performance.

Writing to Files

There are several ways to write to files in Ruby, each with a slightly different use case:

- Using the `File.new` method
- Using the `File.open` method with a block method
- Using the `File.write` method

Let's take a look at each of them.

Using the File.new Method (Initializer)

File.new will return an instance of a file with an open file handle, which means we are able to write to it:

```
file = File.new("new.txt", "w")
file.puts "Hey, nice file"
file.close
```

Calling **puts** on the **file** object here writes the string to the file, although you'll still need to call **close** on the object before you can access the contents of the file from outside the application.

> ### Note
>
> You can actually call **file.puts**, **file.write**, and **file << "my string"** to write to the **File** object and you'll get the same result.

Using the File.open Method with a Block Method

This method allows us to pass a block with the instantiated file object as a parameter. This is a cleaner approach that allows you to create, write, and close a file all in one block of code:

```
File.open("new.txt", "w") do |file|
    file.write("Hey, nice file")
end
```

The section after the **open** statement is a Ruby block and it allows us to encapsulate our **write** logic into a section of code that, when completed, will automatically close the file so we don't need to call **file.close** manually. It looks much cleaner.

Using the File.write Method

```
File.write("new.txt", "Hey, nice file")
```

The **File.write** method is more of a shorthand syntax. The **write** method is actually a member of the parent **IO** class and not the **File** class. It is a quick and short method for opening a file, writing a string to a file, and closing the file with the smallest amount of code. The length of the characters written is returned by the **write** method rather than a file handle.

File.open versus File.new

You will see both of these methods used in examples online. It mostly comes down to personal preference, but **File.open** is the more useful method due to the fact that it supports the ability to pass in a block and immediately iterate over a collection, writing out the results to a file before automatically closing the file when the block exits.

There are times, however, when you may wish to open a file and pass the file reference to another method for processing before closing the file. In this case, you may prefer to use **File.new** over **File.open**.

Both methods will return an instance of **File** (**File.open** is used only when called without a block) and can be used to pass a reference to the open file around the rest of the code base. However, using **File.new** for this specific use case and **File.open** only with blocks can help to make your code easier to understand, as other engineers will know that whenever they see a **File.new** method, there needs to be a corresponding **.close** method call for the instantiated object.

File Modes

We've seen the usage of file modes in the previous examples. To put it simply, they tell Ruby how much access we want to enable for the file we're going to interact with.

There are several file modes that we can choose from depending on the requirement we have for the file. The most common usages are to "read a file mode", **r**, and to "write a file mode", **w**.

The following table is from the official Ruby documentation from the **IO** class and explains the meaning behind each of the modes:

Mode	Meaning
r	Read-only: This starts at the beginning of the file (this is the default mode).
r+	Read-write: This starts at the beginning of the file and does not clear the contents of the file.
w	Write-only: This truncates the existing file to zero length or creates a new file for writing.
w+	Read-write: This truncates the existing file to zero length or creates a new file for reading and writing. It overwrites the existing file if it exists.
a	Write-only: This starts writing at the end of the file if the file exists; otherwise, it creates new file for writing.
a+	Read-write: This starts writing at the end of the file if the file exists; otherwise, it creates a new file for reading and writing.
b	Binary file mode (this may appear with any of the key letters listed): This suppresses the EOL <-> CRLF conversion on Windows and sets external encoding to ASCII-8BIT unless explicitly specified.
t	Text file mode (this may appear with any of the key letters listed except "b")

Figure 7.8: File modes

File Helpers

Aside from reading and writing data, Ruby comes with a bunch of very helpful file helpers right out of the box. These can help you to solve a number of common file-related tasks, such as checking for the existence of files and permissions and deleting files. Here are a few examples of useful file helpers in Ruby.

File.exist?

This checks for the existence of a file. It returns true or false. Use this before creating a new file or opening an existing one to ensure the file exists and to avoid throwing errors.

Dir.exist?

This checks for the existence of a directory. It returns true or false. It is very much like **File.exist?** except for the directories. Use this before creating a new directory to ensure the file exists and avoid throwing errors.

`File.delete`

This deletes a file when given a file path.

`File.size?`

This returns the size of a file. You may wish to use this to report on the size of datasets after importing them or to verify the size of a file before processing it.

`File.truncate`

This truncates (that is, clears) the contents of a file. You can use this to reset a file's content back to empty before writing to it. It is helpful if you wish to reuse a particular file.

`File.zero?`

This returns true if the file is empty. Use this when you want to verify whether a file has any content or not.

`File.birthtime`

This returns the birth time (that is, the time of creation) of a file. Use this when you want to know how old a file is.

> **Note**
>
> You can read more about all the available file options in the official Ruby documentation for the File class here: https://packt.live/35nehxE.

Handling CSV Data

CSV is a very common format for representing tabular data. It is an easily parsable data format to work with and it can be opened in all common spreadsheet applications, such as Microsoft Office and Google Docs, with no need for conversion.

We can represent columns and rows with CSV, much like a relational database or a spreadsheet, which makes it a very handy tool for processing exported database records, generating data to be imported into a database, or creating spreadsheets.

Ruby comes with a full library for handling CSV data out of the box. The Ruby CSV library is actually a gem and is part of the Ruby default gem set. This means that to use the CSV library in your code, you simply need to "require" it.

We can see the **csv** gem with the following **gem list** command:

```
$ gem list | grep csv
csv (default: 1.0.0)
```

Ruby has even published this gem publicly on GitHub (https://packt.live/35qKCUf), just like any other gem.

All modern versions of Ruby (1.9 and later) will have a default CSV gem. The Ruby CSV gem from Ruby 1.9.3 and later is actually based on a popular CSV parsing gem called **FasterCSV**. This was an optional replacement for the core CSV gem before Ruby 1.9.3; however, as it was so popular, the Ruby team simply replaced the default CSV gem with **FasterCSV** as the default CSV gem.

There are other CSV gems out there if you have more specific needs. **SmarterCSV** is another well-known replacement for the default CSV gem that offers parallel import processing for the better handling of larger files.

> **Note**
>
> You can refer to the following for more information on **SmarterCSV**: https://packt. live/2B5xSVk.

Similar to the **File** class we covered previously, the CSV gem has a number of different ways in which we can interact with CSV data and files. Let's take a closer look.

Reading Data from a CSV File Using CSV.read

The simplest way to load CSV data is with the **CSV.read** method. This is an "all-at-once" method that will load the entire CSV document at once into memory and return an array of arrays representing the data.

Let's imagine that we have a **users.csv** file containing the following CSV data:

```
Mike Smith,35,Sydney
James Taylor,42,New York
Susan Jones,29,San Francisco
```

We can read the data with the following:

```
CSV.read("users.csv")
```

This returns the following:

```
=> [["Mike Smith", "35", "Sydney"], ["James  Taylor", "42", " New York"], ["Susan Jones",
"29", "San Francisco"]]
```

Here, we can see that the data has been loaded into an array. We can also see that each row in the CSV data has been represented as an array inside the main array, so we have a nested array or an array of arrays.

We can iterate over this array to get access to the individual rows:

```ruby
require 'csv'
users = CSV.read("users.csv")
users.each do |user|
  puts "name: #{user[0]}"
  puts "age: #{user[1]}"
  puts "city: #{user[2]}"
end
```

This returns the following:

```
name: Mike Smith
age:  35
city:  Sydney
name: James Taylor
age:  42
city:  New York
name: Susan Jones
age:  29
city:  San Francisco
```

This is great. We're able to load data from an external file and interact with it in Ruby with only a few lines of code.

But what kind of problems do you think will arise if we have a wide dataset with many columns or fields? Well, accessing the data with array index positions can get confusing when there are many columns.

The numbers in the square brackets after the **user** variable are **index positions**. As we can see from the preceding array-of-arrays example, each element of the array is another array containing the user information. For each user array, we see that index position 0 is the name, index position 1 is the age, and index position 2 is the city.

As you can imagine, if you have a dataset with many columns or fields, this can get confusing, as you need to keep track of exactly which column is at which index. For example, is **user[18]** the address or is it **user[12]**? Not only is this a bit confusing, but it makes our code hard to read. Wouldn't it be nicer if we could access the data based on the actual field name?

Using Column Headers as Field Names

Thankfully, Ruby makes it easy to refer to row data by the field name, which makes our code cleaner and easier to read.

If, instead, our previous dataset included a header row, the output would be as follows:

```
name,age,city
Mike Smith,35,Sydney
James Taylor,42,New York
Susan Jones,29,San Francisco
```

We can simply pass in the **headers** parameter to the **read** method:

```
headers: true
```

We can now use the heading name to access the row data:

```
require 'csv'
users = CSV.read("users_with_headers.csv", headers: true)
users.each do |user|
  puts "name: #{user["name"]}"
  puts "age: #{user["age"]}"
  puts "city: #{user["city"]}"
end
```

This returns the following output:

```
name: Mike Smith
age: 35
city: Sydney
name: James Taylor
age: 42
city: New York
name: Susan Jones
age: 29
city: San Francisco
```

Much better. How does that work, though? How do you access an array position with a string?

The simple answer is that you don't. Ruby is performing some magic behind the scenes here when the **headers** parameter is supplied, and, instead of returning an array of arrays as we saw previously, it is returning an instance of the **CSV::Table** class:

```
require 'csv'
CSV.read("users_with_headers.csv", headers: true)
=> #<CSV::Table mode:col_or_row row_count:4>
```

The core Ruby documentation describes the **CSV::Table** class (https://packt. live/2OKCIPT) as follows:

"A CSV::Table is a two-dimensional data structure for representing CSV documents. Tables allow you to work with the data by row or column, manipulate the data, and even convert the results back to CSV, if needed."

This simply means that it's a more flexible representation of the dataset than simply an array of arrays. It allows you to interact with the data in different dimensions, be it by row or by column.

> **Note**
>
> While both usability and reliability are increased, there is a performance cost of converting the dataset into hashes and the **CSV::Table** and **CSV::Row** types.For example, we can retrieve the first row with the **by_row** method, as shown in the following code block:

```
users = CSV.read("users_with_headers.csv", headers: true)
users.by_row[0]
=> #<CSV::Row "name":"Mike Smith" "age":"35" "city":"Sydney">
```

This returns an instance of the **CSV::Row** class, which has its own set of helper methods.

We can just as easily return the first column of all rows using the **by_col** method.

To retrieve the values of the first column and return them as an array, we can do the following:

```
users = CSV.read("users_with_headers.csv", headers: true)
users.by_col[0]
=> ["Mike Smith", "James Taylor", "Susan Jones"]
```

Only use the **CSV.read** method when you're dealing with small datasets. Loading large CSV files into memory can cause performance issues and result in excessive resource consumption. We'll discuss the usage of **CSV.foreach** for handling larger datasets in a moment.

Exercise 7.02: Reading Data from a .csv File and Printing a Few Columns

In most cases, we are only interested in a part of the data and not the entire dataset. In this exercise, we will be obtaining only the **city** column from **exercise_2.csv**, which contains other columns too, such as **name** and **gender**. To do so, perform the following steps:

1. Download **exercise_2.csv** from the code bundle. It should contain the following content:

```
name,age,city
Mike Smith,35,Sydney
James Taylor,42,New York
Susan Jones,29,San Francisco
```

2. Create a new file named **exercise_2.rb**, and then load the CSV data into a **users** variable:

```
require 'csv'
users = CSV.read("exercise_2.csv", headers: true)
```

3. Add the code to retrieve a listing of cities from the **users** object and then print them out:

```
cities = users.by_col["city"]
puts cities
```

4. Run the script to see the listing of cities:

```
ruby exercise_2.rb
```

You should see a response as follows:

```
$ ruby exercise_2.rb
Sydney
New York
San Francisco
```

Figure 7.9: Reading CSV data

Reading Data from a .csv File Using CSV.foreach

Previously, we have been using the **CSV.read** method to load all CSV data at once into memory before working with it. However, if you're working with a large dataset, this may cause resource consumption issues.

Processing the data row by row will allow Ruby to manage the memory usage more efficiently on your machine and is generally considered a more idiomatic approach. This can be done by using the **CSV.foreach** method.

Consider the following example:

```
require 'CSV'
CSV.foreach('users.csv') do |user|
  puts "name: #{user[0]}"
  puts "age: #{user[1]}"
  puts "city: #{user[2]}"
end
```

In the preceding example, we call **CSV.foreach** with the filename, just like we did for **CSV.read**, which opens the file. However, instead of assigning the result to a variable, we supply a block that we can iterate over in order to print the results, much like what we did earlier by using **each** to loop over the array.

Once again, we can supply the **headers: true** parameter to invoke the named key functionality we saw earlier, which provides us with a cleaner interface to retrieve the row data:

```
require 'csv'
CSV.foreach("users_with_headers.csv", headers: true) do |user|
  puts "name: #{user['name']}"
  puts "age: #{user['age']}"
  puts "city: #{user['city']}"
end
```

Running both of the preceding **foreach** examples results in the same response:

```
name: Mike Smith
age:  35
city:  Sydney
name: James Taylor
age:  42
city:  New York
name: Susan Jones
age:  29
city:  San Francisco
```

Both **CSV.read** and **CSV.foreach** open the files in read-only mode unless specifically set otherwise by the user. As we're only reading the data, the default read-only mode is all we need.

Response Type Variations

We saw previously with **CSV.read** that, by default, it will return an array of arrays, unless you specify the **headers: true** parameter, in which case it will return an instance of **CSV::Table**, which contains a number of **CSV::Row** instances to represent the row data.

You could be assuming that the **CSV.foreach** method would work in the same way, but it is actually slightly different again.

The **CSV.foreach** method returns an instance of **Enumerator**, which is an internal Ruby class used for iterating over collections. This instance will contain instances of **CSV::Row** to represent the row data in the same way the **CSV.read** method did.

Unlike the **CSV.read** method, however, passing in the **headers: true** parameter does not change the response type:

```
irb(main):001:0> require "csv"
=> true
irb(main):002:0> CSV.read("users.csv").class
=> Array
irb(main):003:0> CSV.read("users_with_headers.csv", headers: true).class
=> CSV::Table
irb(main):004:0> CSV.foreach("users.csv").class
=> Enumerator
irb(main):005:0> CSV.foreach("users_with_headers.csv", headers: true).class
=> Enumerator
```

For the most part, all these slightly different response objects work in a similar way; you can loop over them with an **each** block, perform basic enumerable functions, and treat them much like you would treat a regular array.

It is important, however, to remember that these objects are not simply arrays and, therefore, you may encounter slightly different methods or operations for interacting with the row data depending on the class.

For example, the **CSV::Table** class provides the **by_col** method, whereas the **Enumerator** and basic **Array** classes do not:

```
irb(main):001:0> CSV.read("users.csv", headers: true).respond_to? :by_col
=> true
irb(main):002:0> CSV.read("users.csv").respond_to? :by_col
=> false
irb(main):003:0> CSV.foreach("users.csv").respond_to? :by_col
=> false
```

The preceding **irb** log uses the **respond_to?** method, which simply checks whether an object will "respond to" a particular method name. In other words, it checks whether that method exists on an object or class.

You can imagine that something as simple as changing your CSV import dataset to now include a header row may result in confusion as the response object can change. Simply being aware of these variations can be helpful and save you from having to debug the issue when something unexpected happens.

Writing Data

Writing to a CSV file follows a similar pattern to the **CSV.foreach** method we learned about previously, except that, here, we use the **CSV.open** method and supply a block.

Inside the block, we have access to the file, which we can write to by simply calling **puts** on the opened **csv** variable. In the same way as before, we do not need to manually call **close** as the block will automatically do that for us when it exits:

```
require 'csv'
CSV.open("new_users.csv", "w") do |csv|
  csv.puts ["Sarah Meyer", "25", "Cologne"]
  csv.puts ["Matt Hall", "35", "Sydney"]
end
```

There is an alternative syntax that you may see other people using that works in the same way and makes use of the **append** operator instead of the **puts** method. We do this by using the object << value syntax. Really, **puts** is just an alias for <<, so you can expect it to work in the same way:

```
require 'csv'
CSV.open("new_users.csv", "w") do |csv|
  csv << ["Sarah Meyer", "25", "Cologne"]
  csv << ["Matt Hall ", "35", "Sydney"]
end
```

Both of these examples will generate a new CSV file named **new_users.csv** with the following content:

```
Sarah Meyer,25,Cologne
Matt Hall,35,Sydney
```

The second parameter of the **CSV.open** command is the file mode parameter we learned about in the *File I/O* section. The same rules apply here. In our case, we have passed in **w**, the **write** file mode parameter, which will create a new file each time, overwriting any previous files with the same name.

We could just as easily open the file with the **a** mode and append the file data to the end of the existing file if we were building a larger file over time.

Most CSV methods have a similar parameter structure to the file I/O methods. For the most part, they will work in the same way when it comes to closing files.

Writing CSV Data from an Enumerable

In the previous example, our data was static, meaning there was a line of code for each row inserted into the CSV file. In the real world, however, you're not likely to be doing this (as this would be incredibly time-consuming). It's more likely that you would want to export a collection of records from a database or another data source as CSV data.

This may be hundreds or thousands of rows, but the code should still only be a few lines long.

Let's imagine that we have a table of data that contains the names of cities, the country name, and the number of employees in that city. We want to export that data as CSV.

That data is then handed to our code and we need to iterate over it to generate the data. Here's what it might look like:

```ruby
require "csv"
cities = [
  { name: "San Francisco", country: "United States", employees: 15 },
  { name: "Sydney", country: "Australia", employees: 11 },
  { name: "London", country: "England", employees: 18 }
]
CSV.open("employee_count.csv", "w") do |csv|
  cities.each do |city|
    csv.puts [city[:name], city[:country], city[:employees]]
  end
end
```

In the preceding example, we define an array of cities, where each city is a hash. We define this array as an example, but, as you can imagine, in a real-world application, this may be a very long list returned from a database table.The output from the preceding code will be as follows:

```
San Francisco,United States,15
Sydney,Australia,11
London,England,18
```

The following CSV code is only five lines long and will loop over the entire collection of cities, writing out the data as CSV rows.

We want to highlight here that five lines of code can process thousands of lines of data; we can achieve a very useful result very simply.

> **Note**
>
> There are a number of other pieces of CSV functionality that are available with the standard core Ruby CSV library; you can refer to https://packt.live/2pc66DI for more details.

Exercise 7.03: Writing an Array of Users to a CSV File

Exporting data in CSV format is a great way to retrieve data from your application and share it with other systems or people. In this exercise, we will export an array of users as CSV much like you would export a table from a database in order to process that data with a spreadsheet or another system:

1. Create a new file, **exercise_3.rb**, and **require** the **csv** gem:

   ```
   require "csv"
   ```

2. Create an array of users. Each user will be a hash with the attributes **name**, **age**, and **city**:

   ```
   users = [
     { name: "John Smith", age: 36, city: "Sydney" },
     { name: "Susan Alan", age: 31, city: "San Francisco" },
     { name: "Daniel Jones", age: 43, city: "New York" }
   ]
   ```

3. Open a new CSV file for writing and iterate over the users array, writing the CSV content to the file:

```
CSV.open("new_users.csv", "w") do |csv|
  users.each do |user|
    csv.puts [user[:name], user[:age], user[:city]]
  end
end
```

4. Execute the application and inspect the contents of the **new_users.csv** file:

```
ruby exercise_3.rb
```

You should see the following content:

```
John Smith,36,Sydney
Susan Alan,31,San Francisco
Daniel Jones,43,New York
```

Thus, we have successfully used a Ruby gem to write data to a file.

Service Objects

In previous sections, we learned how to install and include Ruby gems to extend the functionality of our application. We also learned how to interact with files and CSV data. We now know how to read, process, and output data to the screen or the filesystem.

This is useful functionality, although opening files and writing CSV data is something that we would generally consider to be a common functionality that is likely to be shared between classes and can also seem unrelated to the existing classes in our code base.

What do we mean by unrelated? Well, let's assume we have a **User** class and a **Company** class in our application. We want the ability to load user and company data and print it to the Terminal for both of these classes. So, where do we write the code for this functionality? In the **User** class? In the **Company** class? Or, in both classes?

Possible solutions to the common usage code issue are using modules, service classes, and class inheritance.

The answer to the preceding questions is none of the above; neither the **User** class nor the **Company** class is the right place for this code. What we need instead is what's known as a **service object**.

A service object is a class that is created to perform a specific action or set of actions.

A service object is often created in order to **DRY (Don't Repeat Yourself)** up your code, which simply means it contains code that may be used in multiple different places in our application, but by exposing that code from a single central location, our domain model code stays clean and relevant.

The Single Responsibility Principle

Service objects play an important role in fulfilling the **single responsibility principle**.

The single responsibility principle is a well-known and established computer science methodology whereby every class or function has responsibility for no more than a single portion of the code base that represents a single responsibility of the application. This responsibility should be entirely encapsulated within the defined class or module.

Simply put, this is a guideline that means a class or module should only contain logic that relates to that specific class or module.

It is important for the following reasons:

- It makes testing our code much easier as we aren't interacting with a tangled mess of dependent classes.

- It keeps our classes smaller and more specific. For example, **users.rb** deals only with users, not groups, email, or payments.

- It promotes shared functionality. It's a lot easier to reuse code when it doesn't depend on other classes to function.

- It's easier to debug.

- It's easier to refactor. The code lives in a single encapsulated location, not scattered around the code base.

> ### Note
>
> The single responsibility principle is the "S" portion of the SOLID design principles. For more information, you can refer to https://packt.live/2MAFQen.

With this in mind, we can begin to see why we would want to use service objects in our application.

Service Objects versus Modules

By now, you're probably thinking, "Service objects sound very similar to the modules that we learned about earlier."

Sure, there are similarities between service objects and modules, but they are both fundamentally different concepts at their core.

Both service objects and modules will help keep your code clean and focused, both will DRY up your code base, both will promote code reusability, and both will improve the testability of your application.

So, *why do we need both?*

A module is used for sharing stateless functions between your code. Stateless functions typically operate on inputs from method parameters and do not assume any state or variables from the enclosing parent class. A stateless function is essentially like a class method; it does not have access to an instantiated objects variable, but merely whatever state is passed to the function when it's called. They are used as "mixins," which extend the functionality of our classes by "mixing in" the functions defined in the module to the class.

Modules are often thought of in a more "functional programming" aspect. They are stateless and declarative. We don't initialize or instantiate modules; this means that we tend to use them more like helpers.

Service objects are simply classes. Classes can be instantiated. Classes can have instance variables and be passed around to other methods. A service object is just an instantiated class with a specific purpose that generally follows a format for calling the code contained in the class.

A simplified example of a service object is as follows:

```ruby
require "csv"
class CSVPrinter
  def initialize(filepath)
    @filepath = filepath
  end
  def perform
    CSV.foreach(@filepath) do |row|
      puts row.to_s
    end
  end
end
```

In the preceding example, we can see that a service object is just a **Plain Old Ruby Object (PORO)**. Unlike a module, however, here we have an `initialize` method that we can use to instantiate an instance of the class with the `filepath` object passed in and set the instance as a private instance variable.

We then have an instance method called `perform`, which will perform the work of the service object; in this case, it's just simply printing out the rows of the CSV file.

Calling the `perform` method is a somewhat common design pattern that is used to standardize the interface for service objects. The words `execute`, `run`, and `go` are also common. As mentioned in the *The Single Responsibility Principle* section earlier, if we have just one method for executing the logic in the service object, then it helps us to stick to those guidelines. The name of the class is used as the identifier, not the method call.

It's an optional rule that aims to keep our classes simple and clearly defined with a single responsibility; however, it's still just a suggested pattern. You may decide to have a `CSVService` class, for example, with methods named `print` and `print_table` and so on, rather than many individual services with a single `perform` method.

An example of how you might use this service object would be as follows: `CSVPrinter.new("users.csv").perform`.

This is the one-liner way of running the `CSVPrinter` service object. We can see that an instance of the `CSVPrinter` class is instantiated and we immediately call the `perform` method on it.

We could, however, store the instantiated class and call `perform` on it at a later date if need be:

```
csvprinter = CSVPrinter.new("users.csv")
csvprinter.perform
```

Let's take a look at an example where a service object is used.

To highlight where you might want to use a service object, let's examine some slightly more involved code that could do with some refactoring:

```
require "mailgun-ruby"
class User
  attr_accessor :name, :email, :address
  def initialize(name, email, address)
    @name = name
    @email = email
    @address = address
  end
  def create
```

```
    if save_to_database(self)
      send_invite_email
    end
  end
  private
  def send_invite_email
    mailgun = Mailgun::Client.new ENV['MAILGUN_API_KEY']
    params =        from: "hello@myapp.com",
      to: email,
      subject: "Welcome #{name}!",
      text: "Thanks for signing up ...."
    }
    mailgun.send_message 'mail.myapp.com', params
  end
end
```

This is a simplified example that has a single method using the **mailgun** gem to send an invite email after a user is created. In a real-world application, you tend to find many instances of these small, tightly coupled methods that creep into the application over time. Before you know it, your classes are hundreds of lines long and become difficult to manage.

So, what's actually wrong with doing it this way?

Well, to start with, the **send_invite_email** method depends on the user instance's **email** and **name** attributes to populate the recipient and subject fields, so it's dependent on the instantiated **User** object's attributes to function.

When you decide to change the email subject or message or add some additional fields or logic, you'll be editing the **User** class directly, which should really only hold logic regarding the management of **User** objects, attributes, and resources.

We've also required the **mailgun** Ruby gem into the **Users** class as it's a requirement for the **send_invite_email** method to instantiate the **mailgun** client in order to send the email.

But do we really need to **require** an email library in our **User** class? What about when we decide that we want to send Slack messages, upload avatars to S3, or trigger an SMS to the user? Are we going to require those libraries here too?

You can see how this small class can quickly get out of control.

This code also violates the single responsibility principle by defining email-related methods inside the **User** class. Even though it is a user-related email, it does not need to live here. You can imagine that the **User** class of any application is at the very heart of the application and is likely to have a lot of added functionality attached to it in this same way.

Let's refactor this code to use a service object. First, let's extract out the **send_email_ function** function into a service object named **UserInviter**:

```ruby
require "mailgun-ruby"
class UserInviter
  def initialize(user)
    @user = user
  end
  def perform
    mailgun = Mailgun::Client.new ENV['MAILGUN_API_KEY']
    mailgun.send_message 'mail.myapp.com', params
  end
  private
  def params
    {
      from: "hello@myapp.com",
      to: @user.email,
      subject: "Welcome #{@user.name}!",
      text: "Thanks for signing up ...."
    }
  end
end
```

Now let's refactor our **User** class:

```ruby
class User
  attr_accessor :name, :email, :address
  def initialize(name, email, address)
    @name = name
    @email = email
    @address = address
  end
  def create
    if save_to_database(self)
      UserInviter.new(self).perform
    end
  end
end
```

Our **User** class now only defines what it needs to and, in the future, when we decide to change how our invite emails work or what content they contain, we will just be editing the **UserInviter** class. We've also moved out the **require "mailgun-ruby"** statement so it now lives in the **UserInviter** class, which feels a lot more appropriate as this is a class that specifically deals with sending emails.

It's considered good practice to keep your **perform** methods short and concise. In our preceding example, we moved the **params** section into its own private method, which will make testing easier and break down our code into more logical chunks.

Class Method Execution

Ruby is well known for being a highly readable language; it's one of the reasons why developers love the language so much. There is another common design pattern for service objects, which, in true Ruby fashion, sets out to make our service objects just a little bit nicer to work with.

For instance, instead of writing the code in the following way:

```
UserInviter.new(self).perform
```

Wouldn't it be cleaner if we could write it as follows? Let's take a closer look:

```
UserInviter.perform(self)
```

Now that feels more Ruby-like. Let's refactor our service object class one more time:

service_object_class_method.rb

```
1   require "mailgun-ruby"
2
3   class UserInviter
4     def initialize(user)
5       @user = user
6     end
7
8     def perform
9       mailgun = Mailgun::Client.new ENV['MAILGUN_API_KEY']
10      mailgun.send_message 'mail.myapp.com', params
11    end
12
13    def self.perform(*args)
14      new(*args).perform
15    end
```

https://packt.live/2M9n8LY

This looks the same, right? Well, it is, except for the **self.perform** class method:

```
def self.perform(*args)
  new(*args).perform
end
```

This little trick defines a class method named **perform**, which, when called, will simply instantiate a copy of the **UserInviter** class, pass through the arguments to the initializer, and then execute the instance method version of the **perform** method.

We've seen now how service objects can help clean up your code and encapsulate logic into their own classes. Let's try it out now for ourselves by creating a simple service object that lists users and their position in the list.

Exercise 7.04: Building a Service Object

In this exercise, we will create a service object that lists our users. To do this, we will instantiate a new instance of the **service** class with our user list, which establishes our state, and then we'll print our users to the screen using the standard **perform** syntax:

1. Create a new **exercise_4a.rb** file and add the following code. We are essentially introducing a new class to list the users and defining the iterator that will iterate through the list of users and assign index values using the **.each_with_index** method:

```
class UserLister
  def initialize(users)
    @users = users
  end
  def perform
    @users.each_with_index do |user, idx|
      puts "User #{idx}: #{user}"
    end
  end
end
```

2. Create a new file, **exercise_4b.rb**, with the following code to call our service object:

```
require "./exercise_4a"
users = ['John', 'Susy', 'Sarah', 'James']
UserLister.new(users).perform
```

3. Run the **exercise_4b.rb** script:

```
ruby exercise_4b.rb
```

The output should be as follows:

```
User 0: John
User 1: Susy
User 2: Sarah
User 3: James
```

Figure 7.10: Output for a service object

Knowing when to use a module and when to use a service object is more obvious in a real-world application when there are more data objects, functionality, and state objects to think about. Generally, a module is more of a collection of one-time helper functions, such as formatters or converters, whereas service objects can be instantiated with an initial state and can be used to manipulate and mutate data over a series of operations. Instantiated service objects are also available to be passed into methods such as values, whereas modules are "included" in the class with no state.

For example, you may pass an instantiated service object that returns a mutated listing of users into another service object that interacts with the outputted users.

Activity 7.01: Presenting Voting Data in CSV Format Using Ruby Gems

In this activity, we're going to put into practice everything that we've learned in this chapter. We're going to expand our voting program, initiated in *Chapter 4*, *Methods*, to allow the importing of external voting data from a CSV file, and we're also going to improve our user experience by using the **terminal-table** gem to print our vote results to the Terminal in a nice, readable, formatted table.

We will build this new code into service objects so that we don't pollute our models with this extended functionality. Then, finally, we'll write a few new tests to wrap everything up and make sure our code is doing what we expect it to. To do this, perform the following steps:

1. Start by creating a new folder, **services** (at the same level as **models**).

2. Require everything from this directory into our application by adding the **service.rb** file in the top level of our application. In this file, add the following line of code:

```
Dir["./services/*rb"].each { |f| require f }
```

3. Now **require** this file in **application.rb** at the top, underneath the line requiring the **controller.rb** file. It should now look like the following:

```
# require all files in models and controllers directory
require './model'
require './controller'
require './service'
```

4. Create a folder called **fixtures** under the **tests** folder, and then download the **votes.csv** file from https://packt.live/2OzNN6a. It should contain the following data:

```
category,votee,count
VoteCategoryA,Chris Jones,23
VoteCategoryA,Susie Bennet,29
VoteCategoryB,Allan Green,33
VoteCategoryB,Tony Bennet,23
```

5. Create a test to check whether a category exists in the imported **votes.csv** file.

6. Create the service class files, **vote_importer.rb** and **vote_table.rb**, in the **services** directory.

7. In **menu_controller.rb**, add an option to import votes.

8. Add an **import_votes** method to the **voting_machine.rb** model.

9. Add a new **import_controller.rb** controller under the **controllers** folder.

10. Update the **leaderboard_controller.rb** file to now log out tables instead of the raw objects.

11. Create a **votes.csv** file with some test vote data that we can import in the root application directory.

12. Run your solution.

    Here is the expected output:

```
$ ruby application.rb
        ** Welcome to the Employee Of The Month Votathon **
        ** Please enter your choice **
          1. Place a vote for a colleague
          2. See current leaderboard
          3. Add category
          4. Import Votes
          5. Exit
    choice> 4
    Import votes from an external CSV
    Enter the filepath of the CSV file? votes.csv
```

Figure 7.11: Employee of the month voting application

The Leaderboard output would look like:

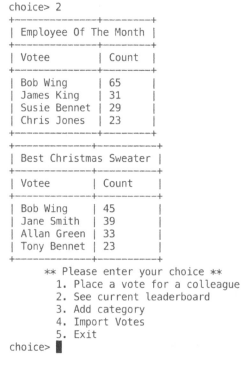

```
choice> 2
+----------------+----------+
| Employee Of The Month |
+----------------+----------+
| Votee          | Count    |
+----------------+----------+
| Bob Wing       | 65       |
| James King     | 31       |
| Susie Bennet   | 29       |
| Chris Jones    | 23       |
+----------------+----------+
+----------------+----------+
| Best Christmas Sweater |
+----------------+----------+
| Votee          | Count    |
+----------------+----------+
| Bob Wing       | 45       |
| Jane Smith     | 39       |
| Allan Green    | 33       |
| Tony Bennet    | 23       |
+----------------+----------+
      ** Please enter your choice **
         1. Place a vote for a colleague
         2. See current leaderboard
         3. Add category
         4. Import Votes
         5. Exit
    choice> █
```

Figure 7.12: Voting application dashboard

> **Note**
>
> The solution to the activity can be found on page 476

Summary

In this chapter, we've covered how to import and export raw CSV data in our application, how to extend the functionality of our applications by including external libraries with Ruby gems, and how to interact with the filesystem using Ruby.

These are powerful tools that can turn our applications from toys into real services with just a few simple lines of code. With these new tools, we can import data from databases, spreadsheets, or any number of other sources and process them programmatically with Ruby in any way we want; the options are endless.

We've also learned some best practices regarding how to structure code that doesn't necessarily fit within our domain models by refactoring them into service objects, keeping our models lean and clean. Your coworkers will thank you for this one, trust me.

An application is only as good as its input and output. We've now learned a few methods by which we can increase how much we input by importing external data, and we've seen how to improve what we output by using external libraries to provide a more user-friendly representation of data.

We can safely say now that we're getting the hang of this. In the next chapter, we will dive a little deeper and go beyond the basics, extending our knowledge of Ruby by looking a little closer at some more advanced functionality.

8

Debugging with Ruby

Overview

By the end of this chapter, you will be able to implement standard logging practices to display application data; create log files and use log levels to segregate and filter logs; perform basic debugging using byebug and Visual Studio Code and use breakpoints and expressions to debug code.

Introduction

In the previous chapter, we learned about extending the functionality of our application with gems, interacting with the filesystem with the `File` and `IO` classes, importing external data using CSV files, and how to wrap all this up in a nicely encapsulated service class.

Software bugs are a fact of life in software engineering. No matter your skill level, bugs always find a way to show up. We can, however, reduce the severity and volume of bugs by improving our knowledge of logging and debugging. A solid understanding of these topics will ensure that, when things go wrong, we're armed with the tools and required knowledge to solve the problem efficiently.

Understanding how and why issues occur is a critical part of software engineering. In this chapter, we're going to learn how to use a proper logging solution to gain visibility of our application's operation rather than just printing variables to the screen.

We'll also learn how to categorize and filter out logs using `log levels`, how to manage the size and retention periods of our log files to prevent our servers from running out of space, and how to customize the appearance of our logs with custom formatters.

We'll learn about some basic debugging tools and we'll also take a look at Terminal-based debugging with byebug, how to step through our code, and how to move through the call stack.

We'll then look at how this is done using a more visual approach, using Visual Studio Code, and how we can conditionally trigger debug breakpoints using expressions.

Logging and Debugging

Logging and debugging are critical aspects of developing and deploying applications in any language. A good log file provides insights into exactly what an application is doing and when.

This is an invaluable resource when things go wrong in a production environment as it enables our applications to be "observed," with the log acting like an activity trace.

For example, when a production application goes down at 3 A.M. and you are responsible for investigating, you will be very happy when you find a nice informative log file waiting for you, as this will be the first place you check.

Effective logging has layers that can be controlled, which allows us to control the verbosity of the log output in order to debug an issue. The perfect logging system provides enough information to be useful, but not so much that it becomes noisy and difficult to read. This is often a hard balance to strike, and this is where "log levels" come into play.

Debugging and logging live within the same realm. They are both diagnostic tools that we can use to observe the operation of our applications. Whereas logging exists at all stages of our application's life cycle, debugging tends to exist mainly in the development environment.

Debugging tools are a critical piece of the puzzle for any software engineer. Without them, we would waste hours and hours of time printing out the values of variables to the screen and manually tracing application behavior.

Thankfully, Ruby has a number of great debugging tools that are at our disposal. We'll cover a few of the most popular ways to perform debugging in this chapter. We'll cover both Terminal- and editor-based debugging so you are fully armed to debug any issues that come your way.

Logging with the logger Class

When you start building a new application, you might intuitively start writing `puts` statements throughout the code in order to expose information to the developer.

We encourage anyone to implement at least a very basic logging framework before you get too deep into a new project. It will save time and hassle later when you decide to implement a proper logging system, not to mention helping you to debug issues earlier.

Most languages either come with standard logging functionality built into the core libraries or have established logging libraries available to be included in the programs.

Python has the `logging` module built into the core language, Java has the excellent `log4j` framework, and Node.js has `Winston` and a number of other packages available for download.

Ruby comes with a very useful `logger` class right out of the box, which makes this job easy.

The Ruby logger is a simple but powerful logging utility that solves multiple common logging problems for you, such as the following:

- **Log rotation**: Rotating or cycling logs is how we prevent our application from creating a huge log file that can't be opened. Log rotation also helps us ensure that logs are sectioned into usable and archivable chunks, rather than one long cumbersome stream of content.

- **Log file size management**: Closely related to log rotation, a good logging solution will also help you manage the size of files. This not only assists us with processing files but helps us to ensure we don't crash a server by filling up its disk space.

- **Logging levels (filtering, development, and production log verbosity)**: In a real-world system, our log file is likely to be full of useful and useless information, depending on the situation and the level of detail you need. A good logging solution gives us control over how to restrict and filter log output.

- **Customizable log formatting**: How do we customize the log output format to be something more to our liking? The ability to make some basic adjustments to how a log is presented can make a big difference when you're reading through thousands of lines of output.

These are common problems for all languages and stacks. Some languages and frameworks will go about solving them in different ways, but any comprehensive solution should at least solve these fundamental problems.

Let's begin with some basic logging fundamentals now.

Basic Logging

Every application log file should include, at a minimum, a few essential pieces of information. The most basic of logging requirements would include some form of category to filter on and a timestamp. Ruby makes this easy for us and gives us a whole lot more.

With just a few simple lines of code, you can implement fully featured standardized logging across your entire application.

Let's look at a basic example:

```
require 'logger'
logger = Logger.new(STDOUT)
logger.debug("User 23643 logged in")
```

Here, we can see the **logger** class being "required" like any other gem, after which we instantiate the class, as the **logger** variable, passing **STDOUT** as the first parameter (more on this soon), and finally, we call **logger.debug** with our message.

When we run this script, we will see the following output:

```
$ ruby logger_basic.rb
D, [2019-08-14T12:17:45.777667 #64647] DEBUG -- : User 23643 logged in
$
```

Figure 8.1: Standard log format

What we're seeing here is the standard log format. This contains:

1. The severity ID
2. The timestamp of the event
3. The Process ID (PID) of the process
4. The severity label
5. The program's name (nil by default)
6. The log message

We get all this information included with every log line, which helps us understand the context of the message.

> **Note**
>
> If you don't like the content or the format of the log output, don't worry – we'll be covering custom formatting options later in the chapter.

Log Levels

A good logging strategy allows for fine-grained control over what goes into our log files and how to filter them. It might feel like searching for a needle in a haystack if you simply dump everything into the log output without any consideration for the severity of the content.

Consider the following example:

```
socket opened - socks 5
closing connection 43463
updated record 45587
updated record 86584
closing connection 56887
updated record 26577
socket opened - socks 5
updated record 67966
closing connection 12433
updated record 67969
closing connection 56887
updated record 26577
updated record 67966
socket unavailable - socks 5
```

```
closing connection 12433
socket opened - socks 5
updated record 67969
closing connection 56887
updated record 26577
socket opened - socks 5
updated record 67966
```

You might wonder what would make this log file easier to read and how we could filter out the informative logs from the error messages.

In this case, there are only 21 lines, but it's still quite hard to spot the error:

```
socket unavailable - socks 5
```

When a log file could be hundreds or even thousands of lines long, you can imagine that it would be incredibly hard to find this line; however, it is the one line in this example that is unique and reporting an error, which makes it an important debugging resource.

So, what would make this better?

For starters, there's no timestamp, so we really have no idea when this error occurred. If we were trying to correlate this error with an error which we detected either upstream or from a client, then this would make it near impossible to line up the timelines.

Next, we have no distinction between what's purely informational and what is reporting critical errors. It's all kind of mixed into one big stream, leaving us with a huge mess we have to dig through manually, reading line by line. We need a mechanism to filter these results or, even better, the ability to enable or disable less relevant logs.

Let's look at this same log file again. This time, as if it had been handled by the **logger** class:

```
I, [2019-07-24T16:15:17 #47525] INFO -- : socket opened - socks 5
I, [2019-07-24T16:15:17 #47525] INFO -- : closing connection 43463
I, [2019-07-24T16:15:19 #47525] INFO -- : updated record 45587
I, [2019-07-24T16:16:22 #47525] INFO -- : updated record 86584
I, [2019-07-24T16:16:23 #47525] INFO -- : closing connection 56887
I, [2019-07-24T16:16:22 #47525] INFO -- : updated record 26577
I, [2019-07-24T16:16:23 #47525] INFO -- : socket opened - socks 5
I, [2019-07-24T16:16:24 #47525] INFO -- : updated record 67966
I, [2019-07-24T16:17:24 #47525] INFO -- : closing connection 12433
I, [2019-07-24T16:27:25 #47525] INFO -- : updated record 67969
I, [2019-07-24T16:17:26 #47525] INFO -- : closing connection 56887
I, [2019-07-24T16:18:26 #47525] INFO -- : updated record 26577
```

```
I, [2019-07-24T16:18:27 #47525] INFO -- : updated record 67966
E, [2019-07-24T16:19:27 #47525] ERROR -- : socket unavailable - socks 5
I, [2019-07-24T16:20:27 #47525] INFO -- : closing connection 12433
I, [2019-07-24T16:21:28 #47525] INFO -- : socket opened - socks 5
I, [2019-07-24T16:21:29 #47525] INFO -- : updated record 67969
I, [2019-07-24T16:22:30 #47525] INFO -- : closing connection 56887
I, [2019-07-24T16:23:31 #47525] INFO -- : updated record 26577
I, [2019-07-24T16:24:31 #47525] INFO -- : socket opened - socks 5
I, [2019-07-24T16:26:32 #47525] INFO -- : updated record 67966
```

That's much easier to read.

Even better, we can use basic shell commands to filter out all the junk and simply show us the errors we're looking for:

```
cat log.txt | grep ERROR
E, [2019-07-24T16:26:16.216648 #47525] ERROR -- : socket unavailable - socks 5
```

We could have thousands of lines in the log file but now we can see those that matter the most in an instant.

So, how is it that we're able to mark these lines as **ERROR** and the others as **INFO**? These are what are referred to as log levels, and when using the `logger` class they are available to us by using the **Logger** instance methods that log specific severity levels. These levels are:

- **DEBUG**

- **INFO**

- **WARN**

- **ERROR**

- **FATAL**

As you may have guessed, these have specific purposes that indicate the severity of the log message. Consider the following example:

```
require 'logger'
logger = Logger.new(STDOUT)
logger.debug("debug")
logger.info("info")
logger.warn("warn")
logger.error("error")
logger.fatal("fatal")
```

The preceding code will output the following log lines:

```
D, [2019-07-29T21:19:54.689147 #71263] DEBUG -- : debug
I, [2019-07-29T21:19:54.689246 #71263]  INFO -- : info
W, [2019-07-29T21:19:54.689261 #71263]  WARN -- : warn
E, [2019-07-29T21:19:54.689271 #71263] ERROR -- : error
F, [2019-07-29T21:19:54.689292 #71263] FATAL -- : fatal
```

As you can see, simply calling the relevant method will output the log line tagged with the particular log level.

Let's study each log level in detail:

- **DEBUG**: This is used for debugging and is generally disabled in production. It is generally used either during the development stages or turned on in order to gather as much information as possible. Typically, this is the information we don't want to log once an application is stable.

- **INFO**: This is used for general messages and often for diagnostic or tracking purposes. It is generally a good choice for regular production logs as we exclude **DEBUG** messages but see everything else.

  Used for standard informational log messages, it may include general information such as diagnostics, process information, job statistics, user authentications, general request information, and so on.

- **WARN**: This is generally used for warning, but not necessarily error messages; for example, `retry attempt #2` or `Slow query detected`.

  If you have particularly noisy logs (say, thousands of lines per minute), this might be a better choice for production systems as the logs will contain only important information. You can always drop back to **INFO** if you need more details to debug an issue.

- **ERROR**: This is used for error messages and exceptions. For example, when capturing an exception, in the rescue block, you would perform a logger error. Another example is when making API calls to an external service; if you receive a non-HTTP 200 response, you may wish to log that as an error.

- **FATAL**: This is used for critical application failures. Log what information you can before the application terminates.

  This is less commonly used in long-running processes such as web servers, but in the case of a console application or a standalone script, you would typically log a **FATAL** error message when encountering a non-recoverable error, just before terminating the program.

Let's look at some more examples of how to use the log levels:

```ruby
require 'logger'
logger = Logger.new(STDOUT)
logger.info("Starting Application")
begin
  0 / 0
rescue StandardError => e
  logger.error(e.message)
end
```

Here's a basic example of handling errors with the correct log level. In this example, we've manually caused an exception by dividing 0 by 0. If we run this code, we'll see the following:

```
I, [2019-07-29T22:01:09.029434 #72692]  INFO -- : Starting Application
E, [2019-07-29T22:01:09.029512 #72692] ERROR -- : divided by 0
```

Let's now solve an exercise with a more interesting scenario.

Exercise 8.01: Logging User Information

A web application allows only three users to be logged in at a time. In this exercise, we'll build a logging system that will display a warning log when more than three users are logged in to the application. The following steps will help you with the solution:

1. Import the **logger** class by using the **require** method:

   ```ruby
   require 'logger'
   ```

2. Define the **logger** variables with the **STDOUT** parameter and display the messages:

   ```ruby
   logger = Logger.new(STDOUT)
   logger.info("Starting Application")
   ```

3. Define the users in an array:

   ```ruby
   users = ["Matt", "Pete", "Brenton", "Geoff"]
   ```

4. Next, we need to state the conditions for the warning log to display the names of the users if more than three users are logged in:

```
if users.length > 3
  logger.warn("Warning, there are #{users.length} users")
end
users.each do |user|
  logger.debug("User: #{user}")
end
```

5. Close the log by using a display message:

```
logger.info("Finishing Application")
```

Thus, we have used the **DEBUG**, **INFO**, and **WARN** log levels.

The output log should look as follows:

```
I, [2019-08-20T05:09:29.250171 #10]  INFO -- : Starting Application
W, [2019-08-20T05:09:29.250198 #10]  WARN -- : Warning, there are 4 users
D, [2019-08-20T05:09:29.250206 #10] DEBUG -- : User: Matt
D, [2019-08-20T05:09:29.250212 #10] DEBUG -- : User: Pete
D, [2019-08-20T05:09:29.250217 #10] DEBUG -- : User: Brenton
D, [2019-08-20T05:09:29.250222 #10] DEBUG -- : User: Geoff
I, [2019-08-20T05:09:29.250226 #10]  INFO -- : Finishing Application
```

Figure 8.2: Log output

At this point, you might be thinking that the **DEBUG** lines aren't so useful and that you would like them to not appear in your logs as it's making them appear too noisy. You could go and remove every instance where you've called *logger.debug* but that would be a pain, and it's possible you might need them again in the near future.

To filter them out, simply add the following line:

```
logger.level = Logger::INFO
```

This statement indicates that we are to display logs that are at the **INFO** level and higher.

If you remember, the log levels listed before those levels are actually in that particular order for a reason:

Figure 8.3: Order of log levels

When we declare the log level as **INFO**, we are saying that we only want to see logs from the **INFO** level and above; that is, **INFO**, **WARN**, **ERROR**, and **FATAL**, but not **DEBUG**.

If we set the logger level as follows, then, we'll only see the **ERROR** and **FATAL** logs:

```
logger.level = Logger::ERROR
```

So, in the preceding example, which lists out our names, we could change the log level to **INFO**, as shown in the following example:

```
require 'logger'
logger = Logger.new(STDOUT)
logger.level = Logger::INFO
logger.info("Starting Application")
users = ["Matt", "Pete", "Brenton", "Geoff"]
...
```

Then, if we run that same code again, we'll see the following:

```
I, [2019-07-29T22:18:07.640570 #72877]  INFO -- : Starting Application
W, [2019-07-29T22:18:07.640647 #72877]  WARN -- : Warning, there are 4 users
I, [2019-07-29T22:18:07.640664 #72877]  INFO -- : Finishing Application
```

We've successfully filtered out all the **DEBUG** log messages with one line of code, and we can just as easily bring the filtered logs back when we need them.

Alternatively, if we want to shorten this code, we can also specify the log level within the call to the initializer, as follows:

```
logger = Logger.new(STDOUT, level: Logger::ERROR)
```

Let's try creating a basic exception logger for ourselves now.

Exercise 8.02: Creating a Basic Exception Logger

In this exercise, we will use the zero-division example from *Chapter 7, Ruby Gems* to demonstrate the usage of log levels:

1. Import the **logger** class by using the **require** method:

    ```
    require 'logger'
    ```

2. Define the **logger** variables with the **STDOUT** parameter and display the messages:

    ```
    logger = Logger.new(STDOUT)
    logger.info("Starting Application")
    ```

3. Now, we'll introduce a zero-division error and log the corresponding error message:

```
begin
  0 / 0
rescue StandardError => e
  logger.error(e.message)
end
```

We should now see the following output, demonstrating an exception being reported at the **error** log level:

```
I, [2019-08-20T05:17:01.456490 #11]  INFO -- : Starting Application
E, [2019-08-20T05:17:01.456530 #11] ERROR -- : divided by 0
I, [2019-08-20T05:17:01.456539 #11]  INFO -- : Finishing Application
```

Figure 8.4: Error log level output

This is how we can build logging systems, depending on the required log levels.

Setting Log Levels by String

You may wish to configure the log level for your application with an environment variable named **LOG_LEVEL** or some sort of configuration file when an application starts. In which case, setting the **logger.level** using the **Logger::Info** constant is a bit tricky. Thankfully, the **logger** class allows us to use a string instead of a constant if we want, so we can configure the log level from an external config input, such as environment variables or a config file. For example, we can do the following:

```
logger = Logger.new(STDOUT, level: "error")
```

Or, we could store this string in an environment variable named **LOG_LEVEL**:

```
logger = Logger.new(STDOUT, level: ENV["LOG_LEVEL"])
```

In this example, the **LOG_LEVEL** environment variable would simply contain a string, such as **error**.

Log Output

Up until now, we've been printing log lines to the console or, more specifically, to what's called **standard output**.

The Ruby **logger** class supports three main output destinations:

- **STDOUT** (standard output)
- **STDERR** (standard error)
- **File** (write to a file)

STDOUT

If you remember, we have been instantiating our **logger** instance with the following:

```
logger = Logger.new(STDOUT)
```

That **STDOUT** parameter passed into the initializer is a Ruby *predefined global constant* that represents the standard output.

> **Note**
>
> You can see global constants defined in the Ruby docs, here:
>
> https://packt.live/33mla0q
>
> As you might infer from the name, standard output is where standard text is sent when you print the text to the console.

Consider the following example:

```
puts "some text"
```

This will simply write **some text** to the standard output, which will appear normally on your Terminal screen.

Another example is the simple **echo** command in your Terminal. Calling **echo test** from your command line will simply write text to the standard output, which appears on your screen like any other output.

STDERR

Living side by side with **STDOUT** is **STDERR**, which represents the *Standard Error output*. As you may have guessed, this works much like **STDOUT**, except that **STDERR** is where you send error output. It provides a way for a program to split regular informational output from error output.

STDOUT and **STDERR**, or the standard output and the standard error output, are what are known as *standard streams*.

Standard streams are a mechanism in computer programming that connects standard input and output channels for a program on an operating system level for the purpose of exporting information from a program or accepting input. There are three main input and output channels, known as **standard input** (**stdin**), **standard output** (**stdout**), and **standard error** (**stderr**).

We don't need to go too deeply into this subject; how these channels work is outside of the scope of this book, although they are common across all languages and operating systems. For now, we just simply want to understand what they are and when to use them.

> **Note**
>
> Streams can be split into separate log files so that **STDERR** logs appear in an **error_log** file and **STDOUT** appears in a log file. This can help get to the root cause of a problem quickly without the need to filter large log files

File

The third output destination is **File**. As you may expect, this is the one we use when we wish to write our log output to a file on the filesystem.

Writing logs to a file is simple using the **logger** class:

```ruby
require 'logger'
logger = Logger.new("log.txt")
logger.debug("User 23643 logged in")
```

Running this script will result in no output to the screen; instead, it will create a new file, **log.txt**, if it doesn't already exist, and write the log line to it:

```
# Logfile created on 2019-07-31 15:32:53 +1000 by logger.rb/61378
D, [2019-07-31T15:32:53.016056 #94993] DEBUG -- : User 23643 logged in
```

You'll also notice that we get a nice little comment line up top there that details the date and time the file was created.

So, what happens when we rerun that same script a few more times? Let's take a look:

```
# Logfile created on 2019-07-31 15:32:53 +1000 by logger.rb/61378
D, [2019-07-31T15:32:53.016056 #94993] DEBUG -- : User 23643 logged in
D, [2019-07-31T15:33:07.560270 #95059] DEBUG -- : User 23643 logged in
D, [2019-07-31T15:33:09.810580 #95096] DEBUG -- : User 23643 logged in
```

As you can see, it will simply reopen the same file and append lines to it rather than creating a new blank file, which is obviously handy if we don't want to reset our log file every time our application restarts.

Log Formatting

Wouldn't it be nice if we could change the way the logs looked? Maybe we don't want all that information or maybe we just find that line hard to read. Thankfully, the **Logger** class has got us covered here again, by allowing us to configure the format of the log output in a few different ways.

Custom Date Formats

The 2019-07-31T15:33:09.810580 date format can be quite confusing to read. This is a commonly understood date format called ISO-8601, which is great for parsing in code, but what about if we just want something more human-readable?

> **Note**
>
> Before implementing a custom date format on your application, always be sure there are no other applications or processes that ingest or process those logs; otherwise, this is likely to result in broken integrations and reports or drastically incorrect times being reported to dependent services.

As an example, let's say we only want the time, in a shorter and cleaner 12-hour format, without the date on the timestamp.

Here is how we can do that:

```
require 'logger'
logger = Logger.new(STDOUT)
logger.datetime_format = "%I:%M:%S%P "
logger.debug("User 23643 logged in")
```

Running this script will output the following:

```
D, [08:43:01pm #78283] DEBUG -- : User 23643 logged in
```

Here is the **logger.datatime_format** line:

```
logger.datetime_format = "%I:%M:%S%P "
```

Each of the % (letter) portions of the string represents a component of the date that we wish to render into a date string. In this case, they are:

- **%I** = Hour of the day, 12-hour clock, zero-padded (01..12)

- **%M** = Minute of the hour (00..59)

- **%S** = Second of the minute (00..59)

- **%P** = Meridian indicator, lowercase (a.m. or p.m.)

Everything else, such as the : and the space are plain string characters.

What about if we wanted the whole date and time but in a much more human-readable format? Consider the following:

```
require 'logger'
logger = Logger.new(STDOUT)
logger.datetime_format = "%h %d %Y - %I:%M:%S%P "
logger.debug("User 23643 logged in")
```

This would give us the following:

```
D, [Jul 31 2019 - 08:58:06pm #78856] DEBUG -- : User 23643 logged in
```

Now that's a very readable timestamp.

This could potentially cause problems with your application considering time zone differences, external systems that ingest the log files, international users, and so on.

> **Note**
>
> There is a large selection of formatting options you can choose from to suit your needs.
>
> You can visit https://packt.live/2nNPx0G for more information.

Dealing with time can be tricky when it comes to the matter of time zones. If your server is set to the UTC time zone, then these times may not appear as you expect. Be sure to check what time zone your server uses so there's no confusion. The **logger** class will use whatever time zone your server is set to by default.

Custom String Formats

Changing the date is handy, but what about if you want to change the whole line? Maybe we want a simpler format that's easier to parse. Well, the **logger** class has got you covered again.

We can do this by using **Logger** formatters:

```
require 'logger'
logger = Logger.new(STDOUT)
logger.formatter = proc do |severity, datetime, progname, msg|
  "#{severity} | #{datetime} | #{msg}\n"
end
logger.debug("User 23643 logged in")
```

This outputs a log line that looks like this:

```
DEBUG | 2019-07-31 21:10:54 +1000 | User 23643 logged in
```

Better yet, when we use the log file, the content will line up nicely, like this:

```
DEBUG | 2019-07-31 21:10:54 +1000 | User 23643 logged in
DEBUG | 2019-07-31 21:10:55 +1000 | another log
DEBUG | 2019-07-31 21:10:55 +1000 | another log again
DEBUG | 2019-07-31 21:10:55 +1000 | and another one
```

Pretty clean, right? So, what's happening here. Let's take a look:

```
logger.formatter = proc do |severity, datetime, progname, msg|
  "#{severity} | #{datetime} | #{msg}\n"
end
```

Here, we're providing a **formatter** in the form of **proc**. A **proc** object is essentially like an encapsulated function that has been scoped to a **local set** of variables. In this case, we have access to the **severity**, **datetime**, **progname**, and **msg** variables, which map to the components of the original timestamp we saw earlier.

We simply put them together to return a string of our own choosing; in this case:

```
"#{severity} | #{datetime} | #{msg}\n"
```

Now, anytime we call a **logger print** function, this **proc** object is executed and the string we choose is the output.

Time Zones and UTC

The current server time zone is used for the timestamp. Simply changing your server's time zone will update the timestamps with the relevant time zone offset; however, you may also wish to include a UTC timestamp. Typically, services that deal with international requirements or integrate with external systems represent time as UTC time as it is not localized and is not specific to any particular country.

We can include a UTC timestamp in the preceding example by simply changing the output line to also print a UTC-cast version of the timestamp, as follows:

```
require 'logger'
logger = Logger.new(STDOUT)
logger.formatter = proc do |severity, datetime, progname, msg|
  "#{severity} | #{datetime.zone}: #{datetime} | UTC: #{datetime.utc} | #{msg}\n"
end
logger.debug("User 23643 logged in")
```

This will output the following:

```
DEBUG | AEST: 2019-08-14 09:56:58 +1000 | UTC: 2019-08-13 23:56:58 UTC | User 23643
logged in
```

Log File Management

`Log files` tend to be one of those things that grow out of control over time.

Our application continues running, doing its job day in and day out until one day it crashes.

You respond and immediately start debugging the issue until you quickly realize there's nothing wrong with the application; the server ran out of disk space – an 80 GB log file being the root cause of the problem.

You can avoid this issue by configuring log retention and rollover. This will ensure that you keep only the number of logs that you specify and you "roll over" what you don't need.

You can take two different strategies here in regard to file retention.

Size-Based Retention

If you have limited disk space to work with, you can specify the exact size of the log files and the number of them to keep before they are erased from disk.

For example, you could say "*I want my logs files to be no larger than 100 MB each, and I'll keep up to 5 of them, for a total maximum of 500 MB of log files.*"

You may wish to have a separate process, such as a **cron** job or a Windows scheduled job to copy or back up your log files to a storage location, such as Amazon S3 or another attached volume for historical records. Once the **Logger** class has reached the file retention limit, the oldest (what would now be the sixth in the preceding example) is deleted from disk.

A simple backup example might be to use a tool such as **rsync** to copy your files to another system for safekeeping.

Restricting the size of your log files is good if you have a fairly consistent workload and you attribute an amount of data to a rough timeline. Say, I know that 10 MB data is roughly half a day.

If you happen to log a lot of information, then obviously you may fill up this fixed size too quickly.

Let's look at the following example:

```ruby
require 'logger'
log_size = 100 * 1024 * 1024
log_limit = 5
logger = Logger.new("log.txt", log_limit, log_size)
logger.debug("User 23643 logged in")
```

It's just that simple to implement log file size retention. We pass the number of files we wish to retain as the first argument followed by the maximum size of the files as the second argument, specified as a number of bytes (100 * 1024 * 1024 = 104857600, which in bytes is roughly 100 MB).

> **Note**
>
> The official Ruby documentation refers to these second and third parameters as the logs **shift age** and **shift size** logs.

The log file looks the same as usual, however, once the log file reaches the size limit (100 MB), then the **Logger** class will automatically create a new file named **log.txt** and rename the previous log file, which is now 100 MB in size, to **log.txt.0**.

This log file has now been "rolled over." So, what happens when the new **log.txt** file reaches 100 MB in size? The same process happens again except **log.txt.0** is renamed to **log.txt.1** and then **log.txt** is renamed to **log.txt.0**, and so on. Basically, you will end up with a history of log files named **log.txt**, **log.txt.0**, **log.txt.1**, **log.txt.2**, and **log.txt.3**.

> **Note**
>
> Some operating systems have this sort of functionality, built in. ***nix systems**, for example, can leverage a tool called **logrotate** to do a similar thing.

Time-Based Retention

The other option for log file retention is time-based retention. Simply put, this means we can roll over our logs on a daily, weekly, or monthly basis. This might be a better choice if the historical value of your logs is important.

For example, if you were informed that, on certain dates, your application was experiencing errors, it would be much easier to narrow down the logs to inspect if you kept daily log files rather than simply keeping 100 MB log files, which may contain any number of days' worth of logs. Here's how we do this:

```
require 'logger'
logger = Logger.new("log.txt", "daily")
logger.debug("User 23643 logged in")
```

Again, we just supply a second argument to the initializer or "shift age." Our options here are **daily**, **weekly**, and **monthly**.

Consider the following example:

```
logger = Logger.new("log.txt", "daily")
logger = Logger.new("log.txt", "weekly")
logger = Logger.new("log.txt", "monthly")
```

Internally, the **Logger** class will evaluate the timestamp of the file and determine whether it needs to roll over the log file or not. When it does, it will append a short timestamp to the end of the filename.

Upon roll over, we should see a file that looks like **log.txt.20190731**.

> **Note**
>
> If you are building an application in a Docker container, your application will need to write all its logs to **STDOUT**. You won't need to rotate log files at the application level.

Exercise 8.03: Creating a Rolling Log File

We've learned about log retention and how it can roll over log files at a specific time or size. Let's put this into practice by creating a log file that will "roll over." We'll set the size to 100 bytes so we can see the log files being created for ourselves each time we call the script:

1. Create the **log_test.rb** file and write the following code:

```ruby
require 'logger'
log_bytes = 100
log_limit = 5
logger = Logger.new("log.txt", log_limit, log_bytes)
logger.debug("Testing Log Rollover")
```

This will instantiate a new **Logger** class, specifying the **log.txt** file as the output. We're also configuring the number of log files to keep and the maximum size of each log file by supplying the second and third parameters to the initializer.

2. Run the following script:

```
ruby log_test.rb
```

3. In the current directory that the script resides in, you will now see a new log file named **log.txt**. There should be only one **log.txt** file. View the contents of this file.

4. Run the script another six times and check the directory. You should see five files named as follows:

```
$ ls | grep log.txt
log.txt
log.txt.0
log.txt.1
log.txt.2
log.txt.3
$
```

Figure 8.5: Rolling log output

Debugging

Debugging is one of the most important aspects of software development. Bugs are simply a fact of life for a software engineer. You can't avoid them, but you can get better at tracking them down and, most importantly, solving them quickly.

Even the best software engineers will write bugs from time to time. Having the right tools and knowing how to use them to solve a problem quickly is one of the most useful skills you can learn with any programming language.

When you start out writing Ruby, you will probably debug your application by simply writing **puts** statements everywhere, logging out the values of your variables to understand what's happening. This will become painful soon enough and you'll want to start using some more powerful tools and interacting with the code at runtime.

We're going to cover the basics of some of the most popular debugging solutions here, both from the command line and from the editor. By the end, you'll have a much better understanding of how to step through your code line by line, evaluate functions midway through program execution, and view the contents of variables without writing a single **puts** statement.

Let's get to it.

Debugging Concepts

We need to understand some basic debugging theory before we get started. This will be referred to throughout the chapter.

Breakpoints, call stacks, and debugger stepping are not specific to Ruby. These concepts are common to most languages, so it's worth taking a moment to grasp them properly.

Let's take a look at some fundamental debugging concepts we will want to grasp before we dive into debugging code.

Breakpoints

A breakpoint is a point in your code at which you can pause program execution and take a look around the current application state.

Variable values and **application state** will be available to view from your debugger at that particular point in time, which is incredibly useful for doing things such as inspecting the value of a variable or calling a particular function from a particular point in the code.

In an editor such as Visual Studio Code, a breakpoint is usually set and indicated by a red dot in the left-hand column of the editor.

The following screenshot shows an example of the Visual Studio Code editor with two breakpoints set on lines **7** and **14**:

```
 4    logger = Logger.new(STDOUT)
 5    logger.level = Logger::INFO|
 6    logger.info("Starting Application")
●7    users = ["Matt", "Pete", "Brenton", "Geoff"]
 8
 9    if users.length > 3
10      logger.warn("Warning, there are #{users.length} users")
11    end
12
13    users.each do |user|
●14      logger.debug("User: #{user}")
15    end
16
17    logger.info("Finishing Application")
```

Figure 8.6: Breakpoints while debugging

When the debugger stops at a breakpoint, we will have access to the variables that have been assigned up until that point.

For example, in the preceding screenshot, when the debugger stops (often referred to as breaking) on line 7, we will be able to access the **logger** object, but not the **users** array. This is because the **users** array has not been assigned yet (we stopped on this line before it was executed).

> **Note**
>
> When we stop at a breakpoint, we have not yet executed that particular line of code. You must step to the next line in order to evaluate it.

However, when we stop on line 14, we will have access to the **logger** object and the **users** array because the **users** array has now been assigned in the previous lines. Furthermore, on line 14, we will have access to the locally scoped **user** variable for that iteration of the **each** loop.

Using breakpoints with Terminal-based debugging is a little different but works in much the same way. Using a Terminal debugger such as **byebug** or **pry**, we can achieve the same breakpoint functionality by inserting a call to **byebug** in our code, which will halt program execution once we reach it and provide us with a command line to look around and inspect the currently assigned objects and variables.

> **Note**
>
> Pry is a more powerful replacement version of IRB that offers some more advanced features, such as source code browsing and syntax highlighting.

Stack Trace/Call Stack/Back Trace

The call stack is the stack of operations at the current time of execution, whereas the stack trace can be thought of as a historical stack of operations that may not be current, it is a representation of a call stack. A stack trace is more likely to appear in an error log. A back trace is just another term for stack trace.

All of these equate to essentially the same thing for our purposes, which is a record of a trail of calling functions up until a given point of time, but for reference, when using a debugger, we're generally interacting with the call stack.

You will often hear people refer to these three interchangeably.

Imagine you drove through the middle of a busy city, turning left, then right, then right, then left again, then straight, then left, and so on. You can imagine that this may be hard to remember, but a call stack, in this example, would be a record of which turns you made at which streets in order to wind up where you are now.

Consider the following example:

```
require 'byebug'
def func1
  func2
end
def func2
  func3
end
def func3
  byebug
end
func1
```

This simple example has three functions that each call the next: **func1** calls **func2**, which calls **func3**. On line 12, we have inserted a breakpoint using **byebug** (we'll cover this more in a moment).

The program will halt at this line and allow us to inspect the environment. At this point, if we were to view the stack trace, we would see the functions listed, and the line numbers at which the code entered the functions, something like the following:

```
"debugger_stacktrace.rb:13:in 'func3'",
"debugger_stacktrace.rb:8:in 'func2'",
"debugger_stacktrace.rb:4:in 'func1'",
"debugger_stacktrace.rb:15:
```

These are sometimes referred to as the "frames" of a stack trace. As you can imagine, when you have a very large application with hundreds or thousands of files – say, for example, a payment processing system or a web application running on top of a framework with many layers of abstraction – a trace like this can be very helpful when tracking down problems. It's like a breadcrumb trail for your application's execution.

Viewing the Stack Trace

When you are stopped at a breakpoint or in a byebug session, you can view the stack trace by simply typing **caller**:

```
    9: users.each do |user|
   10:    byebug
=> 11: end
(byebug) caller
["/Users/cheyne/.rbenv/versions/2.3.8/lib/ruby/gems/2.3.0/gems/byebug-11.0.1/lib/byebug/he
lpers/eval.rb:61:in `eval'", "/Users/cheyne/.rbenv/versions/2.3.8/lib/ruby/gems/2.3.0/gems
/byebug-11.0.1/lib/byebug/helpers/eval.rb:61:in `safe_eval'", "/Users/cheyne/.rbenv/versio
ns/2.3.8/lib/ruby/gems/2.3.0/gems/byebug-11.0.1/lib/byebug/helpers/eval.rb:55:in `warning_
eval'", "/Users/cheyne/.rbenv/versions/2.3.8/lib/ruby/gems/2.3.0/gems/byebug-11.0.1/lib/by
ebug/helpers/eval.rb:31:in `block in multiple_thread_eval'", "/Users/cheyne/.rbenv/version
s/2.3.8/lib/ruby/gems/2.3.0/gems/byebug-11.0.1/lib/byebug/helpers/eval.rb:94:in `allowing_
other_threads'", "/Users/cheyne/.rbenv/versions/2.3.8/lib/ruby/gems/2.3.0/gems/byebug-11.0
.1/lib/byebug/helpers/eval.rb:31:in `multiple_thread_eval'", "/Users/cheyne/.rbenv/version
s/2.3.8/lib/ruby/gems/2.3.0/gems/byebug-11.0.1/lib/byebug/processors/command_processor.rb:
163:in `block in run_cmd'", "/Users/cheyne/.rbenv/versions/2.3.8/lib/ruby/gems/2.3.0/gems/
byebug-11.0.1/lib/byebug/processors/command_processor.rb:168:in `safely'", "/Users/cheyne/
.rbenv/versions/2.3.8/lib/ruby/gems/2.3.0/gems/byebug-11.0.1/lib/byebug/processors/command
_processor.rb:159:in `run_cmd'", "/Users/cheyne/.rbenv/versions/2.3.8/lib/ruby/gems/2.3.0/
gems/byebug-11.0.1/lib/byebug/processors/command_processor.rb:133:in `repl'", "/Users/chey
ne/.rbenv/versions/2.3.8/lib/ruby/gems/2.3.0/gems/byebug-11.0.1/lib/byebug/processors/comm
and_processor.rb:97:in `process_commands'", "/Users/cheyne/.rbenv/versions/2.3.8/lib/ruby/
gems/2.3.0/gems/byebug-11.0.1/lib/byebug/processors/command_processor.rb:77:in `at_return'
", "/Users/cheyne/.rbenv/versions/2.3.8/lib/ruby/gems/2.3.0/gems/byebug-11.0.1/lib/byebug/
context.rb:130:in `at_return'", "byebug_example.rb:11:in `block in <main>'", "byebug_examp
le.rb:9:in `each'", "byebug_example.rb:9:in `<main>'"]
(byebug) 
```

Figure 8.7: Stack trace using caller

The stack trace actually contains a lot more lines than we usually need, including internal Ruby code and debugger library code, but you can generally see your code listed toward the very end of the trace.

StepOver, StepInto, and StepOut

We've learned a little about the call stack now, which leads us to **StepOver**, **StepInto**, and **StepOut**. These are common terms used across all programming languages' debugging tools.

Sometimes, they are labeled differently or have slightly different sounding names, but in general they mean the same thing and that is to move about the call stack in some particular way, generally just referred to as *stepping through your code.*

Not all debuggers use the same terminology for stepping. The concept is the same but the icons or wording may be different.

StepOver generally means to move onto the next executable line of code; however, this will also step over function calls so we can debug the return value without stepping through the sub-function line by line. Consider the following example:

```
1    def func1
2      puts 'test'
3    end
4    func1
5
```

Figure 8.8: The StepOver output

In the preceding example, our breakpoint is set before calling the **func1** method. If we were to **StepOver** at this point in time, **func1** would be executed as normal and the program would end. The call to **func1** will have been *stepped over*.

This does not mean the call to **func1** was skipped from the program execution; the debugger just simply did not **StepInto** the function call.

StepInto means to step into a function and debug it line by line. Be aware that this may mean diving into framework and non-user application code. If you want to trace the full path of code execution, you'll want to use **StepInto**. Consider the following example:

```
1    def func1
2      puts 'test'
3    end
4    func1
5
```

Figure 8.9: StepInto output

Like our previous example, our breakpoint is set before the call to **func1**. This time, we have used **StepInto** instead and the debugger has now "stepped into" the lower function call. This may continue to go deeper and deeper depending on what functions are called next.

To **StepOut**, we'll step back out to the line where the current function was called.

Essentially, it's as if we had called **StepOver** instead of **StepInto** previously, but from a point in the code that we've already stepped into.

Debugging via the CLI with byebug

byebug is a Terminal-based debugger. It's very easy to set up and use and comes with enough useful features to cover most use cases.

To install **byebug**, simply install the **gem** package with the following:

```
gem install byebug
```

If you have ever programmed in JavaScript and used the **debugger** statement, **byebug** will feel similar but with a much more extensive set of features.

So, let's see it in action:

```
require 'byebug'
def reversed(name)
  name.reverse
end
users = ["Matt", "Pete", "Brenton", "Geoff"]
users.each do |user|
  byebug
end
```

Here, we have a basic example: an array of users, a basic function that returns a reversed version of the name parameter, and a loop that iterates over the users' names. We have added the **byebug** statement inside the loop, so we're going to get a **byebug** prompt on every iteration of the loop.

Calling **byebug** like this is a method call so it's not technically a breakpoint. It works in a similar way; however, **byebug** has a different meaning for what a breakpoint is internally and also offers the ability to set breakpoints via the byebug console.

Let's run this code. The output should look like the following figure:

```
$ ruby byebug_example.rb
Return value is: nil

[2, 11] in /Users/cheyne/Dropbox/Ruby-Fundamentals/Debugging/byebug_example.rb
    2:
    3: def reversed(name)
    4:   name.reverse
    5: end
    6:
    7: users = ["Matt", "Pete", "Brenton", "Geoff"]
    8:
    9: users.each do |user|
   10:   byebug
=> 11: end
(byebug) █
```

Figure 8.10: Debugging with byebug

As you can see, byebug has stopped on the line directly after our **byebug** statement. It then presents us with a prompt, with which we can inspect the current environment.

This session is what's known as a **REPL**, which stands for a **READ EVAL PRINT LOOP**. **IRB** and pry are other examples of a REPL in Ruby. REPLs allow you to type and evaluate code in real time without having to rerun the program:

```
$ ruby byebug_example.rb
Return value is: nil

[2, 11] in /Users/cheyne/Dropbox/Ruby-Fundamentals/Debugging/byebug_example.rb
    2:
    3: def reversed(name)
    4:   name.reverse
    5: end
    6:
    7: users = ["Matt", "Pete", "Brenton", "Geoff"]
    8:
    9: users.each do |user|
   10:   byebug
=> 11: end
(byebug) user
"Matt"
(byebug) users.last
"Geoff"
(byebug) reversed user
"ttaM"
(byebug) var local
user = Matt
users = ["Matt", "Pete", "Brenton", "Geoff"]
(byebug) █
```

Figure 8.11: Variable inspection in byebug

From this prompt, we can inspect variables, call functions, and pretty much do anything we would normally do in code.

You can see from the preceding screenshot that we're able to inspect the current user in the iteration by simply typing **user**. We grab the last user of the **users** array by calling the last method on the array, and we even call our own function by reversing the order.

A very useful command byebug offers us is the **var** command, which lists variable values for us. As you can see on the last lines of the preceding screenshot, running the **var** command, the local **var** local prints out the values of all local variables so we don't need to inspect them one by one. Pretty cool, right?

At this point, we want to move on with the program execution. We type **continue** or just **c**, which will continue the program execution until the next time a breakpoint or a call to **byebug** occurs.

In this case, it will be the very next iteration of the loop, which will be the next user in the **users** array:

```
[2, 11] in /Users/cheyne/Dropbox/Ruby-Fundamentals/Debugging/byebug_example.rb
    2:
    3: def reversed(name)
    4:   name.reverse
    5: end
    6:
    7: users = ["Matt", "Pete", "Brenton", "Geoff"]
    8:
    9: users.each do |user|
   10:   byebug
=> 11: end
(byebug) user
"Pete"
(byebug) c
Return value is: nil

[2, 11] in /Users/cheyne/Dropbox/Ruby-Fundamentals/Debugging/byebug_example.rb
    2:
    3: def reversed(name)
    4:   name.reverse
    5: end
    6:
    7: users = ["Matt", "Pete", "Brenton", "Geoff"]
    8:
    9: users.each do |user|
   10:   byebug
=> 11: end
(byebug) user
"Brenton"
(byebug) ▮
```

Figure 8.12: Stepping from one breakpoint to another

In the preceding example, we're essentially stepping from breakpoint to breakpoint.

Conditional Debugging

Using byebug like this is not technically a breakpoint because we're actually just calling a function named **byebug**, which enters the debugging prompt.

This is actually very useful because if we're just calling a method, then we can use it like any other code, right?

Let's look at another example:

```ruby
require 'byebug'
users = ["Matt", "Pete", ["John"], "Brenton", "Geoff"]
users.each do |user|
  byebug if user.class != String
end
```

In the preceding example, we again have the array of users, except for one user in particular, which happens to be an array with a single element. In a real application, this is likely to cause problems and if we attempted to do any sort of string-specific operation on it, we would either get an error or some kind of undesired behavior.

Clearly, this is a bug. Maybe this list of users was generated by some other code and we're trying to track down the cause of an exception. Being able to break and inspect the environment at the exact element that's causing the issue is very useful.

We don't want to step through every single user – there could be hundreds or thousands of records, so instead we use a conditional statement to trigger byebug if we detect that the user is not a string.

When we run the code, we get the following:

```
$ ruby byebug_example.rb
Return value is: nil

[1, 7] in /Users/cheyne/Dropbox/Ruby-Fundamentals/Debugging/byebug_example.rb
   1: require 'byebug'
   2:
   3: users = ["Matt", "Pete", ["John"], "Brenton", "Geoff"]
   4:
   5: users.each do |user|
   6:   byebug if user.class != String
=> 7: end
(byebug) user
["John"]
(byebug) user.class
Array
(byebug)
```

Figure 8.13: Detecting odd characters in the array

As you can see, byebug has triggered on (and only on) the element in the array that was not a string, as defined by our condition, which has helped us to detect which of these elements is the odd one out.

Navigating with byebug

Byebug gives us a number of tools to navigate through our code. We can move up, down, back, forward, and any direction we need to. Here are a few of the most commonly used navigational commands:

- **next** (**n**): The next command will step to the next logical line of executable code, not just breakpoints or calls to byebug. This allows us to step through our code one line at a time and inspect it along the way. The next command will stepover function calls.

- **step** (or just **s**): The **step** command works the same as the next command although the **step** command will step **INTO** function calls.

- **continue** (**c**): This commands until the program ends, hits a breakpoint, or reaches a line. If there are no more breakpoints, the program will run to completion.

- **up**: Moves to a higher frame in the call stack. This may not be the previous line, more the previous calling function's line. If you remember the stack trace, we saw a little earlier, each of those lines are the "frames" this command will step through. You can move multiple frames at a time by passing an integer to the command; for example, **up 3**.

- **Down**: The opposite of **up**. This allows us to move down through the frames of the call stack. You can move multiple frames at a time by passing an integer to the command; for example, **down 3**.

- **help**: You can view the many features available in **byebug** by entering the **help** command from the prompt. You will see a listing of all the available options.

Pry can be integrated with **byebug**, which provides additional navigational commands:

```
(byebug) help

    break       -- Sets breakpoints in the source code
    catch       -- Handles exception catchpoints
    condition   -- Sets conditions on breakpoints
    continue    -- Runs until program ends, hits a breakpoint or reaches a line
    debug       -- Spawns a subdebugger
    delete      -- Deletes breakpoints
    disable     -- Disables breakpoints or displays
    display     -- Evaluates expressions every time the debugger stops
    down        -- Moves to a lower frame in the stack trace
    edit        -- Edits source files
    enable      -- Enables breakpoints or displays
    finish      -- Runs the program until frame returns
    frame       -- Moves to a frame in the call stack
    help        -- Helps you using byebug
    history     -- Shows byebug's history of commands
    info        -- Shows several informations about the program being debugged
    interrupt   -- Interrupts the program
    irb         -- Starts an IRB session
    kill        -- Sends a signal to the current process
    list        -- Lists lines of source code
    method      -- Shows methods of an object, class or module
    next        -- Runs one or more lines of code
    pry         -- Starts a Pry session
    quit        -- Exits byebug
    restart     -- Restarts the debugged program
    save        -- Saves current byebug session to a file
    set         -- Modifies byebug settings
    show        -- Shows byebug settings
```

Figure 8.14: Navigation commands in byebug

We've learned the basics of debugging with **byebug**, how to pause executions, and how to inspect the values of variables.

Let's try it out for ourselves now.

Exercise 8.04: Debugging with byebug

In this exercise, we will now use byebug to debug our code. Take the following steps to complete the exercise:

1. Create the **exercise_byebug.rb** file and let's write some simple code to trigger a **byebug** session when we detect that an element in the array is not an integer:

```ruby
require 'byebug'
nums = [1, 2, 3, "four"]
nums.each do |num|
  byebug if num.class != Integer
end
```

2. Run the script:

```
$ ruby exercise_byebug.rb
```

3. At the **byebug** prompt, inspect the current **var** num by typing **num**. You should see the word **four** as the value of **num**:

```
$ ruby exercise_3.rb
Return value is: nil

[1, 7] in /Users/cheyne/Dropbox/Ruby-Fundamentals/Debugging/exercise_3.rb
   1: require 'byebug'
   2:
   3: nums = [1, 2, 3, "four"]
   4:
   5: nums.each do |num|
   6:   byebug if num.class != Integer
=> 7: end
(byebug) num
"four"
(byebug) num.class
String
(byebug)
```

Figure 8.15: Output for byebug debugging

> **Note**
>
> In this example, we are checking that the **num** class is not of type **Integer**. In Ruby versions prior to 2.4, this will be **Fixnum**. Ruby 2.4 and later replaced **Fixnum** and **Bignum** with **Integer**.

4. Enter the letter **c** (to continue) and hit *Enter*. The program should run to completion:

```
$ ruby exercise_3.rb
Return value is: nil

[1, 7] in /Users/cheyne/Dropbox/Ruby-Fundamentals/Debugging/exercise_3.rb
   1: require 'byebug'
   2:
   3: nums = [1, 2, 3, "four"]
   4:
   5: nums.each do |num|
   6:    byebug if num.class != Integer
=> 7: end
(byebug) num
"four"
(byebug) num.class
String
(byebug) c
$
```

Figure 8.16: Output for byebug debugging with completion

Thus, we have successfully used byebug to debug our code.

Debugging with Visual Studio Code

Debugging with a visual editor is generally a nicer experience, although it can take a little longer to set up.

Debugging with an editor provides you with an interface to click around in, which is a much more visual experience and can feel more comfortable to some users.

Using a similar example to before, here is what debugging within Visual Studio Code looks like:

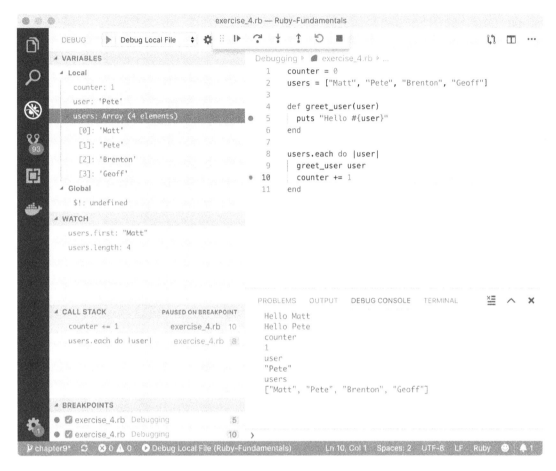

Figure 8.17: Debugging with Visual Studio Code

Here, we see a much more visual experience. All that information we previously had to type commands to reveal is now presented to us from a single interface. It might seem confusing but don't worry – it will make sense soon enough.

Let's take a look through this screen and understand what these individual panels are.

At the top of the main panel, we see a navigation bar with buttons we can click to continue, step over, step into, step out, and so on. There's no need to type any commands:

Figure 8.18 Navigation bar on Visual Studio Code

We can see the listing of local variables and what their current values are. These values are updated as we step through the code. You'll notice that the **counter variable** in this example has a value of **2**. It has been incremented and the interface has been updated to reflect the change:

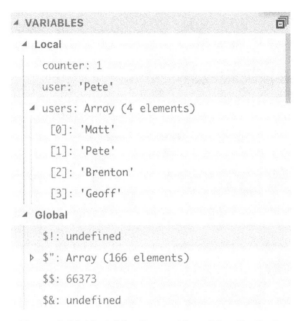

Figure 8.19: Variables list on Visual Studio Code

You can imagine that in a complicated application with more complicated data structures, this can be a very useful tool to see exactly what's happening during the execution of your application.

Below the local variables, we can see global variables. These can be accessed from anywhere in your program and are typically reserved for core Ruby language functionality.

Under the global variables, we have the **watch** panel. The **watch panel** is a useful place where you can pin expressions or variable names that you're interested in keeping track of. This panel will evaluate and display the expression or variable for you on each step. It's much like the **local variables** panel except that you can control what is kept and displayed in the **watch** panel. Think of it as a "Favorites" version of the **variables** panel.

We can use basic expressions as listed here:

- `user == "James"`
- `user.class == String`
- `user.to_s`

The expressions would look as follows in the watch pane:

Figure 8.20: The watch pane on Visual Studio Code

Under the `watch` pane is the `call` stack. The **call stack** or stack trace shows us the trace of method calls up until this point. On the right-hand side, we see the name of the file the breakpoint lives in (breakpoints across all files in your project will show up here as well as the line numbers those breakpoints are set at):

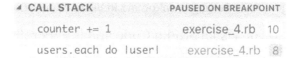

Figure 8.21: Breakpoint information on Visual Studio Code

Lastly, we have a listing of breakpoints, which is very handy when we have breakpoints spread out across multiple files. We can easily enable and disable breakpoints from this panel as we need for our whole project:

Figure 8.22: Breakpoints listing on Visual Studio Code

Setting Breakpoints

As we saw earlier in the chapter, the small red dots on the left-hand side of the main panel are our breakpoints. We can set breakpoints by simply clicking in this column on any line of our code, as shown in the following figure:

```
Debugging ▷  🔴 exercise_4.rb ▷ ...
1     counter = 0
2     users = ["Matt", "Pete", "Brenton", "Geoff"]
3
4     def greet_user(user)
● 5       puts "Hello #{user}"
6     end
7
8     users.each do |user|
9       greet_user user
● 10      counter += 1
11    end
```

Figure 8.23: Setting breakpoints in Visual Studio Code

This is not specific to Ruby or Visual Studio Code and is generally the standard way that most editors, IDEs, and languages implement breakpoints.

Conditional Breakpoints

In the previous section, we were able to conditionally trigger **byebug** by simply adding some conditional logic to the following expression:

```
byebug if <expression>
```

This is a very useful tool and, thankfully, we can achieve the same functionality within Visual Studio Code.

To set a conditional breakpoint:

1. Right-click in the left-hand breakpoint column on the main panel (like you were setting a breakpoint but right-clicking).

2. From the pop-up menu, select **Add Conditional Breakpoint.**

3. You'll now be presented with an expression input box in the right-hand pane, in which you can input an expression just like we did before. This expression can be any short snippet of code; for example, **counter == 3 or counter.class != Integer**:

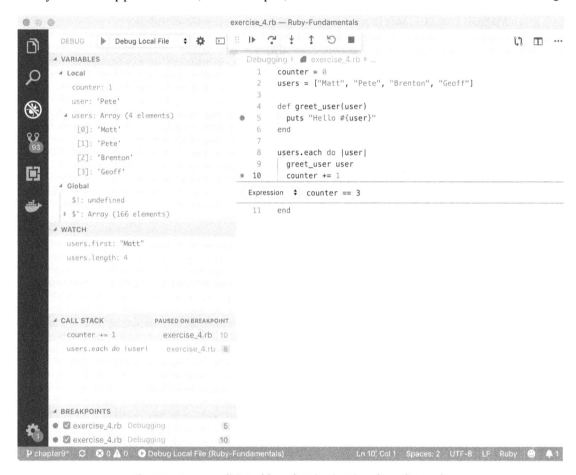

Figure 8.24: Conditional breakpoint in Visual Studio Code

Now the breakpoint will only trigger when the counter equals **3**.

Logpoints

Logpoints are much like breakpoints except they don't "break" into the debugger; they simply log the results out to the debug log for you. This is handy if you want to output some information but maybe don't want to interact with the debugger.

To set a log point, simply right-click, like we did for the conditional breakpoint, in the left column and select `Add Logpoint`:

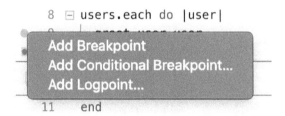

Figure 8.25: Logpoints on Visual Studio Code

For example, maybe you want to view the value of a large list of items. Using breakpoints would be slow and require you to manually continue after each item. With logpoints, you can simply have it write to the debug log, and then inspect the results later.

Logpoints can be controlled like a normal breakpoint. They can be **disabled**, **enabled**, and **conditionally triggered**.

The Debug Console

In the last section, we used the byebug debug console. Debugging with a REPL console like this, as we saw previously, can be a powerful way to test functionality as we can call methods and interact with our code at any particular point of execution in real time, without the need to reload or restart the application:

Figure 8.26: Debug console on Visual Studio Code

Thankfully, we have access to a similar console with Visual Studio Code. Simply click the little Terminal icon in the top left-hand bar or click **View > Debug Console** and you'll see a pane appear at the bottom of the main panel:

```
PROBLEMS    OUTPUT    DEBUG CONSOLE    TERMINAL

Hello Matt
Hello Pete
counter
1
user
"Pete"
users
["Matt", "Pete", "Brenton", "Geoff"]


>
```

Figure 8.27: REPL console

From here, we get access to a REPL console, much like byebug.

When we stop on a breakpoint from this debug console, we will have access to execute code and inspect the values of variables within the context of this line of code.

The debug console is an excellent tool for exploratory debugging when you're not quite sure what you're looking for and you want to have a poke around. Once you find what you're looking for, be it an expression or variable, you can add it to the **watch** panel for quick reference.

> **Note**
>
> The Visual Studio Code documentation covers these topics in greater detail. You can read more at https://packt.live/2VGaYwZ.

It's easier to learn by doing rather than reading in this situation, so let's set up the Visual Studio Code debugger and try it for ourselves.

Exercise 8.05: Debugging with Visual Studio Code

In this exercise, you will learn how to debug application code using Visual Studio Code.

In order to use the Visual Studio Code debugger, first, we need to install the Ruby language tools. We need to install the Ruby language extension. We do this by opening the **Extensions** tab in Visual Studio Code and searching for Ruby. It should be the first one listed, by **Peng Lv**. Click **Install**:

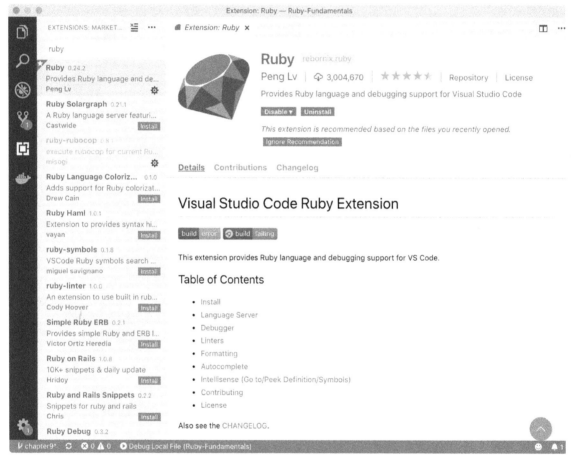

Figure 8.28: Installation of Ruby on Visual Studio Code

Now, perform the followings steps:

1. Install the required debugging gems:

    ```
    gem install ruby-debug-ide
    gem install debase (or gem install byebug)
    ```

2. Create a launch configuration for the Visual Studio Code debugger. This is essentially just a JSON file that tells Visual Studio Code how to execute the debugger and on what files. Click the **Debug** tab in the left-hand column, as shown in the following figure:

Figure 8.29: Debug option

3. In the top dropdown of the debug panel, next to the play icon, click **Add Configuration…**, as shown in the following figure:

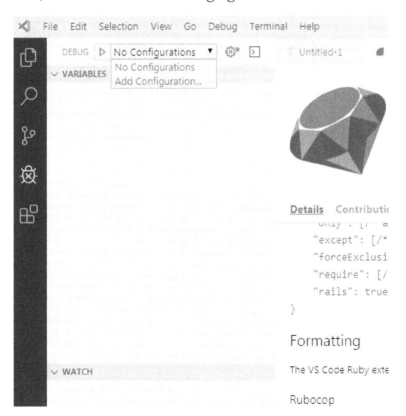

Figure 8.30: Adding configuration

4. Select **Ruby**, then `Debug Local File`.

    In the newly created **launch.json** file, change the program line to **"program"**:
    "${file}"**. Changing this program line to **${file} simply tells Visual Studio Code
    that we want to debug the currently open file and not a fixed file (**main.rb**), which it
    was previously, as shown in the following figure:

```
.vscode ▷ {} launch.json ▷ ...
  1    {
  2        // Use IntelliSense to learn about possible attributes.
  3        // Hover to view descriptions of existing attributes.
  4        // For more information, visit: https://go.microsoft.com/fwlink/?linkid=830387
  5        "version": "0.2.0",
  6        "configurations": [
  7            {
  8                "name": "Debug Local File",
  9                "type": "Ruby",
 10                "request": "launch",
 11                "program": "${file}"
 12            }
 13        ]
 14    }
 15
```

Figure 8.31: The contents of launch.json file

5. There are a number of other variables we can use here to target the correct file. For
    example, if our application always started with a file named **run.rb** at the root of
    our application directory, we would use **${workspaceRoot}/run.rb**.

> **Note**
>
> You can read more about these options at https://packt.live/2IPf9RV.
>
> You can add multiple launch configurations for different purposes. For example,
> one for debugging the application and one for debugging your tests.

6. Create the **exercise_vscode.rb** file with the following code:

```
counter = 0
users = ["Matt", "Pete", "Brenton", "Geoff"]
def greet_user(user)
  puts "Hello #{user}"
end
users.each do |user|
  greet_user user
  counter += 1
end
```

We'll keep things simple here for demonstration purposes.

This code will iterate over an array of names, calling the **greet_user** method each time, passing in the user's name, which will print **Hello <user>**, followed by incrementing a counter.

7. Next, we need to set breakpoints. In the left-hand column (next to the line numbers) in Visual Studio Code, click to add a breakpoint for lines **5** and **10**, as shown in the following figure:

```
Debugging ▷  ● exercise_4.rb ▷ ...
    1    counter = 0
    2    users = ["Matt", "Pete", "Brenton", "Geoff"]
    3
    4    def greet_user(user)
●   5      puts "Hello #{user}"
    6    end
    7
    8    users.each do |user|
    9      greet_user user
●  10      counter += 1
   11    end
```

Figure 8.32: Debugging with VS Code

8. Step through and inspect the code.

Hit F5 on your keyboard or click **Debug > Start Debugging** from the application menu.The first breakpoint should be line **5**. Inspect the value of **user**. It should equal the first element of the **users** array.Click the **continue** button to move on to the next breakpoint, which should be line **10**. Continue to click **continue** and take a moment to inspect the variables and environment at each break. Observe the values changing in the **Local Variables** panel on the left.

Thus, we have successfully used Visual Studio Code to debug the code.

Activity 8.01: Perform Debugging on a Voting Application

In this activity, we'll refactor our voting machine application that we have been building since Chapter 5, Object-Oriented Programming with Ruby, to output a log trail that we can use for debugging purposes.

The voting machine application has reported duplicate votes and categories from our users.

What we would like to do is to have a historical log of when things are happening stored somewhere we can access without needing to see the screen output. What we need is a log file.

The following steps will help you complete the activity:

1. The **Logger** class must be instantiated as method calls are made on the instance of the class. Our **LoggerController** module, is not a class, so we will need to instantiate the **Logger** class somewhere.

2. We can do this by overriding the initialize method in the **LoggerController** module, instantiating the **Logger** class, and then calling **super**. This will ensure we call both the module and parent classes' initialize methods.

3. Extend the **ControllerLogger** module to include a new **log_to_file** method that will write a timestamped log record to a file. Parameterize this method so that we can specify which log level we want the log message to be written out as (set the default to debug).

4. Format the log output to something more user-friendly; it won't just be us reading it.

5. We'll also call this method from our existing log method so that we also capture a timestamped version of any log messages in our general log method.

The output should be as follows:

```
1    DEBUG | 2019-08-04 14:35:10 +1000 | You can vote for: TestCategory
2    DEBUG | 2019-08-04 14:35:10 +1000 | Vote recorded!
3    DEBUG | 2019-08-04 14:58:24 +1000 | Category added!
4    DEBUG | 2019-08-04 14:58:39 +1000 | Exiting...
5    DEBUG | 2019-08-04 15:46:38 +1000 | Category added!
6    DEBUG | 2019-08-04 15:46:40 +1000 | You can vote for: Test
7    INFO | 2019-08-04 15:46:48 +1000 | Vote recorded - Voter: Cheyne Votee: James Category: TestCategory
8    DEBUG | 2019-08-04 15:46:48 +1000 | Vote recorded!
9
```

Figure 8.33: Output for the voting application

> Note
>
> The solution to the activity can be found on page 482.

Summary

Logging and debugging are essential tools for any software project, and while we are learning this in Ruby, the principles are the same for any language.

Logging is one of those things that you don't truly appreciate until you really need it, and when you need it, you'll be glad you spent that extra little bit of time setting it up properly. As we've seen in this chapter, it really doesn't take much effort to dramatically improve your application's logging; even less if you set it up correctly from the very start of a project. With handy classes such as the **Logger** class, we can achieve very useful results with minimal work. We also dipped our toes into the world of debuggers. This is another area that is easily overlooked until you really need it. Once the complexity of an application grows to a certain level, printing out the values of variables is simply not going to cut it.

The ability to step through code execution and inspect the environment along the way is incredibly powerful. It can save you a lot of time and headache when things go wrong. There is a multitude of other functionality built into the standard debugger – enough to fill a books worth of content alone. With these new tools at our disposal, we're ready to tackle any bugs that arise, be they in development or production.

In the next chapter, we will look at a more advanced programming concept, known as metaprogramming. Metaprogramming is like a subset of software engineering that allows code to use other code as input, or in some cases, code that can generate new code. This opens up a whole new world of programming possibilities and expands our software engineering toolbox with an array of exciting functionality and algorithms. When you're ready, let's take our skills up a notch and start learning about metaprogramming with Ruby in the next chapter.

Ruby Beyond the Basics I

Overview

By the end of this chapter, you will be able to use blocks to improve code reusability; implement yield with blocks to maintain control over program flows; implement procs and lambdas with blocks and compare procs and lambdas.

This chapter aims to give you a general overview of metaprogramming.

Introduction

In the previous chapters, we learned how to debug Ruby programs using the `logger` class. In this chapter, we will learn about some of the advanced topics of the Ruby programming language, such as `blocks`, `procs`, and `lambdas`. By now, you must have realized that it's really easy to start writing Ruby code, create sample apps, and get instant gratification; however, every new Ruby developer (and sometimes the experienced ones too) will have a question buzzing in their mind about how it actually works.

We can safely call it the Ruby magic, and that's what we are planning to crack in this chapter. We are going to learn about advanced programming techniques that are present in other languages, but this time the Ruby-specific implementation is our focus. We will tear down the curtain from the syntactic sugar and take a look under the hood to reveal what metaprogramming is. Additionally, we will lay a strong foundation that will allow you to reuse these techniques and enable you to utilize the libraries provided by Ruby. Later, when we learn about Ruby on Rails in the upcoming chapters, it will be easier to comprehend various features and how they operate behind the scenes.

Metaprogramming

You might be wondering what **metaprogramming** actually is. Well, it is utilized by most programming languages. Technically, it's a piece of code that writes code by itself dynamically. With metaprogramming, you can create methods and classes at runtime. It allows you to reopen or even modify classes, as well as add methods to classes on the fly. It helps to maintain the **Don't Repeat Yourself** (**DRY**) principle in programming; however, it is a hard concept to grasp and get right.

Let's imagine the scenario of a chef in a restaurant. This chef needs to know many recipes and be able to put together food for their customers. Each food item requires different steps for preparation. There are some steps that need to be done before, during, and after the food is prepared. In order to create a simulation for these steps to be performed by an automated system, you might consider using the metaprogramming feature provided by the Ruby language.

Metaprogramming makes use of multiple elements available within the Ruby language. Let's take a look at the first building block, which is called **blocks** in Ruby.

Blocks

Blocks are like anonymous functions – **lambdas** – that can be passed into a method. You may also refer to the use of a block as passing a method into a method. The slight difference in blocks and methods is that they do not belong to an object. In other languages, such as C#, Java, or Python, this concept is called **closures**. Blocks are just the Ruby way of implementing closures. Blocks are typically used when we would like to encapsulate functionality that is made up of a sequence of statements. For example, we could encapsulate an "Introduction Letter" email when new people arrive at a company, where we just have to pass a template to a block and it automatically generates and sends the email. The only variable here is the detailed information of the new colleague in the template.

Syntax for Blocks

There are two ways to write blocks: they can be either enclosed in **do/end** or within curly brackets (**{}**). Let's examine a simple example showing how to write them.

With do/end

Consider the following example:

```
(1..5).each do
  puts "I am inside the block"
end
```

The output would be as follows:

```
I am inside the block
I am inside the block
I am inside the block
I am inside the block
I am inside the block
```

Figure 9.1: Output using do/end

With curly brackets (())

Consider the following example:

```
5.times {puts "I am inside the block"}
```

The output would be as follows:

```
I am inside the block
I am inside the block
I am inside the block
I am inside the block
I am inside the block
```

Figure 9.2: Output using curly brackets

Besides this, we can also use the **yield** keyword to write blocks, which we will discuss shortly.

In Ruby, many built-in **class** methods allow you to pass blocks. This helps in enhancing the feature set provided by the built-in methods.

The preceding examples are pretty basic for understanding block syntax. Let's try and understand this with another example of using a block as an iterator variable in order to print something:

```
def star_tree number
  1.upto(number).each do |i|
    puts "*" * i
  end
end
star_tree 30
```

Fire up your Terminal and run this Ruby file:

```
$ ruby block-iterator.rb
```

The output would be as follows:

Figure 9.3: Using a block as an iterator

Let's understand what we have done here. We are calling a **star_tree** method and passing a value of **30** to it, which is then used by the block as an iterator variable number, which helps to create a behavior inside each method. This was a very simple implementation of blocks that is used quite often in real-world programming. Let's learn about **yield** and how to use it with blocks to make really powerful programs.

Blocks can be passed to methods just like any other parameter. We have been using blocks all along without realizing it. Take a look at the preceding code with **.each**. What is running inside a **.each** method is a block, and we define what needs to be implemented in that **.each** method.

The ability of blocks to be passed as parameters makes them a great candidate for applying abstraction, which is a very important concept of object-oriented programming (OOP).

yield with Blocks

The **yield** construct in Ruby is essentially a way to call a block. Wherever you use this keyword, the block code will be executed there. If there is code before the **yield** construct, it will be executed first and then the rest of the code is executed. Other programming languages, such as Python and JavaScript, also utilize the **yield** construct. You can **yield** an empty block; however, nothing will happen as there is nothing to execute.

Let's understand this with an example:

```
def my_method(&block)
  puts "Part one of my_method code"
  yield
  puts "Part two of my_method code"
end
my_method {puts "Yield code from the Block"}
```

The **&block** argument expects a block that will be executed when the control reaches the **yield** line.

The output would be like the following:

```
Part one of my_method code
Yield code from the Block
Part two of my_method code
```

Figure 9.4: Output for yield with blocks

Let's understand this program. We pass a block of code to the **my_method** function which executes the block when the control reaches the **yield** statement. Now, imagine the possibility of using the **yield** keyword to pass a block of code with some operations. With **yield**, you can do all the behind-the-scenes magic we generally associate Ruby methods with.

If we try printing **yield** twice, or maybe after the second **puts** statement in **my_method**, the **yield** construct will call each line of the block that you pass to the program. If you pass two statements, each statement will be executed as many times as there are **yield** statements in the code.

Consider the following example:

```
def my_method(&block)
  puts " Before first yield"
  yield
  puts " After first yield"
  yield
end
my_method {puts "What happens with two yields?"}
```

The output of the first **yield** call with one statement will be as follows:

```
Before first yield
What happens with two yields?
After first yield
What happens with two yields?
```

Figure 9.5: Output for yield with one statement

Now let's take a look at the output for multiple statements:

```
my_method do
puts "First statement"
puts "Second statement"
end
```

The output should be as follows:

```
Before first yield
First statement
Second statement
After first yield
First statement
Second statement
```

Figure 9.6: Output for yield with multiple statements

Exercise 9.01: Building a Simple Calculator

In this exercise, we will be creating a simple calculator that performs basic arithmetic operations such as addition, subtraction, multiplication, and division. We will be using Ruby blocks and **yield** to create reusable code. The following steps will help you complete the exercise:

1. Create a Ruby **block-yield.rb** file.

2. Define our **calculator** block. We use the **yield** keyword, which will use the block of code passed along with the **a** and **b** variables, which are used in the arithmetic operations:

```ruby
def calculator(a, b)
  yield(a, b)
end
```

3. Next, we add the calls for addition, subtraction, multiplication, and division:

```ruby
#Addition
puts calculator(8, 2) { |a, b| a + b }
#Multiplication
puts calculator(8, 2) { |a, b| a * b }
#Subtraction
puts calculator(8, 2) { |a, b| a - b }
#Division
puts calculator(8, 2) { |a, b| a / b }
```

Save the file.

4. Open up the Terminal and execute the following code:

```ruby
ruby block-yield.rb
```

The output should be as follows:

```
10
16
6
4
```

Figure 9.7: Output for the arithmetic operation using yield with a block

The beauty of this program is that we can add n number of operations using the combination of a block and **yield** in our code.

block_given? with Blocks

The **block_given?** method is something we use in tandem with blocks and the **yield** keyword. As the name suggests, it checks whether or not a block for triggering a method or operation has been provided. Let's take a look at its syntax:

```
def my_method(&block)
  puts "Part one of my_method code"
  yield if block_given?
  puts "Part two of my_method code"
end
my_method {puts "Yield code from the Block if block is given"}
my_method {puts "Yield code from the &block if it was passed as argument"}
```

If you execute this code from the Terminal, you will get the following output:

```
Part one of my_method code
Yield code from the Block if block is given
Part two of my_method code
Part one of my_method code
Yield code from the &block if it was passed as argument
Part two of my_method code
```

Figure 9.8: Output for the block_given? method

If we don't pass anything to the **&block** method, we get the following output:

```
my_method
```

The output would be as follows:

```
Part one of my_method code
Part two of my_method code
```

Figure 9.9: Output with an empty block

In this example, we have passed a block of code to **my_method**, which is a print statement, and have also attached **block_given?** to the **yield** keyword. Note that if you remove the block of code and call the method, it will still work and print only two other statements from the method, as seen in the previous example.

If we remove the block of code and also **block_given?** from **my_method**, it will throw us an error as shown in the following figure. This is due to the fact that **&block** is still expecting a block as an argument:

```
Traceback (most recent call last):
        1: from Block_given.rb:10:in `<main>'
Block_given.rb:4:in `my_method': no block given (yield) (LocalJumpError)
```

Figure 9.10: Output for my_method without the block_given? method and an empty block

Exercise 9.02: Building a Flight Status Display System

In this exercise, we will create a method that accepts blocks. If a block is passed, it should call the **logger** function, which is defined in another method. If no block is passed, it will simply print the statements. We call the method twice: once with a block, and then once without a block. This will visualize the updates in the flight status.

The following steps will help you complete the exercise:

1. Create a **basic-logger.rb** file.

2. First, we define the **basic_logger** method, where we are printing display messages that are to be displayed after gaps of 3 seconds:

```ruby
def basic_logger
  sleep 3
  puts "****"
  puts "Changing flight status…"
  sleep 3
  puts "Flight status was changed!"
  sleep 3
  puts "****"
end
```

3. Next, we need to handle a situation in which the program will not fail if no block of code is passed, using the **block_given?** method. We create a method that accepts a block and, inside the block, we have two print statements from the method itself and one **yield** statement, which calls another method. There is a **block_given?** method such that the **basic_logger** method will only be called if a block is passed; otherwise, the code in this method will continue:

```
def my_method(&block)
  puts "Flight Status changer starting"
  yield basic_logger if block_given?
  puts "Flight Status changer ended"
  puts "****"
end
```

4. Finally, let's take a look at how these methods are called:

```
my_method
my_method {puts " Changed Flight status to Departure "}
```

Here, we have called our **my_method** method, once without a block of code and once with it. In both cases, we get the appropriate result.

The output, when we call the method without any argument, would be as follows:

```
Flight Status changer starting
Flight Status changer ended
****
```

Figure 9.11: Output for my_method with an empty block

The output, when we call the method with an argument, would be as follows:

```
Flight Status changer starting
Flight Status changer ended
****
Flight Status changer starting
****
Changing flight status…
Flight status was changed!
****
 Changed Flight status to Departure
Flight Status changer ended
****
```

Figure 9.12: Output for my_method with an argument

If we remove **block_given?** from **my_method**, the **basic_logger** method will be called to check whether we passed a block or not.

The proc Object

The **proc** object is an object of the Ruby class and is used to store a process that can be used later on. **proc** objects are blocks of code that can be set to local variables. Once set, this code can be called in different contexts and can access those variables.

Let's take a simple example:

```
t = Proc.new { |x,y| puts "A very simple proc example" }
t.call
```

The output would be as follows:

```
A very simple proc example
```

Figure 9.13: Output for proc

Another key feature of **proc** is that it can accept arguments. Ruby supports the functional programming paradigm and the **proc** object is one example of this. There are two distinct features that separate blocks from **proc** objects. Firstly, and most importantly, **proc** objects are objects, while blocks are not. Secondly, you can have only one block passed as an argument to functions, but **proc** objects do not have such restrictions.

In other languages, such as Python and JavaScript, **proc** objects are referred to as closures; many languages have their own paradigm for the function of **proc** objects in Ruby. Let's take a look at the syntax of **proc**:

```
def proc_method
    Proc.new
end
simple_proc = proc_method { "Hello World" }
simple_proc.call
```

Here, we first initiate a **proc** object with **Proc.new** inside our **proc** method. This is then called by using **.call** and passing a block of code to it:

```
p = Proc.new { puts "Hello World" }
p.call
```

The output would be as follows:

```
Hello World
```

Figure 9.14: Output for Proc.new

Until the `.call` method is invoked, the **proc** object lies dormant; nothing happens.

> **Note**
>
> Remember that you must always pass a block of code to **procs**, as only then will a **proc** object be instantiated.

In the following exercise, we will discover how to implement **proc** objects in a program.

Exercise 9.03: Performing the sum Function on a Range of Numbers

In this exercise, we will be writing a program to find the sum of a range of numbers. For example, if the start and end of the range are 1 and 6, then the final sum total will be 21.

The following steps will help you with the solution:

1. Create a **proc-sum-range.rb** file.

2. We define a **sum_of_range** variable, which is assigned a value from the output of the block, which is passed to the **Proc.new** construct. Here, the arguments received are used to operate on the numbers, to get the sum of all the numbers between the start and end of a range:

```ruby
sum_of_range = Proc.new do |first, last|
    result = 0
    (first..last).each do |i|
        result += i
    end
    result
end
```

3. Next, the variable that is assigned to the **proc** object is called using `.call` and the arguments are passed to **proc**:

```ruby
puts sum_of_range.call(1,6)
```

4. Open the Terminal and traverse to this file. Run the following command to see the output:

```ruby
ruby proc-sum-range.rb
```

21

Figure 9.15: Output for the sum function using proc

If you have ever wondered how the **inject** method works, then this is a very simple implementation of the same thing, and we achieved it with a few lines of code.

The difference between methods and **proc**, even if they look quite similar, is that while both methods and **proc** are blocks of code, methods are bound to objects while **proc** is bound to the variable it is assigned to. Methods represent the object-oriented part of Ruby, while **proc** represents the functional programming side of Ruby.

Exercise 9.04: Calculating Profit Using proc on an Input Price List

In this exercise, we will create a **proc** object that takes as input a list of prices and returns the new list with a 25% profit.

The following steps will help you to complete the exercise:

1. Open up the **Stocker.rb** file.

2. Create the original price list:

```
original_price = [100,200,300,400,999]
puts "The original price for the stocks: #{original_price}"
```

3. Define the dormant **proc** object:

```
price_profit = Proc.new do |price_list|
    result = Array.new
    price_list.each do |i|
        result << i * 1.25
    end
    result
end
```

4. Create the new list by calling the **proc** object and output the list:

```
new_price_with_profit = price_profit.call(original_price)
puts "The new price for the stocks #{new_price_with_profit}"
```

5. Invoke the script with **ruby Stocker.rb** and inspect the result.

   The output should be as follows:

```
The original price for the stocks: [100, 200, 300, 400, 999]
The new price for the stocks [125.0, 250.0, 375.0, 500.0, 1248.75]
```

Figure 9.16: Output with profit-inclusive prices

Lambdas

Just like **proc** objects, lambdas are also examples of closure in Ruby. Lambdas, just like **proc**, are simply a function with a name. Additionally, just like **proc**, they are objects too. We will be looking at the specific differences between **proc** and lambdas later on in the chapter.

Let's now look at the following syntax to learn more about lambdas:

```
hello = lambda {puts "Hello World"}
hello.call
```

That's really simple. We use the **lambda** keyword to pass a block of code. To call a **lambda** function, we simply use **.call**, in our case, on the variable assigned to it.

There is another very cool and commonly used syntax of lambdas called **stabby lambda**, which is represented as **->**; it was first introduced in *version 1.9*.

The preceding code snippet will change to the following when stabby lambda is used:

```
hello = -> {puts "Hello World"}
hello.call
```

Let's implement lambdas in an exercise. Since **proc** and lambdas are quite close in terms of implementation, to understand them well, let's implement the same problem using lambdas instead of **proc**.

Exercise 9.05: Creating a Program to Sum a Range of Numbers Using Lambdas

In this exercise, we will write a program to sum a range of numbers using lambdas. The following steps will help you to complete the exercise:

1. Create a **lambdas-sum-range.rb** file.

2. Next, we create a lambda using the **stabby lambda** syntax (**->**) and assign it to a variable. If you look at the following code, the arguments that will be passed to **lambda** are next to the stabby lambda syntax and before the **do** keyword. If we had used the classic **lambda** syntax, we would have had to place them otherwise:

```
sum_of_range = ->(first, last) do
    result = 0
    (first..last).each do |i|
        result += i
    end
    result
end
```

3. Let's now call the **lambda** method using square brackets to pass the argument:

```
puts sum_of_range[1,6]
```

4. Open the Terminal and traverse to this file. Run the following command to see the output:

21

Figure 9.17: Output for sum using lambdas

We have successfully used **lambda** to create a **sum** function.

> **Note**
>
> We can use the square brackets with **proc** too, that is, instead of using **.call** when passing arguments to both **proc** and **lambda**.

proc versus lambda

The key difference between procs and lambdas is the way the **return** statement works for both of them. While **proc** ignores the container method, **lambda** does not override it.

A **return** statement in a block of code created using lambda behaves similarly to how a method uses **return**: that is, it simply exits the block handling the control back to the original method. However, in the case of a block of code created using **proc.new**, when the **return** statement is used, it returns from both the blocks of code and the method.

Let's understand this with an example:

```
def my_lambda_method
    lambda { return "Statement from the block" }.call
    return "Statement from the method"
end
```

```
    puts my_lambda_method
    def my_proc_method
     Proc.new { return "Statement from the block" }.call
     return "Statement from the method"
    end
```

```
    puts my_proc_method
```

The output would be as follows:

```
Statement from the method
Statement from the block
```

Figure 9.18: Output for proc versus lambda

If you take a look at the first method of this file, **my_lambda_method**, you will see that it works in a very similar way to any Ruby method, returning the final statement of the method, which even has a lambda with a **return** statement in it.

In the **my_proc_method** method, you can see something different happening. The code is exited altogether after seeing the first **return** statement from **proc**.

This is a very subtle difference between the two methods, but the difference is usually encountered when you are stuck in a bug. Therefore, we need to understand the internal workings of procs and lambdas and how they react to a **return** statement.

The Story of the Chef and the Restaurant

This section will round up metaprogramming with a live example as to how procs and lambdas work in real life. We will define three distinct parts of the operation. The main part of the magic happens in **Chef.rb**, the components are defined in **Recipes.rb**, and we will also have **Order.rb**.

Let's define **Chef.rb**. We will have a list of recipes and some filters. We will have **cook**, the **before** and **after** functions to put together the food, and the **run** function, which will be an abstraction that is used to put together the parts:

Chef.rb

```
1   module Chef
2       def self.included(klass)
3           puts "The Chef is ready for service!"
4       end
5       def recipes
6           @recipes ||= {}
7       end
8       def before_filter
9           @before_filter ||= {}
10      end
11      def after_filter
12          @after_filter ||= {}
13      end
```

https://packt.live/35zkd6X

The entire preceding code should be saved as **Chef.rb** in a directory. This is an abstraction, which is what metaprogramming is all about; we don't know what will be ordered or how to cook the orders. We just want a chef who knows how to fulfill customer requirements.

Now it is time to create **Recipes.rb**; we will define what happens before, after, and during a chicken soup order:

```ruby
require './Chef.rb'
cook "chickensoup" do
  puts "Adding spices"
  puts "Adding water if necessary"
  puts "Waiting for the food to be ready"
end
before "chickensoup" do
  puts "Preparing to cook chicken soup!"
  puts "Preparing bowls, slicing and dicing."
end
after "chickensoup" do
  puts "Cleaning dishes"
  puts "Serving customer"
end
puts "End of chickensoup!"
```

This file can be further extended with more recipes and allows you to customize the orders. This also allows us to detach the functionality of the chef and the orders from the recipes. This makes for a good modular application.

Finally, we can define our **Orders.rb** file, which will be an interface to call the chef to fulfill the orders based on the recipes:

```ruby
require './Recipes.rb'
run('chickensoup')
```

This is it. Save all three files in the same folder and you should be able to invoke the **ruby Orders.rb** command and see the following output:

```
The Chef is ready for service!
Define the ingredients for the recipe: chickensoup
Performing pre cooking steps for recipe: chickensoup
Performing post cooking steps for recipe: chickensoup
End of chickensoup!
Preparing to cook chicken soup!
Preparing bowls, slicing and dicing.
Adding spices
Adding water if necessary
Waiting for the food to be ready
Cleaning dishes
Serving customer
```

Figure 9.19 Output for recipe preparation

Let's now solve an activity, where we will be implementing every topic we have learned about in this chapter.

Activity 9.01: Invoice Generator

In this activity, we will be creating an invoice generator program that will take the customer name, ID, and the amount for two products, then generate an invoice.

The variable names to be used are **cust_name**, **cust_id**, **product1 p1**, and **product2 p2**. Our example will have three functions: **invoice_generator**, **calc_discount**, and **details**.

The following steps will help you with the solution:

1. Create a new Ruby file.

2. Define the **invoice_generator** method and the **p1** and **p2** variables to be used in the method. Implement **&block** and **block_given?** to pass blocks of code for the product prices and customer details.

3. Use the **yield** keyword to pass a block of code only if the first block is passed, and then call the method that will calculate a discount.

4. Define a method to calculate the discount on the product prices and print the final prices. Make sure that you give a flat 20% discount on the sum of the final product prices.

5. Build a method to retrieve and print the customer details and the final product prices with discounts.

6. Implement all the elements together to print an invoice.

The output would be as follows:

```
Enter your Customer Name
John
Enter your Customer ID
123456
Enter Product 1 price
100
Enter Product 2 price
400
Price of Product 1: 100
Price of Product 2: 400
Final amount after 20% discount 400.0
Customer name is John
Customer id is 123456
```

Figure 9.20: The invoice generator output

> **Note**
>
> The solution for the activity can be found on page 484.

Summary

In this chapter, we learned about the key concepts of metaprogramming. We learned about concepts such as blocks and how to use **yield** and **block_given?** to make our blocks of code powerful. We then learned about **proc** and **lambda** and the differences between **proc** and **lambda**, and we also discovered how a subtle difference can help avoid confusion and bugs.

In the next chapter, we will be learning more about metaprogramming in Ruby.

10

Ruby Beyond the Basics II

Overview

By the end of this chapter, you will be able to open classes to add/modify methods; implement monkey patching; use methods such as method_missing and define_method to dynamically create methods at runtime; generate HTTP requests using the built-in Ruby HTTP client net/http; create GET and POST requests using Ruby and create your own gems to share your reusable code.

Introduction

In the previous chapter, we learned about a number of advanced topics, including blocks, procs, and lambdas, which we will use in this chapter when we dive deep into the world of metaprogramming. We will also learn when we should not apply metaprogramming concepts by not always crossing the line into monkey patching (which is changing the behavior of classes and ultimately making the code confusing and unmaintainable).

In the second part of this chapter, we will learn a key programming skill that is required in order to create any real-world application that is communicating with external APIs: how to make `GET` data from a backend server and how to submit data to said server.

The final part of this chapter will help you share and distribute your Ruby code with others. So far, you have learned how to use Ruby gems, but, by the end of this chapter, you will be able to create your own `RubyGem` package and share it with the world.

Metaprogramming – A Deep Dive

We introduced metaprogramming in the previous chapter and defined it as code that generates code. Ruby has numerous powerful methods that make it possible to allow code that writes code. Furthermore, metaprogramming is most often used to create flexible interfaces. This is especially useful when you create Ruby gems that are pluggable Ruby libraries in other Ruby programs. Metaprogramming is also used in creating Ruby-based frameworks, such as Sinatra, Ruby on Rails, or when you create your own framework. Ruby on Rails, the most popular Ruby framework, is loaded with metaprogramming magic.

In the previous chapter, we stated that metaprogramming makes use of multiple elements available within the Ruby language. We discussed three such elements: blocks, procs, and lambdas. In this section, we will take a practical approach in order to understand metaprogramming and discuss topics such as opening classes in Ruby, monkey patching, and some in-built Ruby methods that allow you to create methods dynamically at runtime.

Opening Classes

Opening classes is a way in Ruby that allows us to make changes to methods that reside inside the class or to add new methods. This is also called **functional reloading** or **monkey patching**. In Ruby, a class is never closed; you can always add new methods to an existing class. This applies not just to classes you create, but in-built standard Ruby classes too. Besides adding new methods to further enhance the power of a class, you can also override the in-built methods. This is called **monkey patching**.

You should be careful with open classes, especially when you are modifying or overriding an in-built method. Since that alteration will be valid throughout your application, you must be careful and meticulous while writing such code. It is advisable to alias the method or write a new method altogether. We will learn more about this with the help of examples in the next section.

Now, let's understand the syntax to open a class by means of a simple example. In the following example, we create a Ruby file, **open_class_integer.rb**, and then create an integer class that will add the number **8** to the integer that is provided:

```ruby
class Integer
  def add_eight
    self + 8
  end
end
puts 9.add_eight
```

Run this Ruby file from the Terminal. The output will be as follows:

```
$ ruby open_class_integer.rb
> 17
```

This is a very simple example where we have added a new method, **add_eight**, to Ruby's **Integer** class. So, in our Ruby program, if we call this method on an integer, it will add **8** to it just like in the preceding example, where we have called the method on an integer object with the value of **9**, and the result is 17.

Exercise 10.01: Opening the Ruby String Class to Add a New Method to it

The **String** class is an in-built Ruby class. In this exercise, we will open that class and add a new method, **add_prefix**, to it. This method will prefix whatever string is passed to it. The following steps will help you to complete the exercise:

1. Open the **string** class and add an additional method, **add_prefix**, to it. Inside the **add_prefix** method, we have a default string value added:

```ruby
class String
  def add_prefix
    "My favorite book is " + self
  end
end
```

2. Now, call the method on a string outside the class and you will see the prefix getting attached to the string value:

```
puts "Ruby Fundamentals".add_prefix
```

3. Open the file in the Terminal and check the output:

```
My favorite book is Ruby Fundamentals
```

Figure 10.1: Output for the add.prefix method

Thus, we have successfully managed to add a method to an in-built Ruby class.

Monkey Patching

Another feature of metaprogramming is monkey patching, where we can override the existing method of a class by opening the class and modifying the definition at runtime. For example, if you are using a third-party library that is conflicting with your class method, which leads to a bug, then in this case, we monkey patch that specific method of the class.

Monkey patching is a debatable concept since it places tremendous power in the hands of developers and should be used very carefully, and only in situations where it is really required. Let's now look at an example of monkey patching in order to understand it practically.

An array class in Ruby is an in-built class and includes many out-of-the-box methods. An out-of-the-box feature or functionality (also called OOTB, or off-the-shelf), particularly in software, is a feature or functionality of a product that works immediately, without any special installation, without any configuration, or without modification.

One of the methods most commonly used is **size**, which returns the size of an array.

Now, let's try to monkey patch this method:

```
my_array = ["Hello", "World"]
puts my_array.size
```

Executing this file from the Terminal will provide the following result:

```
2
```

Figure 10.2: Array object size

This was the expected result, since the size of this array object, **my_array**, is clearly **2**. However, imagine we have a requirement where we must always increment the size of an array by **3** for our program. In order to meet such a requirement, we can monkey patch the **size** method of the Ruby array class using the following code:

```ruby
class Array
  def size
    self.length + 3
  end
end
my_array = ["Hello", "World"]
puts my_array.size
```

The output should be as shown in the following screenshot:

5

Figure 10.3: Monkey patching

Here, we are overriding the in-built **size** method and adding **3** to whatever result we get using another array method **length**.

Now, the Ruby program for array object sizes has a new definition, everywhere. This was a very straightforward example to facilitate an understanding of monkey patching.

Let's now add an error to see how much damage incorrect code can do to an in-built class.

We will now add some logic to divide the integer value **1** by **0**, which would result in an error:

```ruby
class Array
  def size
    1/0
  end
end
my_array = ["Hello", "World"]
puts my_array.size
$ ruby monkey_patch_error.rb
```

The output would appear as follows:

```
Traceback (most recent call last):
        2: from prefix.rb:8:in `<main>'
        1: from prefix.rb:3:in `size'
prefix.rb:3:in `/': divided by 0 (ZeroDivisionError)
```

Figure 10.4: Monkey patching

Here, you can see the implementation of incorrect logic using monkey patching and how this would spoil this class for this Ruby program.

Exercise 10.02: Using Monkey Patching to Add/Subtract Values

In this exercise, we will create a program that would add the value **2** to any number passed. Then, we will monkey patch the same class to subtract the value **2** from any number passed to it. The following steps will help you to complete this exercise:

1. Define the **calculation** class. It is initialized with **first_number**, which is used to set the initial value for objects in the **calculation** class. Next, we have a method, **sum**, that adds **2** to the value set in **first_number**:

```
class Calculation
  attr_accessor :first_number
  def sum
    self.first_number + 2
  end
end
```

2. Next, we initialize the object of this class:

```
calc_obj1 = Calculation.new
calc_obj1.first_number = 10
puts calc_obj1.sum
```

3. Next, we monkey patch the **sum** method of the **calculation** class by opening the class:

```
class Calculation
  def sum
    self.first_number - 2
  end
end
```

Note that we only had to modify the definition of the **sum** method, while the initialization of **first_number** stays as it is in the original class definition.

We are subtracting **2** from the initial value, which is set using the **sum** method.

4. Next, we initialize the object of the class:

```
calc_obj2 = Calculation.new
calc_obj2.first_number = 10
puts calc_obj2.sum
```

The output should be as follows:

12

8

Figure 10.5: Output for monkey patching

It is amazing when you first discover that you can modify methods right in the core classes, but monkey patching executed incorrectly can render the program a train wreck. Always think through the edge cases in the case of monkey patching. It is advisable to avoid using monkey patching for core classes and libraries. Its application is preferred in relation to classes created on your own.

method_missing

method_missing is an important tool in the toolbox of Ruby metaprogramming. It is a callback method you can use that gets called when an object tries to call a method that is missing.

Imagine you have created a class that has two methods, and, in your program, you call a method that does not exist in the class. Since this method is not present, then the search moves up the hierarchy, eventually reaching **BasicObject**.

In **BasicObject**, there is a private method called **method_missing**. The system now cycles through one more time to look for **method_missing** in our class and checks whether there are any matches for **method_missing** to produce the desired result.

Essentially, in our class, we are simply overriding **method_missing** from **BasicObject**.

Let's understand this with a simple example by creating a **MyClass** class with no method. Initialize its object, **obj1**, and call the **xyz** method, which does not exist:

```
class MyClass
end
obj1 = MyClass.new.xyz
```

Run this code from the Terminal:

```
$ ruby method_missing_basics.rb
```

The output should be as follows:

```
Traceback (most recent call last):
    prefix.rb:3:in `<main>': undefined method `xyz' for #<MyClass:0x0000000000480940> (NoMethodError)
```

Figure 10.6: NoMethodError

It is quite clear that we have no method as **xyz** in **MyClass**, which we can use with the object, **obj1**.

Let's now modify our class and add **method_missing** to it:

```
class MyClass
  def method_missing(method_name, *args, &block)
    puts "The method you have specified #{method_name} does not exist"
  end
end
obj1 = MyClass.new.xyz
```

Run this code from the Terminal:

```
$ruby method_missing_basics.rb
```

The output should be as follows:

```
          The method you have specified xyz does not exist
```

Figure 10.7: Output for method_missing

When we modified our code and added **method_missing**, we did get a **puts** statement placed in the method instead of giving an undefined error method.

Let's now understand some of the various parameters accepted by **method_missing**:

```
def method_missing (method_name, *args, &block)
end
```

- **method_name**: This is the name of the method you are calling.

- ***args**: These are splat arguments passed to the method.

- **&block**: This is the block of code that defines the functioning of the method.

If you look closely at these three parameters, we can create a method dynamically at runtime, which helps us to create code that creates code, and that is why `method_missing` is a key feature of metaprogramming.

> **Note**
>
> Methods defined using `method_missing` are also known as ghost methods, as there are an endless number of such methods and all can be tackled by defining and responding to calls via `method_missing`.

Whenever we override `method_missing`, it's a good practice to also define `respond_to_missing?`. This method is called when `respond_to?` is called.

`respond_to?` is a commonly used method and, if a ghost method exists, it should return **true**. However, if we do not define `respond_to_missing?`, the computer will return false, even though the missing method is defined.

Let's now look at the following example, where we define a class, **MyClass**, as having the `method_missing` method defined for the method, **xyz**, which returns a string. However, this method does not have `respond_to_missing?` defined:

```ruby
class MyClass
  def method_missing (method_name, *args, &block)
    if method_name.to_s == "xyz"
        puts "You are now in ghost method"
    else
        super
    end
  end
end
obj1 = MyClass.new
obj1.xyz
puts obj1.respond_to?(:xyz)
```

Run this file from the Terminal with the following command:

```
$ ruby respond_to_missing_basics.rb
```

The output should be as follows:

```
You are now in ghost method
false
```

Figure 10.8: Ghost method

Please note that even though we have **method_missing** defined for the method, **xyz**, we still get a **false** value for **respond_to?**.

Let's also define **respond_to_missing?** for any ghost method that starts with an **x**:

```ruby
class MyClass
  def method_missing(method_name, *args, &block)
    if method_name.to_s == "xyz"
        puts "You are now in ghost method"
    else
        super
    end
  end
  def respond_to_missing?(method_name,  include_private = false)
    method_name.to_s.start_with?('x') || super
  end
end
obj1 = MyClass.new
obj1.xyz
puts obj1.respond_to?(:xyz)
```

Run this file from the Terminal using the following command:

```
$ ruby respond_to_missing_basics.rb
```

The output should be as follows:

```
You are now in ghost method
true
```

Figure 10.9: Output for respond_to_missing

Now, we get an appropriate response to the **respond_to?** method.

Exercise 10.03: Managing Ghost Methods for the Company Class

In this exercise, we will be creating a company class that includes employee details, such as name, ID, and location, using the in-built **ostruct** library. We will be implementing **method_missing** to give an appropriate response to methods that start with **employee_**:

1. Create a new Ruby file.

2. Then, we require the **ostruct** library from the in-built Ruby libraries:

   ```
   require 'ostruct'
   ```

3. Next, we create a **Company** class and define the variables – **name**, **ID**, and **location**, within the class:

   ```
   class Company
     def initialize(name, id, location)
       @name = name
       @id = id
       @location = location
     end
   ```

4. Next, we define the employee and also the **new_employee** methods in the same class:

   ```
     def employee
       OpenStruct.new(name: @name, id: @id, department: @location)
     end
   end
   new_employee = Company.new("Akshat", "007", "Tokyo")
   puts new_employee.employee_location
   puts new_employee.respond_to?(:employee_location)
   ```

5. Let's run this program to see the result. Type the following command from the Terminal:

   ```
   $ruby exercise3.rb
   ```

   The output should be as follows:

```
Traceback (most recent call last):
prefix.rb:15:in `<main>': undefined method `employee_location' for #<Company:0x0000000002bb9b60> (NoMethodError)
```

Figure 10.10: Undefined method error

As you can see, we see an error because we are calling a method on the company class object that does not exist. If you look closely, the error itself is indicating to us that there is no method like this, and so we should create one.

We have created an object of the **company** class and then called the **employee_location** method. However, that method does not exist and so the program breaks. We have also called a **respond_to** method on **new_employee**.

If you replace this with the **employee_location** method when called, you will get a **false** value since no **respond_to_missing?** method exists.

6. We will handle all ghost methods that start with **employee_**. Update the code in this file with the following **method_missing** and **respond_to_missing?** methods:

Exercise10.03.rb

```
14    def method_missing(method_name, *args, &block)
15      if method_name.to_s =~ /employee_(.*)/
16          employee.send($1, *args, &block)
17      else
18          super
19      end
20    end
21
22    def respond_to_missing?(method_name, include_private = false)
23      method_name.to_s.start_with?('employee') || super
24    end
25 end
```

https://packt.live/2q8hzVh

Here, we are using regular expressions for matching. Regular expressions help us to match a pattern for a string. The pattern should be between the forward slashes (**/**).

For example, in the preceding code, we are using **/employee_(.*)/**, so anything starting with **employee_** will be matched. The **$** variable will retain the information about the last match.

7. Let's run this program to see the result. Type the following command from the Terminal:

```
$ ruby exercise3.rb
```

The output should be as follows:

Tokyo
true

Figure 10.11: Output for method_missing and respond_to_missing

We have now achieved the desired result. We sent `employee_location`, hence, we got the location as `Tokyo` in our result. Had we called a **ghost** method, `employee_age`, we would have not obtained any result. Play around by creating more ghost methods to see whether there are any changes in the results.

The Define Method

Similar to `method_missing`, `define_method` helps us to create methods dynamically at runtime. Hence, it qualifies as a tool in Ruby's metaprogramming toolbox. Essentially, `define_method` works in tandem with `method_missing` to make the code **DRY** (**Do-not Repeat Yourself**), where, instead of using **def**, we use `define_method`.

Let's look at its syntax:

```ruby
class Factory
  define_method("operate_machinery") do |argument|
    "Starting machines on all assembly lines in #{argument}"
  end
  define_method("package_products") do |argument|
    "Packaging #{argument} products "
  end
  define_method("send_for_distribution") do |argument|
    "Sending for distribution for #{argument}"
  end
  define_method("generate_exit_pass") do |argument|
    "Generate exit pass for #{argument}"
  end
end
  factory = Factory.new
  puts factory.operate_machinery("Manchester")
  puts factory.package_products("healthcare")
  puts factory.send_for_distribution("medical stores")
  puts factory.generate_exit_pass("trucks")
```

If you look here, we have a different syntax for defining a method instead of **def** and **end**; we are using `define_method` and **end**. In the preceding code snippet, we have a class, **Factory**, that has various `define_method` methods that return a statement along with the argument passed.

Let's run this program to see the output. Run the following command from the Terminal:

```
$ ruby define_method_basics.rb
```

The output should be as follows:

```
Starting machines on all assembly lines in Manchester
Packaging healthcare products
Sending for distribution for medical stores
Generate exit pass for trucks
```

Figure 10.12: Using define_method

define_method is best used with lists where we can loop around a list and place define_method in it to keep creating methods when called. We will learn about this in the next exercise.

Exercise 10.04: Creating a Welcome Message Program Using define_method

In this exercise, we will create a Ruby program that will deliver a welcome message to customers across five countries: France, Japan, England, Germany, and Brazil:

1. Create a new Ruby file, exercise.rb.

2. Create a WelcomeMessage class, which has a number of methods that will be generated using a list. We loop over this list and, using the list value, generate methods with the help of define_method:

```
class WelcomeMessage
  countries = %w(fr jp eng de br)
  countries.each do |country|
    define_method("message_for_#{country}") do |argument|
      "Welcome to Ruby Fundamentals, this is a reader from #{argument}."
    end
  end
End
```

3. Outside the class, we create a class object and call various methods, passing the name of the country as an argument. In the define method, we are making use of the list value and argument passed while calling to get the desired results:

```
greeting = WelcomeMessage.new
puts greeting.message_for_fr("France")
puts greeting.message_for_jp("Japan")
puts greeting.message_for_eng("England")
puts greeting.message_for_de("Germany")
puts greeting.message_for_br("Brazil")
```

4. Run the preceding code using the following command from the Terminal:

```
$ ruby exercise.rb
```

The output should be as follows:

```
Welcome to Ruby Fundamentals, this is a reader from France.
Welcome to Ruby Fundamentals, this is a reader from Japan.
Welcome to Ruby Fundamentals, this is a reader from England.
Welcome to Ruby Fundamentals, this is a reader from Germany.
Welcome to Ruby Fundamentals, this is a reader from Brazil.
```

Figure 10.13: Output for define_method

HTTP Requests

HTTP (**Hypertext Transfer Protocol**) is used to make requests and receive responses over the internet. HTTP helps in transferring data from one point to another over a network.

Such requests are most common when you interact with an external server, or APIs, to receive data or submit data to them. Essentially, no real-world applications are possible without making HTTP requests The most common way of organizing APIs is to use the constraints set by REST. **REST** (**REpresentational State Transfer**) is an architectural type that has prescribed standards for various systems to communicate with one another. These APIs are characterized by the separation of concerns between client and server (for example, if we make a Ruby program that interacts with an API, our program with the client and API to which the request is made will be the server).

For now, we will not go into detail about REST, but we will learn how to use it and how easy it makes it to interact with backend APIs.

With REST, there is a proper structure to make a request that generally comprises the following:

- An HTTP verb; these are methods that define what operation should be performed (get, submit, update, or destroy the data)
- A header, information that tells which client passed information about the request
- The path of the resource
- An optional message body that contains additional data

There are five commonly used HTTP verbs that are used to interact with resources when making a request in REST:

- **GET**: The HTTP GET verb is used to react to or retrieve data from a resource.

- **POST**: The HTTP POST verb is used to create a new resource.

- **PUT**: The HTTP PUT verb is used to update a specific resource.

- **PATCH**: The HTTP PATCH verb is used to modify a resource, but not completely. This looks similar to PUT, but there is a slight difference in that the PATCH body also contains a set of instructions.

- **DELETE**: The HTTP DELETE verb is used to remove a resource by ID.

HTTP Requests with Ruby

Ruby has an in-built HTTP client called **net/http**. An HTTP client helps to make various types of HTTP requests using one of the methods explained previously, along with the URL and payload if required. The payload is a set of data that may be required by an external server to take some sort of action; for example, in the case of a search request, the payload could be the search keyword we have punched in the text field and then submitted. Using the in-built **net/http** package, you can make an HTTP request right away.

Let's see how a GET request will look with **net/http**. Let's first understand the syntax of a GET request with Ruby's **net/http** library:

```
require 'net/http'
Net::HTTP.get('example.com', '/index.html')
```

This is a simple GET request made using **net/http**, where we are trying to get a complete **index.html** page from http://example.com. Usually, we save this response and copy the relevant data from it. This technique is used in web scraping to harvest huge amounts of data from other internet websites.

Exercise 10.05: Creating a Ruby Program to Make a Successful GET Request

In this exercise, we will use the Ruby **net/http** library and make use of the https://www.packtpub.com URL to get the data:

1. Create a new Ruby file, **http_get.rb**.

2. First, we require the **net/http** library from the Ruby in-built package:

```
require 'net/http'
```

3. Place the URL in the **URI** method, which is a Ruby module that assists in handling web URLs in Ruby:

```
uri = URI('https://www.packtpub.com')
```

4. Next, we make a **GET** request using this URL and keep the object in a variable response. If the response object has a lot of data, we then print its status code and body using the **response.code** and **response.body** methods, respectively:

```
response = Net::HTTP.get_response(uri)
puts response.code
puts response.body
```

5. Let's now run this Ruby program from the Terminal:

```
$
ruby http_get.rb
```

The output should be as follows:

```
              git:(master)   ruby exercise5.rb
200
 <!doctype html>
<html lang="en">
<head>
<script>
    var BASE_URL = 'https://www.packtpub.com/';
    var require = {
        "baseUrl": "https://www.packtpub.com/static/version1568034315/frontend/Packt/default/en_GB"
    };
</script>
```

Figure 10.14: Get Requests using Ruby

As we can see, with **response.code**, we received the status code **200** for our request from the server, and with **response.body**, we received the data from the GET request we made.

Status Codes

Status codes are provided from the server side, which is in response to a client request made. HTTP status codes are divided into five categories. The first digit of the code defines the class of response. The last two digits do not have any specific class or categorization. The first digit is key to understanding the state of your request. Listed here are five types of status codes:

1xx: Informational

This means that the client request has been received and the process is continuing. This is a client-side status code, and is mainly informational.

2xx: Success

This means that the client request was successfully received, understood, and accepted.

3xx: Redirection

This means that further action must be taken in order to complete the request.

4xx: Client Error

This status code is received in case there has been an error from the client. This means that the request contains incorrect syntax or cannot be fulfilled.

5xx: Server Error

This means that the server failed to fulfill an apparently valid request. This status code indicates that the server is incapable of completing the requests.

> **Note**
>
> Read more on status codes here: https://packt.live/2OP9Rtr.

Exercise 10.06: Creating a POST Request Using Ruby

In this exercise, we will be generating a POST request using the Ruby gem, **httparty**, which simplifies the submission of complicated requests.

Use the following demo URL, **https://my-json-server.typicode.com/typicode/demo/posts**, to make the request.

For parameters of the POST request, use the following format:

```
body: {
id: integer_id, title: ""
  }
```

The following steps will help you to complete the exercise:

1. Create a new Ruby file, **http_post.rb**.

2. Install the **httparty** gem using the following command from the Terminal:

    ```
    $ gem install httparty
    ```

This will install the gem on your system, and you can require it in any Ruby program.

> **Note**
>
> To find out more about this gem, you can refer to its documentation at https:// packt.live/2MfSm42.

3. Now, we require the **httparty** gem in the program:

```
require 'httparty'
```

4. Next, we make a **post** call using a sample API from **my-json-server** (this is a valid API and will work, unless the parameters passed won't get persisted):

```
res = HTTParty.post("https://my-json-server.typicode.com/typicode/demo/posts", body: { id: 5, title: "Ruby Fundamentals" })
```

5. Then, we check the status code received and also the body for the response, which is usually the resource created:

```
puts res.code
puts res.body
```

6. Let's now run this Ruby program from the Terminal:

```
$ ruby http_post.rb
```

The output should be as follows:

```
201
{
  "id": "5",
  "title": "Ruby Fundamentals"
}
```

Figure 10.15: Post request output

As you can see, the output is very clean. We received status code **201**. Since it starts with a **2**, it means we have succeeded, and **201** indicates precisely that the resource has been created. The response body is the value of the data that is used to create the request.

Creating a Ruby Gem

As covered in *Chapter 7, Introduction to Ruby Gems*, a gem is a way for Ruby to package and distribute Ruby programs and libraries. So far, we have been using many open source Ruby gems, which has a positive impact on the speed of development.

In this section, we will learn to create a Ruby gem. Also, **RubyGems** is a package manager for the Ruby programming language and comes with tools baked in by default, which makes it really easy to create a gem and distribute it.

Let's jump right in to creating a simple Ruby gem.

Before you create your first file for your gem, you must make sure to find a suitable name for your gem. RubyGems has official documentation for naming conventions and it is advised to use this for improved programming experiences.

> **Note**
>
> You can refer to this naming convention at https://packt.live/2Bcz1dN.

Exercise 10.07: Creating Your Own Ruby Gem

In this exercise, we will be creating our own Ruby gem, before installing it and then publishing it in a Ruby program:

1. Create two files, namely, **ruby-fundamental-gem.rb** and **ruby-fundamental-gem. gemspec** under the **lib** folder, and place them in a directory, as shown in the following screenshot:

Figure 10.16: Creating Ruby gem files

The code that will be used for our package will reside in the **lib** directory. A good practice is to have one Ruby file with the same name as the gem since, in our case, it will be required as **ruby-fundamental-gem**.

2. Now, we create a class, **RubyFundamental**, and define a method:

```
class RubyFundamental
  def self.hello
    puts "Hello World this is my first gem!"
  end
end
```

3. Next, we move to the **ruby-fundamental-gem.gemspec** file. This file contains information about the gem; for example, the creator, its version number, the contact details for the core team or whoever maintains the gem, and the license:

```
Gem::Specification.new do |s|
  s.name        = 'ruby-fundamental-gem'
  s.version     = '0.0.1'
  s.date        = '2019-06-30'
  s.summary     = "Simple gem to learn how to create gems"
  s.description = "A basic welcome message gem"
  s.authors     = ["Akshat Paul"]
  s.email       = 'akshatpaul@gmail.com'
  s.homepage    = %q{http://www.akshatpaul.com/}
  s.files       = ["lib/ruby-fundamental-gem.rb"]
  s.license     = 'MIT'
end
```

4. Once you have filled in the basic specifications for the gem, build and install this generated gem locally. Run the following command from the Terminal:

```
$ gem build ruby-fundamental-gem.gemspec
```

The output should be as follows:

```
            git:(master)   ruby exercise5.rb
200
 <!doctype html>
<html lang="en">
<head>
<script>
    var BASE_URL = 'https://www.packtpub.com/';
    var require = {
        "baseUrl": "https://www.packtpub.com/static/version1568034315/frontend/Packt/default/en_GB"
    };
</script>
```

Figure 10.17: Creating a gem

5. Now, install this gem locally, which we can then use with any Ruby program locally without a machine. Run the following command from the same folder on the Terminal:

```
$ gem install ruby-fundamental-gem-0.0.1.gem
```

The output should be as follows:

```
                    git:(master)    irb
2.6.3 :001 > require 'ruby-fundamental-gem'
 => true
2.6.3 :002 > RubyFundamental.hello
Hello World this is my first gem!
 => nil
```

Figure 10.18: Installing a Ruby gem

Our gem is successfully installed. Now, let's try using this gem by requiring it. Open IRB and use the following code to test it:

```
$ irb
require 'ruby-fundamental-gem'

RubyFundamental.hello
```

The output should be as follows:

```
                    git:(master)    irb
2.6.3 :001 > require 'ruby-fundamental-gem'
 => true
2.6.3 :002 > RubyFundamental.hello
Hello World this is my first gem!
 => nil
```

Figure 10.19: Requiring a Ruby gem

We have now successfully installed the gem.

6. Publish this gem on the Ruby community; it will be available for use worldwide.

   Log in and set up your credentials using the https://rubygems.org/sign_up URL.

7. Download your **api_key,** which will be used to publish any gem using the following URL: https://rubygems.org/api/v1/api_key.yaml.

   Simply paste this URL in the browser. You will be prompted to add your credentials and the key will start downloading automatically.

8. Create a `.gem` folder in your RubyGem package and add this file but rename it as `credentials.yaml`.

    Run the following command to publish your gem:

    ```
    $ gem push gem_name.gem
    ```

Thus, we have successfully created our own Ruby gem and published it for the world to use.

Activity 10.01: Implementing GET and POST Data to an External Server

In this activity, we will be creating a Ruby program to get JSON data from a public API, and then parse and print the response. Also, we will post new data to the public API.

The public APIs to be used for this activity are as follows:

*   To get data: https://packt.live/33BUM2v

*   To post data: https://packt.live/2MfHItS

Note that the second link will become functional only after the activity is completed. To post data using the preceding backend API, only the name and address fields are required to create new records like this:

```
{
property: {
name: "my_name", require 'ostruct'
address: "my_address"
}
}
```

The following steps should help you to complete this activity:

1. Install and require the **httparty** gem.

2. Create a file for GET requests. Assign a GET request API to a URL variable.

3. Next, make a GET call using **httparty** and display the response using an in-built method, **parsed_response**, which properly parses the JSON response.

    You can implement the same code with a few more lines by using the in-built **net/ http** library and the JSON library.

The output should be as follows:

```
                    git:(master)    ruby get_request.rb
200
{"name"=>"Burj Khalifa", "address"=>"Dubai"}
{"name"=>"Shanghai Tower", "address"=>"Shanghai"}
{"name"=>"Lotte World Tower", "address"=>"Seoul"}
{"name"=>"International Commerce Centre", "address"=>"Hong Kong"}
{"name"=>"Petronas Tower", "address"=>"Kuala Lumpur"}
{"name"=>"Park Avenue", "address"=>"New York City"}
```

Figure 10.20: GET request output

4. Create a file for POST requests.

5. Next, assign our POST API to the URL variable. Make a POST request, along with the URL and a body with proper fields, as per the contract specified in the problem statement.

    The output should be as follows:

```
                git:(master)    ruby post_request.rb
200
```

Figure 10.21: POST request output

6. Check and verify whether the records exist in both the aforementioned URLs.

> **Note**
>
> The solution to the activity can be found on page 486.

Summary

In this chapter, we learned skills that are commonly used in real-world problems, such as metaprogramming, communicating with backend APIs, and creating reusable gems. No Ruby framework or open source library is complete without making use of a lot of metaprogramming. We learned various techniques as well as some of the in-built features of Ruby, including open class, `method_missing`, `respond_to_missing?`, monkey patching, and `define_method`. Next, we learned how to make HTTP requests to interact with external APIs over a network. Lastly, we learned how to package and distribute our reusable code by creating gems ourselves.

In the next chapter, we will learn about the most popular Ruby framework or, should we say, one of the world's most widely used server-side web application frameworks – Ruby on Rails.

11

Introduction to Ruby on Rails I

Overview

By the end of this chapter, you will be able to use the Model-View-Controller (MVC) pattern to create your first Rails application; explain how Action Controller and Action View work together; implement routes, Rails models, and Active Record in a Rails application; save data, set up databases, and create migrations to alter a database schema, create views for web applications quickly with Rails helper methods and use the Rails console and perform Create, Read, Update, Delete (CRUD) operations for a web application.

This chapter aims to equip you with knowledge about Ruby on Rails and the underlying fundamentals that power Rails and make it one of the most popular web application frameworks.

Introduction

In the previous chapter, we learned about advanced topics in Ruby, such as metaprogramming, how to open existing classes and add new methods to them, and how to monkey patch to create dynamic methods on the fly. We also learned about how to interact with external servers by making RESTful calls to them.

In this chapter, we will learn about Ruby on Rails, also known as Rails or ROR. It is a server-side web application framework distributed as a Ruby gem, written in Ruby and first released in 2005. With Ruby on Rails, we can build real-world web applications quickly. Rails is one of the most popular application frameworks for building web applications quickly. It has best practices of web development built into its architecture to create secure, robust, and scalable web apps. Some popular web applications built using Ruby on Rails are Basecamp, GitHub, Shopify, Airbnb, Twitch, SoundCloud, Hulu, Zendesk, and Square – the list goes on.

Ruby on Rails was originally authored by David Heinemeier Hansson (popularly known as DHH) who sourced it from his project management tool Basecamp. DHH then opensourced it in July 2004 and allowed commit rights to the project only in February 2005. In 2007, Ruby on Rails reached a new milestone when Apple announced that it would ship Ruby on Rails along with macOS X. Ruby on Rails is published under the MIT license. It has a core team and a large number of contributors (over 5,000 across the world). In 2005, version 1.0 of Ruby on Rails was released, and the latest stable release is version 5.2, which was released in 2018.

Ruby on Rails is an MVC-based framework that comes with a standard structure for databases, templating engines, web pages, and interacting with databases. It encourages the use of standards such as JSON and XML for data transfer and the use of HTML/CSS/JavaScript for user interfaces. The following are two guiding principles of the Rails philosophy:

- Don't Repeat Yourself (DRY), which means avoiding repetition in code

- Convention over configuration, which means following best practices and following set conventions rather than using numerous configuration files

MVC

MVC is short for Model-View-Controller and is a design pattern that's used to develop web applications. It essentially divides an application in development into three distinct parts – a model, a view, and a controller. They are interconnected in a way that allows maximum reuse of code and effective parallel development, as shown in the following figure:

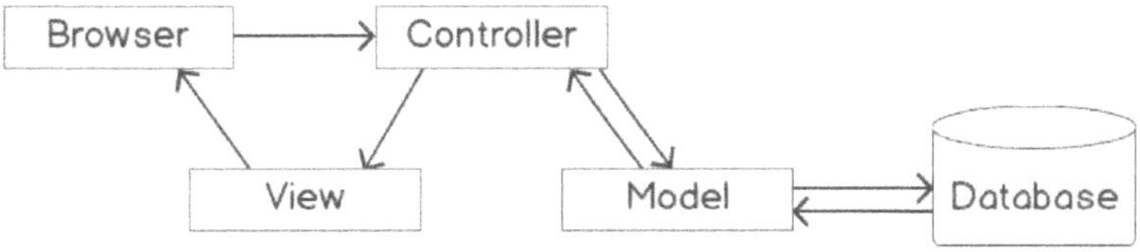

Figure 11.1: Basic architecture of the MVC pattern

In an MVC-based application, a user interacts with the view, which in turn raises an appropriate request with a URL, hitting a controller. The controller handles this request by either interacting with the appropriate model or rendering the required video.

Let's look at each of these components in detail.

Model

The model is the central component of this architecture. It is where we keep the business logic and the rules of the application, as well as being where we maintain the data. Model objects interact and store the model state in a database. The user never directly interacts with a model. Rather, this transaction is only performed through a controller. For example, the data that we see in any web application comes from the model. This could be any calculation or a query that is fetching data from a database.

View

The view is the representation component of the MVC pattern. It is responsible for creating **the User Interface (UI)**. The view displays the data that comes from the model on the UI and also allows the end user to interact with this data. All of this happens via the controller. For example, in the case of web application, the website pages that can be seen form the view.

Controller

The controller accepts inputs and user requests, then converts them into commands to interact with the model or view. The controller is the glue between the model and view; it does much of the intermediary work between the two. For example, it is the controller that processes the HTTP request to generate a web page.

In a nutshell:

- The model is for maintaining data and business logic. It receives input from the controller.

- The view is for the UI, which involves the presentation of data from the model via the controller.

- The controller is a request handler between the view and the model. It also performs various other actions and interactions based on user input.

> **Note**
>
> It is always advised to have a fat model and a thin controller. The concept of a thin controller and a fat model means that we do more work in our model and keep our controller as thin as possible. For instance, we may validate data and simply pass it to the model, while in the model we may define business logic, coding operations, and database interactions. This coding style is very common in an MVC architecture and is a guiding light when developing applications.

In Rails, the MVC pattern is managed by Action Pack and Active Record. Active Record manages the interaction between the model and the database – it is the "M" in MVC, while Action Pack consists of Action View and Action Controller, which represent the "V" and "C" in MVC, respectively.

Action View, Action Controller, and Active Record are packed with helper methods to help speed up development. As we proceed in this chapter, we will use some of them.

Generating Our First Rails App

Now that you've been introduced to the theory concerning Ruby on Rails, it's time for us to create our first Rails application and learn about the anatomy of a Rails app.

Rails commands are built-in scripts that help to speed development by handling most of the everyday tasks encountered in day-to-day development. Some popular ones are listed here:

- `rails new app_name`

  This generates a new Rails application with a file structure for the Rails application.

- `rails server`

  This starts a web server named Puma to host a Rails application. This application, by default, is served on localhost port **3000**. Puma is a web server that comes prepackaged with Rails. It's best suited for local development.

- `rails console`

  This helps you interact with the Rails application using your Terminal. The Rails console is a nifty tool that uses IRB. It's a fast way to test your code for a Rails application.

- **`rails test`**

  By default, Rails comes with a testing framework called **`minitest`**. This command helps to run all the tests.

- **`rails generate`**

  This command provides boilerplate code for various Rails components. For example, **`rails generate controller controller_name action_name`** will set up a controller along with its test and corresponding views for actions. It does the same for generating models and migrations (we will learn more about this in the *Models, Migrations, and Databases* section).

- **`rails db:create`**

  This creates a new database for a Rails application.

- **`rails db:migrate`**

  This helps run migrations on a database.

- **`rails routes`**

  This prints all the valid and available routes of the application to the controller and corresponding actions.

Let's now go through an exercise using these commands to build a more profound understanding of Rails.

Exercise 11.01: Generating a Simple Rails Application

In this exercise, we will create a simple Rails application for a travel-planning and advice application called **`citireview`**. We will serve this Rails application over a web server and access it via the browser.

Follow these steps to complete the exercise:

1. Fire up your Terminal and install the Rails gem using the following command, if you haven't installed it with the bundler:

   ```
   gem install rails
   ```

   > **Note**
   >
   > If you have installed the gems using the bundler, you just have to enable the Rails extension from the Visual Studio Code editor interface. Go to Extensions, then search for Rails and install.

2. Create the **citireview** Rails application using the following command:

```
$ rails new citireview
```

This command initiates the installation of various gems and their dependencies for the application, as listed in the following code snippet. The application is set up in the proper Rails structure, along with the installation of gems and the dependencies included with Rails:

```
chapter11 git:(master) ✗ rails new citireview
```

The following gems and dependencies will be installed after running the previous command:

```
create
    create README.md
    create Rakefile
    create config.ru
    create .gitignore
    create Gemfile
    run git init from "."
Initialized empty Git repository in /Users/akshatpaul/myapps/rubyFundamentals/packt-
github/Ruby-Fundamentals/chapter11/citireview/.git/
    create app
    create app/assets/config/manifest.js
    create  app/assets/javascripts/application.js
```

3. To test whether this application is working correctly, go to the **citireview** directory and run the **rails server** command from the Terminal. This will serve the generated Rails application on a web server called Puma:

```
$ cd citireview
$ rails server
```

The output should show up as follows on the Terminal:

```
[➜  citireview2 git:(master) ✗ rails server
=> Booting Puma
=> Rails 5.2.3 application starting in development
=> Run `rails server -h` for more startup options
Puma starting in single mode...
* Version 3.12.1 (ruby 2.6.3-p62), codename: Llamas in Pajamas
* Min threads: 5, max threads: 5
* Environment: development
* Listening on tcp://localhost:3000
Use Ctrl-C to stop
```

Figure 11.2: Initiating the Rails server

This starts our Rails server and the Rails application is served on localhost port **3000**.

4. Test your sample application by visiting **localhost:3000** on your browser, as shown in the following figure:

Rails version: 5.1.7

Ruby version: 2.4.1 (x86_64-darwin17)

Figure 11.3: Output for the Rails application on localhost

This is the default home page when a Rails application is set up. You might find the Rails and Ruby versions to be different on your machine, but not to worry.

> **Note**
>
> For production applications that are served for your end users, it is advised to go for other web server options, such as Phusion Passenger and Unicorn.

Anatomy of a Rails application

Inside our `citireview` application directory reside the auto-generated files and folders that came when we created our application with the automatic scripts included in the Rails gem. The following are the different components that make up the anatomy of a Rails application, along with their descriptions:

- `app/`

  This folder contains models, controllers, views, helpers, mailers, jobs, and assets for a Rails application. Most of the application-specific code files are placed in this directory.

- `bin/`

  This folder contains various scripts that set up, update, and run the Rails application.

- `config/`

  In this folder, we keep various configuration files related to routes, databases, environments, and initializers.

- `config.ru`

  This file is used by a Rack-based server to start the application.

- `db/`

  This folder contains all the files related to databases, such as migrations, schemas, and seed files.

- `Gemfile`, `Gemfile.lock`

  With Gemfile, you can specify the gem and its respective version number. As the name suggests, Gemfile.lock locks the version number of a gem and its dependencies. This helps to keep the application stable across various environments and during the book of development/deployment.

- `lib/`

  In this folder, we keep any other modules that are used for the application.

- `log/`

  This folder contains application log files.

- **`package.json`**

  Similar to Gemfile, this file contains any Node Package Manager (npm) dependencies used by the Rails application.

- **`public/`**

  This folder contains compiled static files and assets for the application. It is a good place to keep any 404 pages, which appear when there are errors, as well as any other public assets or pages.

- **`Rakefile`**

  This file contains tasks that are run from the command line. It's good practice to keep your custom task inside lib/tasks rather than modifying the default tasks.

- **`README.md`**

  This file contains basic documentation about the application. You may add an introduction to your application or basic steps for how to set it up. This is a markdown file, which is very popular for its text-formatting syntax for documentation.

- **`test/`**

  In this folder, we keep all unit tests for the controller, model, mailers, helpers, and other test files used for the application.

- **`tmp/`**

  This folder contains files that are temporary in nature, such as cache content.

- **`vendor/`**

  In this folder, we keep any third-party code, such as any custom gems.

- **`.gitignore`**

  There are many files and folders that are auto-generated by your computer or IDE that you don't want to commit to your code. Such files should be added in this file so that they will be ignored during the commit to the repository.

- **`.ruby-version`**

  In this file, we declare the Ruby version that is used.

The components will look as shown in the following figure in the application directory:

Figure 11.4: Components of a Rails application

Now that we have generated a Rails application with the default Rails page for when we start the server, what we have at the moment is essentially the home page of our **citireview** application.

In reality, the first thing we would want to do is add our own home page with a welcome message, and this is what we will try to achieve in the next exercise.

Exercise 11.02: Replacing the Default Page

In this exercise, we will be creating a new home page for the **citireview** application, essentially replacing the default home page of the application. Follow these steps to complete the exercise:

1. To create this view, we will also require its corresponding controller. Once again, in Rails, we do have a generator for this. Type the following command to generate a controller with its corresponding views:

    ```
    $ rails generate controller Home index
    ```

    The output should show up as follows:

    ```
    [→ citireview2 git:(master) × rails generate controller Home index
    Running via Spring preloader in process 86850
          create    app/controllers/home_controller.rb
           route    get 'home/index'
          invoke    erb
          create      app/views/home
          create      app/views/home/index.html.erb
          invoke    test_unit
          create      test/controllers/home_controller_test.rb
          invoke    helper
          create      app/helpers/home_helper.rb
          invoke      test_unit
          invoke    assets
          invoke      coffee
          create        app/assets/javascripts/home.coffee
          invoke      scss
          create        app/assets/stylesheets/home.scss
    ```

    Figure 11.5: Generating a controller for the citireview application

    As you can see in the preceding figure, we have created a controller and a route **home** folder in **views** with an **index.html.erb** file, along with tests and assets for styling.

2. Open the view from **app/views/home/index.html.erb** and replace the generated code with the following:

    ```
    app/views/home/index.html.erb
    <h1>Welcome to Citireviews</h1>
    <p>This will be the Index page of our app</p>
    ```

The preceding code is HTML code with **h1** tags, which are header tags. This is usually the largest text on an HTML page to emphasize that it's the heading. Next, we have a **p** tag, which is a paragraph section for this page.

> **Note**
>
> erb, or eRuby (Embedded Ruby), is a template system that is used by default in Rails and allows Ruby code to be embedded with an HTML document.

3. Now open the route file. Since we have to make this view the index page of our application, we would have to make it **root_route**. In a Rails web application, **root_route** is the home page. There is a specific convention to be used for this. Open the route file from **config/routes.rb** and replace it with the following code:

```
config/routes.rb
Rails.application.routes.draw do
  root 'home#index'
end
```

The route file is where all the routes, basically all your application URLs, reside. A route is associated with a controller and an action in that controller. Since it's a home page for our application, we are using the Rails **root** keyword, which means you will serve the application on your home URL.

> **Note**
>
> Routes are written in a specific way, as **controller_name#action_name**. It is important to remember the principle of "convention over configuration," as this is a Rails convention.
>
> **root_route** always routes only GET requests to the action controller.

4. Now start the Rails server with the following command and see the changes on **localhost:3000**:

```
$rails server
```

The application will now appear as follows:

Welcome to Citireviews

This will be the Index page of our app

Figure 11.6: Home page of the citireview application

> **Note**
>
> You can also use alias commands such as **rails g** for Rails application generation and **rails s** for the Rails server.

If you open the controller folder, you will find **home_controller.rb** with an **index** method inside it. Any code related to this view, including its variables or any calculation or minimum logic, will reside in this index action.

Now that we have created our landing page for the application, it is time to add some customization to it. We will now display the heading with a variable value.

Exercise 11.03: Displaying a Page Heading from the Value Served from Its Action

In this exercise, we will add a variable in the **index** action with a string and display an H1 heading on the landing page of our **citireview** application. Follow these steps to complete the exercise:

1. Open **app/controllers/home_controller.rb** and add the following code. We are creating an action for the controller to display the index values with a string that says "Welcome to our Site":

```
class HomeController < ApplicationController
  def index
    @welcome_message = "Welcome to our Site"
  end
end
```

2. Open **/app/views/home/index.html.erb** and add the following code, which defines the index value of the page to display the heading with the value defined with it:

```
<h1><%= @welcome_message %> </h1>
<p>This will be the Index page of our app</p>
```

3. Start the Rails server from the root of this directory:

```
$ rails server
```

The output should show as follows in the Terminal:

```
[→ citireview2 git:(master) × rails server
=> Booting Puma
=> Rails 5.2.3 application starting in development
=> Run `rails server -h` for more startup options
Puma starting in single mode...
* Version 3.12.1 (ruby 2.6.3-p62), codename: Llamas in Pajamas
* Min threads: 5, max threads: 5
* Environment: development
* Listening on tcp://localhost:3000
Use Ctrl-C to stop
```

Figure 11.7: Rails server initialization

4. Open a browser and go to **localhost:3000** to see the output:

Welcome to our Site

This will be the Index page of our app

Figure 11.8: Output for the Rails application

We have successfully updated the heading on the landing page, which is coming from the variable we declared in the index action in the controller.

Extending Our View and Controller

Now that we have the basic Rails application set up, we can add the key features that should appear as part of any review web application. For instance, we will now add a feature to add reviews on the application.

We will create a **Review** resource for our **citireview** application. In Rails, the term "resource" is used to refer to a collection of similar things. For example, if there is a collection of grocery items or a collection of invoices, it is referred to as a resource. We can apply **CRUD** operations for an item of a resource. **CRUD** refers to **Create**, **Read**, **Update**, and **Delete** operations, which are the most fundamental operations applied on any item of a resource at any given time. We will be either creating a record, reading a record, updating a record, or destroying a record.

Rails comes with a **resources** method, which can be used in **config/routes.rb** to declare a standard REST resource. By "REST resource," we mean that all RESTful routes and their corresponding actions will be set up in our routes and we don't have to explicitly add them one by one.

Let's now add a resource to the **citireview** application.

Exercise 11.04: Adding a Resource to the Rails Application

In this exercise, we will be adding a **Review** resource to our application, which will allow the user to add their reviews for a city or specific locations. The following steps will help you complete the exercise:

1. Open the **config/routes.rb** file and add the following code to it. We are essentially declaring the route of our application here:

```
Rails.application.routes.draw do
  root 'home#index'
  resources :reviews
end
```

2. To see what's been set up, type the following command inside your project folder:

```
$ rails routes
```

The output should look like this:

```
|→ citireview git:(master) × rails routes
              Prefix Verb   URI Pattern                   Controller#Action
                root GET    /                             home#index
             reviews GET    /reviews(.:format)            reviews#index
                     POST   /reviews(.:format)            reviews#create
          new_review GET    /reviews/new(.:format)        reviews#new
         edit_review GET    /reviews/:id/edit(.:format)   reviews#edit
              review GET    /reviews/:id(.:format)        reviews#show
                     PATCH  /reviews/:id(.:format)        reviews#update
                     PUT    /reviews/:id(.:format)        reviews#update
                     DELETE /reviews/:id(.:format)        reviews#destroy
```

Figure 11.9: File setup for the resources method

As you can see, we have all the RESTful routes defined for us by default. We need to define their respective actions; otherwise, we will get errors. Remember that these are just placeholder routes; their actions are to be created and defined by us.

Having our resources defined first helps us to implement our CRUD operations. We start with the controller.

3. Generate a **Reviews** controller using the following command:

```
$ rails generate controller Reviews
```

The command output should be as follows:

```
Running via Spring preloader in process 41916
      create  app/controllers/reviews_controller.rb
      invoke  erb
      create    app/views/reviews
      invoke  test_unit
      create    test/controllers/reviews_controller_test.rb
      invoke  helper
      create    app/helpers/reviews_helper.rb
      invoke    test_unit
      invoke  assets
      invoke    coffee
      create      app/assets/javascripts/reviews.coffee
      invoke    scss
      create      app/assets/stylesheets/reviews.scss
```

Spring is a Rails application pre-loader. Its job is to allow an application to run in the background so that there is no need to restart the server every time a task, test, or migration executes. This saves time and results in faster development.

4. Now we will add the required method for our CRUD operations in **app/controllers/reviews_controller.rb**, which, if you take a look now, will be empty. Since we want to create a new record, that is, a new review, we will first define a **new** action in our controller. Open **app/controllers/reviews_controller.rb** and add the following code in it:

```
class ReviewsController < ApplicationController
    def new
    end
end
```

Ruby provides many types of access modifiers, (including private, public, and protected) but all actions must be public. Since action methods are accessed by the view, there would otherwise be an error.

5. Test accessing this action using the URL **http://localhost:3000/reviews/new** we saw with rails route using our browser. Start your server with the following command:

```
$ rails server
```

The error will show up in the output, as follows:

ActionController::UnknownFormat in ReviewsController#new

ReviewsController#new is missing a template for this request format and variant. request.formats: ["text/html"] request.variant: [] NOTE! For XHR/Ajax or API requests, this action would normally respond with 204 No Content: an empty white screen. Since you're loading it in a web browser, we assume that you expected to actually render a template, not nothing, so we're showing an error to be extra-clear. If you expect 204 No Content, carry on. That's what you'll get from an XHR or API request. Give it a shot.

Figure 11.10: ActionController error

Now that is an informative error. The first line gives us a hint as to what is missing: the template. Basically, the application is able to access our **new** action, but there is no corresponding view for it to display. Rails first goes to **reviews/new** to load that template. It then goes to **application/new** to see whether there is a template, since our **ReviewsController** is inherited from **ApplicationController**. So, if you want to add some generic view for the entire application, you can create an application folder and add it there.

6. In this step, we will create a view named **new.html.erb** inside the **view/reviews** folder. The functionality of this view will be to display a form to add a review for our Rails application. Create an **app/views/reviews/new.html.erb** file and add the following code in it, which is a heading with a form to submit a review:

```
<h1>Add new review</h1>
<%= form_with scope: :review, url: reviews_path, local: true do |form| %>
  <p>
    <%= form.label :name %><br>
    <%= form.text_field :name %>
  </p>
  <p>
    <%= form.label :description %><br>
    <%= form.text_area :description %>
  </p>
  <p>
    <%= form.submit %>
  </p>
<% end %>
```

We have now created an **html.erb** page with HTML tags and have embedded the Ruby code within it. We have added the heading in the **h1** tag and have generated a form with a submit button and an action to call.

To inject Ruby code in **html.erb**, use **<%= %>** or **<% %>**. The equals sign indicates that it's an expression and displays the content of the Ruby code. Without the equals sign, the syntax means that the code is a part of the script and the content of the Ruby code won't be displayed.

In order to create a form, we have used a Rails form builder. We used a helper method, **form_with**. This **form_with** helper method is passed with a scope, which is our resource name, **review**, which tells **form_with** what this form is. We have also added the URL, which is the **form** action where the form should pass the parameters mentioned for submission.

reviews_path is another helper method, and it tells Rails to pass the form parameters to a **URI** pattern associated with reviews. The fact that we're submitting a form is how we end up with a POST request instead of a GET request.

Finally, inside the form, we use the **FormBuilder** object, which uses the **label**, **text_field**, **text_area**, and **form.submit** objects to create this form. It is time to make the **create** action in **ReviewsController**, which will interact with a model and save this review in a database.

7. If your Rails server is still up, you have to simply reload the page on your browser at **http://localhost:3000/reviews/new**.

    It should look like this:

Figure 11.11: Review resource added to the application

We have successfully added a review functionality to our application.

You don't need to restart your server again and again after every change in Rails. In development mode, the Rails server automatically detects changes and gives you fresh results. This is one of the key features that powers faster development with Ruby on Rails. However, there are times when you have to restart your Rails server; the rule of thumb is that anything outside **app/**, **config/routes.rb**, or **db/** requires a restart of the Rails server.

Next, try filling in and submitting the form:

Figure 11.12: Adding review

You will get the following error:

Figure 11.13: Unknown action error

As you can see, the application is trying to find a **create** action in the controller.

8. Add the following code to **app/controller/reviews_controller.rb**:

```
class ReviewsController < ApplicationController
    def new
    end
    def create
    end
 end
```

Though it is empty, it is sufficient for now. Go back, refresh, and click on submit again though you won't get any error or success on the browser, check the Terminal and you will see that the request is made. You will see the output as follows:

```
Started POST "/reviews" for ::1 at 2019-09-19 11:30:17 +0530
Processing by ReviewsController#create as HTML
  Parameters: {"utf8"=>"✓",
"authenticity_token"=>"9Ir7+Epf8rnSZCXlx+CJgygomlQ2Ry68riXamfnvdxCKr+FekW9mDoJtkgKZLpFhq4Dym7
Dym9jm/jCdXzuVLQ=="}, "review"=>{"name"=>"The Great Pizza Place", "description"=>"Amazing
pizza's quick delivery"}, "commit"=>"Save Review"}
No template found for ReviewsController#create, rendering head :no_content
Completed 204 No Content in 85ms
```

Figure 11.14: Output for review

We can see that a POST request is made. We can even see the parameters that have been filled in the form. We have received a **204** status code, which means that the request is successful but the client doesn't need to leave the current page.

Since we are not doing anything in the **create** action, the application will be stuck on the page.

Let's now look at building a model and adding a database to our application.

Models, Migrations, and Databases

Active Record is the power behind the model in Rails – the "M" in MVC – which manages data and business logic. Active Record helps in the creation of business objects whose data exists in a database. All this interaction is managed very easily since Active Record is an **Object Relational Mapping (ORM)** system.

> **Note**
>
> To know more about ORM, see https://packt.live/33BjMXZ.

Rails, by default, comes with SQLite support, which is a lightweight serverless database. However, with production applications, it's possible to end up overloading SQLite, so it is advised to use a more stable database, such as PostgreSQL or MySQL. For development, we will also use SQLite, but when we deploy our application for production, we will use PostgreSQL. The switch from SQLite to PostgreSQL is very simple.

To see your database settings, open **config/database.yml**:

```
# SQLite version 3.x
#   gem install sqlite3
#   Ensure the SQLite 3 gem is defined in your Gemfile
#   gem 'sqlite3'
default: &default
  adapter: sqlite3
  pool: <%= ENV.fetch("RAILS_MAX_THREADS") { 5 } %>
  timeout: 5000
development:
  <<: *default
  database: db/development.sqlite3
# Warning: The database defined as "test" will be erased and
# re-generated from your development database when you run "rake".
# Do not set this db to the same as development or production.
test:
  <<: *default
  database: db/test.sqlite3
production:
  <<: *default
  database: db/production.sqlite3
```

As you can see, we have three sections, for the development, test, and production environments, and we can set up different databases for different environments. Also, the switch between SQLite to PostgreSQL is super simple with **database.yml**.

Migrations are a neat way in Rails to create and alter your database schema over time in a simple and consistent way. It uses a Ruby **Domain Specific Language (DSL)** so that you don't have to write raw SQL code, allowing your database schema and its changes to be stable and independent. With the Ruby DSL, the complexities of raw SQL are hidden and we are able to interact with the database using a simple syntax.

Over time, we may have to create a new table, add columns to a table, or make any other alterations. For this, we can use migrations, which create new versions of a database. Migrations always run in order; if we need to roll back, we can simply reverse the order. This convention of migration makes database operation very predictable and stable. A database schema starts with nothing in it. As we proceed, our schema keeps on updating and ends up being a reflection of our actual metal database, which sits behind.

Let's now create a review model for the `citireview` application using a database.

Exercise 11.05: Creating a Review Model for citireview

In this exercise, we will create a review model to store review details in a database table, taking input from the user. Follow these steps to complete the exercise:

1. Create a **Review** model with two attributes. Go to your Terminal and then to the root of your **citireview** directory and type following command. The generator will generate the required files and folders:

```
$ rails generate model Review name:string description:string
```

The output on the Terminal should be as follows:

```
[➔ citireview2 git:(master) × rails generate model Review name:string description:string
Running via Spring preloader in process 88152
      invoke  active_record
      create    db/migrate/20190919062855_create_reviews.rb
      create    app/models/review.rb
      invoke    test_unit
      create      test/models/review_test.rb
      create      test/fixtures/reviews.yml
```

Figure 11.15: Generating model for Review

> **Note**
>
> Just as we have a **generate** command, we also have a **destroy** command, which essentially destroys whatever has been generated by the **generate** command. The "destroy" equivalent of the **generate** command we used is `rails destroy model Review`.

As you can see, this generator has created a **Review** model along with its test files. To seed initial data, there is also a YAML file in **fixtures**. **YAML** is the short form of **YAML Ain't Markup Language**, which is a way to keep configurations in a human-readable format.

> **Note**
>
> To find out more about YAML, see https://packt.live/31l0WCB.

2. We also have a migration that will be used to create our **Reviews** table in the database. Let's open the **db/migrate/20190719200021_create_reviews.rb** file and have a look.

   Note that **20190719200021** is the timestamp of when the file was created, so it will be different for you:

   ```
   class CreateReviews < ActiveRecord::Migration[5.1]
     def change
       create_table :reviews do |t|
         t.string :name
         t.string :description
         t.timestamps
       end
     end
   end
   ```

   In the preceding code, we have our migration, which has the **create_table** helper method to create the **reviews** table in our database. In this method, we are specifying the data type for our two attributes as string. Besides this, we also have **timestamp**, which automatically adds a timestamp for the **created_at** and **updated_at** fields. These are present in all Rails tables by default.

   In our migration file, you can see we have a timestamp, which is placed at the start of the name of the migration file. Inside the **20190719200021_create_reviews.rb** migration file, we have a **change** method, which is used to create and drop the **Review** table with the two attributes, which are the two columns of this table.

   Let's now run a command to run our migration.

3. Go to your Terminal and to the root of your **citireview** directory, then type the following command:

```
$ rails db:migrate
```

The output should look like this:

```
[→ citireview2 git:(master) × rake db:migrate
== 20190919062855 CreateReviews: migrating ====================================
-- create_table(:reviews)
   -> 0.0023s
== 20190919062855 CreateReviews: migrated (0.0024s) ===========================
```

Figure 11.16: Migrating a database

This has created our **Reviews** table in our database. You can check the current status of your database schema at **db/schema.rb**:

```
ActiveRecord::Schema.define(version: 20190719200021) do
  create_table "reviews", force: :cascade do |t|
    t.string "name"
    t.string "description"
    t.datetime "created_at", null: false
    t.datetime "updated_at", null: false
  end
end
```

schema.rb changes every time the state of our database changes. When we add or alter a table in a migration, we actually see the current state of our database.

4. Let's now save the data that we have received from our form. Open the **app/controllers/review_controller.rb** file and update it with the following code:

```
class ReviewsController < ApplicationController
    def new
    end
    def create
        @review = Review.new(review_params)
        @review.save
        redirect_to @review
    end
    private
        def review_params
            params.require(:review).permit(:name, :description)
        end
    end
end
```

Here, we first added a **create** method, which has an instance variable called **@review**, which is creating a new object of the **Review** model by passing all the parameters in a review hash:

```
Parameters: {"utf8"=>"✓",
"authenticity_token"=>"9Ir7+Epf8rnSZCXlx+CJgygomlQ2Ry68riXamfnvdxCKr+FekW9mDoJtkgKZLpFhq4Dym7
Dym9jm/jCdXzuVLQ==", "review"=>{"name"=>"The Great Pizza Place", "description"=>"Amazing
pizza's quick delivery"}, "commit"=>"Save Review"}
```

Figure 11.17: Passing parameters to the Review model

In the next line, **@review.save** will save the **Review** object that we created earlier. We have also added a redirect, which we can modify to the home page of any other view of our application.

We have created a private method where we mention the variables we will be using to save data in our model. Rails has many security features. You have to whitelist parameters that will be used with the model. This is called making strong parameters, parameters that will be allowed to be used in the controller's action.

> **Note**
>
> With strong parameters, the **security feature** parameters in the controller are forbidden to be used in the model for mass assignment unless they are whitelisted. As a rule of thumb, for mass assignment, always make your parameters strong parameters by defining them in a private method. Using a private method is a good practice as it encapsulates the permissible parameters, which can then be used between methods such as **create** and **update**.

5. Let's now run our application to see the output. Run your Rails server and open the following URL: **http://localhost:3000/reviews/new**:

```
$rails server
```

The output should be as follows:

← → C ⓘ localhost:3000/reviews/new

Add new review

Name
Coffee Beans Cafe

Description
Best coffee in town

Save Review

Figure 11.18: Adding a new review

The error output would show up as follows:

← → C ⓘ localhost:3000/reviews/4

Unknown action

The action 'show' could not be found for ReviewsController

Figure 11.19: Unknown action error

When we entered our review and submitted it, we did not get any error related to saving the record; but we did get an error indicating where to go next. This is because we don't have a **show** action and its corresponding view where our app can be redirected.

We can, however, check whether our record has been created or not by using the Rails console.

The Rails Console

The Rails console helps you to interact with Rails applications using the command line. The Rails console uses IRB and allows you to make use of all Rails methods and interact with data. The Rails console is a very useful tool for experimenting with ideas without actually implementing any code.

Let's try this in our application. From the root of the **citireview** application, run the following command:

```
$rails console
```

The output should be as follows:

```
[→ citireview2 git:(master) × rails console
Running via Spring preloader in process 88259
Loading development environment (Rails 5.2.3)
2.6.3 :001 > ▌
```

Figure 11.20: Rails console

Let's check the **Review** model by trying an Active Record query to get all the records from the **reviews** table. Type the following command from the Rails console:

```
Review.all
```

The Terminal will respond as follows:

```
2.6.3 :009 > Review.all
  Review Load (0.2ms)  SELECT  "reviews".* FROM "reviews" LIMIT ?  [["LIMIT", 11]]
 => #<ActiveRecord::Relation [#<Review id: 1, name: "Coffee Beans Cafe", description: "Best coffee in town", created_at:
 "2019-09-19 06:38:40", updated_at: "2019-09-19 06:38:40">]>
```

Figure 11.21: Review model response

We can see clearly that our record, with the correct values for **name** and **description**, has been created. There are some additional columns in this table as well, which are **id**, **created_at**, and **updated_ad**. These columns were created by Rails when we created the migration for this table. The **id** column is autoincremented with an integer value, **created_at** adds a timestamp when a record is created, and **updated_at** adds the timestamp whenever there is a change to a record.

With **Review.all**, we are executing a **SELECT SQL** query to get all the records from the **reviews** table. There are numerous such Active Record methods that can be used to reduce the time spent writing raw queries.

When we submitted the **reviews** form, we got an error because there was an absence of a **show** action and a template. Let's display the review that we have created a view by creating a **show** action.

Add the following code to **app/controller/review_controller.rb**:

```
class ReviewsController < ApplicationController
...
    def show
        @review = Review.find(params[:id])
    end
...
end
```

With a **create** action redirect, we will be redirected to a **show** action. In the parameters being passed, there will be the ID of our newly created record. Using that ID, we will be able to get the record and use its values to display on our view.

> **Note**
>
> The instance variable declared in an action is accessible to the view of this action and its data can be embedded or used with its respective **html.erb** file.

Let's also add a view for the **show** action. Create a new file called **app/views/reviews/show.html.erb** and add the following code in it:

```
<h1>Citireviews Review for </h1>
<p>
  <strong>Name:</strong>
  <%= @review.name %>
</p>
  <p>
  <strong>Description:</strong>
  <%= @review.description %>
</p>
```

Here we have an H1 heading and are using the values in the **@review** instance variable embedded on our **show** view. Load **http://localhost:3000/reviews/new** and make another entry for a review, as depicted in the following figure:

Add new review

Name

Amy baking company

Description

Good deserts bad service
as Gordon said.

Save Review

Figure 11.22: Adding a new review

Click **Save Review** to see the redirection:

Citireviews Review for

Name: Amy baking company

Description: Good deserts bad service as Gordon said.

Figure 11.23: Review a record on a model

We are able to see our saved review, and if we open this URL, with the specific ID of a review, we will be able to see the record in our **show** view.

Let's now add more features to our **citireview** application.

Exercise 11.06: Completing the Reviews Web Application

In this exercise, we aim to do the following with the application:

- Create a view and display a list of all the review titles for the **citireview** application. Also, add a detail button to show a detailed review description.

- Add two links to the home page of the application: one to show a list of all the reviews and another to take us to add a new review.

- Add a back button/URL to take us back to the home page from all reviews, and another button to take us to a new reviews page.

Let's build on the code that we've been dealing with so far:

1. Open **app/controllers/reviews_controller.rb** and add the following code:

```
def index
    @reviews = Review.all
end
```

Here, we have created an **index** action from which we are getting all the records from the **Review** model using an Active Record query and keeping the records in the **@reviews** instance variable. This **@reviews** variable will be used in the **index** view.

2. Create a file called **app/views/reviews/index.html.erb** and add the following code:

```
<h1>All the Reviews</h1>
<table>
  <tr>
    <th>No</th>
    <th>Name</th>
    <th></th>
  </tr>
  <% @reviews.each_with_index do |review, index| %>
    <tr>
      <td><%= index+1 %></td>
      <td><%= review.name %></td>
      <td><%= link_to 'Details', review_path(review) %></td>
    </tr>
  <% end %>
</table>
```

Here, we have added an **h1** tag with a heading for this view. After that, we have a table for listing all the review titles. Then, we are looping over the **@reviews** variable with a helper method, **each_with_index**, where the first attribute, **review**, will be used to show the name of the review, and **index** is the count to maintain, every time we iterate.

3. Load **http://localhost:3000/reviews** on the browser to see the results:

All the Reviews

Sno	Name	
1	Coffee Beans Cafe	Details
2	Coffee Beans Cafe2	Details
3	Amy baking company	Details
4	Amy baking company	Details

Figure 11.24: List of reviews

The review would now look as follows:

Citireviews Review for

Name: Coffee Beans Cafe

Description: Best coffee in town

Figure 11.25: Details of a review

4. Let's now code for the next part of this exercise. Open **app/views/home/index.html. erb** and add the following code:

```
<h1>Welcome to Citireviews</h1>
<%= link_to 'All Reviews', controller: 'reviews' %> <br/><br/>
<%= link_to 'Add new review', new_review_path %>
```

Here we are using the **link_to** helper method, which creates a hyperlink. The first **link_to** method will take us to the **index** action of the **review** controller, which lists all the records from the **Review** model.

The second **link_to** method takes us to the **new** action, which is used to add/create a new record for the **Review** model.

5. Reload the home page of the web application by visiting **http://localhost:3000/** in your browser:

localhost:3000

Welcome to Citireviews

All Reviews

Add new review

Figure 11.26: Adding options for reviews

6. For both of these views, we don't have any way to go back to the home page. Let's add the following code snippet to the two views at **app/views/reviews/index.html.erb** and **app/views/reviews/new.html.erb**:

```
<%= link_to 'Back', root_path %>
```

The output should be as follows:

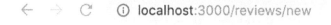

All the Reviews

Sno	Name	
1	Coffee Beans Cafe	Details
2	Coffee Beans Cafe2	Details
3	Amy baking company	Details
4	Amy baking company	Details

Back

Figure 11.27: Redirecting to home page

The **Back** button will redirect the users to the index page, where the reviews are added, as shown in the following figure:

← → C ⓘ localhost:3000/reviews/new

Add new review

Name

Description

Save Review

Back

Figure 11.28: Redirection to the home page

In both of the preceding cases, we are redirected to the home page using a URL.

Let's now add some authentication to the application. We will be using the **devise** Ruby gem for authentication.

The devise Ruby Gem

Using **devise**, we can add authentication to our review application. The goal of the next activity is to implement authentication, and we can use devise for that.

The following are the key features of devise:

- Rack-based
- A complete MVC solution based on Rails engines
- Allows you to have multiple models signed in at the same time
- Modular – use only what you really need

Activity 11.01: Adding Authentication for the Review Application

In this activity, we will be creating an authentication sign-in page for our application using the devise gem.

Follow these steps:

1. Add the devise gem in the **Gemfile** for our Rails application using the following command:

   ```
   gem 'devise'
   ```

2. Open a Terminal, go to the root of the application folder, and install the gem using the following command:

   ```
   $ bundle install
   ```

3. After the gem is installed, type the following command into your Terminal:

   ```
   $ rails generate devise:install
   ```

4. Generate a **User** model to manage user authentication.

5. Update the database schema with every new migration.

6. Add routes for your application.

7. Access the login page and sign in to the application.

The login page should look as follows:

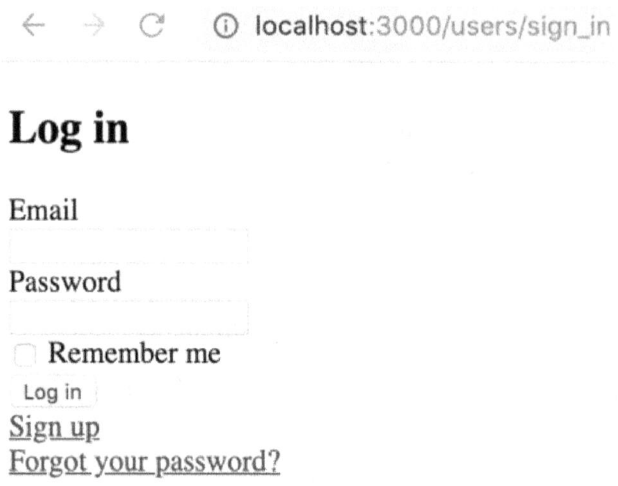

← → C   ⓘ localhost:3000/users/sign_in

Log in

Email

Password

◯ Remember me

Log in

Sign up

Forgot your password?

Figure 11.29: Login page for application

The signup page should be as follows:

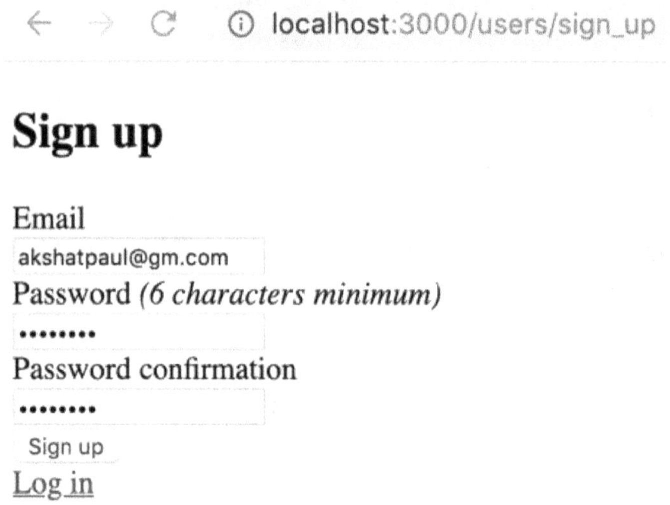

← → C   ⓘ localhost:3000/users/sign_up

Sign up

Email

akshatpaul@gm.com

Password *(6 characters minimum)*

••••••••

Password confirmation

••••••••

Sign up

Log in

Figure 11.30: SignUp page for the application

The index page for the blog should be as follows:

Welcome to Citireviews

All Reviews

Add new review

Figure 11.31: Index page

> **Note**
>
> The solution for the activity can be found on page 488.

Summary

In this chapter, we learned about the most popular Ruby framework-Ruby on Rails. We started with the fundamentals of Ruby on Rails and the MVC pattern it's based on. We then created our first Rails application and discussed the folder structure of an application that uses Rails. We then explored the interaction between a controller and a view using Rails Action Controller and Action View. We set up our model, database, and corresponding migrations, and we learned how easy it is to set up all this with Rails Active Record.

We also learned about routes in Rails and how to set up a root route for our application. Then, we learned how to create views quickly with helper methods and we created our first form. We used this form to save data to a database and create Active Record queries that could do so, too. Similarly, we also learned how to fetch data from the database using Active Record and display the fetched data on a view with **Embedded Ruby (ERB)**. Furthermore, we explored a nifty tool provided with Rails called the Rails console, which can be used for experimenting with ideas without writing much code. Lastly, we secured our application with authentication while working on this chapter's activity.

In the next chapter, we will learn how to associate two tables in Rails with Active Record associations. We will also learn about the various types of validations available in Rails, including how we can trigger or skip them. We will implement validations at the model level. We will learn about Rails scaffolding and how it helps to speed up development time. Finally, we will also learn how to host our Rails application on platforms such as Heroku so that it's accessible to everyone on the web.

12

Introduction to Ruby on Rails II

Overview

By the end of this chapter, you will be able to describe associations and the various types of Active Record associations; implement associations in your application model; evaluate methods that trigger and skip validations; implement model-level validations; develop programs using Rails scaffolding and deploy your application to the World Wide Web using Heroku.

In this final chapter, we'll continue to build upon the previous chapter's application and learn about REST principles and other fundamental features/concepts of Ruby on Rails.

Introduction

In the previous chapter, we were introduced to the Ruby on Rails framework and how the MVC pattern helps us to create a modular web application. We also learned about the fundamentals of the Rails framework, the anatomy of a Rails application, how to save data in a database, how to interact with data using views, and how to test Ruby on Rails code using the Rails console.

In this chapter, we will dive deep into more advanced topics, such as creating associations between models using Active Record association. Like everything else, Rails has built-in helper methods to assist us. Associations are very commonly used in real-world applications. If we take the example of the `citireview` application from the previous chapter, we can easily see a relation between a review and its comments. These are joints that link one model to another with the use of primary and foreign keys. We will learn about six types of such associations provided by Rails.

Then, we will understand how validations work in Rails since validations are a critical feature of any application to avoid garbage data getting into the system, especially in the age of bots, when validations are essential for any real-world application. After that, we will make use of a unique Rails feature called scaffolding, for rapid development that will help generate a model, a view, a controller, and their supporting files all in one simple command. Lastly, we will learn how to host a Rails application on the internet using a popular hosting service called Heroku, because no application is complete unless it goes into production and sees the daylight of the World Wide Web.

Associations

In the previous chapter, we created a review web application where only authenticated users were allowed to write reviews. Ideally, every review would always allow other users to comment on it, and in this section, we will build that feature.

This means we will create a new model called **Comment**, which will be associated with the **Review** model since every review could have many comments, while every comment belongs to one review only. This is called a one-to-many relationship between the two models.

Associations are a set of methods for connecting objects of different models using foreign keys. Associations make it really simple to interact and perform various operations with records using Ruby code.

The following are six types of associations provided by Rails:

- `belongs_to`
- `has_one`
- `has_many`

- `has_many :through`

- `has_one :through`

- `has_and_belongs_to_many`

Let's discuss them one by one.

belongs_to

In the **belongs_to** association, the first model needs to have a one-to-one connection with the second model. This means that each record that the first model has belongs to an instance of the second model, thus creating an association. As can be seen in the following diagram, we have two models, **Review** and **Author**, where every record in the **Review** model belongs to only one author and in order to link **Review** with **Author**, the **id** primary key from the **Author** model acts as an **author_id** foreign key in the Review model:

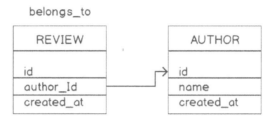

Figure 12.1: belongs_to association

Consider the following code snippet:

```
class Review < ApplicationRecord
  belongs_to :author
end
```

Rails provides helper methods for all associations. In the preceding example, we added the **belongs_to** helper method to the Review model. It is very important to use singular terms for **belongs_to** associations, based on the Rails philosophy of convention over configuration. You would get an **uninitialized constant Review::Authors** error if you used the plural form of an author association in the preceding example. The reason for this is that Rails automatically infers the class name from the association name. Hence, if the association name is in the plural form, then the inferred class will also be in the plural form, which is incorrect.

has_one

The **has_one** association also establishes one-to-one mapping with another model but in a different manner. This association suggests that one instance of a model will have only one occurrence in another model. For example, only one user profile can be created using a particular email address on any portal, as shown in the following diagram:

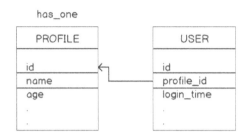

Figure 12.2: has_one association

Consider the following code snippet:

```
class Profile < ApplicationRecord
  has_one :user
end
```

In this example, we have added a **has_one** association to the **Profile** model since every **Profile** can have only one user.

The distinction between **belongs_to** and **has_one** largely depends on where the foreign key is placed. Considering the preceding example, we can call the association **belongs_to** when one user creates user accounts on multiple platforms using the same email address. Here, the foreign key is the email address that is linked to multiple platforms.

has_many

This association generates a one-to-many connection with another model. This is exactly the opposite of a **belongs_to** association. It specifies that each instance of the model has zero or more occurrences in the other model. For example, on a publishing portal, one author may have more than one review, as depicted in the following example:

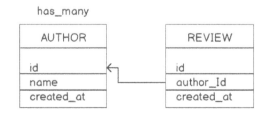

Figure 12.3: has_many association

Consider the following code snippet:

```
class Author < ApplicationRecord
  has_many :reviews
end
```

When declaring a **has_many** association, the name of the other model must be in the plural form.

has_many :through

The **has_many :through** association is used to build multiple connections to another model. This association indicates that the model in which said association is declared can be associated with none or more than one occurrence of another model by progressing through a third model. For example, in a hospital, **Doctors** and **Patients** have interaction via a third model, **Appointments**, as shown in the following figure:

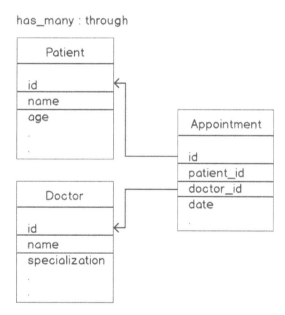

Figure 12.4: has_many: through association

Consider the following code snippet:

```
class Doctor < ApplicationRecord
  has_many :appointments
    has_many :patients, through: :appointments
end
class Appointment < ApplicationRecord
  belongs_to :doctor
belongs_to :patient
```

```
end
class Patient < ApplicationRecord
has_many :appointments
    has_many :doctors, through: :appointments
end
```

Here, we have three models where **Doctor** can have many patients and a **patient** can have many doctors. All of the models link with each other via the **Appointment** model such that **Doctor** can have many appointments and **Patient** can have many appointments, but an appointment belongs to a doctor and a patient. In short, the **Patient** model is associated with the **Doctor** model through the **Appointment** model.

has_one :through

This type of association is used to initiate a one-to-one connection with another model. It indicates that an association that is declared in a model can be linked with an occurrence of another model by using a third model. For example, every **Contractor** has one account on a certain portal, and every **Account** is linked with **AccountHistory**. The association should look like the following diagram:

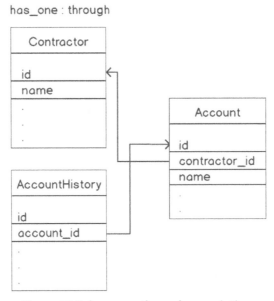

Figure 12.5: has_one; through association

Consider the following code snippet:

```
class Contractor < ApplicationRecord
  has_one :account
has_one :account_history, through: :account
end
class Account < ApplicationRecord
  belongs_to :contractor
    has_one :account_history
end
class AccountHistory < ApplicationRecord
  belongs_to :account
end
```

Here, we have three models, **Contractor**, **AccountHistory**, **and Account**, where every contractor has one account and account history and every **AccountHistory** belongs to an account, while an **Account** has one account history but belongs to a contractor. In short, **Contractor** and **AccountHistory** have one-to-one mapping through the **Account** model.

has_and_belongs_to_many

This type of association builds direct multiple links with another model, without using a third model. For example, a discussion forum may have multiple users and groups within it. Each user may be part of numerous groups and every group may have numerous users who contribute to a discussion, as depicted in the following diagram:

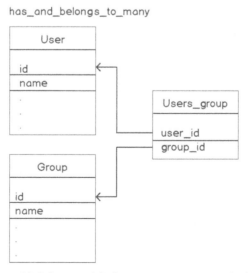

Figure 12.6: has_and_belongs_to_many association

Consider the following code snippet:

```
class User < ApplicationRecord
  has_and_belongs_to_many :groups
end
class Group < ApplicationRecord
  has_and_belongs_to_many :users
end
```

In this example, unlike **HABTM (Has And Belongs To Many)** associations, we use the **has_and_belongs_many** helper method to build an association between the **User** and **Group** models via the **user_groups** model.

Exercise 12.01: Creating a Model to Enable Users to Comment on Reviews on the CitiReview Application

In *Chapter 11, Introduction to Ruby on Rails I*, we built a review application model and added an authentication sign-in page to the model. In this exercise, we will create a comment model and associate it with the **Review** model, and also run the migration. Remember, each review can have many comments but every comment belongs to only one review. We will add a form after a review for users to add comments.

The following steps will enable you to complete the exercise:

1. Go to the root of the project and run the following command from Terminal to generate a model comment:

```
$ rails generate model Comment commenter:string body:text review:references
```

The output should be as shown in the following screenshot:

```
[→ citireview git:(master) × rails generate model Comment commenter:string body:text review:references
Running via Spring preloader in process 90260
      invoke  active_record
      create    db/migrate/20190919081845_create_comments.rb
      create    app/models/comment.rb
      invoke    test_unit
      create      test/models/comment_test.rb
      create      test/fixtures/comments.yml
```

Figure 12.7: Generating a model comment

Here, we have generated a new model comment with **commenter**, **body**, and a **foreign_key** columns for the **Review** model. Let's open the migration file to understand this better. Open the **db/migrate/20190801052630_create_comments.rb** file:

```
class CreateComments < ActiveRecord::Migration[5.1]
  def change
    create_table :comments do |t|
      t.string :commenter
      t.text :body
      t.references :review, foreign_key: true
      t.timestamps
    end
  end
end
```

This migration will create a table, **comments**, with **commenter**, **body**, and **review** attributes.

The **references** keyword is a special datatype for models. The columns that will be created in the database will have their names appended with **_id**, which will hold an integer value of **id** from the **review** table.

2. Run the following command from the root of the project to execute migrations:

```
$ rails db:migrate
```

The output should be as shown in the following screenshot:

```
➜  citireview git:(master) ✗ rails db:migrate
== 20190801060443 CreateComments: migrating ===================================
-- create_table(:comments)
   -> 0.0055s
== 20190801060443 CreateComments: migrated (0.0055s) ==========================
```

Figure 12.8: Rails database migration

3. Next, we need to create an association between two models where every record of the **Comment** model belongs to a review. Open the **Comment** model from **app/models/comment.rb**:

```
class Comment < ApplicationRecord
  belongs_to :review
end
```

Here, we have created an association between the two models where every record of the **Comment** model belongs to a **review**.

4. Now we need to create an associated behavior between the two models **Review** and **ApplicationRecord**. Open the **Review** model from **app/models/review.rb** and add the following code in it:

```
class Review < ApplicationRecord
  has_many :comments
end
```

Once we have added the associations, associated behavior between the two models is enabled. For example, if we have 10 comments belonging to a review and we create a review object such as **@review**, we will get access to many methods that are already available for us to use, such as **@review.comments**, which will give associated comments for this review.

5. Then, we create a controller for comments by running the following command from Terminal from the root of the project:

```
$ rails generate controller Comments
```

The output should be as shown in the following screenshot:

```
→ citireview git:(master) ✗ rails generate controller Comments

Running via Spring preloader in process 35226
      create    app/controllers/comments_controller.rb
      invoke    erb
      create      app/views/comments
      invoke    test_unit
      create      test/controllers/comments_controller_test.rb
      invoke    helper
      create      app/helpers/comments_helper.rb
      invoke      test_unit
      invoke    assets
      invoke      coffee
      create        app/assets/javascripts/comments.coffee
      invoke      scss
      create        app/assets/stylesheets/comments.scss
```

Figure 12.9: Generating the folder structure for the Comment model

This command has generated our required folder structure for the comment feature. Next, let's add a form to submit a comment.

6. Create a form after a review to submit comments. Open the **app/views/reviews/ show.html.erb** file and add the following code:

show.html.erb

```
1  <h1>Citireviews Review for </h1>
2  <p>
3    <strong>Name:</strong>
4    <%= @review.name %>
5  </p>
6
7  <p>
8    <strong>Description:</strong>
9    <%= @review.description %>
10 </p>
11 <h2>Write your comment:</h2>
12 <%= form_with(model: [ @review, @review.comments.build ], local: true) do 13 |form| %>
14   <p>
15     <%= form.label :commenter %><br>
```

https://packt.live/2MLy4OT

Here, we have created a form that will allow the user to submit a comment for a review. On submission, the **create** action will be called in the controller. Before that, we should also add routes for the **comments** resource.

7. Add routes for **comments** by adding the following code in **config/routes.rb**:

```
resources :reviews do
  resources :comments
end
```

These are nested routes that create comments as a nested resource inside reviews.

8. In **CommentsController**, add the **create** action to persist the comment value. Open the **app/controller/comments_controller.rb** file and add the following code:

```
class CommentsController < ApplicationController
  def create
    @review = Review.find(params[:review_id])
    @comment = @review.comments.create(comment_params)
    redirect_to review_path(@review)
  end
  private
  def comment_params
    params.require(:comment).permit(:commenter, :body)
  end
end
```

Here, before we persist the comment, we first find the review that is associated with this comment and create a **Review** object and assign it to the **@review** instance variable. We then make use of the methods available with Active Record associations in order to insert the record into our database. Of course, as implemented in the previous chapter, we allow strong parameters by declaring them in the **comment_params** method.

9. Run the Rails server to test whether the comment has been saved. Run the following command from Terminal from the root of the project:

```
$ rails server
```

Open the browser and access **http://localhost:3000/reviews/3** to find any review. It should look as shown in the following figure:

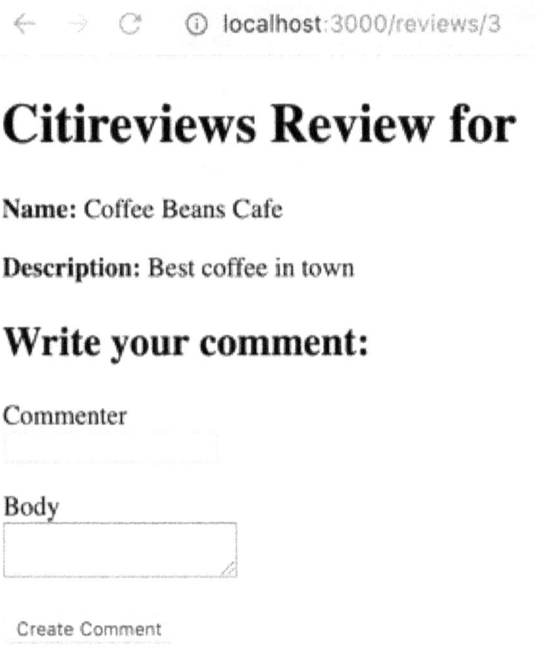
localhost:3000/reviews/3
Citireviews Review for
Name: Coffee Beans Cafe
Description: Best coffee in town
Write your comment:
Commenter
Body
Create Comment

Figure 12.10: Landing page to add comments

Once the comment is added, the **Create Comment** button should be highlighted as shown in the following figure:

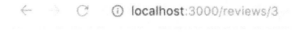

Citireviews Review for

Name: Coffee Beans Cafe

Description: Best coffee in town

Write your comment:

Commenter

Alex W

Body

Totally agree with this
review

Create Comment

Figure 12.11: Create Comment button

Write the review and submit it with **Create Comment**.

We did not get an error, but we cannot see whether our comment was saved or not. Try creating more comments, but to check whether the comments are saved refer to the Terminal window to see a SQL query being executed as shown in the following figure:

```
(0.0ms)  begin transaction
  Comment Create (1.7ms)  INSERT INTO "comments" ("commenter", "body", "review_id", "created_at", "updated_at") VALUES (
?, ?, ?, ?, ?)  [["commenter", "Alex W"], ["body", "Totally agree with your review"], ["review_id", 3], ["created_at", "
2019-09-19 08:24:50.044498"], ["updated_at", "2019-09-19 08:24:50.044498"]]
  (5.3ms)  commit transaction
```

Figure 12.12: SQL query

In the next step, we will display these comments associated with a review and add a few more comments so that you can see them all.

10. Open the **app/views/reviews/show.html.erb** file and add the following code to display the comments associated with a review:

show.html.erb

```
29 <h1>Citireviews Review for </h1>
30 <p>
31   <strong>Name:</strong>
32   <%= @review.name %>
33 </p>
34
35 <p>
36   <strong>Description:</strong>
37   <%= @review.description %>
38 </p>
39 <br/>
40 <strong><i>Comments for this review:</i></strong>
41 <% @review.comments.each do |comment| %>
42   <p>
43     <strong>Commenter:</strong>
```

https://packt.live/2BplYpv

Here, we have added a section to display all the comments associated with this review. Run **rails server** to check it on the browser. It should display as shown in the following figure:

Figure 12.13: Comments displayed

Now, if you submit a fresh comment, it will be displayed immediately in the list of comments associated with this review.

Thus, we have successfully created a `Review` model for the application.

Validations

Validations are added to an application so that only valid data is saved to your database – in other words, only keeping the signal and avoiding noise. For example, a user does not add their name in the age section, but uses a proper email ID format, and adds a proper cell phone number to validate the data on a portal, which is the basic requirement of the portal.

There are various ways and junctures at which we can set these validations in an application before the data gets persisted to the database. Mainly, there are four types of such validations:

- Database validations
- Controller-level validations
- Client-side validations:
- Model-level validations:

Let's look at each of these types one by one.

Database Validations

With database validations, we use database constraints or store procedures to check whether valid data is being stored. This is difficult to maintain since at the database level, changes are difficult to implement and there is more resistance against future changes. However, at the database level, validations such as uniqueness validations absolutely belong to the models as well.

Controller-Level Validations

Validations can be implemented in a controller, but this is against the philosophy of thin controllers, hence it's better to keep them at the model level only. Also, models could be interacted with by different controllers. Data validation is a concern at the data level, which is the model's concern.

Client-Side Validations

These are the first alerts when it comes to a validation example adding constraints right in the form that adds data. However, they are unreliable if they are the only ones to be used since they can be easily bypassed. But in combination with other validations, they are very useful.

Model-Level Validations

This is the best place for adding any validations before your data gets saved in the database. Also, these are database-agnostic validations so, irrespective of which database is used now or is changed later, validations will work. Rails makes it really easy to add validations with lots of helper methods that augment our own custom code.

Methods that Trigger Validations

With Active Record, there are certain methods that trigger validations before saving data in the database. The following is a list of such methods:

- `create`
- `create!`
- `save`
- `save!`
- `update`
- `update!`

Methods that Skip Validations

With Active Record, there are certain methods that skip validations before saving data in the database. The following is a list of such methods:

- `decrement!`
- `decrement_counter`
- `increment!`
- `increment_counter`
- `toggle!`
- `touch`
- `update_all`
- `update_attribute`

- `update_column`

- `update_columns`

- `update_counters`

While the **save** method triggers validation, there is a way to bypass this by adding a flag along with it, as in **save(validate: false)**.

Checking Validations

Rails runs a validation before saving an Active Record object. If the validation criteria are not met, the object is rejected. To test these validations, there are helper methods available: **valid?** and **invalid?**. You can try them on your model in the Rails console.

Consider the following example:

```
class User < ApplicationRecord
    validates :name, presence: true
end
```

The output in the Rails console would be as follows:

```
User.create(name: "Steve Carell").valid? # => true
User.create(name: nil).valid? # => false
User.create(name: nil).invalid? # => true
```

Here, we have created a **User** model, which could have many fields, such as name, age, location, and so on, with validation on the **name** parameter. At the time of creating a record, this record validation triggers, and using the **valid?** and **invalid?** helper methods, we can check whether the result would be true or false.

Exercise 12.02: Adding Validation for the Citireview Application

In this exercise, we will add validation for the **citireview** application such that every review must have a name and a comment body should not exceed more than 50 characters:

1. Open the **Review** model from **app/models/review.rb** and add the following code:

   ```
   class Review < ApplicationRecord
       has_many :comments
       validates :name, presence: true
   end
   ```

   With the presence of validations, if the **name** field is empty, data won't be saved in the database.

2. Start **rails server** from Terminal and open http://localhost:3000/reviews/new in your browser to test whether you can still submit the review without a name:

```
$ rails server
```

The output would be as follows:

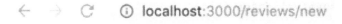

Add new review

Name

Description

This place is awesome

Save Review

Back

Figure 12.14: Saving a review

Redirection to the home page will look as follows:

All the Reviews

Sno	Name	
1	Coffee Beans Cafe	Details
2	Coffee Beans Cafe2	Details
3	Amy baking company	Details
4	Amy baking company	Details

Back

Figure 12.15: Redirection to the home page

Check the Rails server in the Terminal window to see the redirection operation as shown in the following figure:

```
Started POST "/reviews" for ::1 at 2019-09-19 13:58:36 +0530
Processing by ReviewsController#create as HTML
  Parameters: {"utf8"=>"✓", "authenticity_token"=>"20yoyS+taoh0QGUwjGpxPEraKv1h3tY5WC3dZC9quDSlabJv9J3+PyRJ0tfSpGneyXJCM
udrY10Q9jdgib5aCQ==", "review"=>{"name"=>"", "description"=>"This place is awesome"}, "commit"=>"Save Review"}
  User Load (0.2ms)  SELECT  "users".* FROM "users" WHERE "users"."id" = ? ORDER BY "users"."id" ASC LIMIT ?  [["id", 1]
, ["LIMIT", 1]]
   (0.1ms)  begin transaction
   (0.0ms)  rollback transaction
Redirected to http://localhost:3000/reviews
Completed 302 Found in 4ms (ActiveRecord: 0.3ms)
```

Figure 12.16: Redirection operation as seen on the Terminal window

As you can see, the reason why we did not see the review listed is because the record was never created in our database and the transaction was rolled back.

3. Open the **Comment** model from **app/models/comment.rb** and add the following code in it:

```ruby
class Comment < ApplicationRecord
  belongs_to :review
  validates :body, length: { maximum: 50 }
end
```

Similar to the previous step, we have added a validation where we check that the text added in the **body** field is not more than 50 characters.

4. Refresh and open a review and add a comment of over 50 characters:

Figure 12.17: Comment over 50 characters

Submit it to see whether it gets saved and displayed instantly:

Figure 12.18: Failure to save a comment of over 50 characters

The comment failed to save since it was over 50 characters.

Scaffolding

Rails scaffolding is a feature in Rails that helps to autogenerate code. In Ruby on Rails, this refers to the autogeneration of **Model**, **View**, and **Controller** along with CRUD operations, usually for a single database table. This saves a lot of time and is yet another feature of Rails for speedy development.

The following is the **scaffold** command:

```
$ rails generate scaffold ScaffoldName [attributes]
```

This one-line command will set up the model, controller, views, migrations, and test suite – all in one go.

Exercise 12.03: Using Rails Scaffolding to Create a Rails Application for a Store with a List of Products

In this exercise, we will create a Rails application for a store allowing a user to enter a list of products with two fields, **name** and **price**:

1. Create a new Rails application using the following command:

```
$rails new scaffold_app
```

The output should be as follows:

```
 ⇥  scaffold git:(master) rails new scaffold_app
        create
        create   README.md
        create   Rakefile
        create   .ruby-version
        create   config.ru
        create   .gitignore
        create   Gemfile
           run   git init from "."
```

Figure 12.19: Using scaffolding to create a new Rails application

This will generate our new Rails application. Create a **Store** model to save the **name** and **description** of a product using the following **scaffold** command:

```
$rails generate scaffold Store name:string description:string
```

```
  →  scaffold_app git:(master) ✗ rails generate scaffold Store
name:string description:string
Running via Spring preloader in process 92575
     invoke   active_record
     create     db/migrate/20190919083822_create_stores.rb
     create     app/models/store.rb
     invoke     test_unit
     create       test/models/store_test.rb
     create       test/fixtures/stores.yml
     invoke   resource_route
      route     resources :stores
     invoke   scaffold_controller
     create     app/controllers/stores_controller.rb
     invoke     erb
     create       app/views/stores
     create       app/views/stores/index.html.erb
     create       app/views/stores/edit.html.erb
     create       app/views/stores/show.html.erb
     create       app/views/stores/new.html.erb
     create       app/views/stores/_form.html.erb
     invoke     test_unit
     create       test/controllers/stores_controller_test.rb
     create       test/system/stores_test.rb
     invoke     helper
     create       app/helpers/stores_helper.rb
     invoke       test_unit
     invoke     jbuilder
     create       app/views/stores/index.json.jbuilder
     create       app/views/stores/show.json.jbuilder
     create       app/views/stores/_store.json.jbuilder
     invoke   assets
     invoke     scss
     create       app/assets/stylesheets/stores.scss
     invoke   scss
     create     app/assets/stylesheets/scaffolds.scss
```

Figure 12.20: Using the scaffold command to create a model

As you can see, we have a model, controller, views, migrations, and assets all set up in just one command. Earlier, we saw that we had to generate every part using different Rails generators; scaffolding, therefore, saves a lot of time.

2. Run the following command to execute the migrations created in the last step:

```
$rails db:migrate
```

The output should be as follows:

```
→   scaffold_app git:(master) ✗ rails db:migrate
== 201908022003114 CreateStores: migrating
=====================================
-- create_table(:stores)
   -> 0.0007s
== 201908022003114 CreateStores: migrated (0.0007s) =============================
```

Figure 12.21: Executing migrations

As you can see, our **Stores** table is created with this migration, which was generated in *step 2*.

3. Run the following command to serve the application over a web server:

```
$rails server
```

The output should be as follows:

```
[→  scaffold_app git:(master) × rails server
=> Booting Puma
=> Rails 5.2.3 application starting in development
=> Run `rails server -h` for more startup options
Puma starting in single mode...
* Version 3.12.1 (ruby 2.6.3-p62), codename: Llamas in Pajamas
* Min threads: 5, max threads: 5
* Environment: development
* Listening on tcp://localhost:3000
Use Ctrl-C to stop
```

Figure 12.22: Serving the applications on a web server

4. Open the application in your browser – http://localhost:3000/stores/ (since we have created one resource only, which was **Stores**):

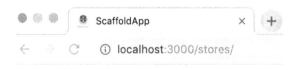

Stores

Name Description

New Store

Figure 12.23: Landing page for the Stores application

At present, there is no data in this application. Click on **New Store** to add data.

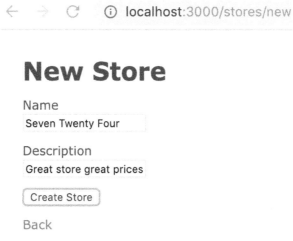

Figure 12.24: New Store option in the application

5. After filling in the form, submit it by clicking **Create Store** as shown in the following figure:

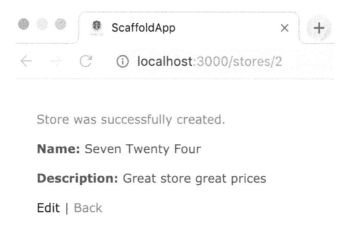

Figure 12.25: Creating a record

Our record has been successfully created.

6. Click the back arrow to see whether the list of data appears as shown in the following screenshot:

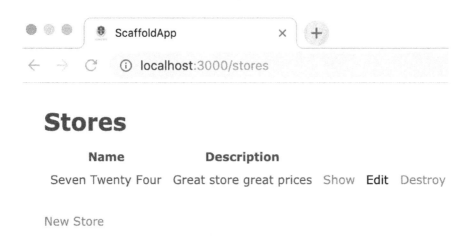

Figure 12.26: List of data on the Stores application

So, on the index page of this resource, we can now see a list of data from this model.

As you have seen, with scaffolding, generating repetitive CRUD operation code is quick and easy.

Activity 12.01: Create a Blog Application and Host It Live on a Cloud Platform

In this activity, we will create an application model for a blogging platform. The activity has to be performed in the following parts:

Part I – Create a blog application with the following features:

1. It should allow the creation of a blog post with a title and content.

2. It should have a comment section to save a comment based on a blog post ID.

Part II – Host the application on a cloud platform such as Heroku so that it is publicly available.

Use the Rails scaffolding feature to build the application rapidly.

The following steps will help you with the solution:

Part I – Create a blog application with the following features

1. Create a new blog model.

2. Use scaffolding to generate an MVC file and a folder structure for posts.

3. Execute migrations and generate tables for posts.

4. Add a root route for adding the index page to display a list of posts.

5. Test your application on the localhost URL, http://localhost:3000.

Part II – Host the application on a cloud platform such as Heroku so that it is publicly available

1. Create a free account on Heroku and download the CLI (Command Line Interface) to set it up locally.

2. Configure **postgres** using the Ruby **pg** gemfile and uninstall the SQLite3 gem.

3. Make sure to update the configuration files with **postgres** specifications.

4. Create a database and run migrations to check for changes.

5. Next, save the application on Git and deploy it on Heroku using the following commands:

```
$ heroku create
$ git push heroku master
```

6. Next, create a database on Heroku and run the following command to check the migrations and generate tables:

```
$ heroku run rails db:migrate
```

7. Lastly, use **https://protected-tor-47977.herokuapp.com** to run the application.

Expected Output:

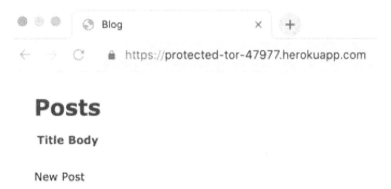

Figure 12.27: Blog post landing page

> **Note**
>
> The solution to the activity can be found on page 495.

Summary

In this chapter, we deep-dived into the Rails framework and learned about features such as Active Record associations, which are essential for any real-world application, and with six associations provided by Rails, working with models and databases becomes easier and more organized. We then learned about validations and the various options Rails provides. After that, we learned about scaffolding in Rails, which is a very powerful tool for rapid application development. Lastly, we learned about how to host our application on the World Wide Web with a popular hosting service called Heroku.

We have learned a lot in the last 12 chapters and we are confident that you will be excited to work with one of the most beautiful and powerful programming languages, Ruby (with the equally powerful Rails framework) – for your next software assignment.

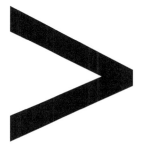

Appendix

About

This section is included to assist the students to perform the activities present in the book. It includes detailed steps that are to be performed by the students to complete and achieve the objectives of the book.

Chapter 1: Writing and Running Ruby Programs

Activity 1.01: Generating Email Addresses Using Ruby

Solution

1. Define and print the first name variable:

```
puts "Enter your first name: "
```

2. Use the **gets.chomp** method to allow the user input to be stored in the variables:

```
first_name = gets.chomp
```

3. Similarly, create a new variable for the last name of the user and print it. Also apply **gets.chomp** on the variable to store the input data:

```
puts "Enter your last name: "
last_name = gets.chomp
```

4. Lastly, use string interpolation to combine the first and last name with the domain name to generate the email address:

```
puts "#{first_name}#{last_name}@rubyprogram.com"
#Output :
Enter your first name:
akshat
Enter your last name:
paul
=>akshatpaul@rubyprograms.com
```

Expected output:

```
Enter your first name:
akshat
Enter your last name:
paul
akshatpaul@rubyprogram.com
```

Figure 1.49: Output for string interpolation

Activity 1.02: Calculating the Area and Perimeter for a Candy Manufacturing Plant

Solution

1. Enter the IRB shell and print the **radius** variable of the candy:

```
print "Enter the radius for the circular candy: "
```

2. Use the **gets** method to get the user input and define the **radius** variable:

```
radius = gets.to_f
```

3. Define the formula for calculating the **perimeter** and **area** of the candy:

```
perimeter = 2 * 3.141592653 * radius
area = 3.141592653 * radius * radius
```

4. Print the **perimeter** and **area** of the candy using string interpolation:

```
puts "The perimeter of the candy is #{perimeter}."
puts "The area of the candy is #{area}."
```

Expected output:

```
Enter the radius for the circular candy: 1.3
The perimeter of the candy is 8.1681408978.
The area of the candy is 5.30929158357.
```

Figure 1.50: Output for area calculator

Chapter 2: Ruby Data Types and Operations

Activity 2.01: Dice Roller Program

Solution

1. We begin by simulating the rolling of a dice. Ruby has an in-built **rand** method, which returns a random number. It takes an argument as an integer and returns a random number. Open **irb** and type the following:

```
rand 2
```

2. Now, repeat that a few more times. You'll notice the numbers you get in response are either **0** or **1**, never **2**. This is what 0-indexing means: the first number is always zero.

3. The problem here is that a die never starts with zero, it starts with one. So, let's create a method for that.

4. Open up **roller.rb** and add the following method to it:

```
def roll
  rand(6) + 1
end
puts roll
```

5. Run that file a few times, and you'll see that we have successfully simulated rolling a dice.

6. Next, roll a dice with any number of sides. Continue to expand on the previous program and add an argument to this method. Open **roller.rb** and add the following code:

```
def roll(sides)
  rand(sides) + 1
end

puts roll(6)
```

7. Now, our program can roll any number of dice, as long as we pass a number of sides to the roll method.

8. Next, roll any number of sides. We will pass another argument along with the sides. For now, let's add the numbers together. Type the following in the **roller.rb** file:

```ruby
def roll(sides, number=1)
  roll_array = []
  number.times do
    roll_value = rand(sides) + 1
    roll_array << roll_value
  end
  total = 0
  roll_array.each do |roll|
    new_total = total + roll
    total = new_total
  end
  total
end
puts "Rolling a 5 sided die!"
puts roll(5)
puts "Rolling two 6 sided dice!"
puts roll(6, 2)
```

9. Run the complete code. You should obtain an output as follows:

```
Rolling a 5 sided die!
2
Rolling two 6 sided dice!
9
```

Figure 2.74: Output of dice roller

Let's now understand the preceding code. We added an argument, **number**, which has a default value of **1**, so that in case we don't pass anything, the program continues to work. We then created an empty array to keep the die we are going to roll, called **roll_array**. The times method of the number variable will create a for loop for us, iterating over the body of the loop a number of times. By default, one iteration will happen. Every iteration will add a new value to our **roll_array** method based on the number of sides our die has. The last part of our function will return the sum of the rolled values with our dice, simple as that.

Chapter 3: Program Flow

Activity 3.01: Number-Guessing Game

Solution

1. Create a Ruby source file called **hilow.rb**.

2. Create the basic program architecture that allows a user to choose to play or exit:

```ruby
play_choice = 'y'
while play_choice == 'y'
  puts "Welcome to HiLow - Shall we play"
  play_choice = gets.chomp.downcase
  if play_choice == 'y'
    play_game
  end
end
puts "Thanks for playing!"
```

3. Implement a single **guess** method that will employ various conditions for guessing a number. It will suggest that the player guesses lower/higher if the guess is incorrect:

```ruby
def try_guess(magic_number, guess)
  if guess == magic_number
    puts "You guess correctly!"
    return true
  elsif guess < magic_number
    puts "Guess higher"
    return false
  else
    puts "Guess lower"
    return false
  end
end
```

4. Put the whole program together with a **play_game** method:

Activity3.01.rb

```
1  def play_game
2    print "I'm going to pick a random number that you will have to guess. Please enter the maximum
   number for the guessing range."
3    range = gets.chomp.to_i
4    magic_number = rand(range)
5    until try_guess(magic_number) do
6    end
7  end
8
9  def try_guess(magic_number)
10   print "What's your guess? "
11   guess = gets.chomp.to_i
12   if guess == magic_number
```

https://packt.live/2MzcGgK

The game will now look as shown in the following figure:

```
Welcome to HiLow - Shall we play? [Y/n]y
I'm going to pick a random number that you will have to guess. Please enter the maximum number for the guessing range.6
What's your guess? 2
Guess higher
What's your guess? 5
Guess lower
What's your guess? 3
Guess higher
What's your guess? 4
You guessed correctly!
```

Figure 3.44: Output for the HiLow game

Chapter 4: Ruby Methods

Activity 4.01: Blackjack Card Game

Solution

1. Write a method to generate a deck of cards:

```ruby
def generate_deck
  cards = (1..13)
  suits = ["Diamonds", "Clubs", "Spades", "Hearts"]
  deck = []
  suits.each do |suit|
    cards.each do |card|
      deck << [card, suit]
    end
  end
  return deck
end
```

2. Write a method to shuffle the deck of cards:

```ruby
def shuffle_deck(deck)
  shuffled_deck = []
  while(deck.length > 0) do
    random_card_index = rand(deck.length)
    shuffled_deck << deck.delete_at(random_card_index)
  end
  return shuffled_deck
end
```

3. Write a method to identify the cards drawn in a hand:

```ruby
def inspect_cards(cards, format: :short)
  hand = cards.map{|c| card_label(c, format: format)}.join(",")
  total = calculate_total(cards)
  "#{hand} (#{total})"
end
```

4. Write a method to label the cards based on their numbers and suits:

```ruby
def card_label(card, format: :short)
  card_labels = {1 => "Ace", 11 => "Jack", 12 => "Queen", 13 => "King"}
  card_suit_labels = {"Diamonds" => "♦", "Clubs" => "♣", "Spades" => "♠", "Hearts"
=> "♥"}
  card_index, card_suit = card
  label = card_labels[card_index] || card_index
  icon = card_suit_labels[card_suit]
  if format == :short
    "#{label}#{icon}"
  else
    "#{label} of #{card_suit}"
  end
end
```

5. Write a method that defines the card value and displays a hand of cards with its total:

Activity4.01.rb

```ruby
75 def card_value(cards, card)
76   case card
77   # face cards are 10
78   when 11..13
79     10
80   when 1 # Ace can be 1 or 11 depending on the rest of the cards
81     # simple algorithm for determining what Ace should count as
82     # get total value of all non-ace cards
83     non_ace_cards = cards.reject{|c| c[0] == 1}
84     non_ace_card_total = calculate_total(non_ace_cards)
85     # If the Ace as 11 busts us, count it as a 1
86     if (non_ace_card_total + 11) > 21
87       1
88     # If the Ace as an 11, gets us to 21, count it as an 11
89     elsif (non_ace_card_total + 11) == 21
90       11
```

https://packt.live/2W7ZTVJ

6. Write a method that governs the gameplay. You will need a way to ask the user whether they want to hit or stay. Hitting means adding another card to the player's hand. Staying means keeping the current hand.

A way for the dealer to determine whether it should hit or stay is for the dealer to follow a fixed set of rules. If the total of the current hand is less than 17, it must hit. If the dealer's hand totals 17 or higher, it must stay:

Activity4.01.rb

```
36 def play(deck)
37   player_hand = deal_cards(deck, 2)
38   dealer_hand = deal_cards(deck, 2)
39   puts "Player has: #{inspect_cards(player_hand)}"
40   puts "Dealer has: #{inspect_cards([dealer_hand[0]])}, <other card hidden>"
41   choice = nil
42   while choice != 'stay' && calculate_total(player_hand) <= 21 do
43     print "Do you want to hit or stay?"
44     choice = gets.chomp
45     if choice == 'hit'
46       player_hand += deal_cards(deck, 1)
47     end
48     print "Your cards are now: #{inspect_cards(player_hand)}\n"
49   end
50   while((dealer_total = calculate_total(dealer_hand)) <= 21 && (dealer_total < 17)) do
```

https://packt.live/2pHa9bp

7. Write a loop that allows a player to continue playing as long as there are enough cards in the deck. The minimum number of cards for a hand is 4 (2 for the player and 2 for the dealer):

```
shuffled_deck = shuffle_deck(generate_deck)
choice = 'y'
while(shuffled_deck.length > 4 && choice.downcase != 'n') do # need at least 4 cards
to play
  puts "Deck has: #{shuffled_deck.length} cards left"
  print "Do you want to play a hand?[Yn]"
  choice = gets.chomp
  if choice.downcase == 'y'
    play(shuffled_deck)
  end
end
# Tests
# puts calculate_total([[12, "Hearts"]]) # 10
# puts calculate_total([[1,"Spades"],[12, "Hearts"]]) #21
# puts calculate_total([[13,"Hearts"],[6, "Hearts"]]) # 16
```

Here is the expected output:

```
Do you want to play a hand?[Yn]Y
Player has: 9♠,Jack♦ (19)
Dealer has: 10♣ (10), <other card hidden>
Do you want to hit or stay?stay
Your cards are now: 9♠,Jack♦ (19)
It's a tie!
Dealer hand: 19 (10♣,9♣ (19))
Player hand: 19 (9♠,Jack♦ (19))
Deck has: 48 cards left
Do you want to play a hand?[Yn]Y
Player has: Jack♥,3♣ (13)
Dealer has: 9♦ (9), <other card hidden>
Do you want to hit or stay?hit
Your cards are now: Jack♥,3♣,7♥ (20)
Do you want to hit or stay?stay
Your cards are now: Jack♥,3♣,7♥ (20)
Player wins!
Dealer hand: 19 (9♦,Jack♣ (19))
Player hand: 20 (Jack♥,3♣,7♥ (20))
Deck has: 43 cards left
```

Figure 4.34: Output for the Blackjack game

Chapter 5: Object-Oriented Programming with Ruby

Activity 5.01: Voting Application for Employee of the Month

Solution

1. Open the Terminal and clone the **Lightweight Terminal Framework** from GitHub:

```
git clone https://github.com/PacktWorkshops/The-Ruby-Workshop/tree/master/Chapter05/
Activity5.01/framework
```

2. Implement the **VotingMachine** model class:

voting_machine.rb

```
1   class VotingMachine
2     attr_reader :month, :year, :results
3
4     class InvalidVote < Exception; end
5
6     def initialize(month, year)
7       @month = month
8       @year = year
9       @results = {}
10    end
11
12    def record_vote(voter, votee)
13      raise InvalidVote unless valid_vote?(voter, votee)
14      results[votee] ||= 0
15      results[votee] += 1
16    end
```

https://packt.live/32CLfrZ

3. Implement **VoteController** to receive votes for the employees:

```
class VoteController < Controller
  attr_accessor :voter, :votee
  def run
    get_input :voter, "What's your name? "
    get_input :votee, "Who do you want to vote for? "
    self.voting_machine.record_vote(@voter, @votee)
    log "Vote recorded!"
  end
end
```

4. Add a controller to **MenuController.rb**:

```
MENU_CHOICES = {
  1 => {controller: :vote, label: "Place a vote for a colleague"},
  2 => {controller: :exit, label: "Exit"}
}.freeze
```

5. Add **LeaderboardController** to count the number of votes against every votee:

```
class LeaderboardController < Controller
  def run
    sorted_results = voting_machine.sorted_results
    sorted_results.each do |person, count|
      log "#{person}: #{count}"
    end
  end
end
```

6. Add **LeaderboardController** to **MenuController**:

```
MENU_CHOICES = {
  1 => {controller: :vote, label: "Place a vote for a colleague"},
  2 => {controller: :leaderboard, label: "See current leaderboard"},
  3 => {controller: :exit, label: "Exit"}
}.freeze
```

7. Add tests to **test_controller.rb**:

test_controller.rb

```
51    def test_menu_controller
52      stubbed_input_method = Proc.new do |variable_symbol, question|
53          instance_variable_set("@choice", $TEST_VARS[:choice])
54      end
55
56      stub_controller with: stubbed_input_method do
57          menu_controller = MenuController.new(nil)
58
59          $TEST_VARS = {choice: 1, display: ""}
60          assert_equal :vote, menu_controller.run
61          assert_match /Please enter your choice/, $TEST_VARS[:display]
62
63          $TEST_VARS = {choice: 2, display: ""}
64          assert_equal :leaderboard, menu_controller.run
65          assert_match /Please enter your choice/, $TEST_VARS[:display]
```

8. Run the test code from **test.rb**:

```
ruby test.rb
```

The output will be as follows:

```
Run options: --seed 51564

# Running:

. . . . . .

Finished in 0.000961s, 6243.4965 runs/s, 23933.4031 assertions/s.

6 runs, 23 assertions, 0 failures, 0 errors, 0 skips
```

Figure 5.44: Output for the test data

9. Run the **application.rb** file. The code in this file will essentially bring together the models and classes we have defined through the activity within a master class. The main program workflow for the application is defined here:

application.rb

```
1  #!/usr/bin/env ruby
2
3  # require all files in models and controllers directory
4  require './model'
5  require './controller'
6  require 'byebug'
7
8  class InvalidChoiceException < Exception;end
9
10 # Create master class called Application
11 # which will be the core class that manages the loop
12 # around the voting machine
13 class Application
14   attr_reader :voting_machine
15
```

https://packt.live/2P8UAE4

Expected Output:

```
** Welcome to the Employee Of The Month Votathon **
** Please enter your choice **
   1. Place a vote for a colleague
   2. See current leaderboard
   3. Exit
choice> 1
What's your name? John
Who do you want to vote for? Mary
Vote recorded!
```

Figure 5.45: Output for voting application

Chapter 6: Modules and Mixins

Activity 6.01: Implementing Categories on the Voting Application Program

Solution

1. We'll begin by first using the code from the previous chapter and writing some tests.

2. Write a new test for **VotingMachine** to add a category:

```
require "minitest/autorun"
require 'minitest/stub_any_instance'
require_relative "../models/voting_machine"
class TestVotingMachine < Minitest::Test
  def test_add_category
    machine = VotingMachine.new(1, 1)
    machine.add_category("TestCategory")
    assert_equal machine.categories, ["TestCategory"]
    machine.add_category("TestCategory2")
    assert_equal machine.categories, ["TestCategory", "TestCategory2"]
    machine.add_category("TestCategory")
    assert_equal machine.categories, ["TestCategory", "TestCategory2"]
    assert_equal machine.send(:valid_category?, "Invalid"), false
  end
end
```

3. Then, implement the **add_category** method on the voting machine. Run tests when complete:

```
class VotingMachine
  attr_reader :month, :year, :results, :categories
  class InvalidCategory < Exception; end
  class InvalidVote < Exception; end
  def add_category(category)
    @categories << category
    @categories.uniq! # make sure no duplicates
  end
  private
  def valid_category?(category)
    categories.include?(category) ? true : false
  end
end
```

The output would be as follows:

```
** Welcome to the Employee Of The Month Votathon **
** Please enter your choice **
  1. Place a vote for a colleague
  2. See current leaderboard
  3. Add category
  4. Exit
choice> 3
What is the category name? Best Christmas sweater
Category added!
```

Figure 6.30: Category addition

4. Write a test for **record_vote** that adds the **category** argument:

```
def test_add_vote
  machine = VotingMachine.new(1, 1)
  category1 = "TestCategory1"
  category2 = "TestCategory2"
  machine.add_category(category1)
  machine.add_category(category2)
  machine.record_vote(category1, "Bob", "Mary")
  machine.record_vote(category1, "Suzie", "Mary")
  machine.record_vote(category1, "Sam", "Bob")
  machine.record_vote(category2, "Jackie", "Sam")
  assert_equal machine.results.class, Hash
  assert_equal machine.results.keys, [category1, category2]
  assert_raises VotingMachine::InvalidCategory do
    machine.record_vote("Invalid category", "Sue", "John")
  end
end
```

5. Amend the **record_vote** implementation to include **category**:

```ruby
class VotingMachine
  attr_reader :month, :year, :results, :categories
  class InvalidCategory < Exception; end
  def record_vote(category, voter, votee)
    raise InvalidCategory unless valid_category?(category)
    raise InvalidVote unless valid_vote?(voter, votee)
    results[category] ||= {}
    results[category][votee] ||= 0
    results[category][votee] += 1
  end
end
```

6. Amend the **test_run_vote_controller** test to include **category**:

```ruby
def test_run_vote_controller
  $TEST_VARS = {voter: "bob", votee: "mary", category: "TestCategory"}
  stubbed_input_method = Proc.new do |variable_symbol, question|
    instance_variable_set("@category", $TEST_VARS[:category])
    instance_variable_set("@voter", $TEST_VARS[:voter])
    instance_variable_set("@votee", $TEST_VARS[:votee])
  end
  # We have to stub the get_input method since this method grabs
  # input from the terminal
  stub_controller with: stubbed_input_method do
    t = Time.now
    machine = VotingMachine.new(t.month, t.year)
    machine.add_category($TEST_VARS[:category])
    Controller.run_controller(:vote, machine)
  end
end
```

7. Implement category choosing in **VoteController**:

```ruby
class VoteController < Controller
  attr_accessor :voter, :votee, :category
  def run
    get_input :category, "Which category are you voting for: #{self.voting_machine.
categories.join(", ")}"
    get_input :voter, "What's your name? "
    get_input :votee, "Who do you want to vote for? "
```

```
        self.voting_machine.record_vote(@category, @voter, @votee)
        log "Vote recorded!"
      end
    end
```

8. Implement the **ControllerLogging** module:

controller_logger.rb

```
1   module ControllerLogger
2     # If you aren't using a framework that gives you logging
3     # out of the box, its usually a good idea to implement a
4     # centralized logging method at the base class so you get
5     # consistent logging and do things like avoid logging output
6     # during tests
7
8     def self.prepended(parent_class)
9       parent_class.instance_eval do
10        def self.inherited(klass)
11          klass.send(:prepend, ControllerLogger)
12        end
13      end
14    end
15
```

https://packt.live/2Pb34KQ

9. Now run the application using the **ruby application.rb** command.

   The application would now be as follows:

```
        ** Please enter your choice **
          1. Place a vote for a colleague
          2. See current leaderboard
          3. Add category
          4. Exit
    choice> 1
    You can vote for:
    Which category would you like to vote for? Best Employee
    What's your name? Jane
    Who do you want to vote for? James
```

Figure 6.31: Voting application with categories

Chapter 7: Introduction to Ruby Gems

Activity 7.01: Presenting Voting Data in CSV Format Using Ruby Gems

Solution

1. Download the **votes.csv** file from https://packt.live/2OzNN6a. Place this under **test/fixtures**. The CSV file will contain the following data:

```
category,votee,count
VoteCategoryA,Chris Jones,23
VoteCategoryA,Susie Bennet,29
VoteCategoryB,Allan Green,33
VoteCategoryB,Tony Bennet,23
```

2. We'll start with our **VoteImporter** service object. Test whether it imports data from the CSV and perform a few basic checks to ensure that the content is what we're expecting. Create the **test_vote_importer.rb** file in the **tests** folder with the following code:

```
require "minitest/autorun"
require 'minitest/stub_any_instance'
require_relative "../services/vote_importer"
class TestVoteImporter < Minitest::Test
  def test_perform
    # Import vote data from our tests/fixtures/votes.csv file
    filepath = 'tests/fixtures/votes.csv'
    results = VoteImporter.perform(filepath)
    assert_equal results.length, 2
    assert_equal results.map{|k,v| k}.include?("VoteCategoryA"), true
    assert_equal results.map{|k,v| k}.include?("VoteCategoryB"), true
  end
end
```

3. Next, we'll write a few tests for our **VoteTable** service object, which will simply check that we're returning a collection of **Terminal::Table** objects and perform some basic checks to ensure that the content is what we're expecting. We'll manually create the **results** object so we're not dependent on any other services. Create a **test_vote_table.rb** file under the **tests** folder with the following code:

```
require "minitest/autorun"
require 'minitest/stub_any_instance'
require_relative "../services/vote_table"
```

```ruby
class TestVoteTable < Minitest::Test
  def test_perform
    # Import votes data from our tests/fixtures/votes.csv file
    filepath = 'tests/fixtures/votes.csv'
    results = {"VoteCategoryA"=>[["Susie Bennet", 29]]},{"VoteCategoryB"=>[["Allan
Green", 33]]}
    tables = VoteTable.perform(results)
    assert_equal tables.length, 2
    tables.each do |table|
      assert_equal table.class, Terminal::Table
      assert_equal table.title.include?("VoteCategory"), true
    end
  end
end
```

4. Define the service object. Create **vote_importer.rb** under **services** with the following code. This code will define the file path of the CSV file from where the count of votes is to be imported. Also, it defines the headers of the CSV file:

```ruby
require 'csv'
class VoteImporter
  def initialize(filepath)
    @filepath = filepath
  end
  def perform
    results = {}
    CSV.read(@filepath, headers: true).each do |row|
      results[row["category"]] ||= {}
      results[row["category"]][row["votee"]] = row["count"].to_i
    end
    results
  end
  def self.perform(*args)
    new(*args).perform
  end
end
```

5. Also, create **services/vote_table.rb** with the following code:

```ruby
require 'terminal-table'
class VoteTable
  def initialize(sorted_votes)
    @sorted_votes = sorted_votes
  end
  def perform
    headings = ['Votee', 'Count']
    tables = []
    @sorted_votes.each do |votes|
      tables << Terminal::Table.new(rows: votes.values[0], title: votes.keys[0],
headings: headings)
    end
    tables
  end
  def self.perform(*args)
    new(*args).perform
  end
end
```

Now we just need to wire them up in our application.

6. In **menu_controller.rb**, add an option to **Import Votes**.

```ruby
MENU_CHOICES = {
    1 => {controller: :vote, label: "Place a vote for a colleague"},
    2 => {controller: :leaderboard, label: "See current leaderboard"},
    3 => {controller: :category, label: "Add category"},
    4 => {controller: :import, label: "Import Votes"},
    5 => {controller: :exit, label: "Exit"}
}
```

7. Add an **import_votes** method that will import and place the number of votes to the **voting_machine.rb** model:

```ruby
def import_votes(filepath)
  @results = VoteImporter.perform(filepath)
end
```

8. Add a new **import_controller.rb** controller to the **controllers** folder to import votes from the CSV file:

```ruby
class ImportController < Controller
  attr_accessor :filepath
  def run
    log "Import votes from an external CSV"
    get_input :filepath, "Enter the filepath of the CSV file? "
    self.voting_machine.import_votes(filepath)
    log "Votes imported!"
  end
end
```

9. Update the **leaderboard_controller.rb** file to now log out tables instead of the raw objects:

```ruby
sorted_results = voting_machine.sorted_results
tables = VoteTable.perform(sorted_results)
tables.each do |table|
  log table
end
```

10. Create some test CSV data as **votes.csv**, which we can import in the root application directory using the following code:

```ruby
require "csv"
votes = [
  ["Category", "Votee", "Count"],
  ["Employee Of The Month", "Chris Jones", 23],
  ["Employee Of The Month", "Susie Bennet", 29],
  ["Employee Of The Month", "Bob Wing", 65],
  ["Employee Of The Month", "James King", 31],
  ["Best Christmas Sweater", "Allan Green", 33],
  ["Best Christmas Sweater", "Tony Bennet", 23],
  ["Best Christmas Sweater", "Bob Wing", 45],
  ["Best Christmas Sweater", "Jane Smith", 39],
```

```
  ]
  CSV.open("votes.csv", "w") do |csv|
    votes.each do |vote|
      csv.puts [vote[0], vote[1], vote[2]]
    end
  end
```

votes.csv will now hold the following data:

```
category,votee,count
Employee Of The Month,Chris Jones,23
Employee Of The Month,Susie Bennet,29
Employee Of The Month,Bob Wing,65
Employee Of The Month,James King,31
Best Christmas Sweater,Allan Green,33
Best Christmas Sweater,Tony Bennet,23
Best Christmas Sweater,Bob Wing,45
Best Christmas Sweater,Jane Smith,39
```

If everything goes well, you should see an option in the menu to import votes:

```
    $ ruby application.rb
            ** Welcome to the Employee Of The Month Votathon **
            ** Please enter your choice **
              1. Place a vote for a colleague
              2. See current leaderboard
              3. Add category
              4. Import Votes
              5. Exit
    choice> 4
    Import votes from an external CSV
    Enter the filepath of the CSV file? votes.csv
```

Figure 7.13: Importing votes

11. Print the leaderboard by selecting the second option:

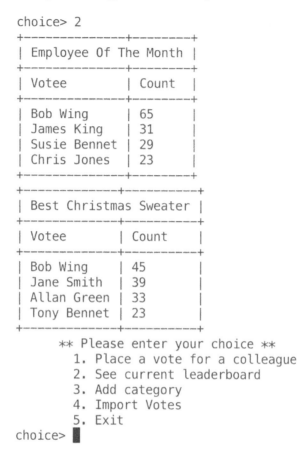

```
choice> 2
+---------------+---------+
| Employee Of The Month |
+---------------+---------+
| Votee         | Count   |
+---------------+---------+
| Bob Wing      | 65      |
| James King    | 31      |
| Susie Bennet  | 29      |
| Chris Jones   | 23      |
+---------------+---------+

+---------------+-----------+
| Best Christmas Sweater |
+---------------+-----------+
| Votee         | Count     |
+---------------+-----------+
| Bob Wing      | 45        |
| Jane Smith    | 39        |
| Allan Green   | 33        |
| Tony Bennet   | 23        |
+---------------+-----------+
        ** Please enter your choice **
            1. Place a vote for a colleague
            2. See current leaderboard
            3. Add category
            4. Import Votes
            5. Exit
choice> █
```

Figure 7.14: The voting application dashboard

Chapter 8: Debugging with Ruby

Activity 8.01: Perform Debugging on a Voting Application

Solution

1. First up, let's write a simple test to ensure that our **Controller** class does indeed have access to the instantiated **Logger** class defined in the **LoggerController** initializer:

```
tests/test_controller.rb
def test_controller_logger
  t = Time.now
  machine = VotingMachine.new(t.month, t.year)
  controller = Controller.new(machine)
  assert_instance_of(Logger,              controller.instance_variable_get('@logger'))
end
```

2. Next, let's extend our **ControllerLogger** module. We'll need to add an initializer first so that our parent **Controller** class can instantiate the **Logger** class. We'll call **super** at the end of the method, which will call **initialize** on the parent class passing through the same parameters (which is the default when **super** is called with no parameters):

```
controller_logger.rb
  def initialize(voting_machine)
  @logger = Logger.new('log.txt')
  @logger.formatter = proc do |severity, datetime, progname, msg|
    "#{severity} | #{datetime} | #{msg}\n"
  end
  super
end
```

3. Now let's define the **log_to_file** method on **ControllerLogger**. This is what we'll use to write to the filesystem via the **Logger** class. We'll want the ability to override the log level. We can use the **send** method to evaluate the level string into a method name:

controller_logger.rb
```ruby
def log_to_file(msg, level = 'debug')
  @logger.send(level, msg) unless ENV['TEST']
end
```

4. Add a call to **log_to_file** in the existing log method so we capture a timestamped copy of the message in our log file:

controller_logger.rb
```ruby
def log(msg)
  puts msg unless ENV['TEST']
  log_to_file(msg)
end
```

5. For some additional logging, let's log out the votes made by users, including some additional information. We'll tag this one as an **INFO** log, so we can filter it out of the logs if we need to:

controllers/vote_controller.rb
```ruby
log_to_file("Vote recorded - Voter: #{@voter} Votee: #{@votee} Category: #{@category}", "info")
```

6. Run the program and create categories, place votes, and so on. Inspect the **log.txt** file.

    You should see output like the following:

```
1    DEBUG | 2019-08-04 14:35:10 +1000 | You can vote for: TestCategory
2    DEBUG | 2019-08-04 14:35:10 +1000 | Vote recorded!
3    DEBUG | 2019-08-04 14:58:24 +1000 | Category added!
4    DEBUG | 2019-08-04 14:58:39 +1000 | Exiting...
5    DEBUG | 2019-08-04 15:46:38 +1000 | Category added!
6    DEBUG | 2019-08-04 15:46:40 +1000 | You can vote for: Test
7    INFO | 2019-08-04 15:46:48 +1000 | Vote recorded - Voter: Cheyne Votee: James Category: TestCategory
8    DEBUG | 2019-08-04 15:46:48 +1000 | Vote recorded!
9
```

Figure 8.34: Output for the voting application

Chapter 9: Ruby Beyond the Basics I

Activity 9.01: Invoice Generator

Solution

1. Create a new Ruby file.

2. Define the **invoice_generator** method and the **p1** and **p2** variables to be used in the program using **&block** and **block_given?**. We call the **invoice_generator** method and pass the product prices along with a block of code:

```ruby
def invoice_generator(p1,p2, &block)
    yield calc_discount(p1,p2) if block_given?
end
```

The **invoice_generator** method has a **yield** keyword, which will only execute the block of code and pass the product prices if the first block of code is passed.

First, **calc_discount** is called and then a block code is executed, which, in turn, passes the customer details to the **details** method.

3. Next, we will define the discount calculator method, **calc_discount**, which will calculate the discount on the products, add it to the product, and print the final price of the product. **calc_discount** is the method where we calculate the sum of the product prices and give a flat discount of 20% on the sum:

```ruby
def calc_discount(p1,p2)
    sum_of_products = p1.to_i+p2.to_i
    final_amount = sum_of_products.to_i*0.80
    puts "Price of Product 1: #{p1}"
    puts "Price of Product 2: #{p2}"
    puts "Final amount after 20% discount #{final_amount}"
end
```

4. Next, we build a method to retrieve the customer details and final product prices with discounts. With the **details** method, we print the customer details, such as **name** and **id**:

```ruby
def details(name, id)
    puts "Customer name is #{name}"
    puts "Customer id is #{id}"
end
```

5. Finally, we bring all the elements together to print an invoice. We take inputs from, say, a store executive to enter their customer name, customer ID, and product prices and save them in the respective variables:

```
puts "Enter your Customer Name"
cust_name = gets.chomp
puts "Enter your Customer ID"
cust_id = gets.chomp
puts "Enter Product 1 price"
product1 = gets.chomp
puts "Enter Product 2 price"
product2 = gets.chomp
invoice_generator(product1, product2) do
    details(cust_name, cust_id)
end
```

6. Let's invoke our script:

```
ruby activity.rb
```

The output should be as follows:

```
Enter your Customer Name
John
Enter your Customer ID
123456
Enter Product 1 price
100
Enter Product 2 price
400
Price of Product 1: 100
Price of Product 2: 400
Final amount after 20% discount 400.0
Customer name is John
Customer id is 123456
```

Figure 9.21: The invoice generator output

Chapter 10: Ruby Beyond the Basics II

Activity 10.01: Implementing GET and POST Data to an External Server

Solution:

1. We first require the gem, and then need to assign our GET request API to a **url** variable. We then make a GET call using **httparty** and display the response using an in-built method, parsed_response, which properly parses the JSON response:

```
require 'httparty'
url = 'https://www.akshatpaul.com/ruby-fundamentals/list-all-buildings'
response = HTTParty.get(url)
puts response.parsed_response
```

2. Run this code from the Terminal using the following command:

```
$ruby get_request.rb
```

The output should be as follows:

```
                    git:(master)    ruby get_request.rb
200
{"name"=>"Burj Khalifa", "address"=>"Dubai"}
{"name"=>"Shanghai Tower", "address"=>"Shanghai"}
{"name"=>"Lotte World Tower", "address"=>"Seoul"}
{"name"=>"International Commerce Centre", "address"=>"Hong Kong"}
{"name"=>"Petronas Tower", "address"=>"Kuala Lumpur"}
{"name"=>"Park Avenue", "address"=>"New York City"}
```

Figure 10.22: GET request output

You can implement the same code without a third-party gem dependency by using the in-built **net/http** library and the JSON library. To try this, refer to the code in the **get_request_net.rb** file:

```
require 'net/http'
require 'json'
url = 'https://www.akshatpaul.com/ruby-fundamentals/list-all-buildings'
uri = URI(url)
response = Net::HTTP.get(uri)
puts JSON.parse(response)
```

You will get the same result as we achieved with much leaner code.

3. Next, let's make our POST request. Create a file, **post_request.rb**. Once again, we require the **httparty** gem, before assigning our POST API to the URL variable. We then make a POST request, along with the URL and a body with proper fields, as per the contract specified in the problem statement:

```
require 'httparty'
url = "https://www.akshatpaul.com/ruby-fundamentals/buildings"
response = HTTParty.post(url, body: { property: {name: "Mr. Ruby Noobie", address: "Tokyo" }})
puts response.code
```

4. Run the following command from the Terminal:

```
$ ruby post_request.rb
```

The output should be as follows:

```
                  git:(master)    ruby post_request.rb
200
```

Figure 10.23: POST request output

5. To check whether our record has been created, we can visit the following URL:

https://packt.live/2MfHItS

If successful, we receive a proper status code and can then verify whether our record exists on the second URL provided.

Chapter 11: Introduction to Ruby on Rails I

Activity 11.01: Adding Authentication for the Review Application

Solution:

1. Add the following gem in your gemfile:

   ```
   gem 'devise'
   ```

2. Open a Terminal, go to the root of the application folder, and install the gem using the following command:

   ```
   $ bundle install
   ```

3. After the gem is installed, type the following command into your Terminal:

   ```
   $ rails generate devise:install
   ```

   The output should be as follows:

   ```
   [→ citireview git:(master) × rails generate devise:install
   Running via Spring preloader in process 88574
         create   config/initializers/devise.rb
         create   config/locales/devise.en.yml
   ===============================================================================

   Some setup you must do manually if you haven't yet:

     1. Ensure you have defined default url options in your environments files. Here
        is an example of default_url_options appropriate for a development environment
        in config/environments/development.rb:

          config.action_mailer.default_url_options = { host: 'localhost', port: 3000 }

        In production, :host should be set to the actual host of your application.

     2. Ensure you have defined root_url to *something* in your config/routes.rb.
        For example:

          root to: "home#index"

     3. Ensure you have flash messages in app/views/layouts/application.html.erb.
        For example:

          <p class="notice"><%= notice %></p>
          <p class="alert"><%= alert %></p>

     4. You can copy Devise views (for customization) to your app by running:

          rails g devise:views

   ===============================================================================
   ```

Figure 11.32: Setting up initial files for the devise gem

This generator sets up all initial files required for devise. There are also some instructions related to customization, which is outside the scope of this activity.

4. Generate a **User** model to manage user authentication. Type the following command in a Terminal:

```
$ rails generate devise User
```

The output is as follows:

```
Running via Spring preloader in process 15790
        invoke  active_record
        create    db/migrate/20190720201553_devise_create_users.rb
        create    app/models/user.rb
        invoke    test_unit
        create      test/models/user_test.rb
        create      test/fixtures/users.yml
        insert    app/models/user.rb
         route  devise_for :users
```

This devise generator has created an appropriate **User** model, along with migrations and routes for our application.

5. Every time we have a new migration, we must update our schema. This will create the required database tables. Type the following command in your Terminal:

```
rails db:migrate
```

The output is as follows:

```
== 20190720201553 DeviseCreateUsers: migrating ===================================
-- create_table(:users)
   -> 0.0031s
-- add_index(:users, :email, {:unique=>true})
   -> 0.0010s
-- add_index(:users, :reset_password_token, {:unique=>true})
   -> 0.0010s
== 20190720201553 DeviseCreateUsers: migrated (0.0052s) =========================
```

6. Type the following command to see where we can access the login page and sign up for our application:

```
$ rails routes
```

The output is as follows:

```
                   Prefix Verb    URI Pattern                 Controller#Action
         new_user_session GET     /users/sign_in(.:format)    devise/sessions#new
             user_session POST    /users/sign_in(.:format)    devise/
sessions#create
     destroy_user_session DELETE  /users/sign_out(.:format)   devise/
sessions#destroy
        new_user_password GET     /users/password/new(.:format)  devise/passwords#new
       edit_user_password GET     /users/password/edit(.:format) devise/passwords#edit
            user_password PATCH   /users/password(.:format)   devise/
passwords#update
                          PUT     /users/password(.:format)   devise/
passwords#update
                          POST    /users/password(.:format)   devise/
passwords#create
cancel_user_registration GET     /users/cancel(.:format)     devise/
registrations#cancel
   new_user_registration GET     /users/sign_up(.:format)    devise/
registrations#new
  edit_user_registration GET     /users/edit(.:format)       devise/
registrations#edit
       user_registration PATCH   /users(.:format)            devise/
registrations#update
                          PUT     /users(.:format)            devise/
registrations#update
                          DELETE  /users(.:format)            devise/
registrations#destroy
                          POST    /users(.:format)            devise/
registrations#create
                     root GET     /                           home#index
                  reviews GET     /reviews(.:format)          reviews#index
```

```
            POST    /reviews(.:format)              reviews#create
 new_review GET     /reviews/new(.:format)          reviews#new
edit_review GET     /reviews/:id/edit(.:format)     reviews#edit
     review GET     /reviews/:id(.:format)          reviews#show
            PATCH   /reviews/:id(.:format)          reviews#update
            PUT     /reviews/:id(.:format)          reviews#update
            DELETE  /reviews/:id(.:format)          reviews#destroy
```

7. So, the user login will use the path **users/sign_in**. Let's open this route in our browser by accessing **http://localhost:3000/users/sign_in**:

← → C   ⓘ localhost:3000/users/sign_in

Log in

Email

Password

☐ Remember me

Log in

Sign up

Forgot your password?

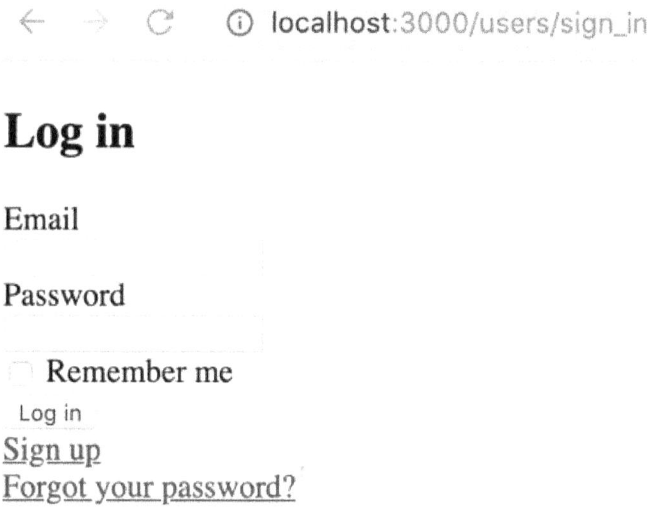

Figure 11.33: Sign-in page for the review application

This is an out-of-the-box view that comes with the devise gem. For a simple application such as ours, this is quite good, but for anything more complex, we can always customize these views.

> **Note**
>
> You won't find this view in your application code; it's coming straight from the gem. To access and customize these default views, you can use `rails generate devise:views`, which will create these views within your application folders, where you can then modify them.

8. Sign up for the application, create your user, then try to log in. The `Sign up` page would look as follows:

Figure 11.34: Signing up on the application

The `Log in` page would look as follows:

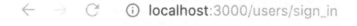

Figure 11.35: Signing into the application

The blog page would look as follows:

Welcome to Citireviews

All Reviews

Add new review

Figure 11.36: Login index page of the application

Signup and login have been successful. However, if we tried to directly access `http://localhost:3000/reviews` without signing in, we'd be able to, since our home and reviews pages are still not under any type of authentication.

9. Add the following code snippet in `app/controller/home_controller.rb` and `app/controller/review_controller.rb`:

```
before_action :authenticate_user!
```

This one line will mean that access to any action in our controller needs to be authorized by devise. Here, `authenticate_user!` is a helper method that determines whether `require` is coming after authentication or not.

> **Note**
>
> `before_action` here is a helper method that is part of a filter. Filters in Rails are methods that are executed before or after a controller action. Filters are inherited from `ApplicationController` and will work with every controller of your application.

Now that we have covered both our **Home** and **Reviews** controllers, if you try to access any URL in our application, it will operate under an authentication system.

Chapter 12: Introduction to Ruby on Rails II

Activity 12.01: Create a Blog Application and Host It Live on a Cloud Platform

Solution

Part I – Create a blog application with the following features

1. Create a new application and run the following command from Terminal:

   ```
   $ rails new blog
   ```

   The output should be as follows:

   ```
   →   activity git:(master) x → rails new blog
           create
           create  README.md
           create  Rakefile
           create  config.ru
           create  .gitignore
           create  Gemfile
   ```

   Figure 12.28: Initializing a new application

2. Go into the **blog** directory and run the following scaffolding command from Terminal to generate MVC files and a folder structure for **post**:

   ```
   $ cd blog
   $ rails generate scaffold post title:string body:text
   ```

The output should be as follows:

```
→  blog git:(master) x rails generate scaffold post title:string
body:text
rails generate scaffold post title:string body:text
Running via Spring preloader in process 25545
      invoke  active_record
      create    db/migrate/20190802221603_create_posts.rb
      create    app/models/post.rb
      invoke    test_unit
      create      test/models/post_test.rb
      create      test/fixtures/posts.yml
      invoke  resource_route
       route    resources :posts
      invoke  scaffold_controller
      create    app/controllers/posts_controller.rb
      invoke    erb
      create      app/views/posts
      create      app/views/posts/index.html.erb
```

Figure 12.29: Using scaffolding to create files and a folder structure

3. The **scaffold** command creates a lot of files and folder structures, essentially creating all the files required for CRUD operations. It has a model, a controller, migration, and views all generated in one go. Scaffolding is very powerful syntactic sugar, doing a lot of repetitive tasks quickly and saving time.

4. Inside the **blog** directory, run the following scaffolding command from Terminal to generate MVC files and a folder structure for **comment**:

```
$ rails generate scaffold comment post_id:integer body:text
```

The output should be as follows:

```
→ blog git:(master) × rails generate scaffold comment post_id:integer body:text
Running via Spring preloader in process 25684
      invoke  active_record
      create    db/migrate/20190802222140_create_comments.rb
      create    app/models/comment.rb
      invoke    test_unit
      create      test/models/comment_test.rb
      create      test/fixtures/comments.yml
      invoke  resource_route
       route     resources :comments
      invoke  scaffold_controller
      create    app/controllers/comments_controller.rb
      invoke    erb
      create      app/views/comments
```

Figure 12.30: Generating MVC files using scaffolding

5. From the root of the project, run the following command to execute migrations and generate tables:

```
$ rails db:migrate
```

The output should be as follows:

```
→ blog git:(master) × rails db:migrate
== 20190802221603 CreatePosts: migrating ========================================
-- create_table(:posts)
   -> 0.0007s
== 20190802221603 CreatePosts: migrated (0.0007s) ===============================

== 20190802222140 CreateComments: migrating =====================================
-- create_table(:comments)
   -> 0.0007s
== 20190802222140 CreateComments: migrated (0.0008s) ============================
```

Figure 12.31: Executing migrations

6. Open the **config/routes.rb** file and add the following code:

```
Rails.application.routes.draw do
    resources :comments
    resources :posts

    root "posts#index"
end
```

Here, we have created a root route, which is the index page of the **posts** controller and will display a list of all blog posts.

7. Test the application by starting the Rails server with the following command and visiting **localhost:3000**:

```
$ rails server
```

The output should be as follows:

```
[➡  blog git:(master) ✕ rails server
=> Booting Puma
=> Rails 5.2.3 application starting in development
=> Run `rails server -h` for more startup options
Puma starting in single mode...
* Version 3.12.1 (ruby 2.6.3-p62), codename: Llamas in Pajamas
* Min threads: 5, max threads: 5
* Environment: development
* Listening on tcp://localhost:3000
Use Ctrl-C to stop
```

Figure 12.32: Starting the Rails server

8. Open the application by loading **http://localhost:3000** in your browser window:

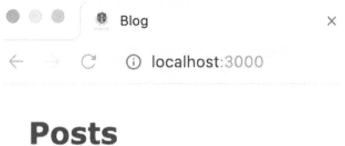

Figure 12.33: Application on localhost

9. Click on **New Post**. The blog should now look as shown in the following figure:

Figure 12.34: New post feature

10. Enter the data for **Title** and **Body** for the new post:

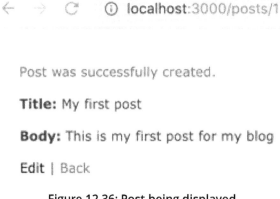

Figure 12.35: Entering data for a new post

11. Click on **Create Post** to submit the form and it will be displayed as follows:

Figure 12.36: Post being displayed

12. The post has been successfully created. Click on **Back** to see a list of all posts:

Figure 12.37: List of posts on the web page

13. Let's add a comment for our first post by visiting the following URL in the browser window: **http://localhost:3000/comments/new**. It will look as shown in the following screenshot:

Figure 12.38: Post being displayed

14. Click on **Create Comment** to submit the form. It should appear as shown in the following figure:

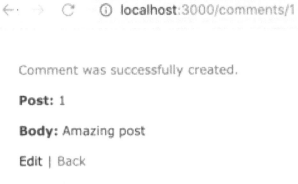

Figure 12.39: Post being displayed

15. The comment has been successfully created. Click on **Back** to see a list of all comments and the post IDs they are associated with:

Comments

Post	Body			
1	Amazing post	Show	**Edit**	Destroy

New Comment

Figure 12.40: Post being displayed

Part II – Deploying your application to Heroku

Before you start deploying your application to Heroku, you need to first create a free account with the Heroku CLI set up locally:

16. Create your free Heroku account by visiting https://signup.heroku.com/.

    Fill in the simple form and create your free account:

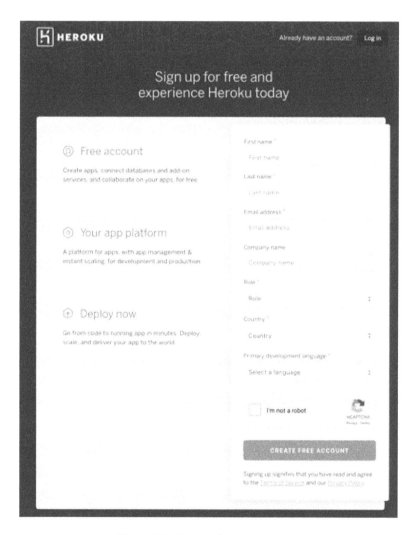

Figure 12.41: Heroku signup page

Note

For our application, we won't require any paid add-ons. This application is available for access for anyone, free of cost.

17. Download the Heroku CLI to set up Heroku locally. There are a number of ways to do that. The following are the ones we recommend but you can choose any of them:

    With Homebrew:

    ```
    brew tap heroku/brew && brew install heroku
    ```

    With **curl**:

    ```
    curl https://cli-assets.heroku.com/install.sh | sh
    ```

    With **npm** (the least recommended):

    ```
    npm install -g heroku
    ```

    Check whether the installation is correct:

    ```
    heroku --version
    heroku/7.0.0 (darwin-x64) node-v8.0.0
    ```

    Log into the Heroku CLI:

    ```
    heroku login
    heroku: Press any key to open up the browser to login or q to exit
     '   Warning: If browser does not open, visit
     '   https://cli-auth.heroku.com/auth/browser/***
    heroku: Waiting for login...
    Logging in... done
    Logged in as me@example.com
    ```

18. We have built our application using **sqlite3** but Heroku does not support it so we will have to use **postgres** with our application. Add the following gem to your gemfile and remove the other gem. Open the gem file and enter the following command:

    ```
    gem 'pg'
    ```

    To remove **sqlite3**, use the following command:

    ```
    gem 'sqlite3'
    ```

Run the following command from the Terminal window:

```
$ bundle Install
```

> **Note**
>
> To set up a PostgreSQL database, please refer to the docs: https://packt.
> live/2MBhC4F.

19. Update the **config/database.yml** file with the following configurations:

```
default: &default
  adapter: postgresql
  encoding: unicode
  # For details on connection pooling, see Rails configuration guide
  # http://guides.rubyonrails.org/configuring.html#database-pooling
  pool: <%= ENV.fetch("RAILS_MAX_THREADS") { 5 } %>
development:
  <<: *default
  database: myapp_development
test:
  <<: *default
  database: myapp_test
production:
  <<: *default
  database: myapp_production
  username: myapp
  password: <%= ENV['MYAPP_DATABASE_PASSWORD'] %>
```

Since the application was running previously, we have to update it with the proper **postgres** configuration.

20. Create a database and run migrations to test that our database changes are successful and that there are no errors. Run the following command from Terminal:

```
$ rails db:create
```

Terminal will show the following:

```
→ blog git:(master) × rails db:create
Created database 'myapp_development'
Created database 'myapp_test'
```

Figure 12.42: Creating a database

This has created our database. Next, let's run migrations:

```
$ rails db:migrate
```

We have successfully migrated our application from **sqlite** to **postgres**.

Thanks to the Active Record ORM(Object Relational Mapping), switching between databases is made very simple. As we saw in this exercise, migrating from **sqlite3** to **postgres** is fast and easy.

21. Specify your Ruby version in your **Gemfile**. Add the following line at the top of your **Gemfile**:

```
ruby "2.6.0"
```

22. Save your application in Git.

Git is required for deploying an application on Heroku. If you don't have Git on your machine, please set it up from https://git-scm.com/ (we won't be doing that since it's beyond the scope of this book).

Run the following command from the root of your application:

```
$ git add .
$ git commit -m "init"
```

23. Deploy the application on Heroku. Run the following command from the Terminal window inside the root of the blog project:

```
$ heroku create
```

```
→  blog git:(master) x heroku create
Creating app... done, ⬤ protected-tor-47977
https://protected-tor-47977.herokuapp.com/ |
https://git.heroku.com/protected-tor-47977.git
```

Figure 12.43: Creating an application on Heroku

This automatically creates a Heroku application on the Heroku server with a deployment pipeline. It also creates a URL for it as you can see at https://protected-tor-47977.herokuapp.com/. After deployment, we will be able to access our application from this URL.

> **Note**
>
> The Heroku application URL for the live site will be different for you than the one mentioned in this activity.

24. Deploy the application on Heroku by executing the following command:

```
$ git push heroku master
```

The output will show up as follows:

```
→  blog git:(master) x git push heroku master
Enumerating objects: 127, done.
Counting objects: 100% (127/127), done.
Delta compression using up to 8 threads
Compressing objects: 100% (112/112), done.
Writing objects: 100% (127/127), 28.83 KiB | 1.52 MiB/s, done.
Total 127 (delta 9), reused 0 (delta 0)
remote: Compressing source files... done.
remote: Building source:
```

Figure 12.44: Deployment on Heroku

The deployment runs for a few hundred lines and takes roughly 30-40 seconds.

25. Set up a database on Heroku. Run the following command to run database migration and generate tables:

```
$ heroku run rails db:migrate
```

The output will show up as follows on Terminal:

```
➜  blog git:(master) × heroku run rails db:migrate
Running rake db:migrate on <2b22> protected-tor-47977... up, run.5571 (Free)
D, [2019-08-02T23:23:34.037665 #4] DEBUG -- :    (13.9ms)  CREATE TABLE "schema_migrations" ("version" character varying
 NOT NULL PRIMARY KEY)
D, [2019-08-02T23:23:34.049448 #4] DEBUG -- :    (8.0ms)  CREATE TABLE "ar_internal_metadata" ("key" character varying N
OT NULL PRIMARY KEY, "value" character varying, "created_at" timestamp NOT NULL, "updated_at" timestamp NOT NULL)
D, [2019-08-02T23:23:34.059064 #4] DEBUG -- :    (5.3ms)  SELECT pg_try_advisory_lock(5137229852418964545)
D, [2019-08-02T23:23:34.093817 #4] DEBUG -- :    (1.7ms)  SELECT "schema_migrations"."version" FROM "schema_migrations"
ORDER BY "schema_migrations"."version" ASC
I, [2019-08-02T23:23:34.096502 #4]  INFO -- : Migrating to CreatePosts (20190802221603)
D, [2019-08-02T23:23:34.114071 #4] DEBUG -- :    (1.8ms)  BEGIN
== 20190802221603 CreatePosts: migrating ======================================
-- create_table(:posts)
D, [2019-08-02T23:23:34.124680 #4] DEBUG -- :    (9.6ms)  CREATE TABLE "posts" ("id" bigserial primary key, "title" char
acter varying, "body" text, "created_at" timestamp NOT NULL, "updated_at" timestamp NOT NULL)
   -> 0.0105s
== 20190802221603 CreatePosts: migrated (0.0107s) =============================

D, [2019-08-02T23:23:34.137485 #4] DEBUG -- :    SQL (4.1ms)  INSERT INTO "schema_migrations" ("version") VALUES ($1) RET
URNING "version"  [["version", "20190802221603"]]
D, [2019-08-02T23:23:34.141634 #4] DEBUG -- :    (3.7ms)  COMMIT
I, [2019-08-02T23:23:34.141794 #4]  INFO -- : Migrating to CreateComments (20190802222140)
D, [2019-08-02T23:23:34.144300 #4] DEBUG -- :    (1.7ms)  BEGIN
== 20190802222140 CreateComments: migrating ===================================
-- create_table(:comments)
D, [2019-08-02T23:23:34.156893 #4] DEBUG -- :    (11.6ms)  CREATE TABLE "comments" ("id" bigserial primary key, "post_id
" integer, "body" text, "created_at" timestamp NOT NULL, "updated_at" timestamp NOT NULL)
   -> 0.0125s
== 20190802222140 CreateComments: migrated (0.0126s) =========================
```

Figure 12.45: Output for database migration

Visit the following URL in your browser to check that your application is live on the World Wide Web; however, when you push the application, this URL will be different – this is a randomly generated URL by Heroku: https://protected-tor-47977.herokuapp.com/

The blog post will now show up as follows:

Figure 12.46: Blog post landing page

We have successfully hosted our application for the world to play with.

Index

About

All major keywords used in this book are captured alphabetically in this section. Each one is accompanied by the page number of where they appear.

W

Z

www.ingramcontent.com/pod-product-compliance
Lightning Source LLC
Chambersburg PA
CBHW060638060326
40690CB00020B/4442